Supply Chain Metrics
That Matter

The Wiley Corporate F&A series provides information, tools, and insights to corporate professionals responsible for issues affecting the profitability of their company, from accounting and finance to internal controls and performance management.

Founded in 1807, John Wiley & Sons is the oldest independent publishing company in the United States. With offices in North America, Europe, Asia, and Australia, Wiley is globally committed to developing and marketing print and electronic products and services for our customers' professional and personal knowledge and understanding.

Supply Chain Metrics
That Matter

LORA M. CECERE

WILEY

Published by John Wiley & Sons, Inc., Hoboken, New Jersey.
Published simultaneously in Canada.

For general information on our other products and services or for technical support, please contact our Customer Care Department within the United States at (800) 762-2974, outside the United States at (317) 572-3993 or fax (317) 572-4002.

Wiley publishes in a variety of print and electronic formats and by print-on-demand. Some material included with standard print versions of this book may not be included in e-books or in print-on-demand. If this book refers to media such as a CD or DVD that is not included in the version you purchased, you may download this material at http://booksupport.wiley.com. For more information about Wiley products, visit www.wiley.com.

Library of Congress Cataloging-in-Publication Data:

ISBN 9781118858110 (Hardcover)
ISBN 9781118938980 (ePDF)
ISBN 9781118938973 (ePub)

10 9 8 7 6 5 4 3 2 1

This book is dedicated to supply chain pioneers who forged the path for the supply chain management profession.

Contents

Foreword

M Y FIRST EXPOSURE to the discipline of supply chain management was in the fall of 1969 when, as an undergraduate business major at the University of Notre Dame, I took an elective course in *Physical Distribution Management*. The text of the same name was by three pioneers: Donald J. Bowersox, Edward W. Smykay, and Bernard J. LaLonde. Less than a year later I would begin a PhD program in Business Logistics at The Ohio State University with the remarkable privilege of having Dr. Bud LaLonde as my program advisor and committee chair.

During the 1960s the academic discipline and eventual career path that would come to be known as supply chain management was effectively in its infancy. Textbooks were only beginning to appear, major fields of study were offered by only a few universities (a scandalous omission that persists to the present day), and the principal international organization of professionals had only recently been founded: the National Council of Physical Distribution Management (NCPDM), later renamed the Council of Logistics Management (CLM) and its present incarnation, the Council of Supply Chain Management Professionals (CSCMP). It was certainly a more innocent time for logisticians, for the management objective in those days was consistent with the course and book titles: balancing a limited set of finished goods distribution costs against selected customer service goals, and almost always for domestic firms.

It was not until 1982 that the term *supply chain* first appeared and it did not gain widespread use until the mid-1990s. But way back in 1963, something remarkable happened. Bud LaLonde did what he would continue to do for decades: he put forth a vision for the profession. In his view *Physical Distribution Management* should be married with *Materials Management* (procurement and manufacturing) and the *whole thing* should be called *Business Logistics*. Revolutionary? Absolutely. Accepted by the profession? Not a chance. Some 13 years later Michigan State researchers would introduce the term *Integrated Logistics* (procurement, manufacturing, and finished goods distribution under a single line-level executive) as one of the attributes for Leading Edge firms. In recent years, notably in the work by Professors Douglas Lambert, Martha Cooper, Keely Croxton, Thomas Goldsby et al. of The Ohio State University and the Global Supply Chain Forum, we have seen SCM developed using the very sophisticated perspective of cross-functional business process integration with relationship management as a key element.

So, five decades later, where are we? Sadly, for many companies not much better off than in the 1970s. We are still crippled by anachronistic functional silos, presided over by vice presidents who fiercely defend their worn-out turf and who measure and reward performance with an endless stream of silo initiatives and ever-changing performance metrics. Supply chain management may be the fashionable verbal coin of the realm, but far too often in practice it is currency that purchases relatively little. Where have we gone astray and what can be done about it?

Enter Lora M. Cecere. As a highly experienced software developer, consultant, and industry analyst she has a wealth of experience from which to draw. And draw she does, introducing the reader to a fictitious company populated with classic executives who are struggling to understand why overall corporate performance lags despite their relentless pursuit of typical performance metrics. In particular, there is a singular focus on growth objectives. Complicating matters further is an impending expansion into Brazil. The executives are all well-meaning, if functionally myopic at the outset. Here, Lora very effectively avoids the obvious trap of overplaying their characteristics to the point of caricature. Rather, at least in my experience, they are very accurately portrayed.

Very early on, Lora introduces the reader to the overarching theme of the book, which is also the title: *Metrics That Matter*. We learn that her selected measures are familiar enough to almost anyone in business, while at the same time we are disabused of a host of other, equally traditional measures. So where is the fundamental contribution? It is with the cross-functional (read that as *corporate performance*) interplay of the measures, the interactions that are not—indeed cannot—be appreciated when one is focused on functional silo performance. It is in this context that we are introduced to the concept of the *Effective Frontier*, the goal of *maximizing corporate performance* by measuring and managing selected metrics simultaneously, not individually. We also learn the critical difference between *efficient* and *effective*, a distinction all but lost in many companies.

If the text stopped here, it might be worthy of consignment to the shelf labeled *Interesting Academic Ideas*. Fortunately for the reader it is only the beginning. For it is in fleshing out the *what*, *why*, and *how* of *Metrics That Matter* that the book truly shines. It is based, first and foremost, on a three-year collaborative effort of Lora and researchers at Arizona State University. The results—presented effectively and at an appropriate level of detail—are startling: industry leaders who are not really leading, accepted practices worthy of the discard pile, conventional wisdom debunked. Along the way we learn what works, what does not, and, most important, why.

For the rest of the book we are drawn into the change process of the company, as the consultant (Lora) gradually introduces new concepts and overcomes the inevitable—sometimes fierce—resistance. This focus on change is one of the most important contributions of the story and, once again, it does not disappoint. For impressive though the research data may be, extensive use of individual case studies and interviews serve to really close the deal. And these are cases with real company names, not some abstract "Company A." There is more than enough evidence to convince even the most skeptical of readers. Finally, Lora emphasizes a critical component of change: the criteria by which we measure, evaluate, compensate, and promote individuals must be revamped as well, lest the silos live on.

There really is a way forward from the morass of supply chain management. Entrenched behaviors are not modified easily. We have unwittingly been chasing either the wrong metrics or the right ones in the wrong combination. But Lora very convincingly shows us that one of Murphy's corollaries is not universally valid: the light at the end of the tunnel need not be the headlight of an oncoming train. Rather, we see in the distance the prizes of substantially improved performance and competitive position. Lora shows us the way to get there via one of the most creative approaches that I have had the pleasure of reviewing in a long time. That is indeed a substantive contribution.

Jeffrey J. Karrenbauer
President
Insight, Inc.

Preface

OVER THE PAST DECADE, *good* business practices did not become *great*. Scorecards were difficult to balance, and leadership teams struggled to evolve. Today, executive boards are disappointed. Even though companies have spent 1.7 percent of revenue on improving technology, they have not been able to maximize the value that they were expecting to earn in the information economy.

In our research, we find that 9 out of 10 companies are stuck. Growth has slowed, and progress on operating margin and inventory turns is difficult. The answers are not as easy to find as promised.

In this book, we tell the story of a leadership team struggling to make progress. The story is fictional, but the characters and the dialogue are a composite of the teams that we have worked with over the past three years. This team, like many that we work with, finds itself seeking the answers to many questions:

- **What drives value in a value chain?** What is value? Different industries have matured at different rates. What can we learn?
- **How do companies maximize value?** Which portfolio of corporate metrics maximizes market capitalization and cash flow?
- **How do we move forward?** The book is the story of a leadership team finding its way.

Each chapter in this book is written to answer specific questions. The goal of Chapter 1 is to answer the question, "How does a company start the journey?" Chapter 2 answers "How do you build a guiding coalition to drive change?" Chapter 3 introduces the concepts of value networks and how metrics can be improved by working collaboratively with trading partners. Chapters 4 through 8 highlight how individual companies have successfully aligned operational strategies to improve corporate results and answer the question of "What is possible?" In each chapter, to make the case, we share research and case studies to give new perspectives on how other companies have worked to drive alignment, balance, and resiliency to improve corporate results.

By analyzing the trends of corporate performance over the period of 2006–2013, in the story, we share insights on the strength, balance, and resiliency of industry peer groups. In the creation of the book, we have developed a methodology to evaluate which companies have been able to deliver the greatest value. More important, we have begun to understand the stories behind these patterns of performance. This analysis is based on three years of research on corporate performance. The reader will gain insights on the management of the value network as a complex system.

Leadership teams want to understand what is possible, and what maximizes value. They want to evolve and mature. Organizations are seeking a road map. Here we provide it. It is our hope that this book can help organizations maximize value and harness the true value of the information economy.

Acknowledgments

WRITING A BOOK is easier said than done, but there is nothing better than smelling fresh ink when you crack the cover of a book that you have completed. While my name is on the front cover, this book would not have been possible without the efforts of a team.

This book took two months to research and a year to write. I owe a debt of gratitude to my team at Supply Chain Insights, who toiled tirelessly on this book. To Regina Denman, my friend and colleague, I give thanks for wrangling the corporate schedules of executives for case studies and interviews.

The story is based on a deep research effort with many starts and stops. I am appreciative for the work of Abby Mayer and Heather Hart. It took many long hours to build the research, refine the graphics, and finalize the work on the Supply Chain Index. I know that it was not easy, and I am thankful for your dedication to see this mission to completion.

I find it easier to type endlessly at my kitchen table than to follow style guides and punctuation practices. Every writer appreciates a good editor, and I am appreciative to Michael Hambrick and Jill Smith for their many, many hours of proofreading and editing. They were an awesome team and I am grateful for the many hours of training on writing styles.

Each chapter of this book was written and rewritten four to five times. When I was stuck (which was often), I would beg friends to read a chapter and give me suggestions. The manuscript was written first as a nonfiction textbook; but, at the urging of my friend, Eric Treworgy, I rewrote the story to give it life through a narrative point of view. This resulted in a four-month delay and a complete rewrite, but I think that the book is a better read as a result. I give thanks to Eric for giving me the courage and inspiration to build the characters that come alive in the chapters that follow.

As a new writer, it is hard to write a book. I am appreciative to Angela Tavares of *Here Booky Booky* for her coaching on narrative style and her guidance on character development. Everyone needs a good coach and her help was invaluable.

Finally, in the middle of a project like a book, everyone needs a good laugh. Lenny Barlow kept me grounded and laughing through the 140,000 words.

I give thanks to all. It took a team! I hope you enjoy the read.

CHAPTER ONE

Starting the Journey

ENERGY FILLED THE ROOM, and excitement reigned. The global team was gathered for this February meeting. It was the beginning of a new year. Many of its members had worked together for years, but never met face to face. They were excited to connect. It was cold outside; but inside the room, the conversation was warm and quickly flowing, as people who previously only knew each other from e-mails shook hands and introduced themselves.

Centered in the front of the room was a flip chart. Placed on the board was a large white sheet of paper. In the center, carefully handwritten with a black marker, was a number. As people gathered over coffee they glanced at the board, and in casual conversation tried to guess what the number 77 might mean.

Joe, a leader in a major global multinational company, was hosting his annual kickoff meeting. It was the launch of his "big, hairy, and audacious goal (BHAG)" for the New Year. He rubbed his hands together as he began his talk. As he unveiled his vision, he was passionate in his argument. He believed in his mission. His speech started with great energy, but then stalled. The group was not buying his message.

The BHAG was an inventory goal. Joe wanted to finish the year with a 25 percent reduction in inventory. This translated to a target goal of 77 days of inventory. His desire was to reduce inventory and return cash to the corporation. The company was in a growth mode, and Joe wanted to deliver on the corporate strategy. As he spoke, the team in the room felt challenged, and a little resentful. Recently the company had experienced layoffs, and today they faced rising costs, increasing demand and supply volatility, and what they felt were ever-changing business priorities. It was hard for them to focus.

As I looked around the room, the group seemed detached and dispassionate. They stared blankly forward into space, occasionally looking at their cellphones. It was as though they had been here before. It was a new inventory goal in the list of many management programs that were being developed without asking anybody about the feasibility of meeting the targets.

I was the guest speaker. As I got up to present, the atmosphere was icy, and the team seemed broken. The mood was despondent. I ruefully went through my presentation, sharing stories and what I thought was my best research. It was difficult. As I made eye contact, I got a few laughs, but the mood was definitely down. As I finished I thought, *What do I do now? Joe is one of my favorite clients. I have known him for years, and he is a great leader. How do I help him?*

As we took a break, I drew Joe aside, put a hand on his shoulder and carefully started a dialogue. I looked him in the eye and said, "How do you know that 77 fewer days is the right inventory target? I know that this is an important meeting for you, but why is this substantial inventory reduction so important for the business? Do you know that the group is struggling with this as a goal?"

Joe returned my gaze and shrugged his shoulders as he said, "It just feels right. I want the team to have a stretch goal. Nothing is ever easy these days. As you know, the company is focused on growth right now. The reduction of inventory would give us dollars to reinvest in research and development (R&D). New products are essential to meeting our growth plan. R&D budgets are being slashed and it now costs us four times more to bring a new product to market than it did five years ago. No one has asked me to do this, but I think that it would help the company. I want to help."

"I know that actualizing the growth agenda is important to you, and no doubt about it, you are a good corporate citizen," I said empathically. "But let's step back. Where are you now? How do you know what is possible? I am just worried about the reaction that I see from your team. They have not bought into the goal."

Joe's mind was cranking on overdrive as he responded, "We have been reducing inventory over the past couple of years, but have had a tough time sustaining it." He then shook his head side to side as he said, "I know that this is a significant cut; however, when I set a stretch goal, I have such a good team that they are able to deliver. I believe in them, and they make things happen. But, to answer your question directly, no, we have not tested to see if this goal is feasible. My thought is that by setting a stretch goal, then the team can achieve it."

"Even so, Joe, I'm worried. How do you know if you can achieve this goal and maintain balance with your other metrics? You know that metrics are tightly interwoven as a complex system. Don't you think that there is a reason you haven't been able to sustain inventory levels before?" I asked quietly.

"I know that we do not have a lot of time now, but I would like to know what you mean by balance. Your concept of a complex system intrigues me. Can we talk later? I would love to know more," Joe said with great intensity.

"Yes, we can talk later. But for now, let me give you a few thoughts. As you and I have discussed many times, the metrics in a company are tightly inter-related," I continued. "There is an intrinsic relationship between cost, service, and inventory. Each organization has its own potential. I think that it makes sense to look at the metrics together as a system to see what this cut of inventory would impact. What do you think?"

"These are all good points. We cut inventories drastically at the end of the recession and it severely impacted customer service. How do I better understand what is possible? What do we want to do today with the group? It appears that we are stuck." he continued.

"I am not sure," I said. "Metrics systems need to be aligned. As a business leader, you are managing a complex system with increasing process complexity. There are finite trade-offs between metrics. Inventory is only one of the metrics in that complex system. I am worried about a goal to attack inventory in isolation. Your company is driving a growth strategy and 37 percent of your products are on product allocation. Demand is outstripping supply, and processes are unreliable. So, why did you pick inventory as the BHAG metric? Why not set a goal to reduce items on allocation as your BHAG for the New Year?

"What if we work together to facilitate a group discussion to see what they think? With the current level of energy in the room, I think that we need to change the dynamic," I continued, while quietly gesturing toward the group gathered over coffee. "Do you think that it would be possible to engage the group in a dialogue to see what they think of your BHAG?"

"Whoa! So many tough questions all at once. The reduction of inventory just seems easier than tackling a broader goal. No doubt about it, process reliability has been a constant struggle for us. I am game to engage the group in a dialogue to get their thoughts, but I am not willing to change my business goal.

My BHAG of 77 stands," Joe said defiantly. "After all, this is a business, not a democracy."

 ## MEET JOE

To understand my interaction with Joe and his team on this crisp winter day, let me introduce Joe. Prior to this team meeting, I had worked with Joe Samparini as a member of a divisional leadership group. This was my first meeting with Joe's global team.

I always enjoyed our interactions. He was full of energy and I was captivated by his infectious smile. At first glance, you'd think Joe was a newspaper reporter because of his slightly disheveled appearance, the dark five o'clock shadow on his jaw, and his loosened tie, rumpled white shirt, and rolled-up sleeves. With his low-key, understated ways, it was easy to take him for granted.

He was a man of few words. Affable and curious, Joe got along with everyone, and people scrambled to be on his team. When tempers flared, he could diffuse anger with humor. It was his wit that set you back and let you laugh at the situation and humanize the people on the team. He was known as a great mentor, and as such it was hard for him to not have direct reports. In fact he was often advised by his human resources team to shed some direct reports and have the team report at multiple levels, but Joe loved people, and people loved Joe. So, currently, he had 40 direct reports. When he gathered the group together, they hung on his every word, and wanted to work hard. They did not want to tell him no. His team relished his smile, and loved to get a pat on the back from Joe when they had done a good job.

He had a lean frame, and stood a bit more than six feet tall. You could tell he was used to being the tallest person in the room by the way he leaned forward when he talked to you. As he would bend down to shake your hand, a loose curl of his dark wavy hair would flop onto his forehead. His eyes were dark brown, and he had the kind of dark circles under them that proclaimed his Mediterranean ancestry. While some people with dark eyes have a sparkle in their eyes or suggest a deep mystery, Joe's eyes looked concerned and interested—he was always a good host.

Joe grew up in a working-class family in Pittsburgh, Pennsylvania. His grandfather was a steel worker, and his grandmother worked in a sweatshop sewing coats. His father and his six uncles and aunts were raised by their eldest sister. Joe's father was raised with a strong work ethic, and by the time Joe came of age, the steel jobs were gone, but his father was a successful owner of an auto dealership. Everyone in Joe's father's family had prospered as the result of hard work and perseverance, defying multiple recessions. The family worked hard, helped others, and spent money conservatively.

Like most of his cousins, Joe had the benefit of a college education. To Joe, the way to succeed was to devote your time and effort to making your employer successful. He was always looking for ways to help the company improve. This was his second company, after he had experienced a reduction in force in his prior manufacturing role just as his career was starting. He realized that the old, unwritten contract of mutual benefit between worker and company was no longer something that could be counted on, and Joe was intent on making himself so indispensable in this new job that he'd never be "downsized" again.

He was a career man. Ethical and strong, Joe could outwork most of his peers, but never wanted to take credit. As a lifelong learner, he was curious and always asked questions and provoked what he called "learning moments." He pushed his team to do well because he genuinely wanted his company to do well in the market. He was a team player, but never a boat rocker. His goal was to retire from the company at 65, and enjoy his bass boat and spend many days fly-fishing. He kept a bright red fly-fishing rod in the corner of his office to remind him that life was not all about work. He had pictures on his desk of himself and his son fishing.

Joe's personal goals centered on living and enjoying the journey. He had a large family. Joe considered himself fortunate to be a dad to nine girls and one boy. The boy was his youngest, and while Joe worked hard, he would also make it known if his son had a ballgame. He was always present at his son's games, sitting on the bleachers rain or shine, cheering and eating peanuts.

His relationship with his boss, Filipe, was tenuous. Joe wished that Filipe had a bit more humility and was more open to learn. Filipe was flamboyant and always wanted to be the center of attention. Joe was different: he knew that he didn't have all the answers and wanted to know more.

SETTING METRICS TARGETS

The story goes on and on. It happens over and over again in corporate America. Operational leaders, like Joe, try to do the right thing but are unable to make progress in metric performance. In this story, Joe is making the mistake of looking at metrics in isolation. He lacks a basic understanding of the inter-relationship of metrics and the need to manage a balanced portfolio. This is common. Most companies lack the understanding of how to drive balance and resiliency in metrics performance and how to improve year-over-year performance.

The examples in this book are based on a variety of experiences. They do not come from one interaction, but instead are insights gleaned from working with many companies. Joe is a fictional character who is a composite of real managers. I find that the questions that different companies ask, and sometimes forget to ask, are eerily similar.

Each leader wants to draw a road map, and they want to know where they are on their journey. There is a quest for excellence, but it is amazing how often leaders do not know *what good looks like.* There is a lack of clarity on the end state. The alignment of metrics to improve corporate performance is easier said than done. There is a struggle to align functional silos.

Metrics That Matter is written for the Joe (or Jane) in every organization who does not want to be average. They want to excel. There is a fire in the belly to understand how operational performance affects corporate performance. They are ready to start the journey and find answers to the question, "What is possible?"

THE JOURNEY

The first step of the journey, for a guy like Joe, is to define operations excellence. The second is to identify the right metrics. The metrics chosen need to reflect all of the elements of the complex system. It is not easy. Putting together the metrics framework requires a clear definition of strategy. There are no cookie-cutter answers. The answer is slightly different for each company.

Figure 1.1 shows how the process for metrics maturity can be iterative. For teams like Joe's, there are five steps. Progress requires continuous learning, refinement, and renewal over many years. It takes a year-over-year focus and discipline by the executive team. Change happens in small increments, not leaps and bounds.

The first step is *awareness* of the need to change. The stimulus is often failure. It could be a missed earnings call, surprises at the end of the quarter, loss of market share, a market downturn, or the loss of business. When this happens, bad news moves like a lightning bolt through the organization. The gap in performance is a wake-up call. Normally, good news will travel fast in the organization while bad news moves slowly. It is only when there is a crisis that bad news travels fast. When the organization recognizes the need for change and is ready for alignment on the metrics that matter, there is an awakening and a *call to action.*

FIGURE 1.1 The Metrics Journey

The second step is metrics *definition*. This decision needs to be based on business strategy. It needs to be a conscious and a set of deliberate choices. The challenge is selection of a few meaningful metrics that represent all of the elements of the complex system. Most companies measure too many things and are not clear on which metrics matter. Gaining clarity is a part of the journey.

The third step is driving organizational *alignment* on the metrics system. This requires building a guiding coalition with a clear vision that needs to be cross-functional. In this step, functional metrics are aligned to corporate metrics frameworks, and targets are established to drive incentives.

The fourth step is to *build organizational potential*. A look at industry performance and accomplishments of industry peer group leaders helps to ground the discussion. The organization can then craft a road map for performance improvement.

The last step, and a very important one, is to *refine and adjust* the metrics to drive strength, balance, and resiliency, over time, in corporate performance.

It is a journey, not a sprint, and it is ongoing. Patience and discipline are essential. Most of the average Joes work in large matrixed organizations within a global company. Progress needs to be measured in millimeters, not meters. Substantial progress happens over the course of many years.

Metrics That Matter at FMC Agricultural Solutions

In the process of writing the book, I have sent the chapters to industry leaders to get feedback. Throughout the book, I will share perspectives from these leaders. Here is an excerpt from an interview with Marty Kisliuk of FMC Agricultural Solutions:

If you don't measure the right things, you will not get better. However, if you measure them, it does not mean that you will get better. There is always tension. If you are not struggling with metrics, then you probably are not using them.

When I think about the metrics that matter, I start my thinking with business strategy. I ask myself, "What is it? And, how will we measure the success of this strategy?" I don't think that any leadership team can deal with more than five to seven metrics at the same time. There is an issue of focus and selective strategy. It varies by industry.

The metrics that matter are going to be the ones that you can take action on. There are two important words implied in the word *actionable*: *action* and *able*. I don't think that any organization can take action on all the metrics simultaneously. We need to start with two or three metrics and move them together.

After being chosen, the metrics cannot align organizations, but they can misalign them. It is only the action by leaders that can drive alignment.

A classic discussion for me is cost versus value. I want to sell value, and I define value as benefit over cost. Cost is only one side of the equation of value. As a result, you cannot have the operations team aligned for cost and the go-to-market teams of sales and marketing driving value. This is nonsense. We have to do it together.

Marty Kisliuk, Director of Global Operations, FMC Agricultural Solutions

Conquering the Effective Frontier

Joe asked me to come back the following week and we continued our talk. The BHAG discussion was still uncomfortable. He had gotten some tough feedback from his team.

As I worked with him, it became clear to me that he, like other executives I work with, was battling a list of ever-changing goals for growth, profitability, and cycles in the face of rising complexity. When this happens, frustration reigns. Arguments abound and tensions are high. Leadership teams want to do the right thing, but it just isn't clear what to do to move forward. The obstacles

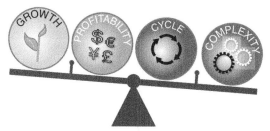

FIGURE 1.2 The Effective Frontier

are large, and the benefits are many. Each organization has a unique potential as defined by the Effective Frontier in Figure 1.2.

As we sat in Joe's office the next week, I tried to explain the concept of the Effective Frontier. "In our last conversation, you asked me about balance. Today, I want to share with you some insights from our research. We find that each company has its own unique potential. The frontier is defined by the interrelationships of growth, profitability, cycles, and complexity. The potential of the company on the Effective Frontier is determined by products, processes, technologies, markets, and channels. Within a company, there are finite trade-offs between interconnected metrics. While there are many definitions and possibilities of metrics for each part of the model, the most commonly used are these four."

I then turned and wrote the following definitions on the whiteboard in his office:

1. **Growth:** Year-over-year revenue improvements
2. **Profitability:** Operating margin (OM), cost of goods sold (COGS), and earnings before interest, taxes, depreciation and amortization (EBITDA)
3. **Cycles:** Cash-to-cash, inventory turns, and order cycle times, days of receivables, days of payables, and production cycle times
4. **Complexity:** Increase in products or channels

After replacing the eraser in its holder, and laughing with Joe about my poor handwriting on the board, I said, "Joe, companies want to power a profitable growth strategy, but often find themselves trapped at the intersection of operating margin and inventory turns. It is a battle of cost versus cash. Leaders like you must forge the operating strategy to help others understand the trade-offs."

"As complexity rises, the potential of the organization decreases. To maintain the status quo, you must constantly redesign operations. As you know, there are many elements that affect operating complexity, like product proliferation, platform complexity, and changes in manufacturing operations." I then paused and looked him in the eye. "As you know very well, these impacts on complexity usually have a negative effect on revenue per employee, return on assets (ROA), return on net assets (RONA), or return on invested capital (ROIC)."

Joe nodded in agreement and said, "This is our struggle. We are constantly being asked to reduce costs and improve working capital, and do more with less, while complexity escalates in the organization. We have no way to push back and manage the metrics that matter. We are not thinking about it holistically as a complex system."

About the Effective Frontier

It is important to note that the name of this model is not the *Efficient Frontier*. Readers who have taken economics courses may have even read it as the Efficient Frontier when speed-reading the page. This mistake is common. Often when I share this model in a lecture, someone will come up and try to correct me.

It is deliberately not named the Efficient Frontier. Why? The efficient organization is not necessarily the most effective. This is an important principle that underlies the research of this book. A singular focus on productivity or cost management can throw an organization out of balance. (An efficient organization is usually defined as one with the highest productivity per employee or the lowest cost per case.)

I had hit a nerve. I started the conversation by passing a piece of research to Joe that is shown in Table 1.1, and saying, "Today, nine out of ten companies are stuck. As shown in the table, when we analyze corporate balance sheet data for companies sorted by Morningstar sector, we find that nine out of ten companies have been unable to move forward for more than three years of sequential improvements on these two metrics. They are not stuck in a good way like a label to a bottle; instead, they are stuck in a bad way like a car in a massive traffic jam going nowhere. They may have made progress on a project, or a focus on singular metrics, but not in the delivery of a balanced metrics portfolio."

Joe flashed his contagious grin and said, "This is certainly the case in my organization."

"Take a look at how industries have changed," I said, shuffling a sheaf of papers and handing to Joe what is shown in Table 1.2. "Growth is slowing;

TABLE 1.1 Percentage of Companies Demonstrating Consecutive Improvement on Both Operating Margin and Inventory Turns for 2000–2012

Morningstar Sector	2 Years Only	3 Years Only	4 Years Only
Chemical (n = 22)	32%	9%	0%
Communications Equipment (n = 94)	33%	13%	2%
Consumer Electronics (n = 11)	18%	0%	9%
Drug Manufacturers—Major (n = 17)	12%	6%	0%
Household & Personal Products (n = 27)	37%	7%	0%
Packaged Food (n = 48)	25%	6%	2%
Packaging & Containers (n = 19)	26%	0%	0%
Semiconductors (n = 76)	33%	5%	1%
Specialty (n = 48)	31%	8%	2%

Source: Supply Chain Insights LLC.

TABLE 1.2 Industry Growth Patterns

Industry	2000–2006 Average	2007–2009 Average	2010–2012 Average
Medical Device Industry (n = 6)	10%	5%	4%
Consumer Packaged Goods (n = 14)	7%	7%	6%
Mass Retail Industry (n = 33)	25%	15%	7%
Chemical Industry (n = 7)	8%	5%	8%
Pharmaceutical Industry (n = 24)	13%	15%	9%
Grocery Retail Industry (n = 37)	13%	10%	10%
Hospital Industry (n = 6)	14%	12%	10%
Retail Apparel Industry (n = 3)	16%	14%	11%
Combined Food & Beverage Industry (n = 32)	10%	13%	12%
Automotive Industry (n = 39)	14%	26%	17%
Brand Apparel Industry (n = 3)	11%	9%	21%

Industry Average comprised of public companies (automotive industry: NAICS 336112), (brand apparel industry: NAICS 31522%, where % is any number from 0 to 9), (combined food & beverage industry: NAICS 3112%, where % is any number from 0 to 9, 311320,311520,311821,311941 & 312111), (chemical: NAICS 325188 & 325998), (consumer packaged goods: NAICS 3256%, where % is any number from 0 to 9), (grocery retail industry: NAICS 44511), (hospital industry: NAICS 62211), (mass retail industry: NAICS 452%, where % is any number from 0 to 9), (medical device industry: NAICS 339112), (pharmaceutical industry: NAICS 325412), (retail apparel industry: NAICS 44812 %, where % is any number from 0 to 9) reporting in One Source with 2012 annual sales greater than $5 billion.
Source: Supply Chain Insights LLC, Corporate Annual Reports 2000-2012.

and as growth slows, organizational tension for metrics improvements increases. Balance and resiliency on the Effective Frontier is tougher with slowing growth. This has been the struggle of many companies in the past three years."

"Okay, I get it," said Joe. "But what do I do? What is my call to action? My organization is clearly stuck, and I see that you are saying it's a mistake to focus on only a single metric like inventory. Help me with the next step. What do I do now?"

I loved Joe's natural curiosity and openness to learn. It was something that I do not see often. I leaned forward and continued, "Getting unstuck requires the management of the Effective Frontier as a system. The metrics are interrelated. There are finite trade-offs. As you learned firsthand in your meeting the other day, the organization must resist the temptation to focus on piece parts, or a singular metric in isolation." I shook my head, "The Effective Frontier needs to be managed as a complex system with complex processes with increasing complexity. As the business increases in complexity, the system needs to be continually redesigned."

"As a leadership team, you must keep a focus on outputs, not just inputs. To drive change, one of the first distinctions that you need to adopt as a leadership team is the difference between functional and corporate performance metrics. This is important if you are to determine the sustainable metrics framework to improve cross-functional success."

Joe nodded in agreement. "This is one of our major issues. We are so entrenched in functional metrics that it's hard for us to also focus on corporate performance. Our incentives are based on what is good for the function. Our sales leader, Frank, is focused on volume while I am incented on cost; and every time that I engage with Lou, our controller, the discussion is about cash. It is impossible for us to maintain a steady course and be balanced. We want to do the right thing by our corporate objectives, and we talk about these at quarterly and annual meetings, but we are not incented to make progress on what you call the Effective Frontier. Shouldn't this be cross-functional as a team?"

"Yes," I said, "You are not that different from other companies that I work with. Trust me, I understand."

"For best-performing companies, it is a series of conscious choices to improve capabilities and push to a new level of the Frontier. However, it happens slowly. It is only after achieving balance and resiliency in the current state that companies can push to a new level of performance. I define this as increasing 'organizational potential.' For this reason, the decision to move to a new level of the Effective Frontier is the last stage in the model," I said, while pointing to what is shown in Figure 1.3.

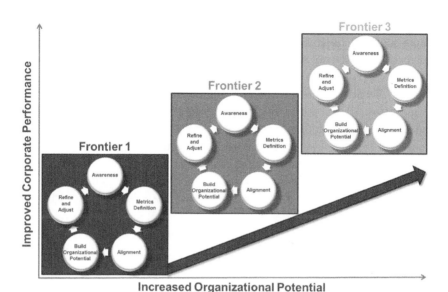

FIGURE 1.3 Moving from One Frontier to the Next

"When a company moves from one frontier to another, it requires a different type of thinking. To effectively make the transition from one level to another, companies have to adopt new mental models. They have to tackle change differently. It could be a new channel strategy or embracing new technologies and processes. Currently, the options abound. The challenge is choice, and working together to build potential cross-functionally."

Joe interrupted. "I have a question. After selecting the right path to move the company to the next frontier, how do companies manage change? The people component is the toughest for us. If others are anything like our organization, the organization is hardwired for incremental, and continuous, improvement. The adoption of a new mental model flies in the face of conventional continuous improvement programs. We are good at the process methodologies of Six Sigma and Lean because they focus on gradual continuous improvement. How do you get the leadership team to risk disruption, to break some eggs, and then put the processes back together again to move to the next level?" Joe asked. "It sounds risky, and as you know, it's hard to get people to agree to risk putting their job on the line."

"People put their jobs on the line all the time, especially by not taking action when action is required," I said. "That's even worse, and plenty of people have lost their jobs because they failed by not even trying. You were the victim of a layoff because the management team did not have the courage to make tough choices."

It was obvious that this point resonated, as Joe quickly retorted, "This is easier said than done. If you are stuck in the management of vertical metrics, you cannot see the big picture."

"This is the secret to building systems with the Metrics That Matter," I said. "You need to engage the entire team in a manner that not only gets mutual buy-in, but paves the future to deliver success. With incremental improvement, oftentimes one metric will win over another metric. Functional areas will become winners and losers. This is the power of defining a new frontier—you are all moving toward a common horizon that you've identified is desirable and attainable. To help you, I would like to share an interview that I recently completed with Marty Kisliuk of FMC. See if this resonates with your team. . . . "

"Good idea," said Joe. "Why, don't we have lunch and continue the discussion?"

The Journey of Managing the Effective Frontier

As leaders, we must move the frontier. It must be done strategically. Many times we get trapped to move one or two metrics instead of the entire frontier. To do this, we must see progress in the metrics that we measure. The rest will be victims of entropy.

To make progress, we have to be good at root-cause analysis. The organization must find the root cause and act quickly.

We must resist the temptation to focus on one or two metrics in isolation. When we do this, we cannot move the frontier to the next level. Instead, as a leadership team, you must find balance and then push to the next level of the Effective Frontier. It is a strategic activity. It is not a week-to-week or a month-to-month initiative. It needs to be focused end-to-end throughout the organization from the customer's customer to the supplier's supplier on an annual basis.

I don't think that we as business leaders recognize that we are on a frontier early enough. It is a paradox. It is the AND. You must move the metrics together while in balance and then redefine the process. Most organizations are not operating at full potential on their frontier and can make continuous improvements. However, when you reach full potential on the frontier, you must force a disruption and change the mental model.

Marty Kisliuk, Director of Global Operations, FMC Agricultural Solutions

The Efficient Organization Is Not the Most Effective

Over faded gray trays in the company cafeteria, I continued. "Computing power and connectivity made greater productivity possible. Over the course of the past decade, the average global multinational company invested 1.7 percent of revenue on information technology." I pulled a recent research study from my purse and pointed to the data (see Table 1.3). "The impact was a dramatic improvement in employee productivity, as defined by revenue per employee, in all manufacturing sectors.

"Technology was an enabler. For many, it was a disruptor. It permitted and empowered companies to increase potential and move to new levels of the Effective Frontier. Today, the belief that the efficient organization is the most effective defies conventional wisdom. The historic focus was to improve efficiency. The belief was that increasing efficiency would lower costs and improve performance." The reduction in labor did not translate to an improvement in operating margin. As I showed him the chart, I said, "However, as shown here, this singular focus had an adverse effect on operating margin and inventory cycles in 7 of the 11 industry sectors." Joe's eyes sparkled. He loved data, and motioned for me to continue.

"In some industries, costs were shifted. Three out of the 11 industries grew sales and general administration (SG&A) expenses. In an effort to spur growth, there was a shift in spending from the back office (manufacturing, distribution, procurement and logistics) to the front office (sales and marketing). There was a belief that we could save money in the back office, and move the money to the front office to fuel growth; however, this level of thinking was flawed. It was not that easy. Teams need to align to win together. Functions need to build potential on the Effective Frontier jointly as a strategy."

Joe asked, "So, since most companies went for improving employee productivity, why didn't margins improve at the same time?" As I stirred my black coffee, I saw that it was as opaque as the answer to his question. "I like this line of questioning. This is something that I am doing more research on, but right now, I believe that it was a misaligned emphasis on the *input* metric (revenue per employee), not a focus on the *output* metric (operating margin). Most companies can put data into systems, but they cannot get data out to measure progress. As a result, the focus is misaligned to concentrate on input, not output. That's why metrics matter so much! Would you agree?"

The Need to Focus on the Right Metrics as a Complex System

On the walk up the stairs back to his office, Joe stated, "I get it. Companies want to increase, or accelerate, inventory turns and reduce cash-to-cash

TABLE 1.3   Industry Progress over the Past Decade

Industry	Operating Margin	Inventory Turns	Cash-to-Cash Cycle	Revenue per Employee (K$)	SG&A Ratio
Industry Snapshots (2000–2012)					
Pharmaceutical Industry (n = 24)	0.19 ↑ 12%	3 ↓ 8%	139 ↓ 1%	462 ↑ 98%*	27% ↑ 24%*
Medical Device Industry (n = 6)	0.16 ↓ 56%	3 ↑ 2%	141 ↓ 4%	270 ↑ 59%*	28% ↓ 3%^
Retail Apparel Industry (n = 3)	0.14 NC%"	5 ↑ 1%"	9 ↑ 627%"	532 ↓ 26%^	19% ↑ 15%^
Brand Apparel Industry (n = 3)	0.13 ↑ 44%	4 ↑ 5%	91 ↓ 15%	254 ↑ 82%*	36% ↑ 14%^
Consumer Packaged Goods (n = 14)	0.13 ↑ 17%	5 ↑ 4%	45 ↓ 45%	333 ↑ 82%*	34% ↓ 15%*
Combined Food & Beverage Industry (n = 32)	011 ↑ 11%	8 NC	41 ↓ 26%	455 ↑ 122%*	19% ↓ 30%*
Chemical Industry (n = 7)	0.10 ↓ 45%	5 ↑ 5%	89 ↓ 16%	458 ↑ 118%*	14% ↓ 32%^
Hospital Industry (n = 6)	0.07 ↓ 11%"	11 ↑ 53%"	−84 ↓ 3215%"	165 ↑ 68%*	12% ↓ −54%*
Mass Retail Industry (n = 33)	0.05 ↑ 20%	8 ↑ 17%	47 ↓ 17%	482 ↑ 173%*	19% ↓ 4%*
Automotive Industry (n = 39)	0.04 ↑ 67%	15 ↑ 5%	44 ↓ 37%	616 ↑ 199%*	8% ↓ 30%*
Grocery Retail Industry (n = 37)	0.04 ↓ 33%	12 ↑12%	−7 ↓ 88%	358 ↑ 31%*	16% ↓ 16%*

Industry Average comprised of public companies (automotive industry: NAICS 336112), (brand apparel industry: NAICS 31522%, where % is any number from 0 to 9), (combined food & beverage industry: NAICS 3112%, where % is any number from 0 to 9, 311320,311520,311821,311941 & 312111), (chemical: NAICS 325188 & 325998), (consumer packaged goods: NAICS 3256%, where % is any number from 0 to 9), (grocery retail industry: NAICS44511), (hospital industry: NAICS 62211), (mass retail industry: NAICS 452%, where % is any number from 0 to 9), (medical device industry: NAICS 339112), (pharmaceutical industry: NAICS 325412), (retail apparel industry: NAICS 44812%, where % is any number from 0 to 9), reporting in One Source with 2012 annual sales greater than $5 billion.
"Calculated from 2001–2012 due to data availability;
*Calculated from 2002 to 2012 due to data availability;
^Calculated from 2003 to 2012 due to data availability;
NC = no change.
Source: Supply Chain Insights LLC, Corporate Annual Reports 2000–2012.

cycles. Improving inventory turns and decreasing cash cycles improves working capital; but, an increase in complexity will decrease margin and reduce inventory turns. They are connected and interrelated. Working these metrics as a complex system while on the effective frontier enables companies to build a road map to drive business strategy. The freeing of capital enables investment. Right?"

I nodded while laughing. Joe walked up the stairs two at a time leaving me out of breath as I struggled to keep up with him while continuing the dialogue. "In the past decade, the use of technology improved the results of large companies greater than $5 billion in revenue. While companies thought that the overall results would be greater, they improved efficiency, not the overall results that they hoped. As we discussed at lunch, it did improve revenue per employee. The adoption of processes and technologies has been slower in mid-market companies with less than $1 billion in revenue. *Whew* . . . " I said, as I leaned my hand against the wall at the top of the stairs to get my breath.

Joe laughed and said, "Sorry, I get carried away. I am so used to the stairs and taking them two at a time that I didn't mean to make you winded. I guess it's just easier for a tall guy to take these stairs fast. Let's take a moment to catch our breath. I appreciate you explaining this to me." We stood on the stair landing for a couple of minutes and talked about his challenges.

Moving Forward, Not Backward

As we walked down the hall, we continued the dialogue. Joe's questions were getting more intense. As he peppered me with them, I stated, "Today, there are more challenges to managing metrics trade-offs while on a frontier than earlier in my career. The pace of change is rapid. Think about it. Today, businesses are larger and more global. Organizations are not aligned. As a result, there is a greater need for focus and conscious choice."

Joe agreed. "I cannot speak for everyone, but I know for us the past decade was turbulent. Demand and supply volatility increased. Markets became more competitive. Merger and acquisition (M&A) activity was rampant. To meet the expectations of financial markets, we pushed costs and elongated the cycles of suppliers. This improved our cash-to-cash cycle by lengthening payables, but is starting to impact margin.

"It is easier to shift costs than improve internal operations," Joe continued. "Over the past year, I had a lot of pressure from my finance team to lengthen payables. However, I keep telling them that it is a penny-wise and pound-foolish strategy, but this is hard for them to see. Pushing costs and waste backward to suppliers and lengthening payables will give short-term benefit; but, I am now seeing that it can cause longer-term issues." The conversation had been as fast as our walk, and we were now back in Joe's office.

Moving to the Next Level on the Effective Frontier

"While this makes sense to me conceptually, it is difficult to orchestrate. As a leadership team, here, we are focused on functional metrics. The concept of the Effective Frontier is a new concept. How would you suggest that we go about adopting the methodology?" asked Joe.

I thought hard and leaned back in my chair. I paused for a moment, and said, "Each organization that I work with has its own unique potential, and is operating on its own frontier. Within each organization, the functional areas also have their own unique potential. The goal is to first recognize it on a corporate level, and then on a functional level, and then define the frontier that best realizes corporate objectives at all levels. The second goal is to know when to move to the next level. This takes training."

"I think that I am getting it. I am trying to absorb the concepts, but it is like drinking from a fire hose," Joe said.

"I know. It's for this reason that most organizations are treading water. It's hard to get the attention of the leadership team. With the rise of complexity in the last decade, most organizations have made unconscious trade-offs," I stated.

"What do you mean?" asked Joe. "Tell me more about unconscious trade-offs."

"Sure, let me explain," I continued. "As complexity increased—products proliferating and service expectations rising—the impact on the metrics portfolio and the potential of the organization is not known. While it can be modeled today using new technologies, most companies do not. It is not a conscious choice. The increase in complexity makes it harder to achieve the same level of operating margin and inventory turns," I said while looking at my watch.

"Why do companies not model it and drive the outcome to maximize potential?" asked Joe.

I shrugged my shoulders and shook my head. "Isn't it ironic that companies design factories, and work for years on the development of those factories, but do not model corporate performance systems? I think that it is because it is a new way of thinking," I stated and stood up and started to gather my papers and pack my briefcase.

"In the face of this challenge, there is a need to drive conscious choice on metrics trade-offs. I can work with you and your team to help you understand how industry leaders that did not modify business processes and assets to drive strength and year-over-year improvement in performance have struggled to deliver a balanced portfolio with resiliency. Joe, do you think that this would be possible?" Joe nodded his head yes, and motioned for me to continue as he said, "I know that you only promised to stay an hour, but I would like you to continue. I am finding this discussion to be very helpful."

"Okay," I said. "Let me make a phone call. Let's take a quick break, and we can work together for a couple of hours."

Getting Off the Plateau

"Thanks for staying," said Joe. "It's just that I don't get a lot of time to think strategically, and I am finding this helpful. Can we pick up where we stopped? Why are companies stuck?" asked Joe.

"The leader of operations knows that inventory cycles and costs need to be managed together. Each industry has a different set of rhythms and cycles. When complexity increases, these change. It is an industry-specific response. Over the past decade, the progress of industries has varied. Most companies are plateaued. Progress in corporate performance is stalled. Companies in the consumer electronics and consumer packaged-goods industries have made the most progress. Other industries, like apparel and automotive, are going backward and losing ground," I said as I showed him Figure 1.4.

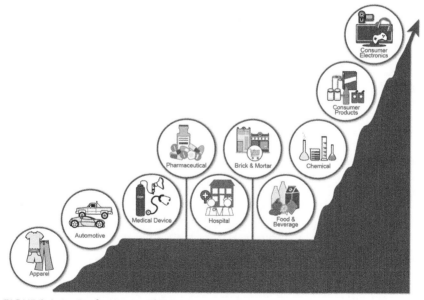

FIGURE 1.4   Performance Plateau
Source: Supply Chain Insights Metrics That Matter Series (www.supplychaininsights.com).

"It is easy to slip," Joe said as he gazed into the parking lot. The sun shone brightly as the bus stopped to let children off onto the sidewalk across the street in front of his office. "One of our issues is alignment. Every meeting is like the first day in school where we're trying to find our place. We have similar tasks but we are competing with each other."

"Yes, I know," I said following his gaze out the window. "To drive organizational alignment, companies need to understand the trade-offs, and what is possible, while defining the Effective Frontier and managing it as a complex system. It's like knowing what needs to be done to graduate to the next grade. They also need to choose the right metrics. It requires going back to school to rethink the basics of business."

TABLE 1.4   Financial Ratios Analyzed to Understand the Effective Frontier

Financial Metrics			
Growth	**Profitability**	**Cycle**	**Complexity**
Common Shares	Cash	Cash-to-Cash Cycle	Altman Z
Employee Growth	Cash Change in Period	Days of Finished Goods	Capital Turnover
Employees	Cash on Hand	Days of Inventory	Current Ratio
Market Capitalization	Cash Ratio TIM	Days of Payables Outstanding	Quick Ratio
R&D Margin	Cash Ratio Quarter	Days of Raw Materials	Return on Assets
R&D Ratio	Cash Ratio Year	Days of Sales Outstanding	Return on Equity
R&D to COGS Ratio	Cost of Goods Sold	Days of Work in Progress	Return on Invested Capital
Revenue	EBITDA	DPO/DSO	Return on Net Assets
Revenue Growth	Free Cash Flow Ratio	Finished Goods Inventory	Revenue per Employee
Revenue Growth TIM	Gross Margin	Inventory	Working Capital Ratio
Revenue TIM	Gross Profit	Inventory Turns	
SG&A Margin	Net Profit Margin	Receivables Turns	
SG&A Ratio	Operating Cash Flow Ratio	Raw Materials Inventory	
SG&A to COGS Ratio	Operating Margin	Work in Progress Inventory	
	OPEX Ratio		
	Pretax Margin		

Source: Supply Chain Insights LLC.

"These trade-offs cannot be determined just by setting up a spreadsheet. It requires the use of more advanced analytics. The use of modeling techniques allows companies to determine the appropriate targets in each metrics area to align against potential. To understand the concept of metrics balance, my research team has been evaluating the progress of each industry based on peer group metrics from each of the areas of the Effective Frontier," I said, while pushing the sheet shown in Table 1.4 across his desk. "These are available from corporate balance sheets and income statements; but we find that there are few repositories of this data to enable analysis of multiple years of data and to capture the patterns, so we've put together a unique data repository of our own from our research."

"Yes," Joe said. "I'm glad the metrics are available, but I'm too busy to try to sort out what's relevant to us. I'd like to take a look at what you've put together on this so we can do some benchmarking." The discussion then turned to a review of the research and what we could do together with his leadership team to build a guiding coalition to support the company's expansion into Brazil. I gave him an excerpt from a new book I was writing about the Effective Frontier to read when he got a minute.

Defining the Research Methodology to Understand Progress on the Effective Frontier

The definitions of ratios most commonly used in the analysis of corporate performance in this book are provided in the Appendix.

This book is the culmination of a three-year research project to understand effectiveness. To write this book, we built a database using public sources of information. We then grouped the data by NAICS codes, and began plotting the intersections of the Effective Frontier manually using orbit charts to understand the trends. We then began to review the patterns of the plots with industry leaders to gain insights into the drivers of the trends.

An orbit chart may seem abstract at first—like a modern art painting of wavy lines—but we have found that it is the best way to study the patterns, or progression, of operational metric performance over time.

Let's take a closer look. Figure 1.5 is an orbit chart example. This is the pattern, or progression, for Walmart for the period of 2002–2012 at the intersection of two metrics: inventory turns and operating margin. The averages for the period are shown in the box along with the stock

(continued)

(continued)

ticker symbol. In each orbit chart, because the metrics can get confusing, we identify which corner of the chart points toward the best scenario. Note that Walmart has made great improvements on inventory, but not in margins. As we will see later, Walmart is an example of a company that has made great strides in improving the efficiency of operations, but not in driving overall effectiveness.

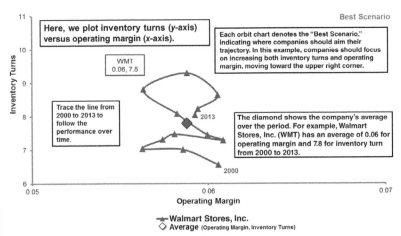

FIGURE 1.5 Example of an Orbit Chart
Source: Supply Chain Insights LLC, Corporate Annual Reports 2000–2013 from One Source.

I continued, "Joe, as we have mined the data, we find three intersections of the financial ratios to have the most interesting patterns. Each offers a distinctly different view, and you cannot assess improvement without looking at the three together." I wrote the three intersections on the whiteboard in his office:

1. Inventory turns versus operating margins
2. Year-over-year growth versus return on invested capital
3. Revenue per employee versus inventory turns

Joe hurriedly scribbled them down. As I worked with Joe, I found that he was writing more and more notes to himself in his black notebook. His intensity amused me. He was such an eager and willing student.

Details Matter: The Nitty-Gritty of the Analysis

"It's hard work," I continued. "In fact, we underestimated the amount of work to do the analysis of corporate balance sheet data and the determination of the Effective Frontier. When we started the analysis, we used absolute numbers, but we ended up using financial ratios. This shift enabled the comparison of companies across currencies and enabled us to better understand the trends of companies of differing sizes. After plotting the trends, we partnered with an operations research team at Arizona State University to help define the methodology to determine balance and resiliency. The data is complex, and we wanted to define a simple methodology to translate abstract patterns into meaningful insights."

"I have difficulty doing this type of analysis, but when I see your research, I love it. I am a fan," said Joe. "It's one thing to talk about corporate performance, and another to understand how it transforms a balance sheet. When I get to the point when I understand this, I will feel real pride."

I smiled and nodded in agreement. "Let me share some insights. One of our first big insights when we started looking at performance results was the danger of using compound metrics in a vacuum. Let me explain: A compound metric is the result of a combination of individual metrics. For example, the two most commonly used compound metrics that one finds in corporate measurement systems are 'cash-to-cash' and 'perfect order.' Let's take cash-to-cash." I then turned to his board and wrote, "Cash-to-cash (C2C) = Days of receivables (DOR) + Days of inventory (DOI) – Days of payables (DOP) outstanding."

Continuing, I said, "So, when you look at progress in C2C, as a leader, you must ask a series of questions:

- What drove the change?
- Did we change the policies with our customers, resulting in a change in DOR, or did we make the terms longer with our suppliers, increasing DOP? Or did we make improvements in inventory (DOI)?
- How have these three elements changed over time?"

Joe agreed, "The answer could be one, any, or even all of them. I see how a compound metric might make it hard to compare one company to another, because they could be getting a similar result for very different reasons!"

"Yes," I said. "For example, we found that the most common driver of cash-to-cash improvements was lengthening the days of payables and paying suppliers later."

Joe rubbed his hands and smiled, and said, "That sounds familiar. It worked for one quarter before it caught up with us. This is a difficult discussion to have with our financial team. When the push for cash is on, it sounds so simple to increase payables; but, I know that we end up eating it when our operating margin rises a couple of quarters after the change."

"Another compound metric is the 'perfect order.' Do you use this for customer service?" I asked.

"We tried it a couple of years ago, but dropped it because it was too hard," Joe said.

I continued, "I understand. This metric lacks an industry-standard definition, and varies from company to company, but many companies try to use it. The most common definition is based on an equation using three metrics."

I wrote on his whiteboard:

Perfect order = Number of total orders shipped for a period

> – (Orders that did not ship on time as per the customer's request date)
> – (Number of orders that did not ship complete with the products ordered)
> – (Number of orders that had damage on receipt)

I spun around and continued, "Similar to the cash-to-cash discussion, if there is a change in the perfect order, the answer is not obvious. Instead, companies have to ask:

- What drove the change?
- How have these three elements changed over time?
- What affected the performance in the three components of this metric over time?

As a result, companies should use caution in using compound metrics and absolute numbers. Compound numbers can drive the wrong conclusions and absolute numbers do not allow the level of comparison needed for benchmarking between companies."

Joe was now pacing. "So much to learn. So much to do. How do we get started?" he asked.

Benchmarking Companies over Time

"There are many ways that we could work together," I said. "The methodology doesn't just apply to the benchmarking the whole company. It can also yield valuable insights at a finer, more granular level by benchmarking divisions. In our work with clients, we find that segmentation of the business by division, and by geographies within the company, yields valuable insights. When we do this more detailed analysis—analyzing divisional and geographic data—the concepts are more quickly grasped by the team."

Then, I showed him an example of this type of analysis as illustrated in Figure 1.6.

"See, Joe, in this example, the patterns of the two divisions of this company are very clear. Division 1 is operating at a higher potential and making year-over-year improvement, while Division 2 is struggling to make clear headway. The use of root-cause analysis to discover the 'why' can help the organization drive continuous improvement and maximize the potential of Division 2 on the Effective Frontier," I said.

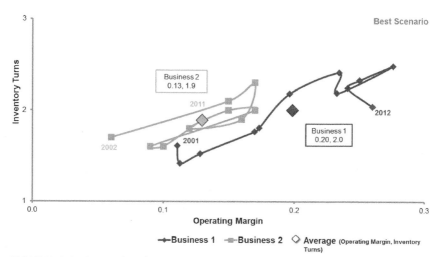

FIGURE 1.6 Example of an Orbit Chart Comparing Two Businesses within a Corporation on Inventory Turns versus Operating Margin
Source: Supply Chain Insights LLC, Corporate Annual Reports 2001–2012 from One Source.

Joe then said, "I love it. I would like to talk to you about doing this type of analysis for all our divisions and geographies. I think that it could help our team. Let's talk about how we could do this. We've put so many systems in place already to try to see patterns in our data, yet we've still not got any insight."

Rethinking Metrics: Using Technology to Manage the Organization in the Information Age

I looked at my watch and said, "I know we only have another hour together, but let me give you a short answer of why I think this has happened, and maybe we can pick it up when we meet again. The ability to drive data-driven decisions has improved through the use of technology. Dashboards, scorecards, in-memory reporting, and visibility technologies make it easier to manage metrics within a company, but companies have to be clear on the metrics strategies. This is the challenge for every Joe like you."

With that, Joe laughed. "So, I am not unique? Do other organizations have the same problem?"

I nodded, saying, "Many times companies will leap to improve metrics through technology without doing the hard work of figuring out which metrics matter and how to align the key performance indicators into a metrics strategy.

"There is also an issue of functional myopia. The views of operations and finance do not easily align. One of the problems is that financial metrics are backward-looking and transactional, while operational metrics are forward-looking based on flows. But the metrics you get from technology are based only on historical data. It's like trying to drive a car on a winding road at 60 miles an hour while looking in the rear-view mirror to steer. Closing this gap requires descriptive, predictive, and prescriptive analytics. While descriptive analytics enable reporting and data analysis, predictive and prescriptive analytics enable the management of operational flows. In contrast, predictive analytics enable operational alerting while prescriptive technologies recommend actions to take. Robust analytics are essential to ensure metrics alignment and are an important step in driving success on a metrics journey."

"This has certainly been one of our issues," said Joe. "We have a guy on the sales team who's really smart and can put together spreadsheets so we can analyze all kinds of things, but they're all about what's already happened, and the sales forecasts. . . . Well, you know, they're really only good about three or four months out, and the sales team always inflates the numbers. It's an ongoing problem."

"When embarking on a project to improve metrics, the average Joe, like you, will need to work with the information technology (IT) department to build measurement systems. This includes self-service reporting, dashboards and scorecards, and alerting systems. Analytics technologies are closely woven into a metrics project to make progress possible. It should be easy, but it is not. I would like to tell you more, but right now I really must be going. As much as I have enjoyed the discussion, I am late." I then suggested that Joe read the article that I had just completed, "Managing Metrics in the Information Age." We agreed to discuss it at our next meeting.

With that, we shook hands and I left my article on Joe's desk. Some excerpts are offered in the following feature.

Managing Metrics in the Information Age

Today, business leaders live in the Information Age. Technologies make new ideas possible. Data flows quicker and computational power enables quicker assessment of complex problems. Decisions can be more data-driven and real-time information enables new capabilities. More and more, metrics can be measured. Targets can be assessed more quickly. However, this only adds value if the technological advancements can be successfully aligned with business outcomes. This is the challenge.

Why is there a problem? Simply put, companies are new at it. We are only 40 years into the Information Age. The adoption of technology in the Information Age followed the Industrial Revolution. The Industrial Revolution was all about mechanization. There was a shift from making things by hand to the mechanization and adoption of manufacturing processes. The focus was on the management of physical assets. It was all about the control of financial assets and liabilities.[1]

The Information Age started in 1975 with the widespread adoption of computers. The practices and policies were a stark contrast to those of the Industrial Revolution that stretched from 1850 to 1975. It makes possible global connectivity and new forms of analytics to drive business insights. Today, most organizations are retiring leaders from the Industrial Age while trying to maximize the potential of the Information Age. This changing of the guard is not easy.

(continued)

(*continued*)

Impact of the Information Age on Metrics and Corporate Performance

This shift was a fundamental change at the core of the organization with intense repercussions:

What drives value. In the Information Age, companies are wired differently. Products and services are enhanced by data. OnStar differentiated General Motors while Pandora redefined the music experience. Around us today, digital data transmission improves the value of molecules and atoms. As a result, manufacturing is more information intensive with less labor and capital dependency. Ironically, workers are more productive today, yet their wage rates are less. Market drivers are constantly changing. Metrics are more complex.

Redefinition of management principles. In the traditional management models of the Industrial Age, investments in people were the primary predictors of a new venture's future performance. This is not so today. It is now possible for a group of relatively inexperienced people—as demonstrated by Facebook, Microsoft, and Twitter—with limited capital, to succeed on a large scale. Metrics help to ignite groups of people to action.

Global workers. As connectivity has removed the friction from borders, workers now compete in a global economy. For example, in the United States, from January 1972 to August 2010, the number of people employed in manufacturing positions fell from 17,500,000 to 11,500,000 while manufacturing value rose 270 percent.[2] In the next decade this pattern will continue. Metrics have different definitions in different countries. With language and cultural issues, it is critical that the metrics are simple and clearly communicated.

Redefinition of the office. More and more employees telecommute. The water cooler is now a virtual experience. In 2012, 2.6 percent of the U.S. employee workforce (3.3 million people, not including the self-employed or unpaid volunteers) considers their home as their primary place of work.[3] As a result, it is more important for companies to have metric dashboards. Leadership teams have to focus more energy on the communication of goals and results. Organizational alignment is more difficult.

Management of the global company. Over the past decade companies have become global. However, companies define "global" differently. While each organization we study defines global governance models slightly differently, they will all agree that the management of a global organization is growing increasingly more difficult. The definitions of regional/global governance, and the evolution of KPIs for a global organization, are critical elements to manage a successful global organization.

Processes that have not caught up with the change in technology. Our technologies are digital. Our processes are not. While the cost of computing has moved from $222 to $.06 per million transistors and storage costs have moved from $569 to $.03 per gigabyte of storage, and Internet bandwidth has improved from $1,245 to $23 per megabits per second, the organization's operational processes remain relatively unchanged.[4] Most companies have digital technologies with analog-based processes. We have not redefined metrics based on what is possible. New possibilities abound. The impact of less data latency and increasing capabilities of mobility and sensor data offer a wealth of opportunities.

Proliferation of data and a need for insights. We are living in the Information Age. Data abounds. Global connectivity transcends borders. Third-generation analytic systems improve workflows. Real-time data is now possible. Yet, as shown in Figure 1.7, companies struggle to use data. Employees cannot get the data that they need. It is their number-one business issue. As a result, metrics need to be defined very clearly while understanding the limitations in data availability.

Data is growing in velocity and variety. However, companies' ability to use data is limited, and the capability of the company to drive performance based on data-driven decisions aligned with metrics is even more immature. It is a limiting factor to actualizing the promise of the information economy.

Will New Technologies Help? Could Big Data Systems Offer Promise?

Many think that the answer lies in new technologies. Some may also allege that the technologies associated with the current Big Data technology evolution may help. We partially agree. It is our view that we need to start with the rationalization of metrics and design of data-driven processes, while avoiding the hype about Big Data technologies.

To clarify the discussion, let's start with a definition. For the purposes of this book, we define Big Data as processes with data volume greater than a petabyte. This large data volume is often coupled with a growing variety and velocity of data.

A petabyte of data sounds like a lot of data, but how much is it, really? A petabyte of data is 1,024 terabytes. A terabyte of data is 1,024 gigabytes. In more graphical terms, a petabyte of data represents

(continued)

(continued)

20 million four-drawer filing cabinets filled with text or the storage of 13.3 years of HDTV video. Twenty petabytes represents the amount of data processed by Google on a daily basis. It also represents the number of hard-disk-drive spaces manufactured in 1995.[5]

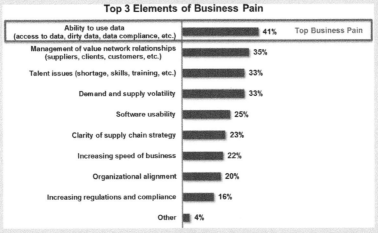

Top 3 Elements of Business Pain

Ability to use data (access to data, dirty data, data compliance, etc.)	41% Top Business Pain
Management of value network relationships (suppliers, clients, customers, etc.)	35%
Talent issues (shortage, skills, training, etc.)	33%
Demand and supply volatility	33%
Software usability	25%
Clarity of supply chain strategy	23%
Increasing speed of business	22%
Organizational alignment	20%
Increasing regulations and compliance	16%
Other	4%

FIGURE 1.7 Employees within Corporations Struggle to Get the Right Data
Base: Manufacturers, Retailers, Distributors, 3Pls, and Other with EDI/XML—Total (*n* = 79).
When it comes to supply chain management, which of these items are the top three elements of business pain for you personally? Please select no more than three.
Source: Supply Chain Insights LLC, 828 Study (June–September 2013).

Unfortunately, the term *Big Data* is the buzzword du jour. While most companies are intrigued with Big Data concepts, companies cannot effectively use the data that they have today, and most do not have the levels of data volume that would qualify for the Big Data definition used in this book. Today, new concepts are emerging that over time could enable disruption to move companies to the next frontier. However, based on current maturity models, the focus today should be the use of technology to improve analytics to drive continuous improvement on the Effective Frontier.

A Future View of Big Data as a Potential Disruptor

When it comes to Big Data, confusion reigns. To drive the opportunity, companies must bypass the hype. Over the next five years, Big Data concepts will become a reality; however, there are three areas of concern to focus on to maximize the value.

1. *New architectures.* Most of the value will come from new forms of data. These new forms of data do not fit well into traditional architectures. Traditional systems use only structured data. The Big Data era will make many of the investments from the last decade obsolete. As these new architectures are defined, many will forget the need to align and design metrics systems to drive data-driven decisions.
2. *Process experimentation.* Big Data offers the opportunity to redefine processes from the outside-in (from the channel back) and define customer-centric operations. This is in stark contrast to the inflexible IT investments installed over the last decade that respond inside-out based on orders and shipments.

   These traditional investments improved the organization's response, but did not allow the organization to sense, shape, or orchestrate processes based on market signals, outside-in, from market-to-market. New forms of data (e.g., pictures, images, social data, sensor transmissions, input from global positioning systems (GPS), the Internet of Things, and unstructured text from e-mail, blogs, and ratings and reviews) offer new opportunities, but they also require new techniques and technologies. These initiatives are promising, but should be seen as experimental. They will slowly take shape and enable opportunities over the next five years.
3. *Skillsets.* To mobilize, companies need to train and develop people with new skills and embrace new forms of technologies. The technologies are immature and the concepts are emerging. As a result, business leaders should see the evolution of Big Data concepts as an investment in the future.

As a result, Big Data technologies are promising, but they are too immature today to help leaders fulfill the short-term promise of the Information Age. For many, it will be a distraction. For the leader, it should be seen as a long-term investment with a promising, but uncertain, outcome. In short, we cannot ignore the trend, but it does not help us today to capture the opportunity of improving the Metrics That Matter in the Information Age. Instead, companies should maximize the use of descriptive, prescriptive, and predictive analytics to improve metrics performance.

The next Monday, my phone rang. It was Joe. He was animated as he explained, "I loved your article. It makes so much sense. I am starting to understand why we are not making more progress. We are looking at technology for technology's sake. We are not clear on how to use data. I think one of our issues is organizational alignment. Can you come back to see me and continue our discussion next week?" I checked my calendar and booked a time for Joe.

Improving Performance

The next Tuesday, I found myself back in Joe's office with a warm cup of black coffee in my hand. Joe was excited to tell me about his week. The team was in the middle of a major transformation to start up a new operation in Brazil and he thought I could help. As we discussed the project, we talked about the issues of organizational alignment.

"When metrics are aligned to the right data, and processes and information are aligned to drive performance, great things happen. For most companies this is the goal. Why, then, have companies stumbled? As you have seen in the case studies in my recent book, *Bricks Matter*, when metrics are well defined and data is aligned, companies outperform their peers, and the organization has greater resiliency. However, when it is done poorly, progress is stalled and metrics performance is halted," I explained.

Joe then asked, "Why is resiliency important? Why do you put so much emphasis on it in your writing?"

"Companies want reliability in performance. Resiliency is a measurement of reliability. When given the choice between fast improvement with volatility, and slower results with more reliability, companies will choose reliability. The environment is tougher, making reliability both more important and even more difficult to achieve. Markets, with impacts from both channel and supplier relationships, are more volatile. When the organization is resilient, as the market shifts, corporate systems, where data and processes are aligned with metrics, can flex to ensure that the desired portfolio of metrics can be managed to drive year-over-year improvements. Make sense?" I asked.

Joe nodded, but I could see that he was still unsure.

Resiliency—the physical property of a material that can return to its original shape or position after deformation that does not exceed its elastic limit.[6]

"Let me give you an example. Maybe this will resonate. During the recession that started in December 2007, organizations were not resilient. The impact varied by industry, but was more pronounced on corporate maturity and metric alignment in industries further back in the value chain. In industries like chemical and plastics, factories were shuttered. Some companies like Chrysler, General Motors, and Lyondell Chemical filed for bankruptcy and survived through restructuring. Some like Smurfit-Stone, a manufacturer of corrugated paper-board, filed for bankruptcy in the middle of the 2007 recession only to trigger an 83 percent drop in stock price. The company was later sold to Rock-Tenn Corporation. It was a stress test for all. The impacts were extreme. Did you feel the impact of the last recession, Joe?" I queried.

"Yes, it was an issue. During this time, I was in the office of the CFO every day. The pressure was intense. I called it my morning thrashing. We didn't know what was happening in the market and we were scrambling. There was a lot of finger pointing," Joe stated.

I continued, "Most organizations lack resiliency. One of the issues is the latency of demand data. The second barrier is the ability to get to data. And the third issue is selection of the right metrics. To become more resilient requires resolving all three issues. Sadly, as companies start to build resiliency, they will be reminded that the promise of the Information Age still lies before us. Much of the data in the corporation is unused. While many will claim that manufacturing companies have been transformed by the Information Age, I take a contrarian view. I believe that companies are evolving. Businesses have changed too much over the past decade to not rethink metrics systems. In fact, the change has been so great that many executives, like you, Joe, are struggling. Did you read my recent article on Verizon?"

Change at Verizon Wireless

Ten years ago there were two mobile phone options. One product looked like a candy bar and one resembled a clamshell. This week, we opened an experience center for customers in a major city. A lot has changed.

This year, we will see the need for micro-segmentation of inventory policy to even a greater degree. We are launching a number of new programs, including same-day delivery and Omni-channel service, and the introduction of new services creates the need for new and different

(continued)

> (*continued*)
>
> approaches to metrics. Our goal is to have any inventory item in the network to service any order for any channel. Making that happen is a challenge. This 10-year evolution in metrics is enormous in scope. The product has moved from being a purchasing afterthought, to being a fashion item, to trying to be a platform for life. The metrics cannot stay the same.
>
> Anne Robinson, Verizon

Joe stood up and paced the floor, saying, "The cell phone industry is a wonderful case study to show change. I remember having one of the clamshells and exchanging it for a brick, and now I have one of these." He opened his drawer to show me the turquoise case of an iPhone. "So much has changed in such little time. Think about the impact of this level of change on Verizon's operations."

Driving Metrics Alignment

"It is difficult to take all of this in at times. It's like change is happening so fast on the outside, and so slow on the inside," Joe said. "We've had the same kinds of issues like Verizon with rapid changes in the marketplace. It causes a lot of tension, especially between sales and operations, but also finance, because we wind up with too much inventory of the wrong type. There are so many moving parts—how do we find time to talk about metrics? Everyone's so focused on their own problems, there's not a lot of interest in getting everyone aligned—today we're too functional to even have that discussion!"

Alignment is the essence of management.

Fred Smith, Federal Express

"I know, it's challenging," I responded. "While many companies talk about alignment, few are able to accomplish their goal. However, when organizations are aligned, things happen more quickly. It takes less effort. People know what to do, and there is a greater bias for action. As a result, the organization can achieve higher levels of results and better withstand the pressures of demand-and-supply volatility.

"Let me share some recent research with you." I flipped an organization chart (Figure 1.8) onto Joe's desk and continued, "It is hard for functional goals

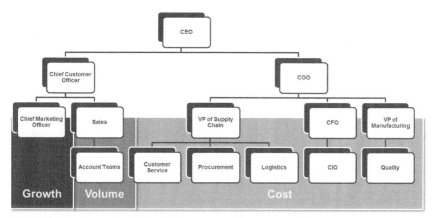

FIGURE 1.8   Functional Goals Overpower Corporate Objectives

not to outweigh and overtake corporate objectives when you see where the bulk of the organization is focused."

I continued, "Groups within an organization see and feel alignment issues very differently. In 2013, we studied three groups within the corporation to understand the perceived differences and similarities of organizational alignment. The three functions were supply chain, corporate finance, and information technology (IT) groups.

"In this research, we observed very different patterns in perceived alignment of the functions. In this study[7] of over 140 participants, we asked each respondent to rate the importance of functional alignment to a business function, and then rank their corporate performance," I said. I shared the results of the study with Joe, shown here as Figures 1.9a, 1.9b, and 1.9c.

Joe took the three sheets of paper and taped them to his wall and sat back and stared. When he saw the pattern, he laughed. "It figures. Look at this data. The supply chain operating team feels more gaps in functional alignment than the finance and IT teams. The supply chain team, by definition, is more cross-functional in nature and feels the impact of functional misalignment more critically in day-to-day operations. The IT teams tend to overstate both their performance and the relative alignment of their business partners, and the finance teams tend to be insular to alignment problems and opportunities. I see this every day." As he thought, he whistled a low shrill note, rubbed his hands together, and said, "This is the case for sure here, but what do we do? What steps do we take? It seems to me that we have to close these gaps if we're going to build a cohesive metrics structure to improve corporate performance."

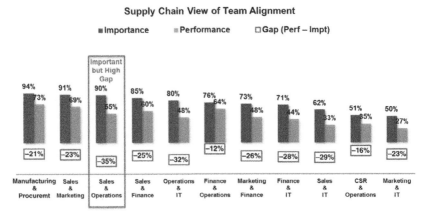

FIGURE 1.9a   Organizational Views on Alignment by Supply Chain
Base: Manufacturers: Supply Chain (*n* = 105)
Q22. In your opinion, how important is it for each of these pairs of teams to be aligned within your company? SCALE: 1 = Not at all important, 7 = Extremely important
Q23. How aligned do you believe that these same pairs of teams actually are with your company? SCALE: 1 = Not at all aligned, 7 = Extremely aligned
Showing: % rated 5–7 on 7-point scale.
Source: Supply Chain Insights LLC, Alignment Survey (March–May 2013).

I loved the dialogue. Joe's natural curiosity made him a great student of research. I continued, "Better alignment happens when companies focus on five things." I then listed these five items on the board:

1. A balanced metrics portfolio with aligned incentives.
2. Horizontal cross-functional processes aligned end-to-end against a business strategy.
3. The definition of a clear operating strategy.
4. The translation of the metrics up and down the organization to make them actionable. They need to be defined for the guy and gal on the plant floor as well as the chief operating officer (COO).
5. Alignment to incentives. Metrics and incentives are tightly woven in change management activities.

"To drive better alignment, companies need to change the conversation. The metrics need to be designed and aligned. It is not about continuous improvement of yesterday's processes; instead, it is about aligning on new mental models within the company to focus on the future."

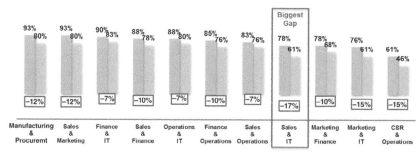

FIGURE 1.9b Organizational Views on Alignment by IT
Base: Manufacturers: IT (*n* = 41)
Q22: In your opinion, how important is it for each of these pairs of teams to be aligned within your company? SCALE: 1 = Not at all important, 7 = Extremely important
Q23: How aligned do you believe that these same pairs of teams actually are with your company? SCALE: 1 = Not at all aligned, 7 = Extremely aligned
Showing: % rated 5–7 on 7-point scale
Source: Supply Chain Insights LLC, Alignment Survey (March–May 2013).

I then looked at Joe, and commented, "Does this make sense?" There was silence in the room. Joe was busy writing in his notebook.

"Absolutely! I am just thinking about how we get from here to there. My boss keeps telling me that we need to be aligned and agile, but he has not defined it. I am thinking about how to approach him with this research. Do you have anything that you could add about agility?"

AGILITY

"Yes, most of the time organizations will use these terms loosely and do not define them enough to make them actionable," I continued. "To achieve metrics resiliency, companies need to improve organizational agility. In our research, we define agility as the ability to achieve the same cost, quality, and customer service given a level of demand-and-supply volatility."

"While many companies state that they want to be 'agile,' they fail to define it adequately enough to make it actionable. There is no industry-standard definition. As a result, without a good definition, the company is not able to make

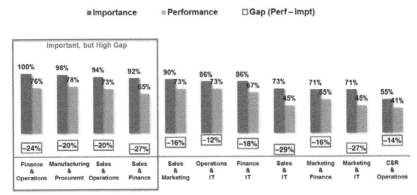

FIGURE 1.9c Organizational Views on Alignment by Finance
Base: Manufacturers—Finance (*n* = 49)
Q22. In your opinion, how important is it for each of these pairs of teams to be aligned within your company? SCALE: 1 = Not at all important, 7 = Extremely important
Q23. How aligned do you believe that these same pairs of teams actually are with your company? SCALE: 1 =Not at all aligned, 7=Extremely aligned
Showing: % rated 5–7 on 7-point scale
Source: Supply Chain Insights LLC, Alignment Survey (March–May 2013).

progress. We find in our study that there are trade-offs between agility and efficiency (as defined as the lowest cost per case or the lowest labor input per unit). By definition, the agile response is also not the most efficient response. The company that designs the most efficient response with the lowest cost per unit, by definition, will not have an agile output. It is about conscious choice. The definitions of a responsive, agile, and efficient response are mutually exclusive. They can be defined by the same metrics systems but require different targets. As a result, to achieve agility, the metrics' targets need to be aligned to drive the right response."

I passed Joe the recent research that I had completed on Agility (shown here as Figure 1.10). I continued, "Based on quantitative studies, we find that the gap in enterprise agility today is high and needs to be a key pillar in the definition of an operating strategy. The focus on the efficient organization has made the organizational response brittle, and unable to flex with market changes."

"Is this the same thing as responsiveness? Or short cycles?" asked Joe.

I shook my head. "No. Agility also cannot be confused with responsiveness. While responsiveness is shorter cycles and a quicker response, the definition of

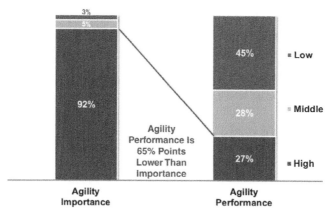

FIGURE 1.10   Importance versus Current Performance on Enterprise Agility
Base: Manufacturers: Total (*n* = 92)
Q12. How important is it for your company's supply chain to be "agile" in 2012? Please base your answer on however your company defines agility. SCALE: 1 = Not at all important, 7 = Extremely important
Q13. How would you currently rate your company's supply chain in terms of being "agile"? SCALE: 1 = Not at all agile, 7 = Extremely agile; Low = 1–3, Middle = 4, High = 5-7
Source: Supply Chain Insights LLC, S&OP (April–May 2013).

agility in enterprise strategy is a much deeper concept. While responsiveness improves cycles, agility improves the potential of the system to absorb volatility and improve resiliency. It is a common misconception. A good example is a footwear company that I worked with in 2005."

Footwear Case Study

We once worked with a footwear company that believed that shorter cycles could improve corporate performance. The company's cycles were shorter than competitors', but the margins were 18 percent higher on average, and their inventory turns were 50 percent worse. As a result, the company had successfully done the wrong things faster, throwing the system out of balance. We see this happen frequently. It is important to get very clear on the definitions of agility and responsiveness.

"My boss, Filipe, thinks that a short cycle solves everything. I would love to have you talk to him," said Joe, laughing.

 ## EVOLUTION

"Let me know when Filipe is available," I stated. "Metrics evolve over time. The portfolio of business metrics needs to be revisited as the business strategy changes. It needs to be grounded in conscious trade-offs. It needs to be managed with systems thinking so that when Filipe is thinking about defining agility, responsiveness, or driving alignment the set-points of metrics are based on the capabilities and potentials of the organization." I then looked at the clock on the wall and commented, "I know that it's getting late. Let me leave you with a story from my friend, Mike. He likes to create bonsai trees, but he also runs a retail store. Here is his take on the development of a metrics system."

> I love to create bonsai trees. I have taken lessons in how to create a bonsai for over 14 years. I also love metrics and the creation of metrics systems. They have a lot in common. My bonsai tree teacher says, "Let the tree speak to you as you care for it, and trim the branches, and you will have a better product." In my view, metrics are the same. You let the metrics evolve, while letting the organization speak to you about what is important. They must evolve slowly and over time.
>
> Interview with a Retail Supply Chain Leader

"I like that study," Joe said, "I'm not sure if I should be proud or embarrassed. . . . I must admit, when I started in my role I was very focused on my own experiences. These were rooted in manufacturing with a commodity orientation. I was blinded by functional metrics. I did not realize then how wrong I was.

"An individual can get so easily baited into a bad set of functional metrics. We should never look at single metrics in isolation. Last month, I made a bad mistake in setting my BHAG."

"Joe, don't be too hard on yourself," I continued. "There is a lot to learn, and there is also a need for continuous alignment. Look at how your organization has changed. Mergers and acquisitions, changing business policies, expansion into global markets, new markets, and channels, the expansion of new product lines, and market volatility top the list of changes. I know the list goes on and on. All metrics can be gamed, but they drive directional alignment. Business leaders, in interviews for my new book, recommend:

- Don't overorchestrate and overthink the metrics. They will never be perfect. There is also an opportunity cost to the organization by trying to make them too perfect.
- Focus on the forward momentum that the metric drives while being aware of adverse behavior that a metric can cause.
- Balance metrics horizontally and vertically, focused on the business strategy.

"Does this make sense?" I asked.

Joe nodded and said, "I wish we could move faster as a team here in driving our strategy. Can you come back a week earlier so we can dig a little deeper? I have some projects coming up that I see now could be a disaster if we don't get the metrics right."

"Sure," I said, "But let me leave you with a thought—just like Rome wasn't built in a day, metrics need to evolve. We believe that strength, balance, and resiliency are important components of a high-performing organization, and they need to get there through organizational alignment, which means getting your whole team operating with the same perspective about these metrics. I think that you now agree."

Joe was still rapidly writing notes from our session in his journal. As he walked me to the door, I asked if I could see his notes. He got a broad-faced grin as I slowly read his writing. Sheepishly, he asked, "Did I get it right?" I gave him a warm embrace goodbye and said, "I wish that all of my students were this quick at capturing the insights." With that, I said good-bye to Joe.

The Notes from Joe's Journal

In the implementation of metrics strategies to improve corporate performance, remember these nine recommendations:

1. Manage the metrics as a system. Design the portfolio of metrics to include the critical elements of customer service, inventory/cash cycles, profitability, and market share. Understand the interrelationships and manage the metrics portfolio as a complex system.

(*continued*)

(continued)

2. Get clear. Be concrete. Drive alignment. Terms like *flexible, responsive, agile, efficient, customer-centric,* and *demand-driven* permeate corporate strategy documents, but they mean different things to different people. Unless the terms are clearly defined and aligned to metrics, they are not actionable. Take the time to define each term and align the desired outcome to a portfolio of metrics.

3. Understand corporate potential before you set targets. Understand your company's potential within your peer group. Study the patterns of industries to determine what is possible. Then use advanced analytics to determine the potential of your division or company.

4. Drive balance in a metrics portfolio. Clearly articulate the business outcome and define a balanced portfolio of metrics to drive improvement. Hold the entire organization accountable for the same portfolio of metrics.

5. Make conscious trade-offs. In the analysis and determination of organizational potential, the interrelationships between growth, profitability, cycles, and complexity metrics will become clear. Use modeling technologies to understand the trade-offs and drive the analysis to make conscious trade-offs.

6. Evolve. Metrics evolve as organizations mature. Review metrics annually and align them with the business strategy. Embrace technology and product disruptors to move the organization to the next frontier.

7. Take care in working with compound metrics. In this chapter we discussed the danger of working with compound metrics. Use them carefully.

8. Stay the course. As a leader, avoid knee-jerk reactions and "programs of the month." Measurements should not be viewed and managed in isolation. Instead, manage individual metrics as integral pieces of a complex system.

9. Be patient. This takes time.

CONCLUSION

As I turned the key in the ignition of my car, Joe's voice was in my head. I kept remembering snippets from our conversation: "Metrics are complex." "Organizations are not naturally aligned." "Analytics can improve measurement." "To move forward, align around a few metrics and manage them as a system, with a focus on a balanced portfolio. Stay focused on your journey."

On the drive out of the parking lot, I reflected on the past couple of days and our discussions about metrics that matter. As I thought, I concluded that as companies mature, they learn that corporate performance cannot be sustained without redesigning the enabling processes. For the organization, this is an intense change management journey. I looked forward to meeting Filipe and working with the larger organization to optimize performance on the Effective Frontier.

Notes

1. A. D. Chandler, Jr., *The Visible Hand: The Managerial Revolution in American Business* (Cambridge, MA: Harvard University Press, 1977); and T. H. Johnson and R. S. Kaplan, *Relevance Lost: The Rise and Fall of Management Accounting* (Cambridge, MA: Harvard Business School Press, 1987).
2. "U.S. Manufacturing: Output vs. Jobs, January 1972 to August 2010," BLS and Fed Reserve graphic, in Fran Smith, "Job Losses and Productivity Gains," OpenMarket.org, October 5, 2010, www.openmarket.org/2010/10/05/job-losses-and-productivity-gains.
3. Global Workplace Analytics, www.globalworkplaceanalytics.com (accessed January 4, 2014).
4. Deloitte, from "Exponential Technologies to Exponential Innovation," Report 2 of the 2013 Shift Index Series.
5. "How Much Is a Petabyte of Data?" *Mozy Blog*, http://mozy.com/blog/misc/how-much-is-a-petabyte (accessed January 4, 2014).
6. The Free Dictionary, www.thefreedictionary.com/resiliency (accessed January 4, 2014).
7. Supply Chain Insights LLC, "Three Techniques to Improve Organizational Alignment," report published July 8, 2013, http://supplychaininsights.com/three-techniques-to-improve-organizational-alignment.

CHAPTER TWO

Managing Metrics on the Effective Frontier

T WAS SPRING. The Kwanzan cherry trees were in full bloom as I walked to Joe's office. While Joe and I had actively communicated over the past three months, this was our first time to meet together face-to-face since our winter session.

I knew as I opened the door to Joe's office that he was thinking hard about the concepts, but he was struggling with how to make them actionable. While he knew that he needed to manage a portfolio of metrics and improve the potential of the organization to conquer the Effective Frontier, his question was, "How?" For him, it was a new way of thinking, and while the concepts stimulated a lot of thought, Joe wanted to take them to the next step. Our goal on this warm spring day was to continue the discussion and formulate a plan to use the concepts as the foundation for his new project.

With so many new products in the pipeline, Joe's company was busy executing a growth strategy. To me, the air in a company feels different when it's growing. It just seems that there is more spring in the step of employees and more enthusiasm. Working with companies in this stage is just more fun. This was the case here: The organization's excitement was running high. The market potential of new products was great, and as a group, they wanted to make a difference.

Joe was being put on a special assignment. While the new position was under wraps, and a secret to the larger organization, he was excited. It was a special job that he was hand-picked for. The selection of Joe for the project represented a big honor, and vote of faith, bestowed by the management team.

His project was to build a new team in Brazil to launch a new product. The project was top secret, but I knew that the market potential was high. His marching orders from his boss, Filipe, were to stabilize his current assignments and get ready to turn them over within the year to a new leader. His new goal was to hit the ground running on building a new business.

THE CONNECTION OF METRICS TO THE BUSINESS STRATEGY

Joe met me in the lobby with a wrinkled tie and a crumpled shirt, and I knew that our session was going to be intense. When we shook hands, there was no small-talk. Joe wanted to get to the task at hand. As we took our seats, he immediately started firing questions at me.

"How do I select the right metrics to stabilize what I am doing here for the turnover? And how do I select the metrics that matter for the new operating team in Brazil?" he questioned. "Today, we have more metrics than we can track, and people are confused. Most of the metrics are functional in nature, and there is no clear dashboard to tie functional performance indicators to corporate performance." In short, he was stuck. Joe was grappling with how to design the right metrics system to deliver the business results.

To close this gap, I showed Joe Figure 2.1, and stated, "Other companies that I work with find this to be a useful model to stimulate thinking." Joe was all ears as I continued, "To maximize success, companies need to start at the ends of the model—the design of channel and definition of supplier strategies—and then work toward the middle. After answering the questions in the model, then the organization can design and align the processes to critical metrics that matter. Without going through this exercise, companies assume that they know "best practices" and they hopelessly pursue process excellence that won't align to business outcomes. As a result, they will work hard and make improvements, but not drive the desired outcomes to improve corporate performance."

Joe wrung his hands and told me a story. "The group that I work with read all of the materials you gave me the last time we met; and after a long debate, we selected five key metrics to define operating performance on the

FIGURE 2.1 Aligning Business Strategy to Operating Strategy

Effective Frontier. While we are unwavering in our commitment to safety, customer service, and human resource goals, we tried to apply your methodology to our business. So, we proposed to our boss, Filipe, that we shift our focus from functionally aligned metrics to a commonly shared set of business metrics for the next year. The proposal is to use your model. We recommended the use of these . . . " he said, as he turned around and wrote the following metrics on his whiteboard:

- Year-over-year growth
- Customer service (on-time and in-full shipments)
- Operating margin
- Inventory turns
- Return on invested capital (ROIC)

"What do you think?" he asked. I smiled and clapped my hands, and exclaimed, "I like it! If you can focus on driving improvement on these five metrics together, and as a system, you will make real progress." I continued, "The best operating strategies and metrics portfolios are built when companies translate business strategy into tactical plans. This sounds easy, but in our research, we find that most companies have defined the business strategy at too high a level to be actionable. We also find that there is an assumption that companies know the best practices of their industry. Both assumptions are dangerous. As a result, without a clear operating strategy and the rethinking of corporate processes, companies aren't aligned to deliver the needed business results.

"The other danger, in an organization like yours, where the team is excellent at driving continuous improvement processes, without clarity on operating strategy, is that the company can do the wrong things well, resulting in performance circling the drain. Have you seen this?" I asked.

Joe laughed, and said, "We see this in spades, all the time! People in the organization talk about driving value, but I find that they're really focused on managing singular metrics in isolation. I see people every day trying to do the right thing, but not able to push forward. In fact . . ." he said, stopping mid-sentence and giving me a wink, "if we're being honest, wasn't that me just three months ago?"

Not wanting to hurt his feelings, I brushed his comment aside, returned the wink, and said, "You've come a long way."

Joe continued, "Let's take this one step further. How could I use this model (shown in 2.1), along with the metrics that matter, to drive improvement in Brazil?"

"The secret, after selecting the right metrics, is to establish reasonable targets, and an agreed rate of improvement over time. For example, in your operating plan in Brazil, you will focus on growth. Growth strategies in new markets require capital. To achieve your goal, you will need to build inventory. To drive growth and minimize inventory, it will be critical to establish the right processes in operations so that you can get and use daily channel data," I said with a twinkle in my eye. "The difficult part of this is redefining the role of sales so that they are comfortable with operations getting and using channel data. Sometimes this can be contentious."

Joe agreed, and asked me to continue to describe the use of the model. I explained, "After establishing your channel strategy, you need to define how you will work with suppliers. Since this is a new operation, and the product sales are very sensitive to weather patterns, you should build supplier relationships that are very responsive to the markets. It will be critical to select the right suppliers with an understanding that they will need to be responsive. To make this successful, you will also have to work on passing the suppliers a good demand signal." I then looked Joe in the eye and asked, "Does this make sense?"

"I think so, but let me play back what I am hearing," Joe stated. "You have told me that I will need to design the system that I'm going to manage. The design starts with the channel. Based on the market and the product requirements, I should start with channel flows and defining customer relationships. After that, you define supplier relationships and information flows. I think that I get it. But, how does this tie to the metrics that matter?"

Grinning, I said, "Let's talk about design. While you have determined a great set of balanced metrics, you don't know the right targets for them in a new operating environment. To set the goals, you will need to benchmark. In this analysis, you will have to determine the potential. For example, the faster that information flows, the quicker you can run your cycles, with less of a need for buffers. This includes your inventory and cash-to-cash cycles. What most leaders miss is the need for design and tuning. The design defines the potential or the achievable goal of the metrics that matter. This is why it's critical to define an operations strategy. The definitions of the business processes flow from the strategy, not the other way around. Does this help?"

"Yes, it does. This is much different from assuming we've got best practices and that all we've got to do to drive improvement is to broad-brush these practices everywhere we operate," he continued. "I am afraid that this flies in the face of what we are trying to do on standardized processes."

In affirmation, I continued, "You are getting it. Let's take another example. One of the things that most companies miss is the relationship between the complexity of the product portfolio and the metrics that matter. The more complex the product line, the lower the potential of the organization at the intersection of operating margin and inventory turns. In short, the answers to the questions in this model define the system, which then drives the targets to support the metrics that matter. Metrics should never be viewed in isolation. They're relative to a system."

"This is much different from the way we operate. We don't actively design our systems, and think about metrics set-points over time based on the potential of the system. Adoption of these principles will require some training. Don't expect us to be at the front of this class," Joe said jokingly.

MANAGING METRICS AS A COMPLEX SYSTEM

"Few companies get it," I said. "Your company isn't alone. I run into many situations where people try to manage metrics in isolation without thinking about them in a system approach. It's an easy trap. It flies against convention. Metrics are necessary to drive performance. The definition of the right metrics—and the alignment of people, process, and technology systems to drive metrics improvement—accelerates corporate performance. When done well, the design of metrics systems, and underlying employee incentives, improves workforce productivity. But, as you know all too well now, if the metrics are managed in isolation, and the organization is thrown out of balance, then bad things happen."

Joe was walking around his office, gesturing with his hands while he said, "We have had enough bad things happening. It's obvious to me now that, for success, metrics need to be managed as a complex system, but this understanding takes a while to build. It requires training and discipline. Most people have been trained to measure a single metric in isolation. It's a leadership challenge to drive continued alignment to build strength, resiliency, and balance on a portfolio of metrics to improve corporate performance. Too few people have this understanding."

"Yes, the management of metrics requires systems thinking. We see that the greatest performance improvement in corporate results happens when it's managed as a whole, and not as individual parts in isolation. Due to the functional nature of the organization, this is a major change management issue. Does this make sense?" I asked.

A complex system consists of many diverse and autonomous, yet interrelated and interdependent components linked through many interconnections. Complex systems cannot be described by a single rule and their characteristics aren't reducible to one level of description. The properties emerge from the interaction of their parts, which cannot be predicted from the properties of the parts.

Joe reached for his black notebook and started scribbling. He was busy for about five minutes, and I felt awkward. Then out of the blue, he looked up and asked, "Is there a model that we could use to organize our thinking?"

"Here is one that has helped other clients," I said, as I rifled through my disorganized red briefcase. I passed a sheet of paper to Joe with a model (shown here as Figure 2.2). "For most organizations, this systems thinking approach is difficult. It is a journey. However, if companies follow this metrics maturity model, these issues are quickly resolved.

"Let me explain the model and let's see what you think," I said, pointing a pen above each item on the paper as I spoke. "In the journey to drive metrics that matter, we find that companies move through five distinct phases. When we started, Joe, your company was deeply rooted in the first stage of

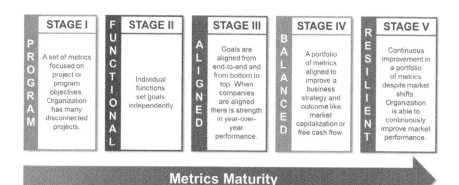

FIGURE 2.2 Metrics Maturity Model

this model. At this stage, companies are managing metrics through isolated programs. As the organization matures, the company moves through five phases, or stages. These are:

1. Isolated programs
2. Functional metrics
3. Aligned metrics for strength
4. Balanced metrics to actualize strategy
5. Resilient metrics to withstand market shifts

"Each stage is progressive—building on the skills learned in the prior stage—but the transition from stage to stage is a change management challenge. The principles of systems thinking become more pronounced in stages three through five. Does this help?" I asked.

Joe beamed with a big smile, closed his notebook, and asked if we could take a break. "Sure," I said. "I would like to spend the morning walking you through examples to define each of these stages so that you can use this model with your team." Laughingly, I continued, "I have built a workbook so that you don't have to do so much writing in your notebook. I don't want your hands to get tired."

It took a while to get to the break room. Joe was a magnet for people, and the team loved Joe. On the way, we were continually stopped by employees who had questions for Joe about the day-to-day operations. When we got back to his office, Joe said, "I love our sessions. It's time to think about what's important. I get so caught-up in the urgent, or the day-to-day details, that I seldom have a chance to do this level of work. I am excited to continue."

USING THE METRICS MATURITY MODEL TO DRIVE CHANGE

As companies move through the metrics maturity model and better understand metrics alignment, they find the design and execution of metrics systems to be a journey. To help Joe, I gave him a workbook to record notes during our morning session.

For each stage of the model, I provided a case study and shared insights regarding the barriers and enablers to make progress on organizational alignment on the metrics that matter. In building the case studies, I was careful to use multiple industries so that Joe could get a broad view. However, as I talked, I never compared the metrics of companies across industries without being sure that I grounded the discussion with their peer group performance. I have a strong belief that companies have to be evaluated within their peer groups based on market drivers.

Stage 1: Isolated Programs

Program- or Project-Based Metrics

As we closed the door to continue, Joe settled back in his chair and again reached for his well-worn notebook, while eagerly grabbing the workbook that I had brought him. He liked to use mechanical pencils and black marking pens in his writing, and usually had one or the other behind his ear. He was ready for more.

"For many companies early in their journey, improvement is focused on projects and programs. Companies have thousands of concurrent projects. This is an output of the Information Age where one of the principles of project management is to meet the threshold guidelines for project approval. Each company has different targets, but most evaluate project opportunities using return on investment (ROI). One of the most common definitions of ROI is based on the DuPont model [shown in Figure 2.3[1]]," I said. I then turned to Joe, and asked, "How do you measure your projects?"

"In a similar way," stated Joe. "Lou, in the finance team, is very proud of his methodology, which is similar to the DuPont model. He keeps a tight grip on spending, acting as if each dollar was the last in his personal checkbook. We have a team of industrial engineers that run these models and each project has to meet the hurdle to be approved. However, as I think about it, I can see that by doing it this way we are not clear how the projects align with each other."

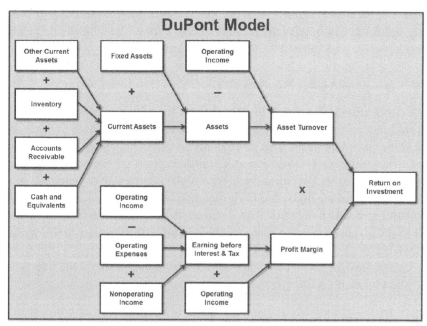

FIGURE 2.3 DuPont Model to Determine Return on Investment

"As a decision tool for projects, the Dupont model is easy to understand. The simplicity of the formula allows the company to freely choose variables. However, since ROI is a compound metric, the aggregate impact of the project decisions on the whole is unknown," I stated in affirmation. "There is no connection to the operations strategy or the management of metrics as a complex system."

"I agree," said Joe. "When these projects are implemented, they're measured and tracked for a short period of time, but the focus isn't holistic. The total impact of multiple programs happening across the organization, focused on different objectives at the same time, can't be appropriately measured as the number of projects can be vast. Can you believe that we had over 15,000 simultaneous projects happening last year? In fact, we get so caught up in project management that sometimes we forget what the goal is. I often think that it's easy to lose sight of the objective as projects take weird twists and turns."

"Isn't that true!" I exclaimed. "At this stage, without the alignment of programs to an overarching strategy and metrics portfolio, companies are unable to make progress to deliver year-over-year improvements on corporate balance sheet metrics. I sense that this may be the case here, Joe. I am interested in your thoughts after we review the barriers and enablers." Joe nodded and pushed back his hair as he turned the page in his workbook.

Barriers to Progress Past Stage 1

"As companies mature, they find that it isn't the review of individual projects that matters. Instead, they find that they need to look at them in aggregate against corporate goals. This more holistic view is necessary and requires a clear definition of business strategy translated into an operational strategy. As we discussed before, most companies make the mistake of defining a business strategy at too high a level to be actionable. When they clearly outline the operating strategy, they find that the projects that look promising as isolated initiatives may not make sense in the overarching program. Make sense?" I asked.

"Absolutely," Joe agreed. "We are a poster child for this stage. We get so caught up in project review that I swear we forget where we are going."

Enablers of Progress to Move to Stage 2

We were making progress. I continued, "Compelling events drive change. The biggest stimulus to focus on the metrics that matter usually stems from organizational failure. When a company stumbles, it's easier for the management team to drive alignment."

"That was the case for us in the last recession," commented Joe. "When the orders did not come in, our project-based approach was meaningless. The organization didn't know what to do."

"When a company is able to articulate an overarching goal through an operations strategy, then the organization is better able to align individual projects to drive success and move to the next stage. However, the management of metrics through a project lens is fraught with issues." I then looked at Joe and asked, "Enough on this? For you this seems straightforward." Joe agreed and we moved forward.

Stage 2: Functional Metrics

I turned the page and continued. "Most organizations are siloed. The metrics are functional. The walls between the silos are strong, and the ability to work together across functions is weak. One of the barriers is getting to data. For example, most companies cannot easily assess total costs. In our research, we

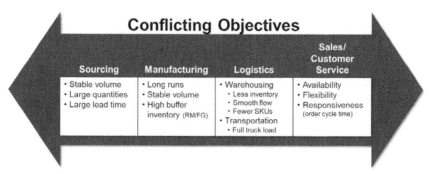

FIGURE 2.4 Functional Objectives in Conflict

find that only 22 percent of companies greater than $5 billion in revenue can easily get to cost data to evaluate cross-functional impacts."[2]

I then pointed to the figure (shown here as Figure 2.4) and stated, "These siloed metrics are often in conflict. This is the dilemma for folks like you, Joe."

At this point, Joe could barely sit in his chair as he exclaimed, "I know this all too well! Sales teams are focused on volume, while logistics organizations concentrate on the lowest cost to transport a product. In contrast, manufacturing groups are making decisions to maximize return on assets (ROA) and procurement is laser-focused on lowest cost. It all sounds good, but we can't work together to achieve a common goal."

"I know," I said. "I see this often. Additionally, as we will see later, a focus on ROA in manufacturing, and a focus in procurement for the lowest cost, won't yield the operating margin or cost of goods sold improvements that organizations seek. And, at the risk of sounding like a broken record, the reason is that functional metrics are in conflict and must be aligned."

Joe laughed, and said, "Yes, I think that the journey from functional to corporate metrics is tough. It is a major issue for our team today. We are unsure how to drive alignment."

I continued, "When leadership teams construct a set of key performance indicators (KPIs) that are aligned and balanced, the organization can move forward to more easily conquer their goals. When operating in silos, each function will look heroic; however, the sum of their efforts on corporate balance sheet results will be disappointing. To make the point, let's take an example. Employees within the Coca-Cola Company laugh and say that they are entrenched within 'camps of feuding landlords.' Functional metrics reign supreme within the company. The organization has created strong functional silos. In contrast, the PepsiCo organization is more aligned to the shelf.

"Consider the impact of this alignment on corporate performance as demonstrated in Figure 2.5. In this figure, I contrast the progress of these two beverage companies in the period of 2000–2013 on inventory turns and revenue per employee. (These are two factors on the Effective Frontier as shown in Figure 1.2.) I think that the patterns tell the story. Notice that during 2000–2013, Coca-Cola's productivity has gone backward from a high of $434,000 of revenue per employee in 2004 to $350,000 of revenue per employee in 2013. Also note the trend in inventory turns. Despite having similar brands, and competing in the same markets, PepsiCo consistently outperforms Coca-Cola on inventory turns. Meanwhile, PepsiCo is making improvements on productivity (revenue per employee), and their pattern is tighter and more reliable," I stated.

Joe was sitting with his legs crossed, tracing the pattern on the orbit chart. He was deep in thought and then flashed his infectious smile. "I love these examples. It helps to make it all so much clearer."

I continued, "The type of pattern shown by Coca-Cola is representative of functional metrics management. In our analysis, PepsiCo outperforms Coca-Cola in both strength and resiliency in the past three years even though

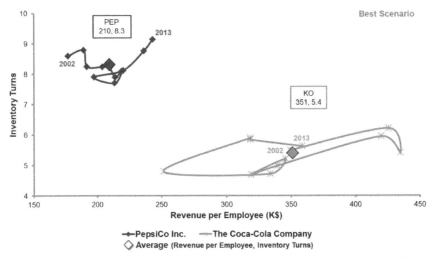

FIGURE 2.5 Coca-Cola versus PepsiCo Corporate Performance Inventory Turns versus Revenue per Employee
Source: Supply Chain Insights LLC, Corporate Annual Reports 2002–2013.

the average revenue per employee metric for Coca-Cola is higher than that of PepsiCo. Note that PepsiCo has an average of $210,000 in revenue per employee while Coca-Cola has an average of $351,000."

"Yes," Joe said. "The averages are misleading. If you just looked at the averages, you might conclude that Coca-Cola is doing a better job on revenue per employee and PepsiCo is doing a better job on inventory turns; but when you look at the pattern and the backward trend of Coca-Cola, it tells a different story. I like the use of orbit charts to measure improvement."

I then rhetorically asked, "So, why is Coca-Cola going backward on revenue per employee while PepsiCo is going forward? There are three drivers. The first is the role of distributors and bottlers. The second is the changing product platform. The third is focus and leadership.

Coca-Cola Case Study

When looking at metrics alignment, it's valuable to look closely at the Coca-Cola Company and the impact of its decisions on corporate performance.

Coca-Cola Enterprises (CCE, Inc.) was spun out of the Coca-Cola Company in 1986. The goal was to consolidate the many independent bottling groups in the Coca-Cola system. The secondary goal was to improve the asset efficiency and revenue per employee productivity of the parent company. On February 24, 2010, just four years after the creation of CCE, The Coca-Cola Company and CCE (Coca-Cola Enterprises) entered talks to sell CCE's North American division back to Coca-Cola. Coca-Cola paid over $15 billion to reacquire CCE in North America, including redemption of Coca-Cola's 35 percent shareholding in CCE.

This was a public admission of channel failure. With the creation of Coca-Cola Enterprises in 1986, Coca-Cola was the darling of Wall Street. The company divested assets to improve return on assets (ROA) and financial fundamentals. What was not obvious then, and is all too obvious now, is that when a company sheds assets, it must redesign to sense and shape demand to drive market performance. The more extensive the supply chain, and the more third-party nodes, the greater the challenge and the more critical its ability to sense demand and service a network.

Coca-Cola learned this the hard way. Battered by retail feedback (five years of falling scores on retailer surveys in North America), declining market share, and rising costs, Coca-Cola declared enough. It announced the repurchase of the bottler. There were three fundamental issues.

(continued)

(continued)

Issue 1: Goal alignment. In the formation of CCE, the bottling operations were incented on volume. It sounded like a good idea then. Who could argue with payment based upon more volume on the shelf? However, when carbonated beverage consumption changed due to consumer health and wellness preferences, the Coca-Cola Company wanted to power growth through selling more new products. The volumes were smaller and the delivery issues more difficult for these new products. Suddenly, there was a problem of functional and channel alignment. The established incentives drove a volume-based response from CCE for more traditional Coca-Cola products. The incentives were not aligned to compensate CCE for the lumpier, lower-volume-demand patterns accompanying new products (iced tea, juices, and flavored water). As a result, the company was not able to achieve the right balance between efficiency and innovation.

Issue 2: Flexibility. When the Coca-Cola bottling system was defined, Walmart was a regional player. As Walmart gained power and established national presence, a regional bottling system became a liability. Walmart wanted a more efficient and responsive system. They wanted to speak with one voice to the customer with flawless execution. The Coca-Cola regional system was riddled with goal alignment issues and could not meet the needs of one of its largest customers.

Issue 3: Technology evolution and adaptation. From 2005 to 2012, while PepsiCo proactively pursued the use of market sensing and advanced analytics in the United States to sense channel shifts, Coca-Cola struggled. The Coca-Cola Company was saddled with trying to fix the near-term channel issues while PepsiCo could focus on more strategic, long-term initiatives. As a result, PepsiCo aggressively built sales overlay analytics systems across the bottlers to gain visibility of channel preferences. PepsiCo reduced the time to sense and respond to channel shifts while Coca-Cola continued to struggle with alignment of the bottlers.

"This case study is a good example of why alignment is essential. While a company may shed assets and outsource to a third party, it must carefully craft strategies to ensure adaptation to the change to gradually evolve processes across the entire network. Functional alignment and channel design are fundamental to accomplish the goals."

"In driving metrics performance, the patterns matter. It isn't about the average value or the data in a point in time. Instead, it's about year-over-year improvement. The patterns of performance need to be measured at the intersection of growth, profitability, cycles, and complexity on the Effective Frontier. It needs to be a systems view. As we look at the progress of other peer groups this is a consistent theme," I concluded.

At this point, Joe put down his reading glasses and closed his workbook for a minute and said, "This makes so much sense when you see it like this, but it's much harder in the real world when we are battling it out between functions."

Contrast with a More Mature Industry

"I know," I said. "This point becomes even clearer when we contrast the pattern of these two carbonated drink manufacturing giants to a more mature organization in a more advanced industry. Take a look at these three companies within the consumer packaged goods (CPG) industry. While both figures (Figures 2.5 and 2.6) contrast revenue per employee to inventory turns, note the differences in the patterns in the two charts. Each of these companies within the CPG peer group is making year-over-year improvements. There is no backward movement. The rate of progress is faster and the trend is more linear.

"The CPG companies are more mature in metric definition and process enablement than those in beverage. There are fewer issues between functional

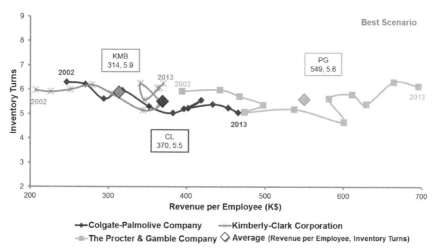

FIGURE 2.6 Consumer Packaged Goods Competitors' Progress on Inventory Turns versus Revenue per Employee
Source: Supply Chain Insights LLC, Corporate Annual Reports 2002–2013.

silos. The channel is owned and managed. The issues with distributors/bottlers in the channel are much less. The processes are more closely aligned from end-to-end," I stated as Joe quickly wrote his notes.

"While most companies know that a focus on functional metrics, and the lack of alignment, is a problem, they don't know what to do about it. It's hard to quantify. They have taken a dead-end view believing that there are best practices. Few companies have taken steps to align metrics and processes end-to-end from the customer's customer to the supplier's supplier. Only 1 percent of companies have a cross-functional leader focused on the definition of processes end-to-end in their processes.[3] As a result, functional management is rewarded. Why? Simply put, it's easier. This is one of the primary reasons why corporations aren't able to actualize greater performance gains through the informational economy." I then stopped to catch my breath.

"Fascinating stuff!" exclaimed Joe. "I love the differences in the patterns that I see in these orbit charts."

"Shall I continue?" I asked.

"Yes," he said. "I like this model. I think that it holds a lot of promise for us. I like the thought of putting the two models that we discussed this morning into an action plan." Joe then turned to his notebook to point out the models that are shown in Figures 2.1 and 2.2.

Barriers to Progress Past Stage 2

"A barrier to moving beyond stage 2 in the model is understanding why functional metrics, and building strong insular silos, can degrade corporate performance. After employees can visualize the impact, they're more capable of thinking holistically end-to-end. Discrete event simulation and the use of 'what-if' optimization in network modeling helps. I find that there is no substitute for plotting the patterns on the Effective Frontier through orbit charts and comparing results to peer groups. However, to drive the transition, companies need to define a leader to articulate and orchestrate cross-functional metrics end-to-end (from the customer's customer to the supplier's supplier). I think in this case, Joe, you are the leader." I continued.

Enablers of Progress to Move to Stage 3

"As we discussed, a compelling market event is a great enabler to align metrics cross-functionally. It's often failure. Or, it can be a transition in leadership. Let me give you an example. One of my favorites is A. G. Lafley's turnaround of P&G starting in 2005. He followed the 'Keep It Simple, Stupid' (KISS) principle of leadership by announcing a simple mantra in 2006 that 'The consumer is boss.' " I continued.

"His efforts aligned the 138,000 P&G employees in 80 countries to two measures of success. The first was defined as 'Was the product available on the shelf when the customer wanted to buy?' The second: 'Was the customer delighted with the product when they used it?' Using these two definitions, he successfully transformed the metrics systems and aligned functions around two moments of truth. This aligned functional silos to a common goal. He drove levels of success that were not possible for his predecessor, Durk Jager. In contrast, Jager had tried to turn the company around by pushing dozens of new products through the R&D pipeline. During Jager's tenure, the metrics were functional and insular. During Lafley's leadership, he broke down functional silos and deemphasized traditional R&D processes. He slashed the number of R&D projects by two thirds, while focusing on outside-in innovation so that the P&G organization could aggressively learn from others. Under his leadership, P&G actively built design networks to fuel innovation. Make sense? Is this a good example?" I asked Joe.

Joe's face again showed that contagious smile. He was taking it all in. "What happens if you don't have a Lafley? You know not everyone can be like P&G," he said.

"Yes, I liken it to me being selected as the model on the *Cover Girl* magazine," I said with a laugh, "You know that some things just are not going to happen. However, I think that some of Lafley's principles are easily applied to any organization. Let's take one that I think is important. In a company where more than half the employees don't speak English as their first language, Lafley said that his 'Sesame Street approach of simple slogans, repeated over and over, kept everyone focused on what's important.' Human beings 'don't want to stay focused,' he said. 'So my job is to get them to focus their creativity around the focus; focus their productivity around the focus; focus their efficiency or effectiveness around the focus.' The moments of truth were simple and compelling. They aligned the organization.

"Don't you think that sometimes we try to make things too complex? And that we miss the mark in communicating to employees?" I asked. "I think that the use of these principles, even if you don't have a Lafley, makes sense. It's a great example of leadership to drive alignment against a compelling mission. The progress on P&G's results in the next sections of the workbook speaks for itself."

"Got it. Makes perfect sense." Joe said. "Let's tackle the next section of the workbook before lunch." Later, as we opened the door to leave for lunch,

Joe's team again flocked to see him in the hall to ask quick questions. It might be a brief conversation or an affirmation of direction, but I could clearly see leadership in action. Joe was a people person. It was almost like having lunch with a celebrity.

Stage 3: Aligned Metrics to Drive Strength

Strength in Year-over-Year Performance

After lunch, we paused to talk about our families and the joys of raising teenagers. We had both struggled with raising teenage daughters over the past year and the experience had taken a lot out of us. While we were commiserating with each other, Joe suddenly snapped into work mode and said, "Let's get started." With that, he again opened up his notebook, picked up his yellow pencil, and said, "I'm ready!"

"Okay, let's now apply the principles," I replied. "Business strategies are different. Not every company has the same potential. They want to make different choices of growth, profitability, working capital cycles and complexity, but orchestrating these trade-offs is easier said than done. Aligning end-to-end and forcing hard choices and trade-offs in functional metrics to align to corporate metrics is difficult. It requires education, commitment, and changes in incentives. When I use the term *alignment*, my definition is to coordinate cross-functionally."

"Yes, like we discussed earlier this morning. Right?" asked Joe. I nodded in agreement.

> When organizations align cross-functionally and to a business strategy, the organization is able to deliver strength in performance. Strength is defined as year-over-year improvements to a company's peer group.

"Leaders make these choices consciously showing year-over-year improvements while laggards lose ground. Let's take the example of Colgate and Procter & Gamble (shown in Figure 2.7). The view at the intersection of operating margin versus inventory turns, as opposed to the view at the intersection of inventory turns and revenue per employee, tells a very different story of operational excellence. If employee productivity is valued, P&G would be seen as the leader, but if the focus is on operating margin, Colgate would be the clear winner. However, today, due to the rise in product complexity, both companies are struggling to make consistent progress on these metrics," I continued.

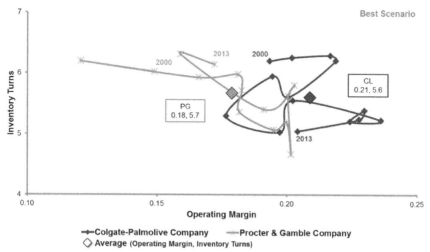

FIGURE 2.7 Comparison of P&G and Colgate at the Intersection of Inventory Turns and Operating Margin
Source: Supply Chain Insights LLC, Corporate Annual Reports 2000–2012.

"Wow! Look at these patterns. I had no idea that they were so complex. To hear others tell it we've been making linear improvements on these two metrics. These are industry leaders and these charts are anything but linear. How do you explain this?" Joe asked.

"In this example, Colgate is making a conscious choice to drive year-over-year improvements in profitability. The functions are laser-focused to drive this metric. It runs deep in the veins of the Colgate culture. There is no company studied in our research that has been as successful in driving year-over-year profitability as Colgate. The company has driven 42 consecutive quarters of improvement in this metric. The goal of the team is to 'self-fund the growth of the company.' Also, it's clear that not only has Procter & Gamble outperformed on revenue per employee, but they have also driven improvements in inventory turns over the past three years. In contrast, P&G is going backward on operating margins. It comes down to what the company values and if they can keep a consistent leadership focus in that area to deliver the desired results," I stated.

"Due to rising complexity—the consumer products industry has added more than 30 percent new products in the past four years—they are unable to balance the improvement in multiple metrics simultaneously. As a result, both companies are struggling to balance a portfolio of metrics—improving a group of metrics together simultaneously—to drive year-over-year improvement. Over the past five years, both organizations have struggled to achieve balance between the two metrics of operating margin and inventory turns. When we find this situation where competitors are struggling to drive balance between metrics, it's time to drive disruption and define a new frontier." I continued by saying, "The story doesn't end here. It requires a peer comparison with a wider group of competitors. When Unilever is thrown into the mix, it's clear that both P&G and Colgate are more resilient than Unilever. Look at the swings in performance by Unilever as compared to its peer group." I then took Joe's pencil and traced the patterns of the three companies shown in Figure 2.8.

"Recently, Unilever has made real progress," I continued. "However, over the course of the past decade, it was a different story. Due to changing management, and ever-changing strategies, Unilever was less resilient at a process level to withstand the impact of the recession. These wilder swings in corporate performance are characteristic of ever-changing priorities. During the period of 2000–2006, both Colgate and P&G had more consistency than Unilever; but now, leadership is up for grabs. That's why it's so important to look at metrics trends over time through the orbit charts."

"This discussion is a breath of fresh air," said Joe. "Most consultants come in and talk about how everyone else is doing things well, and we're not.

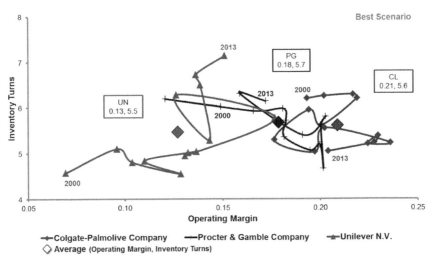

FIGURE 2.8   Progress of Procter & Gamble versus Colgate and Unilever on Operating Margin versus Inventory Turns
Source: Supply Chain Insights LLC, Corporate Annual Reports 2000–2013.

These charts allow me to see the struggle of real companies. There is so much value in comparing companies by peer group."

"I could not agree more," I stated as I continued. "Strength, balance, and resiliency improve as companies mature in their ability to define, align, manage, and fine-tune cross-functional metrics. It requires patience and careful alignment. Leadership needs to be deliberate. The progress is slow but the results are worth the journey."

Barriers to Progress Past Stage 3

"To do this, there needs to be a translation of business strategy to operating strategy to define processes. It isn't easy," I continued. "While one third of companies greater than $5 billion in revenue have created centers of excellence, only one in two are successful. The gap is in the lack of clarity in operating strategy. As we talked in our last session, terms like *agility, flexibility, efficiency, responsiveness,* and *effectiveness* need to be carefully translated into metrics that matter, and the output needs to be defined into operating targets for complex networks of manufacturing facilities, distribution centers, procurement policies, and go-to-market strategies. Holistic and cross-functional thinking drives success."

Joe then opened the pages in his journal to show me his notes from our last session. "I keep on turning to these pages every day and thinking about how to use them. I find these concepts are very valuable."

Enablers of Progress from Stage 3

I nodded my head in agreement and continued, "The alignment of strategy to action improves corporate performance. For example, while Unilever shows a lack of resiliency at the intersection of operating margin and inventory turns, they have successfully balanced metrics as an organizational imperative to drive a more sustainable product portfolio and a lower carbon footprint."

I then passed Joe a copy of Unilever's annual report and asked him to turn to page 12 as I read, "At Unilever we are committed to conducting our operations with integrity and with respect for the interests of our stakeholders." I then looked up and said, "This is an example of translating an operating strategy into the metrics that matter."

I continued with my reading of the Unilever Annual Report, 'We seek to make a positive impact on society through the brands we produce and sell, through our commercial operations and relationships, through the voluntary contributions we make to the community and through our wider engagement

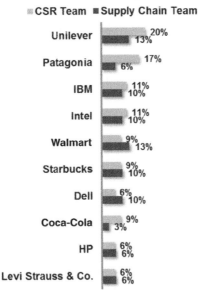

CSR Excellence: Top Mentions*

CSR Team ■ Supply Chain Team

- Unilever — 13% 20%
- Patagonia — 6% 17%
- IBM — 11% 10%
- Intel — 11% 10%
- Walmart — 9% 13%
- Starbucks — 9% 10%
- Dell — 6% 10%
- Coca-Cola — 3% 9%
- HP — 6% 6%
- Levi Strauss & Co. — 6% 6%

FIGURE 2.9   Unilever Corporate Sustainability Performance
Base: Manufacturers, Retailers, Wholesalers/Distributors/Cooperatives with sustainability goals–CSR (*n* = 35), Supply Chain (*n* = 31).
*Showing only companies with over 5% mentions.
Q20: When you think of corporate social responsibility or sustainability excellence in the supply chain, what companies do you think do it well?
Source: Supply Chain Insights LLC, Green Supply Chain (January–February 2013).

with society. We are also committed to making continuous improvements in the management of our environmental impacts and to working toward our longer-term goal of developing a sustainable business.'

"They're making progress," I said. "We survey companies to self-assess who does corporate social responsibility best, and we get a list like this one." I then showed him Figure 2.9, and continued, "Unilever is recognized by their peers as excelling in the definition of an operating strategy to actualize a sustainable operation to drive new opportunities with customers that want a more sustainable planet."

Stage 4: Balanced Metrics to Actualize Strategy

"I like where we are headed in this discussion, and I am a big believer in balanced scorecards, but it's difficult for us to know, as a leadership team, what balance means. Do others have that problem?" asked Joe.

"Absolutely," I continued. "It's for this reason that I want to be deliberate in my definition. I define balance as the organization's ability to manage a group of metrics to enable the business strategy. For me, it's the management of a portfolio of metrics to maximize market capitalization."

"How do you define market capitalization?" asked Joe.

"Market capitalization is a simple definition. It is as defined by the number of shares outstanding multiplied by the market price for the shares. It will move with the market. Make sense?" I asked.

"That is certainly what is important to us as a publicly held company, but do you know which metrics correlate to market capitalization?" asked Joe.

"As a research team, we wanted to figure that out. So, we took six years of market capitalization data and we did quarterly correlations to see which metrics mattered. The results are in your workbook. The highest correlations are at the intersection of inventory turns and operating margin. However, the greatest benefit comes from managing the basket of ratios that drive the cash-to-cash ratio, operating margin, and return on invested capital," I said as Joe and I discussed Table 2.1.

"This certainly helps," Joe commented. "Isn't it interesting that many of the metrics that matter, like days of inventory (DOI), aren't measured by any silo in the discussion of functional metrics, but show up here as so important? Inventory has been our Achilles heel, and it lies between functions. I have a true confession. Since we rewarded return on assets (ROA), we ran up high inventories. While Lou in finance yelled at me to bring the inventories down, I didn't because I was rewarded by my boss, Filipe, to run a high value of ROA. I imagine that there are a lot of organizations like mine that struggle with the same scenario. Isn't it interesting that ROA rates are so low in the correlation while ROIC rates are much higher? And yet, we have been pushing ROA for a long time."

"Indeed. To understand balance, you have to look at the intersection of multiple cuts of the data. In your workbook, I have included three views of BASF to illustrate the point. Note the differences of these three data views for BASF and DuPont for the time period of 2000–2013. Each intersection on the Effective Frontier gives insights into a piece of the story. The insights are about both individual company performance and the relative peer group." We then posted Figures 2.10a, 2.10b, and 2.10c on Joe's wall and discussed the differences and similarities.

Joe and I were speaking all at once when I directed him to one of the figures and said, "What can we see? Both companies are leaders in the chemical industry. BASF is three times the size of DuPont and should have an advantage in economies of scale. Both companies are attempting to redefine their product portfolios and move to a new frontier. The goal is to move up the value stream

TABLE 2.1 Correlation of Financial Ratios to Market Capitalization

Morningstar Sector	Discount Stories	Medical Care	Drug Manufac-turers-Major	Household & Personal Products	Chemical	Packaged Food	Communi-cation Equipment	Medical Devices	Percentage of Industries Demonstrating Correlation per Metric
Number of Companies	**11**	**38**	**43**	**31**	**25**	**56**	**96**	**78**	
Days of Inventory (DOI)	X	X	X	X	X	X	X		88%
Days of Sales Outstanding (DSO)	X	X	X	X	X	X	X	X	88%
Days of Payables Outstanding (DPO)		X		X	X	X	X	X	75%
Return on Invested Capital (ROIC)	X			X	X	X	X	X	75%
Current Ratio (CR)	X	X	X		X		X	X	63%
Operating Margin (OM)	X	X	X		X	X			63%
Working Capital Ratio (WC)	X	X		X			X	X	63%
DPO/DSO (DPODSO)	X		X				X	X	50%
Free Cash Flow Ratio (FCF)		X	X	X			X		50%
SG&A to COGS Ratio (SGAC)		X	X	X			X	X	50%
Return on Assets (ROA)						X	X		25%
Return of Net Assets (RONA)						X	X		25%
Year-over-Year Revenue Growth (YOY)							X	X	25%

Note: Equations based upon data from 2006Q1 to 2011Q4.
Note: The number of companies is the number listed in the Morningstar sector at Ycharts.com when the peer group was defined between March and June 2013. The number of companies included in the analysis may be smaller due to data availability issues.
Source: Supply Chain Insights LLC.

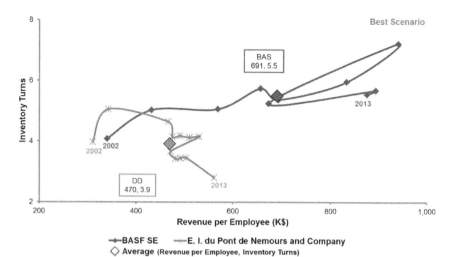

FIGURE 2.10a Contrasting Views of Corporate Performance for BASF and DuPont

Source: Supply Chain Insights LLC, Corporate Annual Reports 2002–2013.

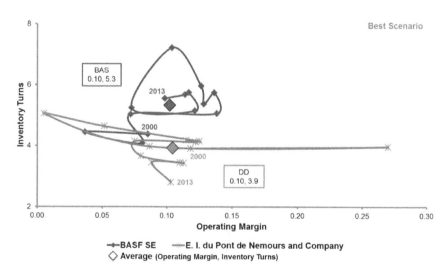

FIGURE 2.10b Contrasting Views of Corporate Performance for BASF and DuPont

Source: Supply Chain Insights LLC, Corporate Annual Reports 2002–2013.

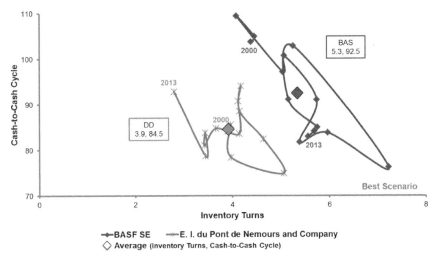

FIGURE 2.10c Contrasting Views of Corporate Performance for BASF and DuPont
Source: Supply Chain Insights LLC, Corporate Annual Reports 2002–2013.

and sell more value-added products and less industrial chemicals. If the companies were in balance, we would see strength, or year-over-year improvement, at the critical intersections of the ratios. When we look at the three data cuts for the two companies in Figure 2.10, we can clearly see that BASF is outperforming DuPont. Here is what this tells me," I said, and turned to the board and wrote three concepts:

1. Inventory turns versus cash-to-cash cycles
2. Inventory turns versus operating margin
3. Inventory turns versus revenue per employee

As I turned around and put the marker down, I asked, "Joe do you remember that the cash-to-cash cycle is a complex metric composed of days of receivables, days of payables, and days of inventory? BASF shows greater strength and resiliency in the pattern at this intersection. The company did the tough work of managing inventories while shortening payables. In contrast, DuPont elongated days of payables, pushing costs backward in the value chain. When you go to Brazil and start up your new operations, I would like for you to be more like BASF and less like DuPont. What do you think?"

"This is clear to me," said Joe. "I also see that all companies in the chemical peer groups were hit hard by the recession of 2007. As a result, there is backward momentum in this pattern during that period. However, note that while DuPont has some wild swings, BASF has a tight pattern. The company lost ground during the recession and then regained it. This pattern for me is a great example of the term *resiliency* that you use all the time. Right?"

"Correct," I said. "BASF, like Procter & Gamble, has strength in performance at the intersection of revenue per employee versus inventory turns, but notice that DuPont doesn't." Joe continued writing, and then looked up and stated, "Looking at the intersections together gives us unique insights. By doing this, I get a much better understanding of balance."

A Closer Look at Cash-to-Cash for BASF and DuPont

Over the past 12 years, both DuPont and BASF improved cash-to-cash cycles, but in very different ways. In Table 2.1, the progress of the three components of cash-to-cash (days of inventory [DOI] plus days of receivables [DOR] minus days of payables [DOP]) is tracked for the two companies for the period of 2000–2012. (Note the lack of resilience for DuPont on days of inventory following the recession as shown in Table 2.2).

TABLE 2.2   Elements of Cash-to-Cash for DuPont and BASF for the Period of 2000–2012

Company (2000–2003)	Days of Inventory	Days of Payables	Days of Receivables
BASF SE	82	50	72
E.I. du Pont de Nemours and Co.	95	51	44

Company (2004–2007)	Days of Inventory	Days of Payables	Days of Receivables
BASF SE	66	38	61
E.I. du Pont de Nemours and Co.	86	49	53

Company (2008–2011)	Days of Inventory	Days of Payables	Days of Receivables
BASF SE	64	30	54
E.I. du Pont de Nemours and Co.	100	66	49

Company (2012–2013)	Days of Inventory	Days of Payables	Days of Receivables
BASF SE	65	31	49
E.I. du Pont de Nemours and Co.	118	76	44

Source: Supply Chain Insights LLC, Corporate Annual Reports 2000–2013.

I agreed and replied, "These are three distinct views with very different patterns. It's for this reason that companies need to map their patterns at the intersections of multiple metrics on the Effective Frontier. This helps to identify what is possible in strength, balance, and resiliency."

Joe said, "I get it now. The examples really helped me. Thanks."

I laughed, and said, "Not all companies that we share the data with are that positive. Let me tell you a story." I recently visited DuPont's senior leadership team. The response was defensive and the discussion was a difficult one. DuPont's belief was that there's little to be learned through the comparison of BASF and DuPont. Their rationale was based in the belief that complexity in their business is higher today since their acquisition of Pioneer Hi-Bred in 1999; and as a result, it's more difficult to maintain balance and resiliency between operating margin and inventory turns. The belief by leadership was "this is just how it is." However, when I asked, "When the business changes, isn't it our job as leaders to continually redesign to absorb complexity to ensure resiliency and balance in corporate performance?" The answer was silence.

Joe was amused by the story, and commented, "Sometimes the natural reaction is defensiveness. Sometimes, the biggest defense is the greatest offense. I wouldn't let that stop you in the work that you are doing."

"Yes," I said. "In contrast, when the metric performance was discussed with BASF leadership, the discussion was more fruitful. The organization shared insights with us that I am now including in my book. Maybe I will bring you this case study when we next meet."

Management of the Complex System to Drive Balance

"Metrics balance can only be achieved when the portfolio is managed as a complex system. Business operations are complex systems with complex processes with increasing complexity. It's easier to state that you have a balanced scorecard than to deliver against one. It requires the management of a portfolio of metrics.

"Industries are different," I continued. "As a result, the correlations are quite different by industry. Likewise, individual corporate performance is very different within each peer group. Both perspectives are valuable. In industry today, the concepts of balance of metrics in a portfolio are less mature than the concepts of functional metrics alignment."

"I get it. That's very clear to me, and it's the case here. What do you suggest we do?" asked Joe.

"It takes time. As companies work on improving the metric balance within a portfolio, they will often find that the processes and technologies need to be reimplemented to improve flexibility and agility. It is a struggle."

"Why?" asked Joe. "What do they find difficult?"

"Remember your comment about your ongoing dialogue with your controller who is always asking you for the lowest cost per case?" I said. Joe responded that this occurred every day, as I continued, "Because companies have mistakenly defined the efficient response as the lowest cost per case and defined that as the most effective response, today many companies have to rectify the fact that they have created inflexible systems that are brittle and unable to drive balance. The efficient response is mutually exclusive with the agile network. As a result, many companies require a process redesign to improve potential," I stated.

Barriers to Progress Past Stage 4

"To move forward," I said, "we need to redefine leadership. A barrier to moving from Stage 4 to Stage 5 is alignment and agreement on the right metrics portfolio to manage. This is hard for a management team.

"The second barrier, as we discussed this morning, is gaining agreement that the team will manage the portfolio using systems thinking as opposed to looking at the metrics as individual and independent measures. The typical organization struggles between functional and corporate metrics alignment. To get past this struggle requires a clear vision, a focus on horizontal processes, and active leadership," I continued.

Enablers of Progress to Move to Stage 5

"I get it," said Joe. "How do we get started?"

"Network simulation and modeling technologies help leadership teams to visualize the interrelationships between these metrics," I said. "I know that you have been experimenting with some of these technologies. These tools also help companies to understand the potential of the business. Through the use of these new forms of technologies, organizations can engage in data-driven discussions cross-functionally as part of horizontal processes. It enables a discussion of what is possible."

Joe was still very engaged in the discussion, and peppered me with myriad questions, but I asked if we could take a quick break before we tackled the last stage of the model. I needed a cup of coffee. Joe asked his assistant to take me to the break room. As I filled my cup, I glanced at the bulletin board to see the key performance indicator reporting on ROA, lowest cost of materials sourced, and the labor cost of manufacturing. I smiled. "Yes," I thought. "This organization is very entrenched in functional metrics. Moving them forward will take some work."

Stage 5: Resilient Metrics to Withstand Market Shifts

As I sat down again, Joe hung up the phone and quickly wrote notes to himself in his notebook, and then crossed his legs and took the position that he had taken in his chair all morning. He asked me to continue.

"Well, Joe, we are almost done today. The last stage of the model, stage five, is the resilient enterprise. You know by now how religious I am on making sure all of the metrics that we use have clear definitions. So, before we start, let me clarify that I define resiliency as a tight and predictable pattern at the intersection of inventory turns and operating margin performance on an orbit chart. Achieving this result requires process alignment to improve agility and flexibility. The processes, through redesign, become more elastic to achieve this goal. Predictability and reliability in these two critical metrics are the goal of the corporation; but most companies fall short of reaching the targets."

I continued, "The swings between operating margin and inventory turns happen when the company is out of balance. The larger the swings, the greater the issue is. It can be driven by increases in complexity or through external factors; but as part of the methodology, we wanted to determine a way to measure resiliency. We believed that companies that were good at market sensing and management of operations would deliver consistency at this intersection.

"We were right," I stated. "Based on plotting data on orbit charts, we see that some companies had very tight patterns while others had wild swings at the intersection of operating margins and inventory turns."

Joe nodded in agreement. "It is so important to see progress over time. I also feel that resiliency is an important metric. I like the concept of being strong, balanced, and resilient."

"It hasn't been easy. In fact, it has taken us over two years of plotting data and analyzing patterns to get where we are today, but we firmly believe that the first design principle of operations is reliability. This includes dependability and consistency in customer service and also delivering on expectations for operating margin and inventory. As defined earlier, I term this *resiliency*. I find that many companies have focused on systems to improve the reliability of customer service, but aren't aware of the erratic nature of results at the intersection of operating margin and inventory turns. When the organization is resilient, the goal is to raise the potential of the system: to deliver reliable and improved customer service while lowering inventories and saving costs."

"It's one thing to say it, and another to measure it. Our goal was to find a way to measure this variability. To do this, we hired a team of operations research leaders at Arizona State University, commonly referred to as ASU, to define a methodology. The details of this methodology are outlined in the back of your workbook (see the Appendix). Based on their recommendation, we calculated the mean distance between points on the orbit charts for all public companies for the period of 2006 to 2013."

As Joe and I discussed the results of the work with ASU (shown in Table 2.3), we were amazed at how different the characteristics of each industry were. The industry segments were listed in the table in the order of

TABLE 2.3 Mean Distance Analysis of Orbit Charts of Inventory Turns and Operating Margins

Mean Distance Analysis of Orbit Chart Performance (Inventory Turns & Operating Margin)					
Industry	Median	Mean	Maximum	Minimum	Standard Deviation
Medical Device Manufacturing (n = 108)	0.7	**1.9**	51.9	0.2	5.5
Consumer Packaged Goods (n = 133)	0.8	**2.8**	118.6	0.2	11.9
Cereal Food (n = 209)	2.1	**5.3**	141.1	0.1	13.2
Pharmaceutical (n = 489)	1.0	**9.7**	1556.1	0.2	75.9
Chemical (n = 181)	1.2	**9.8**	644.2	0.2	59.3
Consumer Electronics (n = 120)	1.6	**11.8**	697.8	0.1	68.8
Contract Manufacturing (n = 1,087)	1.5	**15.1**	10253.2	0.1	313.5
Communications Equipment (n = 431)	2.0	**35.7**	9915.0	0.2	484.4

Based on cooperative work between Arizona State University and Supply Chain Insights LLC.

Industry Average comprises ALL public companies (cereal food: NAICS 3112%, where any % is any number from 0 to 9), (chemical: NAICS 325188 and 325998), (communications equipment: NAICS 3342% where % is any number from 0 to 9), (consumer electronics: NAICS 33431 % where % is any number from 0 to 9), (consumer packaged goods: NAICS 3256% where % is any number from 0–9), (contract manufacturing: NAICS 33441%), (medical device manufacturing: NAICS 339112), (pharmaceutical: NAICS 325412) reporting in One Source.

Source: Supply Chain Insights LLC, Corporate Annual Reports 2000–2013 as available.

most resilient to least resilient. The standard deviation and the range give an overview of the variability of companies within the industry.

Several trends stood out to Joe. He was fixated on the variability of contract manufacturing and stated, "This high variability is a risk to upstream value networks." Excitedly, he said, "While the median number seems reasonable, it's the variability that is the risk. We are not unaware of this risk. The range of corporate performance within this industry is highly variable and I think that it should be actively managed to reduce corporate risk. What do you think?" I agreed.

"Also," Joe said, "I noted in our discussion that the companies with the largest hits on commodity volatility—consumer electronics, communication, equipment, and food—rank the lowest on resiliency. Do you think that the reason is tied to functional processes and companies struggling to orchestrate price decisions market-to-market?"

"Yes, this is clearly the case," I replied. "The inclusion of commodity price variance in go-to-market strategies for price, promotion, and incentive is a gap for most. This should be a major thrust for companies to orchestrate decisions cross-functionally from market to market."

I further explained, "An example of this in practice is the work at Cargill Beef. The company senses the market potential for cuts of beef and orchestrates the go-to-market options based on that potential. As a market-driven leader the company uses price optimization tools to evaluate the potential for beef sales. Before Cargill Beef decides what to package for the market, they first evaluate the market potential for each cut of beef and then optimize how they harvest their inbound herds to maximize the opportunity and minimize the risk. There are 197 ways to cut up beef cattle. Since each breed of cow has a different potential, or finite mix of products—steaks, ground beef, roast, and so forth—Cargill uses the technology in sales and operations planning (S&OP) to drive rancher insights and define which breeds are best for customer demand. This process of being adaptable to trade-offs from market-to-market, based on the use of optimization technologies, is termed *demand orchestration*."

Who Does It Best? Who Is the Most Resilient?

We then turned the pages of the workbook to see which companies were the most resilient at the intersection of operating margin and inventory turns within each industry group. (See Table 2.4.) We talked for an hour on the differences between industries and also between companies within an industry.

I told Joe, "The goal is to deliver strength, balance, and resiliency. Usually, where there is strength and resiliency, there is also balance. The three run hand-in-hand in the definition of operations excellence." We then turned

TABLE 2.4 Comparison of Industry Resiliency Figure

Resiliency Value (Mean Distance) of Selected Companies					
Chemical		Consumer Electronics		Consumer Packaged Goods	
Company	Value	Company	Value	Company	Value
Chemtura Corporation	0.54	Panasonic Corporation	0.51	Colgate-Palmolive Company	0.23
BASF SE	0.55	Samsung Electronics Co.,Ltd	0.59	Beiersdorf AG	0.24
Seiko PMC Corporation	0.55	Bang & Olufsen A/S	0.63	Estee Lauder Companies,Inc	0.31
Nalco Holding Company	0.64	Sanyo Electric Co., Ltd.	0.68	Henkel AG & Co KGaA	0.42
E.I. du Pont de Nemours and Company	0.67	Pioneer Corporation	0.87	Kao Corporation	0.43
W.R. Grace & Co.	0.69	Harman International Industries Inc./DE/	0.93	L'Occitane International S.A	0.43
Lubrizol Corporation	0.71	ILG Electronics Inc.	0.13	Procter & Gamble Company	0.52
Dupont Nutrition BioSciences APS	0.76	Sony Corporation	0.46	Unilever NV	0.74

Based on cooperative work between Arizona State University and Supply Chain Insights LLC.
Source: Supply Chain Insights LLC, Corporate Annual Reports 2000–2013 as available.

to look at the impact of operational decisions for the period of 2000–2012, shown here as Table 2.5. As we contrasted the progress of industry peer competitors for the period of 2000–2012, Joe summed it up well when he said, "A characteristic of an industry leader is to deliver *both* strength and resiliency. Right?"

"Exactly," I said. "That is the beauty of the model."

I then summarized, "Companies rank higher if there is a focus on supply chain excellence and maturity of processes over many years with consistent leadership. The teams that rate the highest have been focused on delivering excellence for at least a decade. They also score better if there is an emphasis on cross-functional processes with shared metrics. There is higher performance when manufacturing reports to supply chain. To do this well, the teams have to be committed to delivering on balanced portfolio metrics. And finally, there needs to be a strong focus on employee development with the building of team capabilities. In contrast, companies with high employee turnover in operations tend to post lower performance."

TABLE 2.5 Contrast of Strength and Resiliency for Peer Competitors for the Period of 2000–2012

Inventory Turns, Operating Margin, Resilience Ranking 200–2012			
Company	Average Inventory Turns	Average Operating Margin	Resilience Ranking
BASF SE	5.3	0.10	0.55
E. I. du Pont de Nemours and Co.	4.0	0.10	0.67
Procter & Gamble Company	5.6	0.18	0.52
Unilever N.V.	5.3	0.13	0.74
LG Electronics, Inc.	6.7	0.04	1.13
Samsung Electronics Co., Ltd.	8.3	0.11	0.59

Based on cooperative work between Arizona State University and Supply Chain Insights LLC.
Source: Supply Chain Insights LLC, Corporate Annual Reports 2000–2012 (through 2013 for select resilience ranking calculations).

Use of Horizontal Processes to Improve Resiliency

To understand the concepts better, I asked Joe to consider the story of two packaging material providers: Sonoco Products and Owens Illinois. Owens Illinois, Inc. (OI) is a $7 billion manufacturer of glass bottles while Sonoco Products is a $5 billion manufacturer of paper packaging. Sonoco Products is over 110 years old. Sonoco is an asset-intensive company employing more than 19,600 employees. In 2012, Sonoco was listed in the top 100 of Corporate Responsibility's 100 Best Corporate Citizens and listed for two consecutive years as one of Fortune's most admired companies.

Comparing the results of the two companies shown here as Figure 2.11, I said, "Both companies are suppliers to the CPG industry. Over the past decade, each of the companies was squeezed on margin. Commodity prices have escalated and their upstream suppliers have been tough negotiators. In an attempt to drive share, both companies initiated a growth strategy. In the period of 2000–2013, OI invested three times more in R&D than Sonoco Products, yet Sonoco had five times greater growth with half the inventory than OI. It also had five times the resiliency. Why?" I turned to write this list of five reasons on Joe's board:

1. Clarity of strategy
2. Alignment on a metrics portfolio
3. Consistency of leadership
4. Management of complexity
5. Strong horizontal processes

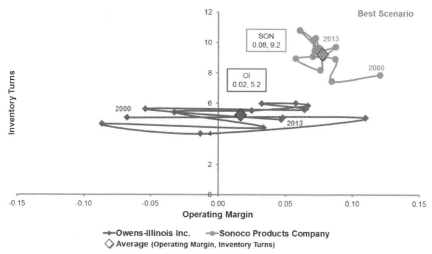

FIGURE 2.11 Contrasting Views of Corporate Performance: Sonoco Products and Owens Illinois
Source: Supply Chain Insights LLC, Corporate Annual Reports 2000–2013.

As I sat down and looked at all of the writing on his board for the session, I laughed. "Wow!" I exclaimed. "I've made quite a mess of things. Look at all of these lists!"

Joe laughed and said, "Putting them on the board helps me to get them right in my notebook. Plus next week, as I work, I can look up at my board and reconnect with the thoughts. Please continue with your story. . . . "

"While OI is functioning in Stage 1 of the metrics model," I began to explain, "Sonoco Products is in Stage 4, moving to Stage 5. The leadership team at Sonoco Products aligned a metrics portfolio against a business strategy in 2010. The goal was growth. The company made a conscious choice to give up margin to gain market share in the tough period following the recession. They worked cross-functionally to maximize asset utilization and improve ROIC while managing inventory and maximizing share.

"It wasn't easy. At Sonoco, there were conflicts between disciplined planning and driving an agile response. Within the organization, there was a faction that wanted traditional production agreements to a forecast with preestablished lead-time agreements with customers. However, to win with customers, the company needed to have a demand-driven order cycle with a short lead-time. To drive balance and resiliency, the team worked to combine both and align the metrics to drive resiliency. They designed the operational systems and made them fit for purpose," I continued.

"As a result, they established two value networks," I stated. They designed their buy-to-plan processes for paper manufacturing and stored roll stock based on forecast accuracy focused on efficiency. They then designed a pull-based system based on agility to convert the roll stock based on customer demand into tubes and cores for composite cans. Each of the supply chains used the same metrics but had different targets in the metrics portfolios. As a result, Sonoco Products improved days-of-inventory performance while improving customer service. Performance reliability is critical in the delivery of cash dividends to shareholders. In 2013, the company increased the dividend to shareholders for the thirty-first consecutive year."

I then stood up, and said, "Since this is the final and most mature stage of the metrics maturity model, you are done. There are no barriers or enablers for stage five of the model; instead, the next sections in your workbook are on how to drive and manage change that accompanies the process evolution. However, before we finish, I wanted to read you some excerpts from an interview that I recently completed with Keith Holliday at Sonoco Products."

Sonoco Products Aligning for Balance

An Interview with Keith Holliday, Director of Supply Chain, Sonoco Products

When you think about supply chain excellence, which metrics matter?

Everything in supply chain is about customer, cost, and cash. For the customer, the big metric is on-time and in-full delivery. Composite metrics do not resonate as well with our leaders. Most consumer products companies are focused on case-fill rate. Industrial customers care a lot less about service than our consumer products. CPG companies have fewer buffers and higher velocity.

The second metric that matters is cash. It matters to our company. I manage two of the three components of working capital: inventory and payables. The commercial teams own accounts receivable.

The third metric is cost: Everyone cares about it, but no one knows how to measure it. It is tough to measure total cost. So, we go after a good surrogate. We focus on distribution costs.

The problem is that financial metrics are backward looking. Supply chains need to be forward looking, but we do need backward metrics to look at root cause.

How have metrics changed over your tenure?

It used to be all about costs. Then there was a focus on cash. And then it focused on customer service. This seemed to come very late. Prior to that the customer was important, but you did not worry about it until the customer was complaining.

What have you learned?

Every time that I talk about the supply chain to one of our commercial leaders, they say "supply chain is really complicated." They see the supply chain as a function. What they did not realize is that the supply chain is the core process of a manufacturer. It is about the commercial processes and how that gets translated into scheduled. The focus on the process of supply chain is tough to get the leaders to grasp. So, we focus on what they care about. . . .

Unfortunately, manufacturing companies tend to be in silos. Each one of the functions worked independently. You cannot get truly excellent unless you have something that fits together so that the whole gets better. You must answer the question of "How do I really put all of this stuff together?"

 ALIGNING ON ASSET STRATEGIES

It was late, but I had one more important point to make with Joe before I left. I asked, "Do you have a minute to think about the measurement of asset strategies?" He gave me a thumbs-up, so I continued, "One of the metrics that can throw a company out of balance is the measurement of asset effectiveness. As complexity increases, asset utilization will decline."

D efinition of Asset: A resource with economic value that an individual, corporation, or country owns or controls with the expectation that it will provide future benefit.

"There are a number of ways that companies can account for assets and align for value. In our research, the three most commonly used are ROA, RONA, and ROIC. Getting clear and driving alignment is essential because each has a different implication with far-reaching impacts. The formulae for ROA, RONA, and ROIC are shown in your workbook. Notice how different they are?" I asked. (See Table 2.6.)

"While ROIC has a better correlation to market capitalization, most operations leaders measure themselves by ROA." To understand the difference, and how dramatically different the outcomes are, I asked Joe to look closely at the numbers for the food industry peer group. I spread out the tables shown here as Tables 2.7a, 2.7c, and 2.7b.

He rubbed his hands. I had Joe's attention. He had spent years being beat over the head to improve ROA. Joe responded, "ROIC isn't only a measurement

TABLE 2.6 ROA, RONA, and ROIC Formulae

Equation Definitions	
Return on Assets	Net income/Total assets
Return on Invested Capital	365 × (Operating income + Income tax total)/Period length/ Total shareholder's equity
Return on NetAssets	Net income/(Property, plant, equipment + Total current Assets−Total current liabilities)

Source: Supply Chain Insights LLC.

TABLE 2.7a Comparison of Return on Assets

Return on Assets				
Company	2000–2005	2006–2011	2012–2013	2000–2013 Average
Anheuser-Busch InBev N.V.	2%	4%	8%	**4%**
Campbell Soup Company	11%	13%	9%	**11%**
ConAgra Foods, Inc.	5%	6%	4%	**5%**
H.J. Heinz Company	7%	8%	8%	**8%**
Mondelēz International, Inc.	5%	4%	5%	**5%**
Nestlè S.A.	7%	13%	8%	**10%**
PepsiCo Inc.	13%	14%	9%	**13%**
The Hershey Company	11%	11%	15%	**11%**
Unilever N.V.	5%	11%	10%	**8%**

Source: Supply Chain Insights LLC, Corporate Annual Reports 2000–2013.

TABLE 2.7b Comparison of Return on Net Assets

	Return on Invested Capital			
Company	2000–2005	2006–2011	2012–2013	2000–2013 Average
Anheuser-Busch InBev N.V.	4%	9%	12%	**7%**
Campbell Soup Company	17%	13%	11%	**15%**
ConAgra Foods, Inc.	7%	7%	5%	**6%**
H.J. Heinz Company	13%	14%	13%	**14%**
Mondelèz International, Inc.	8%	5%	5%	**6%**
Nestlè S.A.	9%	8%	8%	**9%**
PepsiCo Inc.	16%	13%	10%	**14%**
The Hershey Company	17%	13%	16%	**15%**
Unilever N.V.	10%	13%	13%	**11%**

Source: Supply Chain Insights LLC, Corporate Annual Reports 2000–2013.

TABLE 2.7c Comparison of Return on Invested Capital

	Return on Net Assets			
Company	2000–2005	2006–2011	2012–2013	2000–2013 Average
Anheuser-Busch InBev N.V.	11%	37%	73%	**31%**
Campbell Soup Company	−4%	57%	40%	**28%**
ConAgra Foods, Inc.	14%	17%	14%	**15%**
H.J. Heinz Company	25%	33%	31%	**29%**
Mondelèz International, Inc.	29%	36%	36%	**33%**
Nestlè S.A.	30%	63%	43%	**46%**
PepsiCo Inc.	38%	38%	30%	**37%**
The Hershey Company	22%	24%	28%	**24%**
Unilever N.V.	83%	124%	94%	**102%**

Source: Supply Chain Insights LLC, Corporate Annual Reports 2000–2013.

of assets, but also the use of capital. Look at the results for Mondelēz. The company is performing below the peer group on Return on Assets, but has lengthened payables and performs well on RONA. However, when the total cost of capital is considered, on ROIC it performs below its peer group. I can clearly see what you are saying."

"If the cost of capital is 7 percent, then the top performance would go to Campbell Soup Company and Hershey," I stated.

"Yes," said Joe. "And the teams at ConAgra, InBev, and Mondelēz should be having the discussions of why they are underperforming to market on asset strategies[4] with their operating committees. I would hate to be a part of that discussion."

I concluded, "With a few exceptions, overall, the use of assets in the food industry isn't improving. While many have driven improvements through the increase of payables, the company that has done the hard work to improve potential is Hershey. Hershey has improved the use of their internal physical assets of plant and equipment while reducing inventory. Sadly, several of these companies don't look bad when you look at ROA; but when you look at ROIC, it's clear that they are operating at a level below the market cost of capital. Based on our research, we strongly believe that ROIC is a metric to consider when companies are building their balanced metrics portfolio."

Colgate: A Leader in Improving ROIC

Colgate prides itself on ROIC performance. The company has posted more consecutive quarters of increased operating margin than any other company studied. It ranks higher on resiliency than its peers, but is stuck on its ability to deliver a balanced portfolio. Here is an excerpt from an interview with Mike Corbo, the supply chain leader at Colgate:

Excellence is easier said than done. Our business is complex. We have worked hard to get good at understanding the financial levers of operations. We are disciplined in making capital investment decisions. We base them on return on invested capital. As a result, we seldom outsource manufacturing.

We take pride in our innovations in manufacturing. Today, 95 percent of manufacturing is directly managed by the Colgate team and we have taken steps to vertically integrate some of the operations. For example, we make the tubes for our toothpaste. This enabled us to improve operating margin, and return on assets, but has hurt us in delivering on the revenue per employee productivity numbers in your analysis. It's about conscious choice.

You are what you measure. We are diligent in metrics. We pay attention from case fill to the customers' feedback on on-time deliveries and plant efficiencies and forecast accuracy.

Michael Corbo, leader of Supply Chain, Colgate-Palmolive

MANAGING CHANGE

"This journey, and the management of change, is often underestimated. The transition, as the organization matures, requires a zealous focus on having the right stuff. Initiatives to improve corporate performance are a lightning rod for change. This will be most of your challenge," I advised.

Joe agreed and then added, "Success requires a conscious and deliberate approach and that is easier said than done."

I turned a page in his workbook and pointed to a figure that might help. "Building on J. P. Kotter's change management model (seen in Figure 2.12[5]), we find that having the right stuff includes: having a shared vision, providing the right skills, defining employee incentives, enabling the right resources, aligning on a common and shared plan, and management by enlightened leadership. When organizations don't align and actively manage change management, issues abound. This includes confusion, anxiety, false starts, employee frustration, or gradual change."

"We have certainly had a lot of false starts and anxiety," said Joe. "This is a wonderful chart for me to put right here on my board next to my phone. When I move into action, I should ask myself if I have put together all of the right parts to drive the right change."

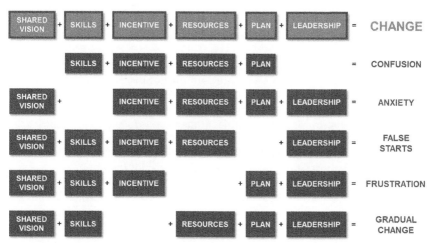

FIGURE 2.12 Managing Change
Source: Based on concepts from *Leading Change* by John Kotter (Cambridge, MA: Harvard Business Review Press, 1996).

I replied, "Yes, I find that the elements in this model are essential. In our research, we can see and hear the leaders from each of these companies. The companies that have driven the best results on strength, balance, and resiliency have had leadership consistency. They have also had a shared vision and shared metrics. No doubt about it, the management of change means that companies have to have the right stuff. All of the boxes in the model have to align for success."

It had been a long day. Joe was still energized and asked, "Don't you want to check out my notes and make sure I got things right?" He then winked, mocking me for checking out his book the first day. I played along, and read his notes. I am always impressed by Joe's ability to hear and translate insights into action.

The Notes from Joe's Journal

Clearly written in mechanical pencil, "Making progress on the metrics journey takes time. It requires a deliberate focus and leadership consistency is essential. There needs to be education to build the guiding coalition and this will require the onboarding of the greater organization. I am not sure how to do this, but the clearer and the more compelling the message, the easier it is to build a metrics framework. To make the journey, I think that these are the right next steps:

1. Translate the business strategy into the operating strategy. Using the framework (outlined in Figure 2.1), clearly define the operating strategy and the metrics that matter framework and the Effective Frontier. Focus on five to seven metrics that are interrelated and can be used to drive the business strategy. After deciding on these metrics, align the functional metrics to the corporate performance metrics. These serve as input metrics into the higher level corporate metrics, or output metrics. Connect the corporate metrics to cross-functional incentives and educate employees on why Metrics Matter. Then work to understand how to set the metrics targets.
2. Understand your potential. Get clear on definitions. Realize that excellence must be defined. While most companies talk about excellence, too few define it. It's easier said than done. The definition of excellence is hard work for the leadership team, but it's essential. There are many factors to consider. Also, as a leadership team, spend time to agree and gain consensus on the 'gold standard.' This will be the company's performance that you most want to emulate. This activity will drive clarity and help to drive a foundation for workforce communication.

3. Plot your results at the intersections of the Effective Frontier. To understand your current state, understand the patterns. Plot the intersections of growth, profitability, cycles, and complexity. Each intersection offers a new learning opportunity. After doing this analysis, analyze the patterns and gain insights on the business drivers and the market factors. Compare the results of your company to the relevant peer groups and gain insights into what is possible.

4. Analyze patterns and perform a root-cause analysis by business unit. After understanding the patterns for your company, plot the divisional and geographic unit data. Spend time as a group discussing the patterns and focusing on a root-cause analysis. In light of the analysis, it's often helpful to reflect on the past years' performance. After doing this, agree on the targets for the metrics that matter.

5. Train the teams on the metrics maturity model. The evolution of the Metrics That Matter maturity model takes time to learn and understand. Spend time helping employees to understand the goals, the metrics that matter, and the processes for development.

6. Use new forms of analytics to enable cross-functional analysis and Alignment. After determining the prior steps, build a model to help simulate 'what-if' analysis to help employees to understand the trade-offs and the interrelationships of the metrics.

7. Ask for help from human resources. Tap into your change management experts. Employees are vested in personal incentives and historic performance. Changes in metrics and performance incentives shouldn't be tackled without help from a change management expert."

CONCLUSION

I looked at my watch. So much left to do, but as I walked down the hallway, I reflected on my day with Joe. I liked these sessions. I was hoping that he learned that after selecting the metrics that matter, the goal is to drive strength, balance, and resiliency in corporate performance, all of which need to be defined and aligned cross-functionally. Functional metrics are input metrics to the process. They cannot be the output.

After achieving balance, strength, and resiliency on the Effective Frontier, companies can think about moving to the next level of performance. The processes of metrics maturity, while on the Effective Frontier, involve continuous improvement. The movement to a new Frontier requires disruptive thinking and the engagement of a new mental model.

Joe wanted me to come back and work with him some more to discuss how to build the guiding coalition. I looked forward to continuing the discussion.

 Notes

1. H. Thomas Johnson and Robert S. Kaplan, *Relevance Lost: The Rise and Fall of Management Accounting* (Cambridge, MA: Harvard Business School Press, 1987, 1991).
2. Supply Chain Insights, "Infographics," December 2013.
3. Supply Chain Insights Report, "Voice of the Supply Chain Leader" (February 2014), www.supplychaininsights.com/9/23/2013.
4. "Cost of Capital," New York University, http://pages.stern.nyu.edu/~ada modar/New_Home_Page/datafile/wacc.htm (accessed March 9, 2014).
5. Figure based on concepts from John Kotter, *Leading Change* (Cambridge, MA: Harvard Business Review Press, 1996).

CHAPTER THREE

Using Value Network Strategies to Move to the Next Level on the Frontier

T WAS AUTUMN. Scarlet leaves swirled in the air as I walked to dinner. It was time for Joe to develop his strategy for the New Year, and he invited me to help.

As we sat down, we laughed about his BHAG session the prior January. We celebrated how far he'd come on his journey. The mood was exuberant as he celebrated his team's recent award for driving significant improvements in operating margin and reducing inventory levels. When I congratulated him, Joe laughed and said, "I am slowly conquering the Effective Frontier, but I have a lot more work to do."

Joe now wanted to push performance to a new level. For him, it was all about growth and building a guiding coalition to drive change. He was excited about defining the new frontier with his new project. Based on the success with his team, he was starting to gain momentum with his peers. Humbly, Joe would always say that they were at the beginning of their journey. He continued to be worried about the gap between his company's performance and their peer group. Even though he was driving improvements, he felt that there was still a lot to do to solve nagging customer service problems. His team didn't feel that they could bridge the difference in performance without a redesign of the business network and redefining how the company did business.

The evening's discussion was on how to change the mental model within the company. Joe wanted to make a compelling case for change with his boss. He was to meet with the division vice president, Filipe, soon, and Joe wanted to prepare. As we shared a glass of wine and laughed at some of the recent discussions between Joe and Filipe, I knew that getting ready for this important meeting was the impetus for our one-on-one session the next day.

MANAGING WHAT YOU CAN'T CONTROL

As dinner was served, Joe spoke of his new opportunity. "Based on emerging growth opportunities in Brazil, I need to build a global operations footprint. I feel that the opportunity is substantial; but to seize it, I need local manufacturing and distribution capabilities, and I know that they will need to be outsourced," he continued. "The reason I have scheduled our work session tomorrow is because I'm worried about how to do it right. I know that my work will be dependent on setting up meaningful multitier relationships to drive value." During dinner, he discussed the need to establish new distributor relationships and work through third-party agents to penetrate the channel.

His goal was to use third-party trading partners to enter the market and then build his own sales team. He also needed to outsource much of his manufacturing and distribution processes. As a result, his future results were now going to be more dependent on others: He had to control what was not under his control. This worried him.

To be successful, he knew that he needed to crack the nut of managing value networks. He was worried as he shared a story. "In one of the other divisions within the company, the shift to outsourcing happened quickly. The goal was to lower the cost of manufacturing through the use of low-cost labor. The change happened faster than the organization could absorb and the processes are still in flux today. As we outsourced to China, we decimated the division's results. Just as they were starting to get the organization back on its feet, the cost for manufacturing wages in Mexico dropped 20 percent (in constant dollars).[1] The world economies had shifted before the division even finished building a network in China. It was sad," Joe concluded.

"As easy as it sounded at first, the impact was pervasive." He looked me in the eye as he continued, "It was one of those projects where the savings were compelling on a spreadsheet; but, you know how these things go. It proved more difficult than originally believed. Today, lead times are longer for the division and the processes are less flexible."

He folded his napkin and laid it aside. "Yes, we reduced labor costs, but total costs climbed precipitously. To use your words, consistent results on customer service and operating margin on the Effective Frontier became tougher to deliver. As a result, the organization has a bad taste in its mouth for outsourcing," Joe then reached down into his briefcase and pulled out one of my recent research studies, shown as Figure 3.1.

"I like this chart," said Joe. "It speaks volumes to me."

Joe felt that there was great room for improvement in his processes. He believed that the company was reactive, slow, and traditional and that the processes were cautious and built from the inside out. Joe wanted to build a value network that could serve multiple regions with different market conditions. He wanted more agility and alignment in the design of his new project in Brazil

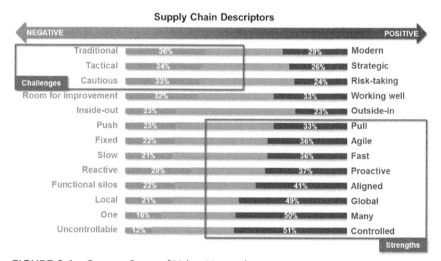

FIGURE 3.1 Current State of Value Networks
Base: Manufacturers, Retailers, Wholesalers/Distributors/Cooperatives, Third Party Logistics Providers, Consultants, Academics and Other—Total (*n* = 30).
Q27. For each of the pairs of words, please pick the one word or phrase that best describes [your][a typical] company's supply chain. SCALE: 5-point scale with one word on either end.
Source: Supply Chain Insights LLC, Cross-Survey Analysis 2012–2014.

and he felt that it was essential to sense channel flows based on outside-in processes.

Joe continued, "It's the same old story. Business conditions change, and we're stuck. We just can't move fast enough. It happens over and over again. We are just too traditional."

In Joe's business, in the past year, the product lines quadrupled and they entered new markets. As the transit times got longer and the business became more complex, it was harder to get a clear demand signal to ship the right products to the right markets to deliver products on time and in full to meet customer expectations.

"It shouldn't be this hard," Joe said as he looked at me intently. "But today I have a longer, less flexible source of supply in the face of rising demand volatility. How do other companies do it? How can I better manage demand? What can I learn about how they have built effective global networks?"

While Joe's goal was to propel growth, and not to chase low-cost labor, he realized he faced many of the risks that he saw first-hand in the other division. He wanted to build the right information technology (IT) systems to power a network so he could better use data to drive balance between growth, profitability, cycles, and complexity in these new and volatile markets.

"I just think that traditional approaches are a recipe for disaster," Joe said quickly with intensity.

I then reached into my briefcase to show Joe a piece of recent research, and put it on the table. I took out my pen and drew on it to make a point (see Figure 3.2). "You are not alone," I stated. "Most companies face a similar dilemma. It's no longer about the design of a process within a company's four walls. Instead, it's now an opportunity to design value networks that sprawl across the world. Outsourcing is today's reality. Today, 9 out of 10 companies outsource a major part of their operations. As you can see here, 30 percent outsource at least half of manufacturing with 55 percent outsourcing at least half of logistics."

The research helped Joe gain perspective. "Outsourcing changes the organization's focus and the underlying processes," I said while straightening my napkin. "As a company transitions from direct management of operations to building processes with third parties, it can have a major impact on the organization. It can go either way. We see that the shift can either dramatically improve or denigrate the organization's ability to meet corporate performance targets. It is both an opportunity and a risk. What makes the difference?" I probed. "In short, Joe, it's building an effective network. It is critical to

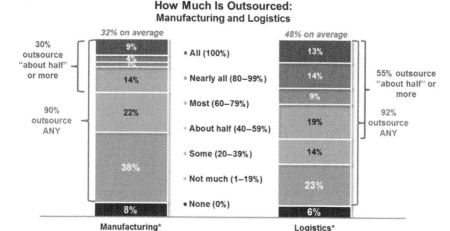

How Much Is Outsourced:
Manufacturing and Logistics

FIGURE 3.2   Current Levels of Outsourcing
Base: Manufacturers, Retailers, Wholesalers/Distributors/Cooperatives and Third Party Logistics Providers—Total (*n* = 78).
*Manufacturing: 3% answered "don't know" (not shown on chart); Logistics: 1% answered "don't know" (not shown on chart).
Q7: In 2013, how much of your company's manufacturing is outsourced? Your best estimate is fine.
Q9. In 2013, how much of your company's logistics is outsourced to a third-party logistics (3PL) provider? Your best estimate is fine.
For the purposes of this survey, a third-party logistics provider is a company that processes orders and ships goods on your behalf.
Source: Supply Chain Insights LLC, Supply Chain Visibility Study (October 2013–January 2014.

approach it as an opportunity and design the network based on your operating strategy."

Joe nodded in agreement as I continued, "Consider the case of two apparel manufacturers, Hanes Brands and VF Corporation (shown in Figure 3.3). Both Hanes Brands and VF Corporation are performing below their peer group industry average of apparel companies with more than $5 billion in revenue. As you can see from this diagram, the results are circular with both Hanes and VF going backward in performance. While VF is closer to industry averages of peer group performance than Hanes Brands, neither company has the strength or resiliency in corporate performance on the Effective Frontier that you saw in the consumer packaged goods peer group. A primary issue is that they outsourced manufacturing, but they did not redesign their systems to translate and manage demand."

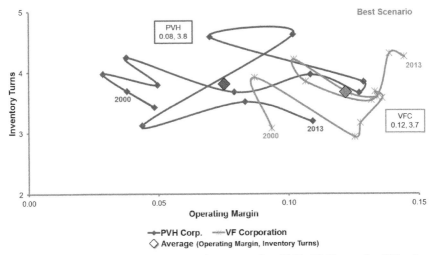

FIGURE 3.3 Apparel Company Performance for 2000–2013 on the Effective Frontier
Source: Supply Chain Insights LLC, Corporate Annual Reports 2000–2013.

I continued. "They are not alone. These companies are characteristic of the apparel industry. The industry introduces a new line each year, and the consumers' purchasing patterns are fickle. Demand is uncertain, but to minimize labor costs, manufacturing is outsourced.

"With the opening of global trade in 2002–2005, apparel companies rushed to take advantage of the lower costs of labor and the opportunities of tax-free manufacturing zones. While it sounded like a good idea, as you can see, apparel companies have steadily lost ground on the Effective Frontier over the past decade," I stated.

"We have not had to outsource to reduce labor costs, but I'm going to need to outsource both manufacturing and logistics and depend on third-party distributors in Brazil. I know that I need to build effective networks. It worries me. I can't afford to stumble," Joe said, looking concerned.

I put my hand on his arm reassuringly and asked, "How can I help?"

Joe's issue with Filipe was deep. When the company made the decision to chase low-cost labor, there was no consensus. At that time Filipe was leading the division, and he single-handedly dictated the shift. As a result, he received praise for courage and leadership, and it was one of the primary reasons why he was now leading Joe's team—hence the dilemma.

"It is amazing," Joe continued. "Filipe got all the glory and his team inherited a mess. Today, when I discuss the transition with Filipe's old team, no one remembers the discussions about the associated risks and need for investment. I find it amazing that there is no organizational memory of the potential impacts of the shift on future corporate scorecard performance. Since then, the division has struggled. In-transit inventories and safety stocks have grown, total costs have escalated, and the order-cycle times have skyrocketed with a deterioration of customer service. While Filipe's decision to outsource was heralded as a great idea five years ago, and he received great accolades because of it, the division is now in trouble.

"I think that I should rename Filipe the Teflon man. It seems that nothing sticks to him," continued Joe. "He made a change and moved on and now the division is having to live with it, but the design is not right. Filipe drove down costs, but he didn't improve value, and now I work for him. See the problem?"

> The discussion and analysis is important, because no one will remember the agreement when the results roll in two years from now.
>
> *Robert Cantow, Senior Director of*
> *Supply Chain Operations, Biogen*

"Yes, we are going to have to tread carefully here, aren't we? I like these kinds of challenges. I am looking forward to working with you on this." I said with a grin.

It was clear to Joe that he needed to build a network to capture the growth opportunity in Brazil. For him, it was not a question of when; instead, it was a question of how. When Filipe made the change to lower the cost structure in his prior role, he failed because he didn't build the supporting infrastructure. The organization could not flex with business changes. As a result, the efforts had failed. Joe was searching for an answer on how to build an effective trading partner network and he knew that after he achieved that, he then faced a tougher battle of convincing Filipe to invest in trading networks.

I told him this story from my recent interview with IBM. As we talked through the story after dinner, it helped him gain insights on how to design business networks to drive the right organizational behaviors. I shared, "Joe, while you think that it is about IT infrastructure, I want you to listen to this story to understand that the bigger challenge lies in change management."

IBM's Work on iBAT

I met with one of IBM's Director of Operations at a supply chain conference in the spring of 2014. He was presenting the story on how IBM had used analytics through an IBM Research designed tool named iBAT (the IBM Buy Analysis Tool). iBAT made substantial improvements managing end-to-end inventory within IBM's Business Partner sales model, resulting in millions of dollars of real bottom line PTI improvements.

"iBAT started due to challenges in the United States. We had too much inventory in the channel, and it created a lot of costs. If a Business Partner has too much inventory and the price is coming down, then there is a problem. We would price-protect the Business Partners for forty-five days, but when the price protection expired, they stopped buying. So, we extended the price protection.

We were spending millions to get the inventory out of the channel while we were pushing inventory into the channel.

Worst still, at times we would be running out of supply. The distributors would have many weeks of supply, but the wrong stuff. So, they would miss sales. It was a constant struggle. So, we asked the IBM Research team for help.

I was in the demand planning group at the time that iBAT started. We worked with the Research team to get channel data. They ran a simple regression on the channel information. They determined the rates of sales per channel node based on historic data. It then evolved to include lead times and seasonality, and variability on the product and insights on how the product should sell. The iBAT system that they created came up with a recommended supply level for each Business Partner. The Business Partners liked that. In fact, they used it to beat us over the head, and fought with our internal sales team to rationalize the channel inventory levels.

Changing the Behavior

Things got better, but the behavior did not change.

My job was to come up with a way to get Business Partners to use the iBAT tool in the channel to actually make purchasing decisions. We came up with a min and max range (reasonable range) by product that was linked to our price protection terms. We told our distributors that if they had a part, and the item was within the min-max range of iBAT, then we will price protect it forever. We proposed this in 2008, and they agreed to do it. It was summer 2008 and, if you recall, in September 2008, we had a macroeconomic thrust to help us. The economic downturn, in a twisted way, helped as there was more pressure than ever to lower inventory levels. We were able to reduce the channel inventories from a six-month supply down to the min-max levels.

Within a few months, we were reaping the benefits of moving to shared decision making between IBM and our channel partners, based on true analytics. Tying this behavior to price protection had finally changed behavior. Within a year, we had reduced price protection expense by 80 percent, aged inventory by 30 percent, returns were cut in half, and in a remarkable twist, despite running with one-third less inventory, our serviceability actually improved by ten percent.

What made it better was the kick-in of the stimulus money in September 2009, and our business came back with a vengeance. We took share in the channel as the economy came back. It made doing business with IBM easier. We had an unemotional third party—the network tool iBAT—that had the facts.

iBAT gave us sound wisdom to manage the network versus humans trying to make their business targets and the channel buyers to make their cost targets. As a result of iBAT, it was not a person winning. Instead, it was a voice of truth that enabled everyone to win.

Evolving the Use of iBAT around the World

Coming off the experience in the US, iBAT was a great story on how to use analytics. In Europe we had 100 Business Partners. In early 2010, we rolled it out in Europe, but didn't roll out qualified price protection. We made it optional. We gave them a choice because we didn't have the same inventory issues, but, the advantage of the program was that it became easier to do business with IBM because all trading partners had the same data and we were aligned on outcomes. This was significant. It allowed us to manage the inventory end-to-end in.

We then focused on Brazil and India.

Once you get stuff into Brazil, you can't get it out. We had a ton of inventory there. The model was different. In the rest of the world, we were build-to-order, but in Brazil, we pushed finished goods into the region, and waited for the order. The sales team ordered in Brazil based on different data sets without good data. As a result, they had all the wrong stuff. We decided to try to use iBAT in Brazil to improve the decision making. We decided to stock in country inventory levels that the analytic tool predicted and lo and behold, we saw the same results.

(continued)

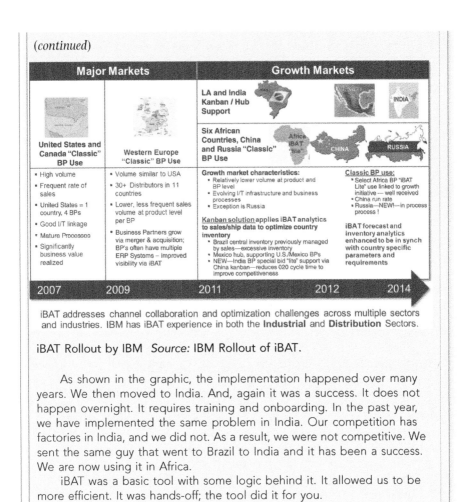

(continued)

Major Markets			Growth Markets	
United States and Canada "Classic" BP Use	**Western Europe "Classic" BP Use**	**LA and India Kanban / Hub Support** **Six African Countries, China and Russia "Classic" BP Use**		
• High volume • Frequent rate of sales • United States = 1 country, 4 BPs • Good I/T linkage • Mature Processes • Significantly business value realized	• Volume similar to USA • 30+ Distributors in 11 countries • Lower, less frequent sales volume at product level per BP • Business Partners grow via merger & acquisition; BP's often have multiple ERP Systems – improved visibility via iBAT	**Growth market characteristics:** • Relatively lower volume at product and BP level • Evolving I/T infrastructure and business processes • Exception is Russia **Kanban solution** applies iBAT analytics to sales/ship data to optimize country inventory • Brazil central inventory previously managed by sales—excessive inventory • Mexico hub, supporting U.S./Mexico BPs • NEW—India BP special bid "lite" support via China kanban—reduces O2O cycle time to improve competitiveness		**Classic BP use:** • Select Africa BP "iBAT Lite" use linked to growth initiative — well received • China run rate • Russia—NEW!—in process process ! iBAT forecast and inventory analytics enhanced to be in synch with country specific parameters and requirements
2007	2009	2011	2012	2014

iBAT addresses channel collaboration and optimization challenges across multiple sectors and industries. IBM has iBAT experience in both the **Industrial** and **Distribution** Sectors.

iBAT Rollout by IBM *Source:* IBM Rollout of iBAT.

As shown in the graphic, the implementation happened over many years. We then moved to India. And, again it was a success. It does not happen overnight. It requires training and onboarding. In the past year, we have implemented the same problem in India. Our competition has factories in India, and we did not. As a result, we were not competitive. We sent the same guy that went to Brazil to India and it has been a success. We are now using it in Africa.

iBAT was a basic tool with some logic behind it. It allowed us to be more efficient. It was hands-off; the tool did it for you.

"This case study helps me," said Joe. "It is a great example of moving from a sales-driven to a market-driven approach in the management of value networks. It's a shift from inside-out to outside-in processes that can only happen through value network automation. I think, if I have it right, this is what you've been advocating. Right?"

"Yes," I said. "In a sales-driven process, the behavior in the channel is driven by sales teams of the business partner with the most power. While in a market-driven value network, the business partners are aligned and incented based on market drivers. Together, the partners work together while using common and well-understood data sources in a collaborative process. IBM's iBAT is a good example of what I am talking about. The value network gives a common view, and aligns processes for not only volume, but also value."

"It is becoming clearer to me," Joe said. "However, I am bothered by two things in this case study. First, it took many years to change organizational behavior. This was *even* after they had a technology in place to guide replenishment decisions. I don't have years. As you know, I need to do it quickly. Secondly, there are few companies with the size and scope of IBM. It *even* took IBM seven years to roll out these processes around the world; and you know that we are not IBM."

"No doubt about it, I continued. "This type of change is hard work. You must first change the sales behaviors. This takes leadership, and I don't think that IBM was deliberate and forceful about making this change at a leadership level. Instead, it was a project in a line of other projects. Joe, we are talking about tough issues here. As you know, in most organizations, sales has carte blanche to do what they want in the channel, and many times that means doing what they need to do to make their quarterly bonuses. Stuffing the channel is not good for anyone. While it may improve the sales teams' bonus checks, it is detrimental to channel relationships in the longer term. However, the change, because it is so fundamental, cannot happen overnight. Like in the IBM case study, there needs to be a compelling reason to rethink how business is done," I continued.

"It is getting late. Want to continue this dialogue tomorrow?" I asked. Joe grinned, and said, "Yes, I could keep you up all night talking about this stuff. I don't mean to be rude. I find stuff like the IBM case study fascinating. We also have some very perplexing issues with our sales teams that I am not sure how to tackle. I think that this issue of sales working well with operations is a common problem. Can we pick this discussion back up tomorrow when we get to the office?"

Building Effective Networks with Trading Partners

The next day Joe was relaxed. As I sat down in my familiar chair, and he took out his notebook, he was ready. He wanted answers. His mind had worked in overdrive during the night, and it was not clear to him how to drive organizational alignment to support value networks. He was especially concerned about redefining the roles of internal sales and procurement groups to support the network. He felt that this was critical to his success in Brazil.

I asked him to open the workbook that I had brought for today and said jokingly, "Class is in session! Let's get started."

I smiled as I continued, "Joe, there are three basic types of value networks: demand, supply, and design. The IBM case study is an example of a demand value network. Filipe's outsourcing is an example of a supply network."

I stated, "A fundamental capability for a value network is visibility. It comes in different forms. As you have so rightly pointed out, the issues are many with roots in organizational design. Since the channel behavior is usually sales driven—interaction between a buyer and a seller acting on individual incentives—the traditional dynamics focus on what is best for the salesperson, not what is best for the channel relationship. As a result, like in the iBAT case study, we often have situations that are out of control as well-intended sales personnel try to sell more product. It takes many forms: The purchase orders can constantly change; the payment terms are elongated; product designs can shift; or product lines are extended. However, in short, it all comes down to one thing: What sales is selling is not in line with the shifts in the market. Outsourcing supply makes it even more difficult to keep everything synchronized. Your role is to redefine these processes and the role of sales and procurement to focus on serving the network. It is hard."

"As you have rightly pointed out, you also need to define the right IT infrastructure. This is the second nut to crack following a redefinition of sales and procurement roles." As I was speaking, Joe was taking copious notes. I paused to let him catch up.

"A common mistake that companies make is to think that the network can work well through tight integration. This is not true," I continued. At this point, Joe raised his eyebrows and looked at me over the top of his glasses and continued his ferocious and frenetic writing in his notebook. "Instead, it requires synchronization and harmonization of data. Companies learn the hard way that integration isn't sufficient. The more trading partners and the more changes, the greater the need to automate the trading network, and the more that this becomes an issue."

Joe turned his chair to stand up, and looked at me and stretched his long arms, and said, "Okay, maybe I'm slow, but help me here. What is the difference between integration and synchronization? And, what in the heck is harmonization of data? And, as you tell me, please go slow. Remember that I am not an IT guy!" he said with a wry smile.

Definitions

- Integration: The electronic connection of data from one system to another.
- Harmonization: The normalization of data elements item name, item number, customer, etc. to ensure context and meaning across trading partners.
- Synchronization: In the integration of data, the characterization of time elements—day, time, beginning and end of week and month—of data elements to ensure matching context in data integration of business networks.

"I understand. This may seem like a nuance, but getting this right is extremely important in the design of value networks. While a tightly integrated network connects data sets, a network that synchronizes and harmonizes data makes sure that the data that is connected has the right context for the *what*, the *when*, and the *how* of data. Let's take some examples. When you sell something to a distributor, your product code is different than that of the distributor's. Right?" I asked. Joe shook his head in agreement as I continued. "To record this sale correctly, the distributor's item code needs to be harmonized with yours. It would make no sense to your IT systems for you to record the data in the nomenclature of your distributor. So, instead, you need to translate the item code of the distributor into your selling unit. This is termed harmonization. Now let's define synchronization."

After I took a deep breath and searched for a good example, I continued, "When you sell the product, you are physically located in the eastern part of the United States and the distributor is in Europe. Each of you work in different time zones and the data needs to be synchronized to be sure that we have the right date of sale. Likewise, your average purchase order changes three times. The changes in the purchase order must be synchronized to be sure that we are working from the same sheet of music in the network. Synchronization is about time. Am I making sense?" I asked again while continuing. "While we used to pass data in the network through simplified EDI messages, now we are seeing the growth of business-to-business networks that enable the synchronization and harmonization of data through an integration layer termed a canonical. The canonical layer is programmed to ensure data translation and synchronization can happen correctly across data exchange formats. It is a great advancement in business-to-business networks that makes the integration layer much more flexible than the traditional passing of EDI messages or the direct connection of enterprise resource planning (ERP)."

"Okay, let me cry 'Uncle,' I get it," grinned Joe. "You are now a bit out of my league on a technology front. My take-away from this discussion is make sure I've got a good team in IT to help me when I go to Brazil. While I am not sure of what you said, I realize that our traditional approaches are not going to be equal to the challenge. Let me think more about the differences between integration, synchronization, and harmonization and get back to you."

"No problem," I said. "I know that I am throwing a lot at you all at once. One of the problems companies face is that when outsourcing decisions are made, the technology strategies are not aligned to enable frictionless processes within value networks. You saw this happen when Filipe did his outsourcing. As a result, visibility is poor, and companies cannot make the critical decisions that need to be made in a timely fashion. Instead, decisions are made late on missing data, and the gaps between what is important and the current level of performance are large. This is a barrier to driving higher levels of corporate performance. In fact, Joe, did you know that there are eight definitions of the common word *visibility?*" We then studied what is shown in Figure 3.4.

"I understand. Most of our energies within my company to date have been in the automation of transactions within my four walls," Joe said as he motioned to the walls around him. "While we have outsourced logistics and manufacturing, we have not built the networks to meet the business requirements for network visibility, and that is one of my current problems. Right?" asked Joe.

"Yes, that is correct," I replied. "As most companies learn too late, outsourcing is easier said than done. We need to move from inside-out processes to outside-in value networks. The greater the dependency on outsourcing, the more important planning is to the organization. Data is the lifeblood. It needs to be clean and near real-time with little latency.

"You cannot get there with a traditional approach to technology," I stated. "New investments in infrastructure are needed to power inter-enterprise

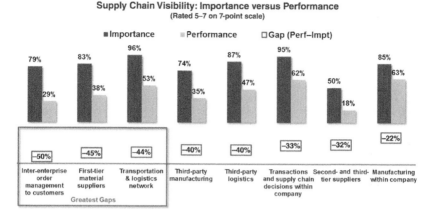

FIGURE 3.4 Visibility Requirements of Business Networks

Base: Manufacturers, Retailers, Wholesalers/Distributors/Cooperatives and Third Party Logistics Providers—Total (*n* = 78).

Q15. Please think about supply chain visibility. How important is it for your company to have visibility of the supply chain in each of the following areas? SCALE: 1 = Not at all important, 7 = Extremely important.

Q16. How well do you think your company performs on having supply chain visibility in each of these same areas? SCALE: 1 = Poor, 7 = Excellent.

Source: Supply Chain Insights LLC, Supply Chain Visibility Study (October 2013– January 2014).

visibility and enable new processes. As a result, most organizations struggle to get data and make the right decisions. When they can't, they try to bully their way around the network, managing outsourcing relationships with trading partners based on buy-sell relationships focused on individual incentives using spreadsheets. As you know from your own experiences, spreadsheets are not up to the task. Instead, we have spreadsheet jockeys and planning ghettos that need to be automated."

Joe knew that he needed to get help from his IT group. While they wanted to lend a hand, their energies were being consumed by the demands of multiyear enterprise projects. Their budgets were squeezed and resources were scarce. This is where Joe wanted Filipe's help. He needed to make the case for investment to build inter-enterprise business network systems. This would take some work, and we agreed to set up a time when we could meet with Filipe face-to-face.

Case Studies of Value Networks

Joe's focus shifted as he furrowed his brow and clapped his hands, "Enough said. Who did it well? What were their results on the Effective Frontier?"

> We live in a world where supply chains, not companies, compete for market dominance. But companies often have diverging incentives and interests from their trading partners, so when they independently strive to optimize their individual objectives, the expected result can be compromised.
>
> *Hau Lee, Stanford University*

He was ready to learn more. I watched intently as he settled back in his chair with his notebook, and moved into active listening mode to hear about the case studies. As he settled in and got comfortable, I smiled and began, "In the past decade, the most effective value networks were built by Taiwan Semi-conductor Manufacturing Company (TSMC) and Walmart. A failure was the building of the Boeing 787."

Joe then quickly asked, "What made TSMC and Walmart successful? What can I learn from the Boeing failure? I need to know more."

My answer to Joe's question was simple: "TSMC and Walmart were successful in building and executing value networks because of five critical success factors." I stood up and wrote these five factors on his board:

1. They were designed with the end in mind. They were fit for purpose. Each partner gained value.
2. Each network was a critical part of the business strategy.
3. Corporate commitment became a way of life.
4. Alignment. The design of the value network drove trading partner alignment.
5. Enabling technology infrastructure.

"Makes sense," Joe said scribbling furiously in his notebook. "We certainly don't have these characteristics here; however, this is great insight into what I need to build." He then looked up and smiled, and stated, "I am sure that you have some case studies of these to share with me. Your bag seems to be always packed with more materials than I can absorb. I look forward to learning more, but right now I need coffee. Can we take a break?"

We agreed that it was time for coffee and, together in the break room, we reviewed the case study of the building of a design network by TSMC. In the semiconductor market there are pure-play semiconductor foundries, like TSMC, that do not produce a significant amount of their own integrated circuit products, but instead produce integrated circuits for other companies based on their design.

Example of a Design Network: Taiwan Semiconductor Manufacturing Company (TSMC)

Founded in 1987, TSMC was the semiconductor industry's first pure-play foundry. In this role, the company made no product of its own and focused all of its efforts in making semiconductor chips for third-party manufacturers. Today, the company is one of the world's largest foundries serving over 450 customers and manufacturing more than 8,800 products for a variety of applications in computer, communications, and consumer electronics value chains.

In the semiconductor industry, a foundry is a major investment with a short lifecycle and high cost. A good rule of thumb in the industry is to plan for 18 months to build a foundry and 6 to 12 months to reach a level of production reliability. The capital cost to build a foundry has doubled with every two generations of semiconductor chip development.

It's a market with intense competition. In the period of 1997–2000, the company attempted to be the most efficient producer. However, TSMC quickly learned that the future success of the company was in the transition to service. As a result, the company has invested in a long lineage of service-based offerings to drive open innovation for the customer's network, positioning themselves as a partner, not a supplier or a competitor.

In 2001, TSMC launched an integrated library, Reference Flow, with a single goal in mind: Provide the shortest time possible to design and ramp-up the production of new products. These libraries were a network to support time to market for upstream customers. The library included TSMC-tested semiconductor designs and also validated the designs of third parties. By 2004, 75 percent of TSMC's customers used the company's library in their upstream designs. They also launched services to reduce the costs of testing and introducing new techniques, like

(continued)

(continued)

parallel mask production, to reduce the cycle time of wafer fabrication. They also developed direct communication systems to improve customer visibility for work-in-process material status and online testing results.

In later years, they renamed the service the TSMC Open Innovation Platform. It retained many of the original concepts, but used more modern technology to enhance customer collaboration with suppliers on design. It's a substantiation of TSMC's Open Innovation model that strives to bring together the thinking of customers and partners to drive a common goal of shortening design time, minimizing time-to-volume of innovation, and speeding time to market. Today, TSMC is the market leader in the global contract manufacturing semiconductor market with a 49 percent market share. The closest competitors have a 12 percent market share, demonstrating that companies win when they put more value in the value chain for trading partners.

The results for TSMC on the Effective Frontier of corporate business results versus Intel and Western Digital are shown in Figures 3.5a, 3.5b and 3.5c. While TSMC didn't achieve the revenue/employee of Intel, note that it did outperform the two competitors in margin and inventory turns. For the period of 2000–2013, TSMC averaged a 31 percent margin with nine inventory turns while Intel averaged a 24 percent margin with five turns.

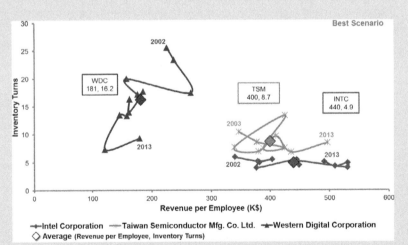

FIGURE 3.5a TSMC versus Intel and Western Digital Performance on the Effective Frontier—Inventory Turns versus Revenue per Employee
Source: Supply Chain Insights LLC, Corporate Annual Reports 2002–2013.

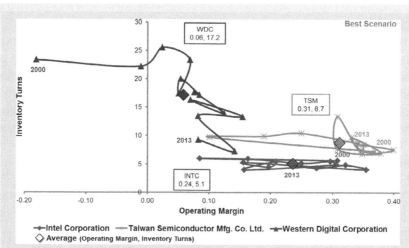

FIGURE 3.5b TSMC versus Intel and Western Digital Performance on the Effective Frontier—Inventory Turns versus Operating Margin
Source: Supply Chain Insights LLC, Corporate Annual Reports 2000–2013.

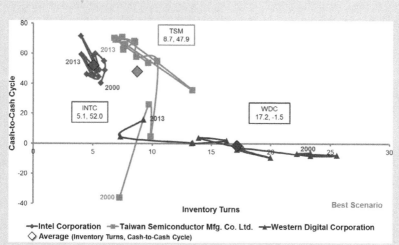

FIGURE 3.5c TSMC versus Intel and Western Digital Performance on the Effective Frontier—Cash-to-Cash Cycle versus Inventory Turns
Source: Supply Chain Insights LLC, Corporate Annual Reports 2000–2013.

"I love that story!" exclaimed Joe. "The network became so integral to the fabric of the company. I am wondering how we do the same thing here."

"Yes," I said. "For many, it comes down to leadership. Consider the quote from TSMC's chairman and CEO, Morris Chang, 'The main thing that we have learned is that a foundry needs to be a service-oriented business, so we are molding ourselves into a service company.' Can you imagine how hard a transition this was? An asset-intensive company like a semiconductor company transformed into a service organization powered by a design network?"

Joe nodded in agreement and asked if we could review the case study of Walmart. I continued, "I have a lot of respect for what Walmart has accomplished. The Walmart case study is an example of automating the supplier network. It is what Filipe should have done. Walmart named their network Retail Link, and the building of the network and the automation of the supplier base gives them channel power."

Example of a Supply Network: Walmart

Walmart now tops the Fortune 500 list. For the past 25 years, the company has outperformed competitors. One of the reasons is Walmart's investment in supply chain management. A competitive advantage is Walmart's building and usage of a supplier network termed Retail Link. Today, you wouldn't think of being a supplier to Walmart without the use of Walmart Retail Link.

Founded in Rogers, Arkansas, in 1962, the company has progressively invested in technology and new approaches for supply chain management. It was not a big-bang approach, but a steady investment focused on building sustaining value through the automation of stores and building supplier networks.

Early investments in inventory management were foundational for the supplier network. In 1975, the company installed inventory control systems to produce income statements for each store. This investment in store execution level to see inventory on a daily basis underpinned Walmart's soon-to-be supplier network. (For reference, today only 60 percent of North American grocery stores have perpetual inventory management systems installed at the store level.)

Subsequent investments formed the basis for Walmart Retail Link. In 1977, the company implemented one of the first companywide computer networks to order merchandise from suppliers. In 1982, the company was an early adopter to use bar codes to scan point-of-sale (POS) data. In 1992, Walmart rolled out the Retail Link network system to strengthen supplier partnerships. The system provided daily data daily on sale trends and inventory levels. In 1996, Walmart made Retail Link and EDI available via the Internet and began using the Internet as an application platform. In 2005, the Retail Link system had approximately 100,000 registered users running more than 350,000 queries a week.

Today, Walmart Retail Link is a critical element of doing business with Walmart for a supplier. It has also been adopted as an integral part of Walmart's global expansion. Each country has its own Walmart Retail Link providing daily data daily on sales (52 weeks of point-of-sale data), store insights with consumer demographics, perpetual inventory changes, store voids (no product available), and shifts in demand patterns.

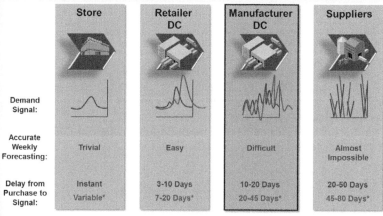

Red Text/Lines = Emerging Economies with Distributor Trade

FIGURE 3.6 Bullwhip Effect: Data Latency and Distortion across the Network
*Red represents emerging economies with distributor trade.

Supplier networks can decrease the bullwhip effect's impact in the supply chain and improve replenishment. The sharing of daily data daily in the supply chain with suppliers can decrease demand latency by up to 80 percent. As a result, suppliers can see and respond to channel demand requirements more quickly. The concept of the bullwhip effect is outlined in Figure 3.6. Without a value network to enable trading partners to see channel inventories, they're dependent on orders and shipments that have inherent demand latency (the time that it takes to trigger the order replenishment from a downstream partner based on an order-reorder point). This creates distortion and latency of the demand signal.

(*continued*)

(continued)

The impact of Walmart Retail Link to improve value was pervasive and can be clearly seen in Figures 3.7a, 3.7b, and 3.7c.

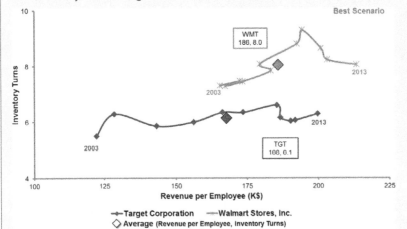

FIGURE 3.7a Walmart versus Target on the Effective Frontier—Inventory Turns versus Revenue per Employee

Source: Supply Chain Insights LLC, Corporate Annual Reports 2003–2013.

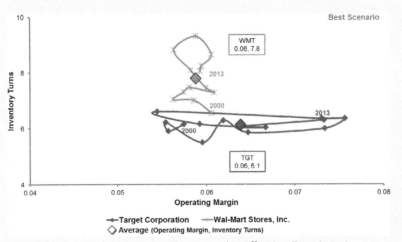

FIGURE 3.7b Walmart versus Target on the Effective Frontier—Inventory Turns versus Operating Margin

Source: Supply Chain Insights LLC, Corporate Annual Reports 2000–2013.

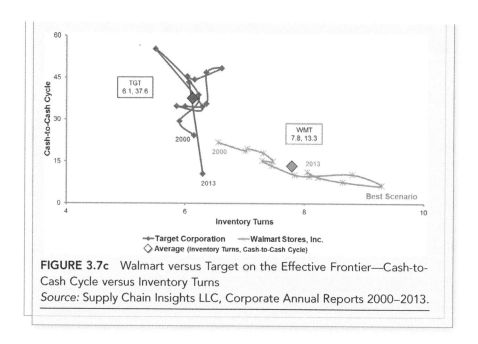

FIGURE 3.7c Walmart versus Target on the Effective Frontier—Cash-to-Cash Cycle versus Inventory Turns
Source: Supply Chain Insights LLC, Corporate Annual Reports 2000–2013.

Joe picked up a towel and wiped the table. We had lingered in the break room, and had a vigorous discussion on the case studies. As a result, we had many marked-up napkins and used paper coffee cups lining the counter. The dialogue went longer than we both imagined, and Joe was now intent on figuring out how to drive value through a network with trading partners. He spent most of the time fervently writing notes and asking me questions. He was narrowing in on a theme. He believed that the largest challenge for him was to change the mental model of his organization.

I concluded the discussion by stating, "Just remember, Joe, the building of Walmart Retail Link was not altruistic. Let's not fool ourselves. It was a smart business move for Walmart. As a result of these efforts, Walmart has outperformed its closest competitor, Target, on the Effective Frontier. The company has been able to give its suppliers better terms than Target—an average of 10 days faster payment in the period of 2000–2013—while operating its stores with one third less cash." Joe and I reviewed Table 3.1 before returning to his office.

"This is compelling. Look at these numbers," Joe stated as he stared at the chart on the clean table. "Target averaged 38 days on their cash-to-cash cycle while Walmart averaged 13 days. In parallel, Walmart had 7.8 inventory turns versus 6.1 for Target. While both companies had the same operating margin

TABLE 3.1 Walmart versus Target: Performance on the Components of Cash-to-Cash on the Effective Frontier

Company (2000–2003)	Days of Inventory	Days of Payables	Days of Receivables
Target Corporation	62	57	32
Walmart Stores, Inc.	52	36	3

Company (2004–2007)	Days of Inventory	Days of Payables	Days of Receivables
Target Corporation	60	64	39
Walmart Stores, Inc.	49	38	2

Company (2008–2011)	Days of Inventory	Days of Payables	Days of Receivables
Target Corporation	58	53	41
Walmart Stores, Inc.	42	37	4

Company (2012–2013)	Days of Inventory	Days of Payables	Days of Receivables
Target Corporation	59	48	31
Walmart Stores, Inc.	45	40	5

Source: Supply Chain Insights LLC, Corporate Annual Reports 2000–2013.

average, Walmart was more resilient, having a 1.0 value on the resiliency index while Target had a value of 1.3. Powerful!" he said, while tapping his fingers on the table. "Filipe is all about numbers."

When we got back to his office, Joe said, "Okay, we have seen two case studies where companies drove significant value, but I know this is not all a bed of roses. What about Boeing? Didn't you say that this one was a failure?"

"Yes," I answered. "I think that we often learn more from failure than success. Boeing is a wonderful reminder that while we can outsource our value network, we cannot divorce ourselves from the responsibility of managing and owning the network. This is a key point that I want you to get from this case study."

Boeing: Fixing a Value Network after Catastrophic Failure

Boeing is the world's largest aerospace company. The company is a manufacturer of commercial jetliners and defense, space, and security systems. Boeing's products and tailored services include commercial and military aircraft, satellites, weapons, electronic and defense systems, launch systems, advanced information and communication systems, and performance-based logistics and training. Boeing employs more than 170,000 people across the United States and in 70 countries. It's comprised of two business units: Boeing Commercial Airplanes and Boeing Defense, Space & Security. Boeing has manufactured commercial jetliners for more than 40 years. With the merger of Boeing and McDonnell Douglas in 1997, Boeing's leadership in commercial jets, joined with the lineage of Douglas airplanes, gave the combined company a 70-year heritage of leadership in commercial aviation. Today, the main commercial products are the 737, 747, 767, and 777 families of airplanes and the Boeing Business Jet. New product development efforts are currently focused on the Boeing 787 Dreamliner, and the 747–8. The Boeing 787 is a long-range, midsize jet airliner. It was unveiled on July 8, 2007, and was targeted to enter service in May 2008. It entered commercial service on October 26, 2011.

Attractive to the market, the Boeing 787 is a superefficient airplane designed for passenger comfort. The fuel-efficient design enables the plane to fly with 20 percent less fuel consumption. On introduction, demand was high. Early orders exceeded expectations. Then the schedule started slipping. And, orders were canceled. Negative press started to flow. What happened? How could the Boeing supply chain have such a major miss in a delivery?

The story is one of an innovation-driven company trying to collaborate with third-party suppliers to bring multiple innovative technologies—composites, new design, energy-efficient software, and more effective engines—to market simultaneously for the launch of a new type of aircraft. The revolutionary design was lightweight due to the extensive use of composite materials. Composite materials made up 50 percent of the aircraft, and the design of a one-piece fuselage eliminated 1,500 aluminum sheets and over 40,000 fasteners. This simplified the design and made it lighter for better fuel consumption. Innovative engines from General Electric and Rolls-Royce enabled even more efficient fuel consumption.

The work started well. Boeing commissioned 50 suppliers at over 136 sites around the world to design and assemble subassemblies for a final build at Boeing's Everett Washington facility. The suppliers designed subcomponents around the globe using a new computer-aided design (CAD) solution.

The issue was holistic execution and quality control. The Dreamliner launch had multiple public delays due to a shortage of fasteners. Conflicting specifications, compliance issues, and coordination issues plagued the program, which translated into delay after delay. As a result, orders were canceled, renegotiated, and pushed out.

(continued)

(continued)

In 2011, Boeing shipped three completed 787 planes and finished the year with 857 unfulfilled orders. The company publicly stated that "Our goal in 2012 is to ensure that 787 production is stable and reliable, while maintaining focus on execution as we deliver an increasing number of airplanes across all our programs." Through a redesign of the supply chain, Boeing established goals to increase production of the 787 by 300 percent. To do this, the company invested in supplier assistance teams, adding two hundred engineers and supply-chain specialists over the past two years to orchestrate the supplier network.

Boeing is learning from the mistakes in the production of the 787. The Boeing executive responsible for the *737* program is quoted as indicating that they will take a "fundamentally different" approach with this new program. Rather than a top-down approach to setting supplier requirements and milestones, the company is actively pursuing supplier development programs. This work will focus on ensuring that suppliers have the right skills, capabilities, and resources.

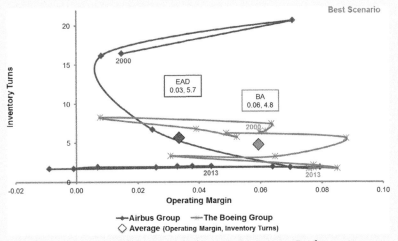

FIGURE 3.8 Impact of Boeing's Failure on Corporate Performance
Source: Supply Chain Insights LLC, Corporate Annual Reports 2000–2013.

Why did Boeing fail? Boeing outsourced design and carefully developed a supply network to deliver a superior new aircraft. The focus was on features: the best engine, the lightest composites, and superior performance of each supplier's work on subassemblies. The new engines worked well, but the issue became one of network orchestration and management of the holistic design effort. The network was not set-up for control of quality, manufacturing, and testing. As a result, quality control and design coordination plagued assembly. Boeing learned the hard way that the more outsourcing in a network, the greater the need for quality control processes to ensure network orchestration. While subassemblies manufacturing and supply can be outsourced, the process for network orchestration is essential. The coordination requirements are even greater when working on new products or new technologies through a value network. While a company can outsource its network, it can't outsource the responsibility for coordination.

Building Outside-In Processes

As we discussed the IBM, TSMC, Walmart, and Boeing case studies, the impact on business results was obvious. Based on the size of the prize, Joe questioned, why there were not more companies in other industries building effective value networks? He also questioned why companies still tried to power processes inside-out, and call them "best practices." We laughed and I retorted, "The answer lies in changing mental models." We agreed to tackle this after lunch.

Joe commented, "My stomach is as empty as my head is full."

I joked, "I hope that this is a good thing!" Joe swung around from his chair and patted me on the back and said, "Absolutely! Let's talk more over lunch."

We both laughed as he opened his door, with his notebook in hand. "Joe, you can't leave the notebook behind, can you?"

"No," he said. "I think that we're on a roll. We have a lot more to cover before we are done today! Besides, I don't get many days to sit and think. This conversation challenges me to think harder about how to run the business more effectively."

M etrics help to form the mileposts by which you can measure how far you have come and where you need to go.

Robert Cantow, Senior Director of Supply Chain Operations, Biogen

Dancing with the Long Tail

We sat with Joe's team over lunch, and the group was commiserating about the rampant addition of new products into the spring product line. It was getting more difficult to plan production and have the right inventory.

Joe asked me, "What do others do? How do they manage the product line to reduce complexity?"

"Complexity comes in many forms," I stated. "It looks different by industry. Aggression in go-to-market activities, those of marketing and sales, or the extension of the product line can add to complexity. To drive balance, the operations team needs to continuously redesign the network and realign processes to deliver results in the face of changing market drivers and go-to-market programs. As complexity increases, customer service usually plummets and it is more difficult to achieve balance in the metrics portfolio. It is for this reason that companies use modeling technologies to understand the impact of the long tail on operations to proactively manage expectations."

"Long tail?" Joe questioned. "That is a new term for me. What do you mean by the long tail?" His team laughed.

Taking a pen from my purse, I drew what is seen in Figure 3.9 on a napkin. Tracing the curve, I said, "As complexity in the product line increases through product extensions, the order frequency decreases and the demand pattern becomes lumpier, or more sporadic. It is tougher to plan, and the products in the long tail represent a disproportionate amount of inventory. As a result, as the tail gets longer, there is a greater need to build value networks."

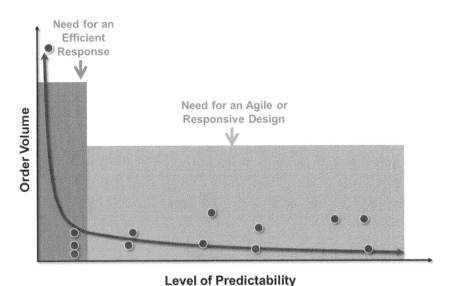

Level of Predictability
Based on forecast accuracy vs. actual order profiles

FIGURE 3.9 Definition of the Long Tail

> When I ask my team about customer service, I get high-five reviews. However, when I meet with my customers, I get thumbs-down feedback. I find the measurement of customer service to be one of the most difficult metrics to measure.
>
> Division Vice President, Confectionary Manufacturing Company

"I see," stated Joe. "While I have never thought about it quite like this, the concept makes sense. Right now, within the organization, the pressure is on. We are trying to hit on all cylinders to grow. We have myriad creative programs cooking at once. Price, distributor incentives, promotions, new product launch, and marketing activities are all being thrown at the problem to stimulate baseline demand. I can see how this contributes to the current problems that we are experiencing."

I said, "The complexity of go-to-market programs and product line extensions need to be viewed together. Recently, we worked with a company that had delivered a 40 percent reduction in the product portfolio based on some excellent work on product rationalization. At the same time, the marketing programs accelerated ramping up the pace of go-to-market activities. The team committed to the delivery of operating savings and inventory turns based on the product rationalization, but failed to meet the goal because they didn't look at the impact of the two forces together."

At that point, one of his team members spoke up, "That sounds like what happened in Project Ontario. We simplified the product line, but sales kept changing the program. We could never get good at predicting demand and costs escalated."

"Yes," said Joe. "And look at the inventory write-offs from that project. I have a meeting today to talk about how we could get it so wrong. I can see now how we went off course."

"As the tail becomes longer, and the demand becomes lumpier, with more ups and downs that are less predictable, the demand latency increases," I said.

"Can I ask," quipped Joe's lead demand planner, "what is demand latency?"

"Sure," I said. "It is not a well-understood term, but it's the time that it takes for a channel partner to hit a reorder point and trigger a replenishment. The longer the long tail of the order pattern, the greater the latency of the demand signal. It just takes longer for the replenishment signal to make it through the network. As a result, as the tail becomes longer, it's more critical to build value networks and align metrics to reinforce agility or responsiveness. Make sense now?"

"Can't we just deal with this problem through shorter cycles?" asked another member of Joe's team.

"Not really. Shorter cycles are an important component, but they are not the entire answer. You must figure out if you need an agile or responsive value network."

"Aren't they the same?" asked Joe. "I use these terms interchangeably."

"No," I continued. "A responsive design focuses on shorter cycles. This is needed when the response to the market stimulus is known, but it is a question of the timing of the demand trigger. An example of this is an allergy drug.

"Companies know the quantity of the demand, but they do not know when hay fever season is going to hit," I said with a grin. "An agile network design is unsure of both the quantity and the timing. This happens in new product launch, or a new market. In this case, it takes more than short cycles to keep balance on the Effective Frontier. Instead, it is about the design of buffers, the form and function of inventory, and postponement. In the agile network, when the market event happens, if designed correctly, the networks can adapt."

Joe said, "Okay, let me see if I can sum this up. As product platforms proliferate, companies need to redetermine metric set-points to ensure that they have a feasible plan. However, to keep the same level of performance with an increase in demand latency, companies need to drive a redesign and build value networks. Correct?"

"Absolutely correct!" I answered. "And as we will see after lunch, the greater the complexity the more vulnerable the company is to economic cycles and market downturns. Very few companies today understand this interrelationship."

Withstanding Economic Downturns

As we walked back to Joe's office, he remarked, "Your comment on demand latency struck a chord. The recessions of 2002 and 2007 were wake-up calls for us. As channel demand slowed, we were slow to respond. Despite a decade of investment in IT architectures, and the advancements in connectivity, we could not stay in sync with market changes. Why? We were focused on being in alignment with customer orders, but we could not sense the market shifts. We were caught off-guard by the downturn."

"I know, it was you and everyone else," I said. "It should have been a lightning rod to drive change for all of manufacturing, but unfortunately many people went back to their old inside-out processes and haven't been able to synchronize operations with channel demand."

"For example, did you hear about the DuPont plant closures?" I asked. "As you know, DuPont prides themselves in running some of the toughest processes to run anywhere in the world. They are recognized as the best at designing and operating plants that others consider to be too hazardous to run. For them to shut down factories was a major statement. The ripple effect and the time for recovery were larger than expected for everyone. Companies were caught with their pants down and a major factor was not being in sync with market demand."

In December 2008, DuPont announced plans to address rapidly deteriorating market conditions and strengthen the company's future competitiveness. Plans are focused on generating cash by better aligning cost, working capital, and property, plant, and equipment expenditures to the revised demand signals of the fourth quarter. These plans include a restructuring program with associated fourth-quarter pretax charge of $535 million, with expected pretax savings of about $130 million for 2009, and about $250 million annual savings thereafter. The company also outlined 2009 plans to achieve a $1 billion in net working capital reduction and a 10 to 20 percent reduction in capital spending.[2]

When we got to his door, Joe asked, "Was it bad for everyone?"

I replied, "Leaders that used market signals in enterprise processes sensed channel changes faster and aligned with market demand. The IBM iBAT case study is an example of a leader using a value network to sense demand, and what should be done today. Unfortunately, less than 6 percent of companies today have this capability. Demand sensing improves balance and resiliency in corporate performance. Let's take a look at some of the research in your workbook. . . . " Joe and I then studied the research chart shown in Figure 3.10.

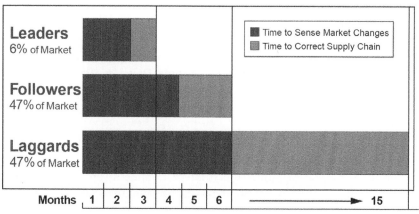

FIGURE 3.10 Importance of Sensing in a Market Downturn

I continued, "Because most companies can't sense and translate demand, an economic downturn is a wake-up call to get serious about the alignment of metrics. However, most companies cut the fat, but do not improve the muscle. Companies that operate functionally and are not aligned can't achieve the right balance between costs, asset utilization, and inventory cycles. In addition, companies without value networks can't survive economic cycles."

> Demand sensing is the time that it takes for an organization to sense true market changes in the channel. If the organization relies on orders as the primary market signal, the latency of the demand signal can be delayed by weeks. It varies by industry. It can be one to three weeks in consumer products and four to eight weeks in pharmaceutical value networks and 8 to 12 weeks in the service parts industry. The longer the tail of the demand curve and the further back in the channel that a company is, the more critical it is to build value networks to sense demand.

Joe stated, "Well, this is another selling point for our presentation for Filipe. We also struggled in the recession of 2007, and we cannot sense channel demand today. We are not in your 3 percent."

"Don't worry, you're in good company. The concepts of demand sensing and translation are not readily understood by conventional executive teams. There is a general belief that the order is a good representation of demand. Only the more advanced management teams understand that the order is poor proxy for demand, and that they need to own the channel and sense the flows through value networks in the channel to be sure that they can match the rhythms and cycles of the enterprise operations to market demand. If you do this, I will put you in the leaders' category," I said with a grin.

"Look at it this way," I continued. "On a positive note, an economic downturn is a wake-up call. Most companies make more progress on balancing and improving results at the intersection of operating margin and inventory turns during major recessions than at any other time. However, the results can't be sustained because they fail to build the muscle to operate at a new level on the Effective Frontier." Joe then studied what is shown as Figure 3.11 in his workbook.

"Yes," I continued. "Companies can use an economic downturn to drive new discussions on mental models. It's a time when the need for market sensing is crystal clear to the executive team. It can be a wonderful opportunity to build outside-in processes. We need to emphasize this point to Filipe."

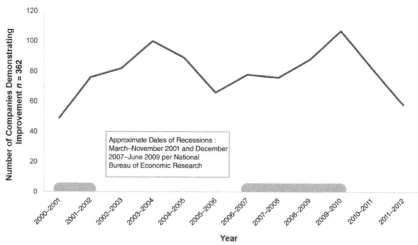

FIGURE 3.11 Improvement in Both Operating Margin and Inventory Turns Following an Economic Downturn

Morningstar peer groups: chemical, communication equipment, consumer electronics, drug manufacturers–major, household, and personal products, packaged food, packaging and containers, semiconductors, specialty chemicals available at Y Charts Professional, www.ycharts.com.

Source: Supply Chain Insights LLC, Corporate Annual Reports 2000–2012, National Bureau of Economic Research.

Use Failure to Your Advantage

It's easier to build a guiding coalition in times of failure than success. As I discussed with Joe, there needs to be a reason to drive change. The output of the burning platform needs to drive value and align to the corporate strategy. Following are some examples that I included in his workbook:

New drugs are the lifeline for large pharmaceutical companies. In 2005, when R&D funding was slashed, the procurement group of GlaxoSmithKline set a goal to fund the growth of a new drug. The team identified the average cost of a new drug, and developed a corporate savings programs to return enough money to the corporation to fund R&D efforts for a new drug program. They were successful in achieving their mission.

(continued)

(continued)

In 2009, the Kimberly-Clark operations team was facing increased competition and declining sales. The team set a target to drive growth through the alignment of operations processes with retailers. The operations team tracked net new sales through improved processes to deliver on new programs while maintaining cost and inventory balance. As you will see in the following chapters, they beat their goal by two years while improving their operating margin and inventory turns.

In 2010, Greenpeace attacked Nestlé, manufacturer of Kit Kat chocolate bars, for accelerating deforestation of the Amazon by their procurement of palm kernel oil. The Greenpeace attack went viral. The team had to respond quickly. They built a guiding coalition to align and reverse public sentiment in a two-month timeframe.

Management of Commodity Volatility

"It is not just about demand; leaders also find that it is important for supply," I continued. "While companies have decreased dependency on labor as an input into the value chain by improving productivity and outsourcing, one of the major obstacles for companies to improve operating margin is commodity costs. It's both the rise in costs and the volatility of commodity prices—they have never been higher. Unfortunately, the automation of the procurement function has created less alignment of procurement with operational processes, and the processes are not up to the challenge of reining in this risk."

"So true," stated Joe. "We run our businesses like they were designed when oil was $25/barrel. I just can't get my procurement team to shift from a focus on purchased cost to landed cost. We *so* need them to work collaboratively with suppliers to build value-based relationships."

As I reviewed the data in Figure 3.12, we discussed how automation of the supplier network is an opportunity for most companies.

I continued, "The focus on vertical processes within a function cuts down on the ability for a company to balance the impact of commodity volatility on cross-functional processes and balance them with go-to-market strategies. We need to talk to Filipe on how to bring these inputs into critical horizontal processes like sales and operations planning (S&OP) to improve the metrics that matter."

"Now if we could just get Filipe to buy into the fact that we need both a demand and a supply network for Brazil, we would be all set," continued Joe.

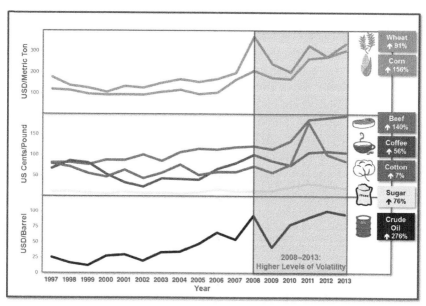

FIGURE 3.12   Commodity Volatility
Source: IndexMundi, based on annual data from January of each year; percent increase based on comparison of 2013 versus 1997.

"I would love to see that," I stated. "If you could sense the shifts in the channel and translate them through the supply networks, you can raise the potential of your new operation in Brazil on the Effective Frontier. It's more critical to build effective value networks and outside-in processes now than ever before!"

Aligning the Team for Action

Based on the conversation, it was clear to Joe that he needed to align the team for action. He wanted to build a guiding coalition to move to the next stage of the Effective Frontier. We worked through the afternoon to build a presentation for Filipe to support the need to build a value network and automate the channel and provide supply visibility to first and second tiers of suppliers. Due to the volatility of the product that he was making, and the lack of insight about his new market, he felt that it was even more important to do it now to get ready for the launch.

"We should think about building a guiding coalition, or a larger team, to drive the change. Any thoughts about how we could do that?" I asked.

"You are reading my mind. I think that this is important, but do you have any comments on how others have done this?" asked Joe.

"I have had success with several companies with these steps," I replied. "First you need to get clear on the market drivers and reduce organizational friction by tackling the alignment issues through the design of an operating strategy. After agreement on an operations strategy, the next step is to build the balanced portfolio of metrics. This is like the one that we spoke of in our last meeting. The focus needs to be on defining metrics that drive balance and resiliency. However, in this process to build the guiding coalition, the leader must skillfully avoid traps and build the burning platform for change. Let's take a look at these in your workbook. . . . "

As Joe turned the page, I stated, "The statement for change needs to be clear, compelling, and concise. There can be no ambiguity. It must hit employees in their hearts, driving action, and avoiding these traps."

Seven Traps to Avoid

1. *Singular metrics.* Avoid looking at metrics in isolation. Use analytics to understand the interrelationships. Inventory targets need to be based on demand and supply volatility, and operational inputs based on form and function of inventory. They should never be set based on arbitrary or historical targets.
2. *Functional metrics.* Use the Effective Frontier and the alignment of corporate metrics as a discussion to build a metrics hierarchy that starts with corporate metrics, and then align functional metrics and then personal incentives.
3. *Focus on inside-out.* As demand and supply volatility increases, often as the result of the implementation of growth strategies, it becomes important to focus on the value network from the customer's customer to the supplier's supplier. The metrics need to be aligned outside-in. Focus on network profitability, inventory, and cash-to-cash cycles while minimizing complexity. Define relationships so that they're win-win.
4. *Complexity.* Complexity isn't free. Understand the cost of complexity. Embrace good complexity that drives market share and aligns with the corporate strategy, but reduce bad complexity that adds costs but does not improve market share.
5. *History.* Learn from history, but look forward. Focus the metrics journey based on forward-looking views. Learn from history, but understand the power of real-time market sensing. Adjust organizational focus based on market shifts.

6. *Too many metrics.* Hold the organization accountable for a few metrics that represent revenue, profit, asset utilization, inventory cycles, and customer service.
7. *Continuous improvement.* While continuous improvement is the driver to improve performance on the Effective Frontier, new mental models and disruptive thinking are necessary to get to the next level of performance. They're different organizational behaviors. Don't confuse the two.

"Hopefully, you understand by now how important this is," I stressed. "You can't move forward until you build this guiding coalition, align on metrics, and move these metrics into employee incentives. We need agreement and alignment with corporate finance teams. Since the financial teams tend to view operations based on transactions, and the business leaders within the operations teams view the business in forward-looking flows, this requires substantial work. Many leaders are naïve and underestimate this journey."

"I get it," said Joe. "This is the life that I lead. What I think most people don't understand is the concept of the Effective Frontier and the fact that you can increase the potential of the company to perform on that Frontier by working these metrics as a system and empowering them outside-in through value networks. Am I close?"

Building the Team

"Yes, but it is not a onetime process. In the formation of the leadership team, each new member added to the group will come with their own definition of what drives excellence in corporate performance, and there needs to be a continual evolution," I stated. "Many times it's so clear based on their prior experiences that they will have little patience for the discussion; however, since this is a new way of thinking, you need to be sure that you drive the discussion."

I looked him in the eye, and continued, "To drive the guiding coalition for change, you must force the discussion each time that you add a new member."

"Okay, I get it. I have added this to my notes. So, tell me more. How does this process work?" Joe asked.

"All groups go through the normal steps of Tuckman's Group Development Model of forming, storming, norming, and conforming to perform,"[3] I said. "Often we will work with teams as they form and observe circular discussions

	Forming	Storming	Norming	Performing
Individual Issues	*"How do I fit in?"*	*"What's my role here?"*	*"What do the others expect me to do?"*	*"How can I best perform my role?"*
Group Issues	*"Why are we here?"*	*"Why are we fighting over who's in charge and who does what?"*	*"Can we agree on roles and work as a team?"*	*"Can we do the job properly?"*

FIGURE 3.13 Stages of Tuckman's Group Development Model
Source: Adapted from Bruce Tuckman's Group Development Model (1965).

because they're not aligned on terms and definitions." We then discussed the model shown in Figure 3.13.

I continued, "These differences can be substantial. To better understand this point, let me share the perspectives of two senior business leaders as they come together to form a team. At the time of the interviews, Philippe Lambotte was at Merck and had not made the transition to Mattel. Peter Gibbons had just moved to Mattel from Starbucks. As you read the two interviews, note how these more advanced leaders see the metrics that matter. We hope that their perspectives—how they both contrast and complement each other—clarify the need for onboarding and alignment of business leaders in the metrics journey as a fundamental step to drive corporate performance."

Meet the New Mattel Team

Mattel is focused on achieving their vision of "Creating the Future of Play." Every day, the leadership team at Mattel is a guiding force for 28,000 worldwide employees. The senior leadership team of operations is new. Philippe Lambotte, former senior vice president, Supply Chain of Merck and of Kraft Foods, is now an SVP at Mattel working for Peter Gibbons, executive vice president of Operations. At the time of the interview, Peter had been at Mattel for a year. Peter had recently joined from Starbucks, and Philippe was getting ready to join the team. Note the differences in perspectives, history, and beliefs as they come together to build the guiding coalition for Mattel.

Let's start with Philippe's perspective and then learn from Peter:

Philippe, which supply chain metrics do you think matter?

When I think of metrics, I think of an equilateral triangle: On each corner is a different metric. The corners of the triangle are costs/unit, cash (inventory cycles and working capital), and revenue/growth. In the middle of the triangle is customer service. It's the major customer-centric outcome required to balance the three metrics.

I think of customer service as delivering on customer success. I see it as "What do customers think about you?" I look for progress in both transactional and nontransactional interactions. Keeping the triangle sides equal is fundamental to drive success. You need to maintain balance while improving your metrics.

How do you balance metrics?

It's all in the sequence. The order of focus on how you improve them and what is your starting point. In the management of operations, cost most often gets the first focus. This is the one metric within a manufacturing company that supply chain/logistics organization, manufacturing, and procurement organizations easily align to. They have clear targets and responsibilities to achieve cost targets and missing them has critical implications. However, my philosophy is to focus on service first and optimize the costs at a given service level. I believe it's very difficult to be efficient with a mediocre service. It's even more difficult to improve your cost continuously where service isn't reliable.

Can you improve service and reduce costs simultaneously?

Absolutely, it can be done. However, you need to do it with a holistic viewpoint. I encountered situations when cost was overemphasized and reducing transportation costs by filling trucks led to late promotional deliveries, which had a much more negative impact on our company and our customers. On the opposite, I experienced cases when service trumped any other metric and express and unplanned deliveries became the norm, leading to shipments with negative margins. To find the optimal trade-off, it's critical to involve customers in defining service through their eyes.

What does this mean? For example, if you ship your product through a wholesaler or directly to a physician, the on-time shipment targets should be different. I had an experience where the on-time target was plus/minus

(continued)

(continued)

four hours for all channels and all customers. When we looked closer, we found our distributors needed complete shipments from us only once per week to synchronize with their other suppliers on-time and optimize their own shipments. However, the delivery frequency and on-time expectation of physicians we delivered to directly was much more stringent: They had no storage space in their practice and were scheduling our shipments in relation to their patient visit, so they needed to work within a narrow delivery window of a few hours. We learned that by adapting our behavior and metric to customer requirements, we did really obtain the best of all worlds.

After service and cost, what is next?

Once you have the right controls on costs and service, the next level of optimization focus is the cash conversion cycle management. Payables are the place to start because it requires mostly work with external partners. Receivables are hard to change because of the market requirements per country. Working capital and inventory optimization together is the Holy Grail of a balanced scorecard because it deals with both internal and customer-facing impact.

The more business lines or products produced by your company, the greater the number of external challenges and customer channels, the more challenging this balance is to achieve. There is no one size fits all.

An example of segmentation in the pharmaceutical industry: Vaccine supply chains deal by definition with live cells and require high investments to be successful. They require cold chain distribution, long-term planning, late-stage differentiation opportunities, and business is done with a high amount of time-bound tenders. As a result, lead time is often long and inventory needs to be produced long in advance. Drugs for diabetes, which is a growing health issue in the world, have requirements that are very different from vaccines: generally a more straightforward manufacturing process, greater volume with ongoing customers, and ambient temperature distribution. While metrics are defined similarly for both businesses, the metric trade-offs required to get to the optimal balance in the metric triangle are different.

Another example is in the consumer goods industry: coffee. Soluble coffee manufacturing is hugely asset intensive with important capital expenditure plant infrastructure. Their high asset utilization is critical to drive fixed costs down. The plant has to run almost continuously, independently of demand. Hence you must be able to work with high inventories since any slowdown of the production line will drive important cost increases at the shelf. Roast and ground coffee on the other side shows a different picture: Manufacturing roasting beans is simpler, less capital-intensive, and highly commodity driven at the market level. This means a high promotional environment with fluctuating prices requiring high packaging flexibility and low inventory to be able to react. It implies that asset utilization of manufacturing lines as well as inventory targets should be much lower in roast and ground compared to soluble coffee. One size won't fit both coffee businesses.

Companies that successfully manage segmented supply chains integrated with their business requirements are the ones that are successful.

What derails metric performance?

I would say mergers and acquisitions (M&A) and lack of specific focus were the two key obstacles I encountered. Getting to best practice in balancing the metrics triangle I mentioned gets even more difficult when step changes occur to greatly modify your business systems (such as in M&A periods). The companies I worked with, Procter & Gamble, Kraft Foods, and Merck, each had specific challenges as they grew through M&A. In this transition, it is key for companies to maintain good performance in mature parts of the business and then focus on the parts of the businesses that need reengineering.

Second, as companies become more complex and larger, the talent and focus get spread over more areas; the tendency is to go for common target and supply chain designs, especially if pressure grows to deliver on synergies and cost reduction. At some point, a company like Kraft used to own biscuits, cheese, pizza, confectionery, beverage, and meats with products delivered directly to stores (DSD), through the customer warehouses or via wholesalers across more than 100 countries. It was extremely challenging to drive one common practice around metrics. Now Kraft is split between a company focused on North America and warehouse-delivered products (Kraft Foods Group) and a company mostly focused on emerging markets with snacks with a lot of direct store distribution (Mondelez International). This company split also enabled us to segment supply chains and adapt metric targets for the relevant business requirements.

Is there an overriding message needed to keep the metrics that matter healthy?

Focusing on making your customer successful is a key principle. Beyond delivering on time and in full shipments, retailers often measure service differently and you need to understand what is key for them. For some retailers it's all about missed sales derived from on-shelf availability. For others it's all about In-stock at the back of their store. The ability of a manufacturer to understand what matters to their customers and create a joint partnership focused on improving products for what our joint customer—the shopper—needs and wants is critical for success.

"Now, let me contrast the views of Philippe with the beliefs of Peter," I stated. Joe and I had a rich discussion on the differences as we read the interview with Peter Gibbons together.

Peter Gibbons is the executive vice president, Global Supply Chain for Mattel, Inc. He is responsible for manufacturing, procurement, supply chain planning, logistics, quality, social responsibility, and final product engineering. Philippe reports to Peter.

Peter, which metrics do you think matter to supply chain excellence?

For me, fulfillment is the fundamental measure of end-to-end supply chain performance. I believe that the challenge for the supply chain is to deliver exactly what the customer asks for the first time. Therefore I use the "perfect order" metric to assess our overall performance and to "peel back the onion" and ask questions about what we need to do to satisfy customer requirements and demand. In my experience this has been a powerful metric to generate profound change.

Of course, the achievement of 100 percent "perfect order" performance isn't possible. But, that isn't the point. It's a goal. We want to strive for ultimate performance to understand what needs to change or improve to allow our supply chain to satisfy customers—and some of those changes may have to come from the customer—to be reflected in how we manage demand.

I have come across customer service metrics and fulfillment metrics that overstate performance. Previously, we had a definition that didn't truly reflect what the customer was asking for (an example is case fill rates versus perfect order fill rates). Many organizations have encouraged allowances and adjustments that inflate the service numbers, but all this does is create a false sense of organizational confidence and tension between supply chain organization and sales and marketing.

No matter the metric, I like to measure performance "in a manner that provokes improvement," focusing on processes and not on people. My mantra is "let the metrics measure the process but let the people improve it." As leaders, when we remove fear and instill confidence, it's easier to go fix the process.

How do you define the metrics that matter? And, what have you learned?

There are three metrics at the core of how I lead supply chains: safety, customer satisfaction, and total delivered cost. Approached correctly,

I have found them to be effective levers that get to the heart of how the supply chain is performing.

Safety is about ensuring your people go home after their shift as well and healthy as when they arrived. It measures how much you care for your people, the control of your physical processes and the alignment of your leadership team. It's hard to be world-class at anything if you can't be world-class at safety.

We touched on *customer satisfaction* already. Considered broadly it becomes a lens for how you view quality, new product launches, product promotions, and supply chain design changes as well as day-to-day business. It measures if the end-to-end machine (the supply chain) is operating the way we need it to.

Total delivered cost means capturing the end-to-end cost of the global operation: inbound freight, material purchases, inventory losses, yield losses, internal and external manufacturing, distribution, interfacility freight, outbound freight, overhead, duties, taxes, tooling, and so forth. When it comes to the total supply chain costs, I want to measure the "global financial footprint" and not be constrained by how the enterprise manages the accounting or the ownership of cost centers or legal entities. It's easy to become trapped in cost accounting and lose your way.

These three metrics can create transparency ("How are we doing?"), the motivation to change ("We can do better"), and the signal that we are making progress ("Results matter").

Finally, over the years I have learned that while businesses are complex and dynamic it's best to keep things simple:

- Are our processes in control—are they reliable and predictable?
- Are we improving—are we delivering improved customer satisfaction, launching more new products, helping grow the company's sales, improving our profits?
- Do our people think we are a good place to work—is their environment improving?

What have you learned?

It's important to think about how best to align metrics and how you manage them with the culture of the company. Companies are different.

For example, ICI was a highly technical and analytic company. So when we reviewed metrics, the numerical outcome (say 70 percent) was likely to be provocative. We were driven more by trends and data; and less by emotion.

Starbucks was different. It's a more relationship-based company focused on creative outcomes. There, we talked less about the number and more about the impact on the success of the store employees.

(continued)

(continued)

Guaranteeing the right delivery every day to a store meant that when the store manager opened the store for business, they could focus on delivering a successful Starbucks experience to the customer. We wanted no distractions due to replenishment issues.

In short, every business is different. It's important to align with the key cultural and business drivers.

Finally, talent is the foundation of our success. I believe in investing in talent and developing people from the earliest stage of their careers. I also believe in providing challenging jobs and tasks early in careers. I want to make sure that entry-level supply chain professionals have "water up to their chins," but no higher.

You build capabilities by stretching people in challenging assignments, and showing that you trust them and have faith in their potential.

"Joe, tell me what you hear." I asked, "What are the differences and similarities on the metrics that matter that you hear in the two interviews?"

"Very interesting," said Joe. "While both leaders are very aligned on customer service and cost, Peter does not mention cycle metrics in the interview. Each leader has a great background and understanding, but they have a different philosophy based on prior experience. To maximize success, this new team will need to spend some time aligning their views of current performance on the Effective Frontier and how they will push the company to its next performance plateau. This example helps me. I often find that leaders will align quickly on issues of costs and customer service, but have very different views on cycles."

"I agree," I stated. "And with a highly seasonal product, like toys, in an outsourced model, value networks and outside-in processes are a key element to drive performance to the next level of improvement. To align, these leaders will need to work together to build an operations strategy as we discussed in your last session."

BUILDING THE GUIDING COALITION

"So, how do we get started?" Joe asked. "I am anxious to get this going."

I continued, "After education, and getting agreement on the corporate metrics system, the next step is to build the guiding coalition to drive change. This group will lead the journey to determine the metrics set-points for different value networks and operating centers. They will also ensure that the metrics are aligned top-down and bottom-up, congruent with corporate performance incentive systems. They will also need to ensure alignment with strategic business partners."

"The first task is to define the burning platform. Since metrics systems affect incentives and progression opportunities, change management issues abound. The burning platform must be compelling. To accomplish this goal, it must be succinct and clear. As a lightning rod, it needs to align the team around the cause that they can all agree on and make actionable. Do you have a burning platform, Joe?" I asked.

"I'm not sure," Joe continued. "I have never thought about it in these terms."

Definition of a Burning Platform

The term *burning platform* is used in the business lexicon, which emphasizes that immediate and radical change is needed due to dire circumstances in the company. The origin of the term stems from a story about a man on an oil platform in the North Sea. One night he is awakened by an explosion and fire. Striving to escape the encroaching flames, he is able to find his way through the chaos to the edge of the platform.

As the fire envelops the platform, he must use split-second decision making to do something or die a horrible death. His only option is to jump more than 100 feet from the firey platform into the freezing North Atlantic waters.

If the dangerous jump doesn't kill him, he will surely die from exposure within minutes if not rescued. With no other rational alternative, he jumped!

Fortunately the man did survive the jump from the platform and was rescued shortly thereafter. His philosophy had been "*Better probable death than certain death.*"

The point of the story is that it took a blazing platform to cause a major change in behavior. This story emphasizes the point that radical change in people only occurs when survival instincts trump comfort zone instincts.[4]

 EDUCATING THE ORGANIZATION TO TAKE THE FIRST STEP

As we sat down to map our steps to take the burning platform of the launch into Brazil, and then expose the entire leadership team to the concepts of the

Effective Frontier and Metrics That Matter, Joe and I agreed that education was the right next step.

Once again, Joe was sitting in his chair with his workbook in front of him, a whiteboard full of notes, and a wall covered with sketched models. He was deep in thought. "It's so simple to say, and so hard to do," he stated. "But education is foundational and necessary. These concepts will be foreign to the team that I work with. I think that it's critical to drive a common understanding to drive change. I think that education is the building block to anchor the journey to power our new levels of corporate performance.

"I agree," I stated. "To drive success, the organization needs to feel the fire of the burning platform. It needs to be internalized. The passion of the mission has to overcome fear. It has to be a clear statement grounded in business reality. Along the way, there are many obstacles and hurdles to navigate. This one with Filipe needs to be one of our first obstacles to tackle."

"I am not sure whether it is Filipe's surety of best practices or sales protection of the status quo that will be the toughest nut to crack," Joe said as he broke into a wide grin. "Anyway, I believe in what we have discussed today. I am ready to take on the challenge!"

"As a next step, let's review whom we should try to reach out to in our efforts to build the guiding coalition," I stated. "In your workbook, I have shared some principles or tenets from Kotter's work to help guide our discussion."

Four Tenets to Building an Effective Guiding Coalition[5]

In putting together a guiding coalition, the team as a whole should reflect:

1. *Position power:* Enough key players should be onboard so that those left out can't block progress.
2. *Expertise:* All relevant points of view should be represented so that informed intelligent decisions can be made.
3. *Credibility:* The group should be seen and respected by those in the firm so that the group's pronouncements will be taken seriously by other employees.
4. *Leadership:* The group should have enough proven leaders to be able to drive the change process.

Aligning with the Leadership Team

The concepts I reviewed with Joe are initially foreign to most leadership teams that I work with. As we talked, gaining acceptance and driving adoption were Joe's fears. His organization had a strong history of functional leadership; but, they didn't understand the implications of managing operations in an extended value network. The corporate mission for growth made the business more complex, and the competition in the channel was fierce.

As a result, we agreed that Joe would begin the discussion with the team on what he needed to improve reliability in operations in the United States and then start to define the prerequisites for Brazil. As a result, the initial focus was reliability in customer service, with a drive for consistency in delivering operating margins and inventory targets. Together, we strategized how to approach his team. On his office whiteboard after break, we listed the team and added descriptors to jumpstart our afternoon discussion on how to build a guiding coalition and a leadership team for his company:

Finance team: Joe's finance team relished numbers. They were conservative, and most of their analysis was transactional and backward-looking. They wanted to control, and as a result Joe often fought the setting of arbitrary targets. In contrast, Joe's operations teams were the opposite. They were focused on analyzing the probability of supply and demand with a forward-looking view. It was a very different perspective. It was tough to align the two different outlooks, which resulted in constant tension.

Chief operations officer (COO). Filipe, Joe's boss, was a traditional operations officer. He grew up working his way through manufacturing. He struggled to drive cross-functional and horizontal processes. Due to the fact that most of the emphasis was on vertical excellence, this was a consistent theme in Joe's organization.

Vice president of sales. For Joe, this was a key stakeholder to influence. The vice president of sales was the heir-apparent to the chief executive officer (CEO) position. He was under the gun to deliver growth, and many considered him a bit of a prima donna. His teams were aggressive and relentless. The recent issues in customer service had created tension between sales and operations.

As I stepped back from the board, I said to Joe, "This dynamic is normal. The intricacies and interrelationships of metrics are not clear because the

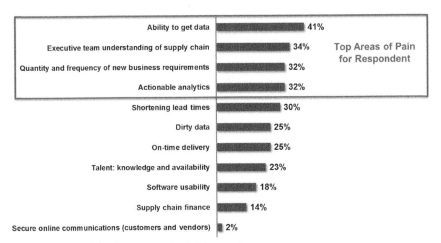

FIGURE 3.14   The "Average Joe's" Struggle
Base: Distributors, Manufacturers, Retailers (*n* = 44).
Q5b: When it comes to supply chain management, which of these items are the top three elements of business pain for you personally? Select no more than three.
Source: Supply Chain Insights LLC, Talent-L (August–September 2012).

conventional view of functional silo metrics is divisive. While many believe that this can be solved through better analytics and clarity of an operating strategy, when the rubber hits the road, it is what you measure and reward." Together, we discussed how paralyzing this is for an organization. Joe liked the research shown in Figure 3.14.

As Joe looked at the board, he admitted, "Sometimes what should be *so* easy is *so* hard. How can we be a team to drive the business if we're not aligned about what we reward? It sounds so simple, but this will be very hard to fix."

To help drive clarity for the leadership team in his next presentation to them, Joe planned to share some of the orbit charts that we had developed together. We built a PowerPoint for Joe to present to Filipe.

In the afternoon, he even had his team build a network model with several scenarios to show the interrelationships of the metrics in several of his business segments. He used "what-if" analysis and "discrete event simulation" to help the leadership visualize how changes in the complex system drive surprising outcomes. In playing with the models and changing the inputs, the team was able to see the impact of the recent shifts. They were also better able to set metrics targets for a number of measurements in the portfolio. As a result, Joe felt better prepared.

What-if simulation enables the use of optimization technology to test alternative outcomes through parallel optimization scenarios, whereas discrete vent simulation tests the feasibility of an optimization outcome by testing.

Some Background on Joe's Team: Changing Mental Models

Bucking the trend flies in the face of culture, especially at Joe's organization. His team is built on the concepts of continuous improvement of inside-out processes. Incrementally, and reliably each year, the team has successfully driven results to help the company to fund growth programs. The team has a mindset of process improvement and moving forward incrementally. The focus is on driving momentum and accelerating efficient operations. As such, the team culture was well prepared to propel lean processes.

When it came to driving change, I shared Joe's concerns. There was no doubt that the team was seasoned. No one sitting at the table in Joe's leadership team meeting had less than 20 years of experience. They grew up in the culture and, as career employees, their interactions were steeped in history. Over and over again, they wanted to take the safe and conservative path forward to ensure a safe retirement.

It was now clear to Joe that the required change to improve corporate performance in U.S. operations was not incremental. It needed to be disruptive, and the operation in Brazil needed to be quite different from the one in the United States. The discussions on building effective value networks stimulated his thinking on how to be outside-in. There was a fire in his belly that the company should be more aggressive in the adoption of new mental models. Joe had heart for the mission and over and over again he spoke of "the need to break a few eggs in order to make an omelet."

Joe knew that he needed more support from his leadership team to help him align organizationally to drive higher levels of corporate improvement; but his question was still "How?" He remained committed, but nervous. He was ready to take the next step. We polished the presentations for his team and formatted the research to try to sell the work that we had done together to his leadership team.

As I left, because I was partially curious and in a teasing mood, I asked Joe if I could see his notebook.

"Checking up on me? Wanting to see how I am doing? Okay," he said with a grin, "here are my insights from today."

The Notes from Joe's Journal

- Define value cross-functionally. While many companies talk about a balanced scorecard, few have defined what balance means. The journey from a functional set of metrics to value as delivered based on alignment, balance, and resiliency requires a cross-functional guiding coalition. I need to think about who this should be.
- Extend this value proposition to trading partners through the building and participation in value networks. Today's organization is more dependent on trading partners and requires the exchange and sharing of operational data across the value network. The building of the value network should come before the dependency on third-party networks for distribution, manufacturing, logistics, or procurement. The longer the value network with more complexity, the greater the need to first move with the infrastructure and a set of aligned metrics across trading partners. This design is critical to improve the potential of the company to deliver higher levels of performance.
- Build the burning platform and educate the organization to drive the guiding coalition. I need to work on the "statement for action." The best statements are usually short, meaningful, and relevant. For example, a major consumer products company defined a goal of delivering 2 percent to the top line through improved customer service. It was communicated to their channel partners and the team worked to gain alignment to win together. This goal was tracked and success celebrated when the team beat the goal by reaching it two years faster than the target.
- Tackle change management barriers. Teams are siloed. They're deeply entrenched in the definition of excellence as defined by their career experiences within a function within a company. Incentives have history. Respect the history and work on cross-functional alignment to the burning platform. The creation of the burning platform has to be compelling because the functional leaders feel that they can better control their earnings potential if the metrics are functional and within their control. The alignment of incentives and the creation of corporate metrics systems shouldn't be started without heavy involvement of a change management specialist.
- Use failure as a platform for change. In the depths of failure, a business leader has the greatest opportunity to build the guiding coalition to drive change. Seize this opportunity.

CONCLUSION

It was a good day. With my empty red briefcase on my shoulder, I was walking down the hall, thinking about all the ground that we had covered in our discussion. It was my hope that Joe learned that the journey to implement the Metrics That Matter starts with alignment on the metrics. It then requires education and alignment to enable action. Continuous improvement programs help you progress on the Effective Frontier, but getting to the next level of the Frontier requires new models.

With the increase in complexity, the building of trading partner networks and incentive systems are an important technique to drive performance to the next frontier. It's becoming more critical today as more and more services and products are outsourced.

To understand and embody new models, teams often need a strategy day, or workshop, to enable them to internalize the concepts. The new mental models are tough to actualize. Building the guiding coalition is essential to ensure that the efforts stick and drive results. Aligning for action will be Joe's challenge.

As I reached for the door, Joe sent a text. "I have booked our next meeting to work with the leadership team. We have a lot to do. I look forward to partnering with you to make it happen!" I smiled as I walked into the parking lot. There was a lot to do with Joe's leadership team, but I was looking forward to the interaction.

Notes

1. Pan Kwan Yuk, "Mexican Labor: Cheaper than China," *Financial Times*, April 2, 2013.
2. 2008 Annual Report, DuPont.
3. Bruce Tuckman, "Developmental Sequence in Small Groups," *Psychological Bulletin* 63, no. 6 (1965): 384–399.
4. Problem-Solving-Techniques, "The Burning Platform," www.problem-solving-techniques.com/Burning-Platform.html (accessed April 7, 2014).
5. Kotter International, www.kotterinternational.com/our-principles/change steps/step-2 (accessed March 2, 2014).

4

A Strategy Session on Managing Value Networks

T WAS A BRIGHT winter day when I met Joe in the lobby for our next planning meeting. As I opened the door the icicles hung precariously from the roof of the conference center. The weather was harsh, and the icicles were massive. It had been three months since we'd last met. A lot had changed.

"Look at those icicles," Joe said as we sat down at the conference table with our coffee. "They are finally starting to melt. I hope that spring is just around the corner. This has been a tough winter. We've got a lot to do."

"I know," I said. "The plane cancellations and storms have been brutal. We've got a lot of catching up to do on the project and the work that I've planned to do with the team. I am anxious to get started and find out how you, and your work, are progressing."

As we talked, we could see the icicles slowly melting. The sound of the drops against the window dominated the room but soon faded into the background as we focused on the task at hand.

Joe opened the discussion. "The meeting last fall went well with Filipe. You know that I was worried. Those operations guys are very detailed. They tend to drive me crazy. I am a big-picture guy, and Filipe tends to pick apart all the details. So, when you work with them on the strategy day you really need to be prepared! The orbit charts really started a new conversation. Filipe was confused at first and then he got it.

"Just like me, it took him awhile to get used to a new way of looking at metrics. But he started to like the approach once I showed him how to read the charts. As a result, he got his team together and we spent most of the winter analyzing the patterns. We met every week for an hour and talked. We started interviewing other companies to learn more. Filipe even set up a discussion group on email to collect our thoughts. Isn't it funny how a new concept feels strange at first and then becomes accepted," stated Joe as he sprawled in his chair. I loved the excitement in his voice as he continued.

"At first, I was really afraid that once we started getting into the drivers and trends in our business that it would cause some finger-pointing. As an organization, we tend to be so defensive that it is often difficult for us to have a cross-functional discussion. However, the orbit charts were novel enough that everyone had to work together to just figure them out. It was a puzzle. By the time we were done, we'd somehow leapfrogged the finger-pointing to have a holistic discussion. As a result, everyone became more curious about the performance of companies in our industry, and how they performed on the metrics that matter in the same time frame."

I nodded my head in agreement. "One of the beautiful things about using orbit charts is that it forces companies to look at history in a new way. It helps companies to understand how interconnected the business is." I said, "The trick now is to understand which metrics you can use to run the business so that you get the results you want."

Joe smiled and said, "You are so right! When we had our December update call, you told me that we needed to start looking at metrics holistically, and as a system. We are just beginning to build our guiding coalition. You'll be happy to hear that we have now developed a first cut of the metrics that we want to measure. Our next step is to drive alignment." At that point Joe grinned, and said, "And you'll never guess what we named the project."

"Okay, surprise me," I said.

Joe laughed. "Our new project is named Project Orbit! What'cha think?"

I clapped my hands with glee and we proceeded with the task at hand.

 ## ADDRESSING ORGANIZATIONAL TENSIONS

When it came to reviewing the plan for Joe's expansion into Brazil, he encountered problems. The organization had a long legacy of driving channel behavior through sales incentives. The sales team was powerful. The concept of managing the channel through the use of a value network was difficult for the organization to accept. As he socialized the concepts in the IBM iBAT case study, the executive team questioned whether it made sense. They wanted Joe to use a more traditional technique to manage the sales channel in Brazil. To Joe's leadership team, the investment in network architectures just seemed like a waste of money.

"I know that we need to do something different," Joe said quietly to me. "The team will not admit it, but Filipe's prior work to build a new channel in Mexico just didn't work. This expansion involved distributors, and we were not clear on what was selling when in the channel. We need to have a much better handle on channel data when we expand into Brazil so we can manage the whole supply chain." He paused and then said, "But my real challenge is getting the management team to see past quarterly objectives to look more holistically at the longer-term opportunity.

"Let me tell you a story. The other day, Frank, our vice president of sales, stopped me in the hallway and made a snide comment. Frank put his finger in my face and said to me, 'If you had all this channel data, what would you do with it? You can't manage what you have now.' I didn't like Frank's attitude when he said, 'I am tired of orders being cut and continually being asked questions on service failures in the field.' "

Joe held up his hands, and said, "In summary, Frank thinks that we're naïve to think that information on channel sales will improve our on-time deliveries."

He continued, "It got more difficult during the first meeting in December when I discussed the concepts of being more demand-driven in the design of processes for the expansion into Brazil. In the discussion, the issues between Frank and I came to a climax. The executive team was uncomfortable.

"In the meeting, Frank banged his hands on the table and told me that I was tying his hands behind his back. He looked at me directly and said that if we implemented what I was asking, he wouldn't be able to manage end-of-quarter sales objectives." At this point, Joe hung his head, and said, "This is very hard. Pushing sales on the last week of the quarter to make our numbers is very ingrained in our culture. We almost make it a game. There is a lot of sales bravado around pushing at the end of the quarter. How do I help them to understand that we need to manage the channel and the flows?" asked Joe.

"But this was not all," Joe said. "Frank continued to make his case claiming that we would never be able to trust the distributors to manage fixed inventory targets based on what is selling in the market. Trust is an issue for us in South American markets. Frank is pushing back hard on me stating that managing the channel is the role of sales.

"This discussion then led to heated debates about the current levels of customer service within North America. These arguments are uncomfortable. Today, we have way too much inventory, but it never seems to be in the right place. The issues with case fulfillment are rising and the number of cases being cut from orders worries the team. We are always reacting to a shortage, or transferring a product from one distribution center to another to avoid a major outage or customer service failure. Sometimes, we can't get out of our own way," continued Joe.

"In the meeting, Edgar Simpson, our division president, listened quietly to the discussion with Frank as it unfolded. As you know, Edgar is a polished, seasoned leader, and he wants the sales team to be aggressive. He did not rein in Frank's behavior, but I know from private dialogue that he wants greater reliability in sales," Joe continued in telling the story. "So, Edgar took me aside and told me that he thought that I had made a good case for being more demand driven, and trying new techniques on managing channel demand as part of the geographic expansion, and that he wanted to move forward. As a result, Edgar told Frank that he wanted to do a workshop together so we all can agree on the best approach. He asked me to set up something. As you know, he is practical and wants to be sure that we focus on how other companies have tackled the issues. He wants to leave the session being very clear on how to build balance, strength, and resiliency into the operations.

"So that's how that meeting went," Joe said ruefully to me. "I left it wondering if Frank's protests were really a change management issue. To me, they are a real red flag. Is Frank thinking that he's losing control of sales, or does he really disagree that demand-driven value networks managed by balanced metrics will work?"

I replied, "Let's put together the strategy workshop for the executive team. I think we'll be able to find out the answer to that question pretty quickly."

We then went to the whiteboard together and listed the goals for the meeting:

- The role of sales in market-driven value networks
- How to manage metrics that matter on the Effective Frontier
- The role of horizontal processes in driving alignment

As we worked through the goals on the board, Joe made several points. He felt that the organization was too functionally focused, and he was not sure of the best way to drive cross-functional alignment. Joe and I brainstormed options. Could we drive balance and alignment through the use of horizontal processes? We thought that it was worth a try.

Joe emphasized that the session needed to be pragmatic. The case studies that I shared with Joe in the fall prompted heated dialogue with the team. The discussion of the IBM case study of iBAT had been intense. The question top of mind for Joe was, "Why was a value network needed? Why could we not drive the same behaviors through the change in sales incentives? What does it mean to be market-driven? Why was it important?"

The session could not be academic. The team wanted to discuss company case studies. Their desire was to better understand how other companies had struggled to achieve balance. They wanted to understand how others were successful in building organizational alignment. The team sought an understanding of how a team at another company worked together to improve corporate performance.

As we finished the planning for the session, Joe questioned how we would tackle a major issue. In driving alignment, functional metrics need to be traded-off to improve overall metrics. The problem was that all functional groups want to excel; as each group pushed its own excellence programs, the emphasis shifted to optimizing the parts, but not the whole.

Sometimes, to get lower total costs, the functional groups had to consciously make the choice to not have the lowest cost. Joe spoke of the recent decision to increase manufacturing cost targets to improve distribution costs. As a result, the manufacturing plants were consciously running shorter runs with higher costs to ensure that truck loading could be optimized to drive lower transportation costs.

The decision was tough for the organization to swallow, but it was the right strategy. Getting there was difficult. Joe's questions were, "Who in the organization should make those choices? And what processes could enable the groups to understand and align functional goals to enhance corporate performance?" He thought that this was an important discussion for the four goals of the strategy workshop. We scheduled it to follow their annual meeting in two weeks.

I shook Joe's hand. I thought that we were prepared for the session.

Meet the Team

In the preparation for a strategy day, I wanted to understand the individuals on the team. Within an organization, each person has his or her own set of social, emotional and political drivers, and this organization was no different. In the development of the agenda, we wanted to make sure that the entire team felt comfortable.

The team was diverse and action oriented. Each member was a strong personality. They were newly formed; as a result, group interactions were

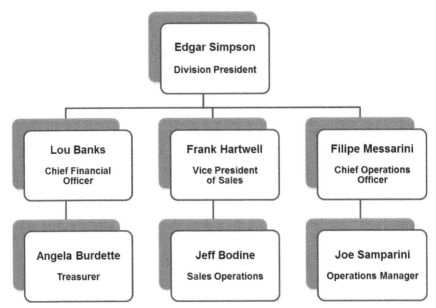

FIGURE 4.1   The Organization
Base: Employees of Undisclosed Major CPG Company (Revenue > $58) (*n* = 148).
Q20: In your opinion, how important is it for each of the pairs of teams to be aligned within your company? SCALE: 7 = Extremely important, 1 = Not at all important.
Q21: How aligned do you believe that these same teams actually are within your company? SCALE: 7 = Extremely aligned, 1 = Not at all aligned.
Source: Supply Chain Insights LLC, CPG Employee Survey (September 2013).

rough. Few in the leadership group had operations experience. Joe carefully outlined the characteristics of each person on the team as shown in Figure 4.1.

Edgar Simpson: Division President

It was easy to think that Edgar Simpson—at 5 feet 4 inches and 140 pounds—was a pushover, but nothing could be further from the truth. He had a brilliant smile that he used often, and he spoke in a calm and deliberative manner. He had always exceeded performance expectations, and people clamored to be on his team. At 15, he had been one of the youngest high school graduates ever to be accepted into Yale. He worked his way through undergraduate school, then graduate school at the Harvard School of Business. His office walls were covered with photographs of the teams he'd worked with all over the world—the new factory in Brazil, the fast-track production project in China, the inventory crisis in Rotterdam, and many more. In all of them, Edgar was standing to the side, giving the team prominence, because he knew that without their efforts nothing could be accomplished.

Maybe it was the experience of growing up in East Harlem with his grandmother that gave Edgar his people skills. Edgar was well liked. He knew that to survive on the streets, he not only needed to be smart about life, but also about people. He had a natural empathy and was expert at motivating people. The key was to understand people's motivation, and find a way to use it to achieve common goals. Edgar had a natural instinct combined with street smarts, intellect, and analytical skills that made him a juggernaut in the business world. His phone held hundreds of contacts, and he always returned his phone calls on the day they were received.

Edgar had a natural way with people. One day he'd be sitting at lunch talking with a plant operator in Brazil, asking her about her family; the next day he would be talking to a *Financial Times* reporter. Edgar always made time for people. This was not because he knew that he needed them to succeed, but because he was genuinely interested in their success. He cared. His warmth always permeated our discussions.

Edgar knew how to ask hard questions, and didn't have a lot of time for dithering. He was decisive. It did not take him long to get to the root of the matter, and he had the influence to bring others along with him. Edgar had been watching Joe for a long time and was pleased that Joe was taking the initiative to look at inventory and balance it with corporate performance metrics. He was actively mentoring Joe and watching his project closely.

Today, his costs for capital were just too high and there was pressure from the treasury division to take action to correct this. So, he'd been pleased when Joe came to him and told him how he wanted to help the division's bottom line.

Seeing the conflict between sales, operations, and finance, Edgar knew he needed a catalyst for change, and this project had been a springboard for action. One thing was clear: To get to that next level of performance, to be more effective, change had to come from within. The group had some of the brightest minds in the company, and if anyone was going to solve the issue of how to grow, how to delight customers while minimizing costs, it would be this team. He was confident that this was possible, and he knew with the right level of support, Joe could get the job done. When Joe asked if he could bring in an outside expert, Edgar was pleased, because the team needed more perspective and some new ideas to drive their thinking.

At this juncture in the business Edgar's reputation was at stake, but it wasn't the first time. Every project that he'd encountered depended on his ability to inspire and facilitate a team to succeed, and when they did, he made sure that credit was given where it was due. The number of pictures on his office walls kept increasing, and the contacts in his phone were growing. Edgar knew where his company's most valuable assets were, and he knew from experience that his future accomplishments would come from their success.

He knew that only leaders can lead. History told him that the wrong metrics can lead to misalignment. He had walked that road before. Edgar was there to bring the same clarity of purpose that he felt earlier when he led a division at GE Healthcare. He felt that GE knew how to run a sound business.

Frank Hartwell, Vice President of Sales

Frank Hartwell was a big man with gigantic ambitions. At 6 feet 5 inches, he dominated the room.

He was handsome. He had dark hair and dancing, bright blue eyes. He could turn heads, and was used to getting his way. People gave him a wide berth. He had a temper and used it often.

His eyes could turn from friendly to ice-cold in an instant. He had an incredible ability to alternate between charm and intimidation. Frank liked to be the center of attention in a meeting, because he believed that if a company was growing, it was due to the sales team's efforts. Everything else just supported the sales strategy.

He made it no secret that he was on a track to become a candidate for CEO. It would be at either this company or another. He was driven. Frank had beaten the odds of a short tenure in sales by driving his sales team hard, focusing on exceeding sales goals, and never giving up. His career ambition depended on it.

Frank also had an eidetic memory—he could remember the details of a rare encounter from years before—and he knew every sales deal intimately.

As a manager, he was extremely protective of his team. Frank had hand-picked his regional managers and personally interviewed each salesperson. He knew that his continued success depended upon keeping his team motivated and well paid. That was his mission.

At a first meeting, it would be easy to dismiss Frank as a cliché, with his expensive suit and tie, platinum bracelet, and watch from an obscure and extremely expensive Swiss boutique in Manhattan. But Frank was deadly serious about business, and he had demonstrated quarter-after-quarter results. No doubt about it: He could deliver. This gave him power and the ear of the CEO and the board. He had dedicated his life to the work and paid the price with two divorces and three children needing and not getting the attention he wanted to give to them. He had everything invested in his job and his work, and was determined that Sales would never come up in a quarterly report as anything but exceeding expectations.

Frank was attending these meetings because he felt that if the company didn't fix the out-of-stock issues, pretty soon sales would start to really suffer. He had recently taken a trip to Cleveland, Ohio, to placate a very unhappy customer, and his phone was starting to ring with customers making demands. It reminded him of his days at Procter & Gamble before A. J. Lafley took the helm.

He was busy. Frank loved operating on overdrive. As a result, he had a history of sitting in meetings, multitasking with his laptop in front of him, texting on his smartphone, and jumping in and out of the conversation seemingly at random, but with surprisingly germane contributions. It was hard to figure out how he did it, and while it was rude, nobody dared to tell him to stop. Maybe it was his photographic memory that allowed him to master the multitasking, because he was always prepared and on point.

He just wanted operations to do their job. Frank was convinced that the customer service issues were someone else's problem to solve. The customer service problems needed to be fixed, and he was going to hold the operations team responsible. He was fed up with excuses.

Frank didn't feel that the longstanding customer relationships were at risk, although he had been forced to make some credit concessions lately. The bigger issue was the opportunity cost. The unhappy customers took too much of his team's time. As a result, they were distracting his team from the larger task at hand. Customers were complaining about the more and more frequent stock-outs of popular lines.

Frank was not about to take any of his salespeople out of the field to attend these meetings, but he did bring his sales operations director, Jeff, who was his expert in forecasting, pivot tables, and all of the technical tools that he didn't have the time or interest to learn.

Jeff Bodine, Sales Operations

Jeff was as smart as a whip. A corn-fed kid with flaming red hair and wire-rim glasses, he never missed a beat in a meeting. He was as humble as Frank was arrogant.

His dedication to the company was without question. He grew up in a two-room house. He wanted to get ahead but not at the expense of others. He graduated from an Indianapolis community college and considered himself fortunate to get such a great job.

Jeff had found his niche. He found Frank amusing and tolerated his antics, but he was well-loved by the entire sales team, and he thrived in a sales organization. While you would never want to put Jeff on the front line selling, there was no one better to support the sales function.

In meetings, he was a sponge. He had a constant fascination with global operations.

Jeff took pride in his spreadsheets. The sales team would fondly call him the backbone of the operation. His tribal knowledge was housed in three massive spreadsheets that detailed the pipeline, recurring revenue, and future market potential. He was Frank's right-hand man, and the go-to contact for sales and operations to get questions answered.

Recently, Jeff had become very health conscious and started working out at lunch and riding his bike to work. As an overweight kid, he now watched what he ate and was very focused on building the potential of his body. He wore a heart rate monitor and was constantly comparing notes with the triathletes in the building on his training plans.

In his personal life, he was pragmatic. His family came first. As a new father, with a pregnant wife and a new boy on the way, job security was important. While he wanted to help, he didn't want to rock the boat.

Like Frank, he saw the operations team as complaining. After all, he gave them the numbers each month. Why couldn't they just execute against the plan that he gave them? And why were they always asking him questions about his data? It just didn't make sense. Sales was the closest to the customer, and he felt that the operations team just needed to buckle down and make what sales told them to make. He begrudgingly agreed to come to the meeting and was hoping that it would help to stop the customer service issues.

Filipe Messarini: Chief Operations Officer

Filipe is known in the organization as a "climber." Short in stature but long on intellect, it was well understood that he was competing with Frank for the divisional president role. The tension in the room climbed when the two interacted.

He had over 30 years with the company. His first job was at the factory in Mexico City. Frank was proud of his accomplishments, and frequently spoke of how the real work happened on the floor of the manufacturing plant.

He was born to a family of proud migrant workers. He vividly remembers moving from city to city as the crops came in and scrambling to keep up in school. Filipe had become an American citizen five years ago. Today, he is proud to hold two passports.

He was driven. In high school, he worked with his guidance counselor to get a scholarship to Stanford. He was grateful for the experience but hungry with ambition to help his family have a better life. He did not want his wife and two children to ever have to endure the hardships that he had experienced picking strawberries in southern California.

His best friend worked at Dell and he was enamored with their processes. He wanted to lean-out the supply chain and outsource operations to improve the return on assets. He admired the Dell organization for their success in achieving a negative working capital cycle. For him it was all about cost management and shortening the cash cycle by lengthening payables.

At the age of 55, Filipe felt confident in his capabilities and his ability to lead an operations team. His focus was on what was urgent and completing the task at hand. Filipe worked long hours and would often be the last person out of the building at night and the first person to open the office in the morning. His days were heavily booked with meetings. He had little time to build relationships and foster cross-functional networks. But he had a keen sense of humor and could disarm Frank in the meeting with his wit.

His wife was good friends with Edgar's wife, and the foursome frequently met at Filipe's house for a barbecue. He prided himself on his skills to deliver a great meal on the spit, and he and Edgar had spent many a Saturday night drinking beers and laughing about the team. Edgar was the godfather of Filipe's son.

Lou Banks: Chief Financial Officer

Lou Banks at 60 years of age is a 30-year veteran of the company. A man of medium build, his intense brown eyes command attention beneath a pair of enormously bushy eyebrows. The mop of prematurely gray hair that he had since the 1970s disappeared with the new millennium, and he now sported a polished bald pate. Unlike many of the corporate transitions that Lou had seen come and go, his transition from thinning hair to shaved head happened overnight. Lou was never one to delay a decision. While it might have elicited comment around the watercooler, nobody dared to mention it to Lou's face. It wasn't that Lou was unfriendly—he had a great string of stories and jokes, and he sat on several community nonprofit boards. He just cultivated a vibe that said that he was all about business; any deviation would be at his discretion and on his schedule.

To say that Lou was intimidating wouldn't be an understatement. He had an air of J. Edgar Hoover about him, and you felt when his gaze fixed upon you that you were either doing something you shouldn't, or that he knew about something that you should know. One was never caught unprepared for a question from Lou Banks, because if you were, he would first raise his left eyebrow, then his right, then wiggle them alternately, taunting you with the comical spectacle as if daring you to laugh. Then he'd go for the kill, boring into your soul with those dark brown eyes until you felt as small as a pea.

Everyone felt that Lou was next in line for CEO and all were shocked when he was apparently passed over when the new CEO was hired from the outside last year. What they didn't know was that Lou had been offered the job not once, but twice, and had declined. Lou's highest priorities were his family and his community work, and he depended upon his team to keep his professional life efficient. His organizational skills remain legendary, and his team of analysts and administrative assistants work together like a small orchestra.

Lately Lou has been finding that his team is working harder and harder, and doesn't seem as prepared as he would like with answers to simple questions. Last week, he even had to get on his computer from home and attempt to sort out some inventory and production results that didn't make sense. Things have always been complex at the company, but lately it seems that the spreadsheets are not agreeing with one another, and he has more and more pages of data to wade through that never seem to agree. He is becoming less sure of his statements during the quarterly analyst calls.

Lou loved pistachios, and he always had a dish of nuts in the shell on his desk. He shared generously, and when he came to meetings, he always brought a huge bowl of them for everyone. When he concentrated on a puzzle, he'd sit at his end of the conference table, biting on the shells to crack them open, both eyebrows wriggling furiously while he was chewing.

He was never one for sitting down and relaxing. In a meeting, he would frequently pace the room, rubbing his hands as he walked. This drove Frank crazy.

Angela Burdette, Treasurer

As the only woman in the room, Angela knew what it was like to survive in a man's world. Her taste in suits was exquisite and she was always on time. In the 1980s, when Angela joined the company, she was meticulous about not taking on tasks that the male-dominated culture relegated to women. She was very conscious about the glass ceiling for female executives. So when coffee or catering, or back then, typing, came up, she made herself scarce. She had worked very hard to cultivate her professional image and as a result had risen through the ranks to become treasurer. She enjoyed the respect of her colleagues and was now very comfortable doing things her way. One of her pet peeves was lack of organization, so lately she'd thrown out her old restrictions and made sure that the caterers had set up coffee, that the room was set with agendas, and that the menus for lunch were available. Sometimes if you want to get something done, you get it done yourself, whether that means going to the field to get the latest numbers on a construction operation, or making sure that you don't starve for lunch. Angela had gotten to the point where she was respected on her own terms, and now ran things the way she saw fit.

Angela was Lou's sergeant-at-arms and managed the corporate treasury function. She was a high-ranking employee who was slated to replace Lou when he retired. Even though the rest of the team did not know that Lou's retirement was imminent, Lou was busy training and mentoring Angela, and Edgar was 100 percent behind her.

In a meeting, Angela was a woman of few words. She listened intently and often took notes. Her memory was excellent and she was constantly watching the body language of the participants. A natural collaborator and team player, Angela wanted the team to move forward and kept focused on the goal.

In the evenings, she gathered with a small group of women and took advanced ballet. Her focus at the ballet barre equaled her intense composure at work. With excellent posture and poise, she had equally mastered both a triple pirouette in fourth position in ballet and how to close the books with ease at work. No one knew the balance sheet better than Angela.

Getting Ready for the Workshop

Over lunch in the cafeteria, Joe and I talked about the team dynamics.

"The meeting should be interesting," Joe said, biting into his bean burrito. "They get together once a quarter after the books close. Even a good quarter creates some fireworks. After Edgar came, the meetings quieted down a lot, though."

"It's a challenge when each member of the team has a different definition of process excellence," I said. "If you can align the team on a common definition, you can make those quarterly meetings a lot more productive."

At the end of the day, we reviewed the agenda with Filipe and Edgar and got ready to drive new insights with the team. As an output of the workshop, the team would make its own decision on how to drive alignment on the Metrics That Matter.

THE STRATEGY DAY

Edgar kicked off the workshop.

"I want the team to come out of this workshop with a clear operating strategy," he said in his quiet, compelling voice. "It is even more important that you combine your strengths here, so I'm expecting you all to work together on this."

"I understand; but at the end of the day, the sales team needs to sell," Frank interrupted. "If the organization wants to grow, it needs sales. We need the other functions to just hunker down and focus on supporting sales growth."

Jeff wiggled uncomfortably as Frank continued, "The lack of operations reliability and customer service effectiveness is a barrier. We need to face facts. Today, the company has a performance issue. The operations team just isn't delivering the reliability that we need. I don't know why we're wasting time today on this meeting when the real work needs to be done to fix operations."

Edgar calmly sat back and beamed, signaling for me to get started.

I swallowed hard and began. "Thank you for your support, Edgar. In my preparation for this meeting, and in my discussions with all of you, including Frank's comments just now, it is clear that the company is on a divergent path.

"You have increased product complexity to drive opportunistic sales while simultaneously making the operations team more efficient," I continued. "As a result, you are unable to be effective in delivering what Frank's team has been selling."

At this point Angela smiled, and Joe nodded his head in affirmation. The team relaxed. I asked for them to bear with me to define the basics of operations excellence and process evolution. I spoke of the need for cross-functional alignment to drive higher levels of performance. To try to build a guiding coalition in the first hour of the workshop, I walked the team through the steps of process evolution.

The group discussed the steps of process evolution of value networks within organizations. I shared that progress happens through discrete steps of the model, shown here as Figure 4.2. The team listened intently to the explanation of each phase.

Efficient: In the efficient organization, there is a focus on producing goods and services at the lowest cost. As goods become lower in cost, companies sacrifice customer service. As fill rates start to decline, the focus shifts to the building of a reliable supply network. I asked Filipe to consider if this was one of the company's current problems.

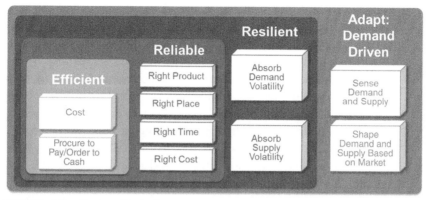

FIGURE 4.2 Process Evolution

Reliable: The focus of the reliable network is to reach the right balance between costs, inventory, and service. It is often termed the right product at the right place at the right time. However, if the network is too lean, without inventory buffers and push/pull decoupling points, companies find that they are vulnerable to market swings. This was the case for the company in the recession of 2008.

As we discussed this, I asked Jeff to consider that, while he might be delivering numbers to the operations team, the accuracy on the mix of products mattered. While the demand numbers on volume were accurate, the changes in the type of products in the portfolio were not. Over the past two months, the mix of products to be made by contract manufacturers with long lead times had varied significantly. As the number of products grew and markets became more complex, sensing actual market consumption grows in importance.

Resilient: As a result of the great recession, and with the rise in volatility, companies started designing networks to absorb demand and supply volatility. Before the outsourcing of manufacturing, companies had two buffers: manufacturing and inventory. However, with the outsourcing of manufacturing, inventory became the sole buffer. As a result, inventory strategies grew in importance. Today, there is a greater need to design the form and function of inventory. In this area, the company was behind. I then asked Filipe to think about the impact of outsourcing in his last assignment and the inflexibility of the operations redesign when manufacturing was outsourced. We had a healthy discussion on why the design of the network mattered and why the need for information grows in importance as more and more operations are outsourced.

Demand-driven: With his P&G background, Frank waxed eloquent about the need for the company to be demand driven. However, his interpretation was a sales-driven, not a demand-driven, strategy. We discussed the difference. We talked. Frank struggled. The grimace on his face became even more apparent and he was taken to task by Angela. She spoke of the irrational pushes by sales on product at the end of the quarter to make sales bonus incentives and the cost to the rest of the organization. Products were returned, orders were transported at higher costs, and customers were angry to have been talked into orders that they did not want or need. At the end of the discussion, the team clearly understood why being demand-driven is an aspirational journey for most companies.

Being demand-driven requires the building of outside-in processes, from the channel back to the enterprise. It requires the redesign of sales and challenges the power structure within the organization.

In this process, the company aligns to the flows of the channel. This change transformation contradicts the traditional sales techniques of large promotions and stuffing the channel. Companies that are more demand-driven have the greatest advantage in driving incremental revenue, but it only becomes possible when companies learn the differences between sales-driven and demand-driven strategies.

This process change requires a redefinition across the organization. Traditional processes today are inside-out and driving demand-driven processes is about much more than forecasting. In the session, we discussed five fundamental shifts.

1. **Implementation of demand sensing technologies.** Demand sensing is the use of advanced analytics to visualize and translate demand patterns with minimal demand latency. Technology reduces the time needed to sense actual channel sales. The use of demand sensing technologies enables the reduction of inventory, the growth of sales, and the reduction of freight costs. This made sense to the entire team.

2. **Active management of demand shaping programs.** Demand shaping varies by industry, but is usually the combination of price, promotions, trade incentives, marketing programs, and new product launches. In a demand-driven organization, the effectiveness of these programs is tightly evaluated in revenue management programs. On this point, Angela spoke up. She cautioned Frank that there needs to be better discipline in the management of trade

funds. She was having problems with accruals and asked Frank to help.

3. **Translation of demand with minimal latency into operational processes to drive an intelligent response to sense market changes.** This was a hard concept for the team to understand. So, we tracked the time that it took from a customer buying an item to the point when it translated into an order. They were surprised to find that it varied by 15–45 days for their company. Angela quickly translated this *bullwhip effect* of order translation into company working capital impacts.

4. **Ownership of the channel.** The management of a value network through the channel with a focus on the end purchase. The shifts in flows are translated into organizational incentives. The visibility decreases demand latency and improves customer service. Frank had not thought about the impact of demand latency and mix inaccuracy on the ability to source and manufacture products.

"Okay," Frank interjected. (I was amazed that it had taken this long before he stopped me.) "I see how the IBM iBAT case study makes sense if you put it in perspective of processes for the entire company. I can try to help get channel data if I know that we will really use it. At the end of the day, you guys need to reassure me that this will help me to grow topline sales." At that point, he gestured to the team.

Joe looked at Frank and quickly retorted, "It would help us a lot. Seeing what is really happening in the channel is very important. If I can see what you are selling quicker, I can have materials on hand and manufacture products more quickly with less inventory. This will make us more nimble and we can better respond to your rush orders. You know those midnight specials?" Joe said with a wink.

I smiled. Progress was happening with the team. They were a tough group; but, ever so slowly, change was happening. This was especially between Frank and Joe. After the interchange of thoughts on sharing channel data, we continued with the agenda and discussed the fifth shift.

5. **Horizontal processes to use and translate the channel demand signal.** While the conventional processes use demand data within the function of sales, marketing, and supply chain, the demand-driven processes bring the outside-in mapping of demand shifts into the horizontal processes of revenue management, sales, and operations planning

(S&OP), supplier development, corporate social responsibility (CSR), and risk management.

Now that Frank had broken the ice to start a discussion, Angela spoke up. "Today, we are flying in the dark with little visibility of the operational impacts of decisions. For example, I need better visibility on both sales and operations so I can source capital at the best rates—this can make or break a quarter when margins are slim. Improved forward visibility will be really helpful in treasury function as well. You have my support."

At that point, Lou Banks grabbed a handful of pistachios from the bowl, cracked one, and tossed it into his mouth. He wiggled his eyebrows and looked at Frank. His voice rumbled when he said, "I know that the finance team needs to serve the business, but sometimes it seems like we're the gatekeeper or protector of the balance sheet. I feel that this should not be the case. There are ways we can support your efforts, but. . . ." His voice faded as Lou looked intently first at Frank, and then at Filipe, "You guys need to own the business. I am tired of the fighting. It isn't the role of the finance team to drive operational decisions." He settled back in his chair and munched on his pistachios, satisfied that he'd made his point.

The discussion then turned back to the IBM iBAT case study. It was a good example of a demand-driven process evolution. While traditional sales incentives can stimulate growth through the first three steps of the model, in the movement to be outside-in, the organization has to shift from conventional sales-driven to demand-driven processes. Being demand driven reduces waste and improves alignment but to reach this goal requires a change in behavior. It took IBM 10 years to drive this type of behavioral change. At this point, Frank was beginning to nod his head in agreement, and I could tell from Edgar's body language that he was beginning to feel better. The tension in the early part of the session had run high. The emotions in the room were starting to calm.

The team agreed that they were currently in an "efficient" phase of process definition in the model. Lou admitted that the finance team owned part of the problem. They had recently pushed the organization to produce at the lowest cost per case, not understanding the greater issues with demand and supply variability and the need for buffers. Filipe offered that his singular focus on lean operations had played a role.

While the concepts made sense to the team, they wanted to discuss a case study of a team that had made progress. So, right before lunch, we reviewed the case study of Company PDQ.[1] It made the need for outside-in process design crystal clear for the team.

A Market-Driven Journey

Company PDQ prided itself on being marketing-driven. As a food and beverage leader, they had a long legacy of launching successful products and penetrating global markets. The focus of the marketing team was on demand insights. They were good at managing focus groups to understand the effectiveness of advertising programs, trade promotions, and new product launch potential. Ivy League marketing graduates flocked to the company looking for a job.

The corporate focus was on functional excellence. The silo walls between functional groups were strong and the investments in technologies made them even tougher to penetrate. The belief was that if the functional groups were delivering their goals, then the company would outperform their peer group. The finance team was strong and heavy-handed. They were very focused on tightly managing costs within the corporation. The team prided themselves on outperforming the market on return on invested capital. As shown in Figure 4.3, they had achieved their objective.

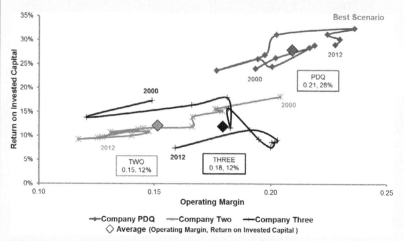

FIGURE 4.3 Company PDQ Performance against Peer Group on ROIC Versus Operating Margin
Source: Supply Chain Insights LLC, Corporate Annual Reports 2000–2012.

The culture had little turnover, and very little cross-functional career movement. In many ways, they were isolated. With strong bonus performance and good retirement incentives, people within the

(continued)

(continued)

organization were cautious and conservative. They did not want to rock the boat. As a result, when the finance organization said "Jump," they asked, "How high?"

They also had a decade of delivering operations excellence. With a strong performance on costs and reducing cost of goods sold, they had built closely coupled and vertically integrated global manufacturing centers. The operations team prided itself on delivering over 30 consecutive quarters of cost savings. The company had come to depend on it.

As global markets opened, they were there first. The company delivered high market share with an entrepreneurial spirit. The operations team managed three categories in nine major regions. However, this market expansion carried a cost of complexity. The board of directors of Company PDQ challenged the team to do more. They wanted the team to deliver even greater savings to continue to fund corporate growth. However, as the team evolved the strategy they found that they were out of balance. They were struggling to manage inventory and reduce cash-to-cash (C2C) cycles. As shown in Figure 4.4, they had also recently struggled with case-fill rates. In meetings, the sales team was grumbling because their customer service performance was declining. They were losing the faith of retailers in regions of modern trade.

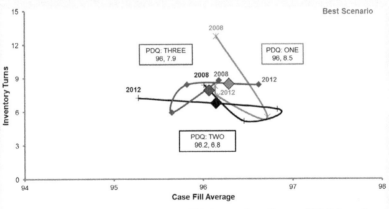

FIGURE 4.4 Company PDQ Customer Service versus Inventory Turns by Category
Source: Supply Chain Insights LLC, Corporate Annual Reports 2008–2012.

The reason for the loss of customer confidence confused them. They were not clear about the root cause. The team had reduced the number of items by 38 percent; yet the inventory and customer service results were going backward.[2] The difference was not insignificant. The days of inventory of company PDQ was unfavorable by 10 days compared to their peer group.

The organization of Company PDQ was proud of a number of achievements. They had rolled out a global planning system and had focused on driving improvements in forecasting. The team had also invested in an inventory management system. They were sure that if they just worked harder on the projects that were underway, they could drive high ROIC and operating margin while delivering on customer service and inventory levels.

What the team did not realize was the following,

Sources of complexity were increasing. While the group had decreased the number of items in the product line, they had simultaneously increased the number of special promotions and price incentives to the trade to stimulate sales. Sales teams were aggressive in demanding specialized packaging and smaller product sizes, and this added to the complexity, pushing the company product line further and further out on the long tail of the supply chain.

Despite the increase in inventory, the customer service levels were declining. While many believe that higher inventories deliver better customer service, the fact is that it has to be the right inventory. High inventories in a company often accompany poor customer service results. The reason? Company PDQ was not actively designing the form and function of inventory and managing the inventory buffers. If the network isn't properly designed and demand is translated on a near-real-time basis, then the wrong product will be available at the wrong place.

The most balanced business category was a regional operational team. In Figure 4.4, the category that was most in balance on cost, inventory, and customer service was a regional product line with one instance of enterprise resource planning (ERP). (ERP is a system to capture transactional workflows of the company. Visibility across ERP instances is hard to manage.) The company had three ERP instances. People could not get to the data. The number of global planners trying to manage these global categories numbered over 400. As a result, most of the work was done on spreadsheets. They were unaware that they could not effectively manage the Effective Frontier using a spreadsheet.

The system was out of balance. The strong focus on results had pushed functional metric performance that was out of balance. There was strength in performance, but the organization viewed results in spreadsheets and could not see the interrelationships between the metrics. At no place in the bonus hierarchy was any employee rewarded

(continued)

(continued)

for inventory management. As a result, inventory hung in the cracks of the organization as a symbol of lack of alignment. There was no accountability in the metrics to drive balance in metrics performance.
Horizontal processes were immature. The sales and operations (S&OP) process was 20 years old and had a sexy four-letter acronym name. But, as outlined in Figure 4.5, the system was out of balance. The majority of employees (53 percent) thought that it was biased toward a sales/marketing perspective and only 56 percent of employees considered the process effective, yet the organization was very proud of the process.

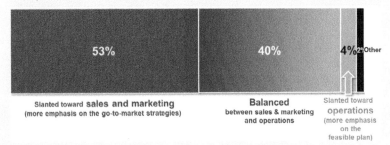

| 53% | 40% | 4% 2% Other |

Slanted toward **sales and marketing**
(more emphasis on the go-to-market strategies)

Balanced
between sales & marketing
and operations

Slanted toward
operations
(more emphasis
on the
feasible plan)

FIGURE 4.5   Evaluation of Sales and Operations Planning by Company PDQ Employees

Base: Employees of Undisclosed Major CPG Company (Revenue > $58) Involved in S&OP Process (*n* = 45).

Q17. When you think about the S&OP process, what is your personal assessment?

Source: Supply Chain Insights LLC, CPG Employee Survey (September 2013).

In S&OP, there was more focus on sales and marketing. The operations team was told what to do. As a result, the company could not reach balance on the development of a feasible plan. This resulted in case-fill and inventory issues. Because of difficulty in sensing demand, as shown in Figure 4.6, there were myriad never-ending and conflicting priorities. They were always chasing their tail, rewarding the *urgent* and having no time for the *important.*

In addition, the organization had a strong positive forecasting bias, which led to overforecasting of new products and trade promotions.
Channel data was not being used. The company had channel-data-sharing relationships with over 30 retailers and had built a global system to capture distribution inventory and shipment changes in modern trade. However, the data was not being used cross-functionally, and the focus was not holistic. Sales used the data in spreadsheets, but did not

want to share the information. They were not sure what anyone would do with it. It seemed like information overload to the sales team at Company PDQ.

This is a new way of doing business.

Financial Leader at Company PDQ in Discussions on Demand Sensing

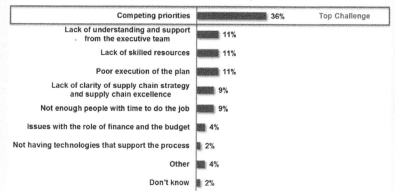

Top Challenge in Building an Effective Sales and Operations Planning Process

Competing priorities	36%	Top Challenge
Lack of understanding and support from the executive team	11%	
Lack of skilled resources	11%	
Poor execution of the plan	11%	
Lack of clarity of supply chain strategy and supply chain excellence	9%	
Not enough people with time to do the job	9%	
Issues with the role of finance and the budget	4%	
Not having technologies that support the process	2%	
Other	4%	
Don't know	2%	

FIGURE 4.6   Competing Priorities a Top Challenge in S&OP
Base: Employees of Undisclosed Major CPG Company (Revenue > $58) Involved in S&OP Process (*n* = 45).
Q18. What is your company's single largest challenge in building an effective S&OP process?
Source: Supply Chain Insights LLC, CPG Employee Survey (September 2013).

The focus of Company PDQ was *sales*. The commercial teams were using the retail data for sales reporting and the development of category management plans for weekly sales briefings, and the sales operations teams were using the global distributor data to manage monthly incentives. There was no accountability for bias.

Within customer service, there were over 30 vendor-managed inventory (VMI) programs, but the data was not being used in the development of a forecast or as a demand-sensing signal. Instead, it was being used to build orders and shipments for specific shipments. As a result, the company was blind to the shifts in channel demand. The flows were not analyzed.

The organization did not understand the concepts of demand latency. Their best-selling item had a demand latency of seven days while their

(continued)

(continued)

long-tail items had latency of 40 to 45 days. Often new product launch items had a latency of 30 to 35 days. As a result, the success rate of new products was hard to read. It took the marketing team two to three months to analyze market data and develop trade programs.

When they began to understand the concepts of demand latency their minds started to shift. They did not realize that marketing processes were monthly and worked on market data that was two months old. To roll up data for global market share, the marketing team had to work in 700 systems.

They also did not realize that the sales department was working on weekly data that was only one week old. The sales processes were weekly, but did not analyze daily sales trends or weekly shifts across retailers. This was a contributing fact to the lack of alignment between sales and marketing that was higher than competitors.

While there was closer alignment between Company PDQ's operations and finance teams, and operations and procurement, there were greater gaps between sales and marketing, and sales and operations. These gaps are shown in Figure 4.7.

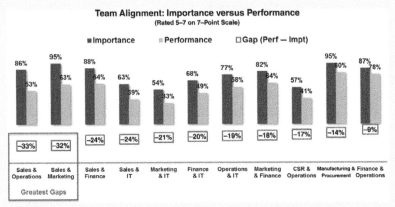

FIGURE 4.7 Functional Alignment of Company PDQ

Base: Employees of Undisclosed Major CPG Company (Revenue > $5B) (n = 148).

Q20: In your opinion, how important is it for each of the pairs of teams to be aligned within your company? SCALE: 7 = Extremely important, 1 = Not at all important.

Q21: How aligned do you believe that these same teams actually are within your company? SCALE: 7 = Extremely aligned, 1 = Not at all aligned.

Source: Supply Chain Insights LLC, CPG Employee Survey (September 2013).

The company was constantly changing priorities based on differing data views of the leadership team and market understanding. The processes were inside-out with a focus on vertical excellence. As a result, as shown in Table 4.1, the company lacked alignment.

TABLE 4.1 Functional Alignment Company of PDQ to Industry Benchmarks

Gaps in Team Alignment		
	Company PDQ*	Industry Benchmark
Sales and Marketing	−32%	−23%
Sales and Operations	−33%	−35%
Manufacturing and Procurement	−14%	−21%
Operations and Finance	−9%	−12%
Sales and Finance	−24%	−25%
Operations and IT	−19%	−32%

They also did not realize that the order was carrying 7 to 45 days of latency. This latency is due to the replenishment rules and channel flows in the channel. Their operations processes were built based on order replenishment. Consequently, the organization was responding to data that was 7 to 45 days late. As they better understood the long-tail of the supply chain and the need to manage complexity in the channel, the "ah-ha" moments began. The longer the tail the more important it was to decrease demand latency.

After the design of outside-in processes, the company now understands that they are on a five- to seven-year journey to become demand-driven. They also more clearly see the implications of sales-driven or marketing-driven processes. To drive the journey, they have focused on building a training program and actively educating the teams on the differences of being sales-driven versus market-driven. They also have a new appreciation of the damage that demand latency can have on alignment and performance balance.

Demand latency: The time that it takes for channel demand to roll-up through the channel to an order for the corporation. This includes the velocity of sales in the channel that trigger a series of channel reorder points and shifts in order fulfillment due to policies (e.g., transportation load building, full-pallet ordering policies, credit authorization, and price incentives).

After reviewing the case study, Joe's team wanted to know why more companies had not made more progress on becoming demand-driven. The reason was simple. It is a new way of doing business and the concepts are not well understood. They fly in the face of conventional process definition.

Companies traditionally have worked well within silos. It is only when complexity increases on the Effective Frontier, and growth slows, that there is a need for horizontal alignment to develop end-to-end processes. The greater the shifts in the business, the more important it is to move people from a functional to an end-to-end value network mindset.

The question for the team was then "What is next? What can we expect in the future?" With rising commodity volatility, they were feeling the pinch of both commodity price increases and volatility that the demand-driven concepts needed to be extended with bidirectional orchestration of demand and supply volatility from buy-side to sell-side markets. So, we discussed the concepts of a market-driven value network. Joe's team liked the build-out of the model in Figure 4.8.

A market-driven value network senses and responds market-to-market. It is horizontal and bidirectional to continually test and learn and orchestrate processes cross-functionally from buy-side to sell-side markets. The focus is holistic to maximize opportunity and mitigate risk.

Joe inquisitively asked, "What is the difference between becoming demand-driven and driving market-driven processes?"

My response was quick: "Joe, while demand-driven processes are from the channel back, market-driven processes operate cross-functionally from

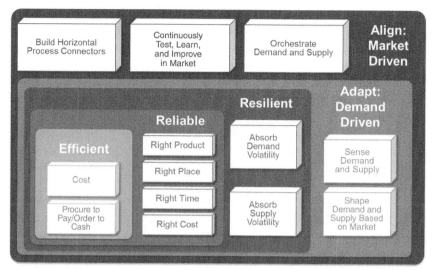

FIGURE 4.8 Market-Driven Process Evolution

buy and sell relationships. There is volatility in both the sales channel and your purchases of materials. While the market-driven processes build on the demand-driven concepts, as you become more mature you will use horizontal processes to orchestrate the response market-to-market. For example, as materials become more expensive, you may change your go-to-market channel strategies to change price, or alter the bill of materials to provide greater value at a lower cost for the customer. To do this, you need to be outside-in in both sales and procurement, and orchestrate volatility, constraints, and price cross-functionally to make better decisions to maximize volume while protecting margin. Make sense?"

"Absolutely. I like the concept of orchestration. Will we talk about this more?" asked Joe.

"Absolutely," I said. "But for now why don't we break for lunch?"

As the catering was arranged and Angela paid the bill, Edgar took Filipe and Frank to the side and began a conversation in low tones, but as I stood to the side, I overheard their discussion.

"Frank, I like what I'm hearing about you being more open to some of these concepts—I feel as if you're developing a plan that will help the sales team exceed performance expectations, and I want you to keep an open mind about how to work with operations." Edgar paused, and then continued, "Filipe, I know that you feel like you're getting whipsawed all the time by sales, but that is the market environment we live in. We need to figure out how to get better visibility so you can have more predictability." He then reached up and put one hand on Frank's shoulder and his other hand on Filipe's. "I know that you both are going to put your personal battles within the organization aside to close this alignment gap. It's not just me who is counting on you—it's the employees and shareholders, and I want Joe to succeed on this project."

These "Edgar moments" had become legendary in the organization. The friendly shoulder grip, just a little tighter than necessary for emphasis, was all Edgar needed to do to make sure he had someone's complete attention.

The conversation over lunch was fun. They told stories about misalignment, customer service failures, and bad decisions. The good thing was that now they could laugh about it. They were starting to jointly own the solution. After lunch, they decided to brainstorm together and capture their key insights from the meeting:

Ten Common Misconceptions That Are a Barrier to Improving Performance

1. Market-driven isn't the same as marketing-driven.
2. Sales-driven isn't the same as being market-driven.
3. Orders and shipments do not represent "true" market demand.
4. We believe that if we improve the forecast, then we will become demand-driven. While it helps, it isn't sufficient. We need to focus on understanding the "mix" of items being sold in the channel at the time that they are sold.
5. Demand latency is a bigger barrier to driving improved performance than we thought.
6. Tight integration of companies can be problematic. To be effective, the data needs context. To drive excellence data needs to be synchronized, harmonized, and translated across organizational functions.
7. The most effective operations strategy isn't always the most efficient.

Edgar then commented on the concept of the Effective Frontier. He liked it. The simplicity of the model appealed to him. He asked the team to consider the impact of managing the organization using a few cross-functional metrics on their dashboards. He recommended that they focus on channel sales or revenue, days of inventory (DOI), case fill rate, return on invested capital

(ROIC), and operating margin. He liked the concept of driving improved balance, strength, and resiliency into operations through the process changes.

Joe stepped back from where he had been writing on the board and said, "This workshop is starting to feel like that big icicle that Lora and I saw hanging on the roof when we were planning this meeting." He held his hands up, nearly a foot apart. "It was this big, but by the time our meeting ended it had melted and fallen to the ground. I am glad to see that our tensions are also starting to thaw."

There were some encouraging nods around the table, and some nervous chuckles. "Yes," Filipe said, getting into the poetry of the moment, "an icicle can take many days to form during the cold days of winter but as the seasons shift, it can quickly melt and fall to the ground." He continued, "Maybe it won't take so long to thaw out next time."

Everyone laughed, which was a welcome relief from the tension of some of the morning's discussions.

Joe could see that the group was thawing, but he also knew that it would take many days of discussion before they could internalize the concepts and make them actionable. He believed that this was their secret to future success. It was important to cast off old paradigms and embrace new thoughts. They just had to find the right mechanisms to take the concepts and move them into action.

THE JOURNEY: BECOMING MARKET-DRIVEN

The team agreed that this work could push them to a new level of the Effective Frontier. After reviewing the Company PDQ case study, it was clear that they needed to make the transition. No doubt about it. They were sales-driven. As a result, driving continuous improvement on their current frontier could lead to lower levels of corporate performance.

Their question was, "How do we get started?" As a first step, I encouraged Joe's team to use the large white wall in the conference room to plot their "oops" moments from 2013. An *oops moment* was a time where they were surprised by market demand. It could have been either up or down; but it was a significant deviation of expected demand resulting in either a shortage of product in the channel, or missed shipments, or obsolete inventory.

At the same time I encouraged the team to plot the impact of a commodity price/availability issue, and think about the concepts of a market-driven value network market-to-market. They were also to map commodity shortages. The energy was high as they worked together to recount the number of issues that they had encountered throughout the year. Angela volunteered to set up the session and Jeff asked if he could provide the data.

As Jeff and Angela worked with the group, they found that there were many issues. Each oops moment was documented on a separate piece of paper and taped to the wall. In fact, there were so many areas to document that we had to take a break to allow the team to get more paper.

During the prior year, there were many major misses in the market. Things had happened, but they did not understand why. Cross-functionally, there was no forum for the leaders to flesh out the root cause of their gaps in performance. It was now gaining clarity. Frank and Filipe sat back and listened.

As they reviewed all of the times that they were surprised by market results, it became clear that they were reacting to late market signals, and their response was functional and reactive. It was not aligned and responsive. As a result, their metrics and bonus systems were not driving cross-functional collaboration.

"Filipe and I've concluded that we can't keep doing what we're doing. While we talk about being aligned, today we are functional. While we're talking about consistency in direction, today we are constantly changing company direction," said Frank. "We don't have clear market signals and, like Company PDQ, we are out of balance on metrics. Sometimes we shift demand to meet quarter-end goals and then preload the channel."

Filipe chimed in, "We leaned-out the organization too far in order to meet financial goals. But now we don't have enough flexibility to change as the market shifts. My teams don't have enough direction to be more responsive to their channel."

Frank and Filipe were sitting next to each other now, not opposite each other. Angela noted their body language was less confrontational. They were realizing that they needed to work together to solve the problem that had been created by working as two separate organizations instead of one. They had their "a-ha" moment—they had not understood until this moment the impact of demand shifting on the company's performance on the Effective Frontier.

At the break, Edgar had walked into the meeting. He was quietly sitting at the back of the room smiling.

Angela spoke up. "If you think about Joe's project in Brazil, it's important to get this right. We're agreed that we need to adopt market-driven initiatives there. But just as we put on the whiteboard, this is something that hits all of our divisions. I think we need to make this a corporate transformation project, not just a regional initiative."

Lou added, "But you've got to focus on action. This can't just be another initiative that sinks under its own weight because it's too big and too hard to do."

Jeff looked up from his spreadsheets. "What about the risk management project? It's impacting everything that we are doing, and we have to develop a sales and operations planning model to support it."

"We might as well add in the corporate social responsibility project," Lou said, "I need help on that one and it's pretty much a risk management issue in any case."

Joe said, "If it can expedite what I need to do in defining how we get these processes in place in time for the Brazil project, I'm all for it, but I don't want it to get lost."

As they thought about Joe's new venture and the expansion opportunity, they agreed that they could not just adopt the market-driven initiatives there. Instead, they needed to make it a corporate transformation. They believed that this was not a functional project, or a regional initiative—instead, it needed to be a new way of doing business. The focus needed to be end-to-end from the customer's customer to the supplier's supplier. Data sharing and outside-in processes were essential. The belief was that they could quickly integrate the new direction into their development of horizontal processes.

Their goal was to orchestrate decisions and go-to-market strategies, end-to-end, bidirectionally. They wanted better cross-functional alignment and balanced decision making. They decided that using the risk management, CSR, and S&OP initiatives might save them all a lot of time and provide a good focus and jumping-off point. Joe, Angela, and Jeff agreed to spearhead an initiative to evaluate the use of these processes to drive cross-functional alignment.

RISK MANAGEMENT: A CATALYST FOR DRIVING BALANCE AND RESILIENCY?

The team's interest in risk management was not just happenstance. It was a real issue that had become critical to operations in most sectors, partly as a result of lean initiatives that had focused solely on efficiency in the prior two decades.

In preparation for the discussion, I shared some industry statistics with the group on risk management. In 2013, 80 percent of companies had a material supply chain disruption, and the average company experienced three

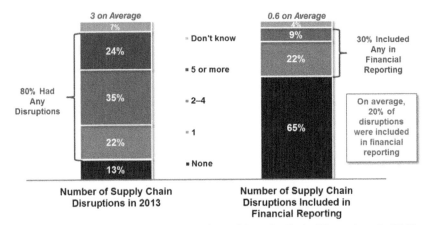

Number of Supply Chain Disruptions in 2013

Number of Supply Chain Disruptions Included in Financial Reporting

FIGURE 4.9   Risk Management: Number of Supply Chain Disruptions in 2013

Base: Manufacturers, Retailers, Wholesalers/Distributors/Cooperatives, and Third-Party Logistics Providers—Total (*n* = 46).

Q15: Now please think just about last year, 2013. How many supply chain disruptions, if any, did your company experience in 2013? A supply chain disruption is an unplanned event or an occurrence that had material consequences on your supply chain. Your best estimate is fine.

Q16: How many of your supply chain disruptions in 2013 were material enough to be included in your financial reporting? Your best estimate is fine.

Source: Supply Chain Insights LLC, Supply Chain Risk Management Study (February–March 2014).

disruptions, as shown in Figure 4.9. To put this in perspective, the average company has a gap of 28 percentage points on current performance versus desired state on risk management.

Joe's group had experienced disruptions in both Hurricane Sandy in the United States and the Japanese tsunami. Angela mentioned the benefits that they would achieve in better insurance premiums if the team could improve their preparedness. They were currently working on improving their risk management programs. They believed that they could use their work on risk management to help them to be more proactive. They liked the idea of connecting the use of better demand data to a tangible objective in their risk management program.

"Progress has been slow on the risk management project," Angela said. "Jeff and I've been struggling to get the team to adopt risk management practices to drive outside-in processes." She paused and considered.

"The biggest challenge we've had is that we don't have a consistent definition and set of practices. As an organization we focus on the urgent, not necessarily the important. We need to be proactive on the important."

Jeff added, "If we're more market-driven, maybe it will help us drive some of the thought leadership and orchestration that we need in order to agree on what's important."

At that moment I gestured and accidentally knocked over my coffee. I was such a klutz. Edgar was sitting next to me and saved my papers with a fast swipe of a napkin. They all laughed when I said, "The companies that are the most mature in risk management learned the hard way. They had a disruption."

It was also the case here: The team agreed that they had historically learned the hard way. Angela decided that she would take leadership of this team, and create an education process of the impact of their major disruptions and drive cross-functional readiness programs to be sure that they were better prepared in the future.

The workshop broke for the day. The team was exhausted by the amount of territory that they had covered, but very satisfied that they had reached a consensus and had an action plan for how to proceed. The whole team got individual emails from Edgar at 11:00 that night, telling them that he was proud of the progress that they were making.

The next day we started the workshop a little later to give the team time in the morning to catch up on emails and work that they had missed the previous day.

I cautiously put my coffee on the table in front of me and we went around the table to check in, to see if everyone was still focused and aligned on the approach we'd agreed to take the previous day. We were going to delve into risk management, social responsibility, and S&OP as mechanisms to create some of the processes needed to be a value-driven network.

Defining Risk Management in the Value Network

They liked the idea of starting with a definition for the risk management team. For Angela, it was *the proactive identification and resolution of potential risks to the organization*. The key word in this sentence was "proactive." They all agreed that they were too reactive. Their systems would respond, but they could not sense. Performance is measured by indicators, not by performance predictors. They wanted to change this.

The team was hard-wired for supply. They could wax eloquent about the work that they are doing on "control tower" or "supply chain visibility," but up until this workshop, they did not see demand as a risk management issue, or as something that they could manage.

Filipe said, "We need to change. Demand volatility is a huge issue for the whole organization. Take a look at this map of risk drivers." He then showed them the chart I had given them the prior day in Figure 4.10.

He continued, "Today, we are dipping our toes into turbulent waters."

I added, "The largest gap in risk management expected over the next five years, in the face of rising demand volatility, is the management of global operations."

FIGURE 4.10   Risk Drivers

Base: Manufacturers, Retailers, Wholesalers/Distributors/Cooperatives and Third-Party Logistics Providers—Total ($n = 46$).

Q8. What do you see as the top three drivers of supply chain risk at your company today? Please select no more than three.

Q9. What were the top three drivers of supply chain risk at your company five years ago? Please select no more than three.

Q10. What do you expect will be the top three drivers of supply chain risk at your company in five years? Please select no more than three.

*Others with consistent low risk not shown: Corruption, Intellectual Property Right, Water Scarcity, and Computer Security.

Source: Supply Chain Insights LLC, Supply Chain Risk Management Study (February–March 2014).

The team collectively felt that they were not prepared as an organization for future risks.

As Filipe finished, Joe smiled. "Maybe this is why a project like IBM's iBAT can help with our global expansion. There are two major risks that go hand-in-hand—global operations and demand variability—that a demand network can help us solve"

Here's what Joe was referring to.

1. **Increasing complexity of operations.** With a decade of building global supply chains behind them, the company was feeling the impact. Local regulations, fair labor, variability in shipping lanes, new materials, out-sourced manufacturing, and faster product development cycles were all contributing to the pain. The financial stability of contract manufacturers and third-party logistics firms was a growing risk factor.

   The team agreed that they could not look at it as just one factor. It was many. They also agreed that they were better at managing regional supply chains than tangled, knotty global ones. The organizational dynamics and politics make regional/global governance difficult. They understood better now how a project like iBAT could help them to better manage global operations.

2. **Demand variability.** The biggest surprise to the risk management team was the role of demand uncertainty on risk. This was something that they had not considered. Jeff commented that this gave him a new appreciation of the importance of his job and the need to decrease demand latency in data sharing.

   This gave the team more impetus to push back on sales-driven and marketing-driven concepts to get real market data with minimal latency and use it in cross-functional processes. This discussion helped to align the group.

At the end of the hour of reviewing the research, the risk management team agreed that this initiative was a good horizontal process to focus on in the market-driven transformation. They thought that through the redefinition of processes they could get greater awareness of the impact of demand latency on risk and the need to drive balance and resiliency in corporate performance. The belief was that connecting to this initiative would help to socialize the concepts for greater understanding.

The team turned to the second initiative that they had decided to include in Project Orbit: corporate social responsibility.

CAN CORPORATE SOCIAL RESPONSIBILITY BE AN IMPETUS TO DRIVE ALIGNMENT AND BUILD MARKET-DRIVEN VALUE NETWORKS?

"Supply chain sustainability" is the management of environmental, social and economic impacts and the encouragement of good governance practices, throughout the lifecycles of goods and services.

Supply Chain Sustainability (definition)—United Nations Global Compact

Lou had led the CSR initiative for the past two years. He had fought to get recognition within the company. It fit his personal social responsibility agenda but also, from a finance standpoint, he had seen first-hand the impact that social responsibility and sustainability issues can have. His mantra: A single photograph of an issue of fair labor or pollution from a far corner of the world can have an immediate impact on sales and suppliers.

Within an organization, supply chain sustainability can be known by many names: the green supply chain, the good citizenship report, CSR policy, or fair trade. The programs may have different names, but the goals are focused on creating a better balance between the corporation's efforts to manage profit, people, and the planet. For many, this can be in stark contrast to the traditional supply chain goals of the right product, at the right place, at the right time.

This was Lou's challenge. To meet the stated corporate goals for sustainability programs, he knew that it was critical for operations and corporate sustainability teams to work well together. The success of one is dependent on the success of the other. Over the past 10 years, corporate sustainability goals have transformed supply chain objectives, causing companies to rethink their definitions of supply chain excellence. Much was in flux. After our strategy session, Lou set up a session with Frank and Filipe to talk about the CSR program and asked them for their help to make it more impactful. He was pleased that they were open to help.

"Gentlemen," Lou rumbled as he pried apart a pistachio shell with his thumbnails, "we have some significant disconnects on our sustainability initiatives, and I need your help in fixing them.

"The first is that we aren't even coming close to meeting our goals. As you know, Frank, we have a few of our customers who have insisted that we have a program in place. That is why we initiated this program three years ago.

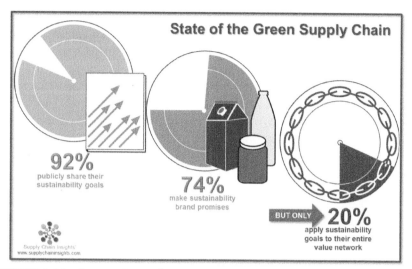

FIGURE 4.11　Current State of Corporate Sustainability Initiatives
Base: Manufacturers, Retailers, Wholesalers/Distributors/Cooperatives with sustainability goals (*n* = 66).
Source: Supply Chain Insights LLC, Green Supply Chain Study (January–February 2013).

Unfortunately, today, every time we're asked to report on progress, I feel like we're fudging the results."

"At some point that's going to come home to roost," Frank said. "They are going to either switch suppliers or ask for some kind of penalty price concessions. Either way, it is bad news for us."

"It's almost impossible to meet the objectives they're setting and to meet our production volume and cost goals," Filipe replied. "Something has got to give and until I'm told otherwise, I'm minimizing production costs and maximizing volume, because that's how I'm measured."

"Well, there's good news and bad news." I said, pulling up the research shown in Figure 4.11. "The good news is that you're not alone, but that's also the bad news. In the research, we find that 92 percent of respondents surveyed have a public statement or declaration of goals and policies for corporate sustainability. It has also grown in importance to redefine the brand promise. Today, 74 percent of respondents surveyed connect their success in sustainability to their brand statements. The opportunity is to use sustainability as a brand advantage. A good example of this is Unilever."

Lou stated, "I think we're more vulnerable than we think on this issue. The greatest impact on our corporation is outside our four walls, yet we are only focused on our own operations. We need to do both."

I agreed. "You are not unusual. In our research, only 20 percent of respondents were focused on the entire value network (from the customer's customer to the supplier's supplier). While the most common focus is on the enterprise, the greatest corporate risk lies outside the four walls of the enterprise, and companies are staking both their corporate and brand reputations on their abilities to deliver. When they focus on the end-to-end results, they can do both."

"We can't afford this. Over 65 percent of nonrenewable resources are outside the walls of our operations. And that smells like trouble to me." As Lou spoke, his pate was a little shinier than normal, the sweat a physical reminder of his passion on this subject.

Filipe poured coffee as Lou continued, "The second disconnect is in decision making. The two sets of goals—corporate social responsibility and operations— lack common processes and definitions for governance. Many of our decisions are ad-hoc. As a result, when given a policy choice between operations and corporate sustainability, our answer is to address the urgent one. The primary drivers of the decisions are profitability and customer service. I think that we need to develop a better and more proactive decision process or we'll never catch up on this issue. As a result, it will be a bigger and bigger sales and financial liability."

I added that progress on corporate sustainability is easy at first. "Initially, the traditional supply chain and the sustainability objectives closely align. As companies adopt CSR programs, initial results reduce costs and decrease waste. However, as the programs become more systemic, especially in the area of supplier development, pressures on program alignment become more difficult. For example, the "greenest" decision, given a choice of suppliers, may not result in the lowest cost. Today, all companies are struggling with the right mechanisms to achieve balance and alignment between the two programs."

Then Lou countered, "But operational processes are decades in the making, while sustainability processes are less than a decade in maturity. As companies have become larger and more global, aligning these two important teams becomes more and more complex."

"Yes," I said, "It is important to drive balance in corporate performance through horizontal processes."

I looked at the group, and then continued, "Alignment and progress on CSR requires different metrics. Not all the levers are equal with varying degrees of difficulty for measurement. The measurement of energy is easy while carbon and water are the most problematic." The group studied the research shown in Table 4.2, and concluded that the management of these metrics on the Effective Frontier would drive a holistic discussion on balance and alignment that they were struggling to achieve right now.

TABLE 4.2 Measurement in Corporate Sustainability Initiatives

	Have Goal	Importance*	Performance*	Top 3 Easiest to Track*
Energy usage	97%	92%	69%	72%
Water reduction	88%	79%	60%	53%
Carbon footprint	79%	75%	48%	40%
Water usage	74%	65%	37%	51%
Recycled content	42%	75%**	61%**	46%**
Conflict minerals	41%	37%**	37%**	11%**
Green buildings	36%			
Fair labor	30%			
Fair trade	11%			

Base: Manufacturers, Retailers, Wholesalers I Distributors I Co-operatives with sustainability goals—Total (*n* = 66).
*Top 2 Box (7-point scale); bases vary by element—showing only elements with base size = 25+;
**Small base size—interpret with caution.
Q4. In which of these areas does your company have any goals for 2013? Please select all that apply.
Q11. How important is each of these elements to your company's overall sustainability goals? SCALE: 1 = Not at all important, 7 = Very important.
Q12: How would you rate your company's performance on meeting your goals for these same elements? SCALE: 1 = Poor, 7 = Excellent.
Q13: Please select up to three elements that are easiest for your company to track, in terms of progress.
Source: Supply Chain Insights LLC, Green Supply Chain (January–February 2013).

> The management of the supply base requires us to do hard work in managing the relationship to a greater degree than we have had to do in the past 15 years.
>
> Vice President of a Dairy Operation

Over the last year Lou and Angela had begun to work together to make subtle changes. At first they met with purchasing and began a supplier development effort to measure carbon, water, and waste impacts. They then started talking to Filipe about how the inclusion of CSR metrics into the corporate metrics would improve balance.

Recently they had started including Frank in the discussion. It was their belief that progress on CSR was going to matter to customers. They wanted him to be ready. Their goal was to use it to drive a brand advantage. They wanted to be a good corporate citizen, but they also wanted to create a real, sustainable competitive advantage for the brand. Once again, the team realized that metrics that matter span multiple objectives and can work together for a common objective.

After reviewing the work, Edgar thought that it would be a good idea to place carbon usage in the value chain as a metric, along with growth, operating margin, inventory levels, case fill rate, and return on invested capital, on their corporate scorecard.

SALES AND OPERATIONS PLANNING TO DRIVE BALANCE AND RESILIENCY

Like most companies, Joe's company had an S&OP process. S&OP processes are now in their fourth decade of maturity, but as in most companies there was not just one process; instead, there were many, and each was in a different state of maturity.

In our afternoon session on S&OP, Edgar joined us. He had commented in the strategy session that while most organizations have redesigned their processes many times over the past four decades, he felt that they were operating the same process that they defined in 1968. He commented that back then he had long hair and bell-bottom pants and danced to the Rolling Stones. (The image resonated.) The team laughed. The goal he felt was to redefine the process and move it forward quickly. He felt that it was critical to get it right today.

Edgar had felt it important enough to reconvene the entire working team of Project Orbit for this session. He felt that cross-functional alignment was critical to having an effective and proactive S&OP process.

He stood up and began speaking to the group. "Manufacturing and operations processes are getting more complex. I think we can all agree on that one. Global expansion is adding more complex channels, and our progress is slow in responding. We keep on creating these spreadsheet ghettos to try to fit these new go-to-market strategies into our old S&OP process. We have to have an effective process and that starts with alignment on what metrics we are operating on today, not those that we used in 1985."

Edgar continued, "Good planning matters now more than ever, because things are more complex and a lot more volatile. We all need to take a systemic approach to building our new S&OP process. The big barrier, frankly, is the executive team. This includes me. We need to start measuring these metrics for balance as a complex system. We need to understand more about how we operate today so we can develop the right S&OP process."

He then turned and asked me to walk through the basics. The goal was for everyone to be on the same page.

I asked the team to stretch. It had been a long day. I then continued, "Sales and operations planning aligns and connects the functions of the company. It drives balance. Horizontal processes are essential to becoming market-driven and building effective value networks. A mature S&OP process improves agility and alignment. (I showed them Figure 4.12.)

"Just to be sure that we are on the same page, let's start with a definition," I said. "Sales and operations planning is defined by the Association of Production and Inventory Control Systems (APICS) as 'a process to develop tactical plans that provide management the ability to strategically direct

FIGURE 4.12 Impact of S&OP Maturity on Alignment and Agility

Base: Manufacturers Total (*n* = 92), "Have S&OP Process" (*n* = 74), "Have Mature S&OP Process" (*n* = 30), "Mature S&OP goal = Maximize opportunity and mitigate risk" or "Determine the most profitable plan." Other answer options included "Match demand with supply" and "Develop a feasible plan" (www.supplychaininsights.com).

Source: Supply Chain Insights LLC, Green Supply Chain Study (April–May 2013).

its businesses to achieve competitive advantage on a continuous basis by integrating customer-focused marketing plans for new and existing products with the management of the supply chain. . . . ' For manufacturers, retailers, and distributors, it has become a critical process to power growth, improve resiliency, and drive efficiency improvements. In the past decade, it has seen a renaissance of activity.

"The S&OP process helps guide organizations in an uncertain world. It enables the visualization of risk, and yields a cross-functional understanding of opportunities. In the face of increasing demand volatility, S&OP helps. Additionally, S&OP processes are becoming more strategic in building effective trading partner relationships. As companies attempt to drive differentiation through partnerships, organizational alignment and effective data sharing grows in importance. The maturity of an S&OP process can easily be determined by answering five questions." I then turned and wrote them on the board:

1. What is the S&OP goal?
2. How is balance achieved between demand and supply?
3. How are decisions made?
4. How does the organization measure success?
5. How is S&OP tied to execution?

I then turned around, and asked, "Does this make sense? Any that you think that I am missing?"

A group discussion followed. They agreed with the points on the board, and Joe and his team believed that they were immature in their S&OP process and that the larger team needed education. They also thought that the improvement in agility and alignment could help their performance on the Effective Frontier. However, they wanted to know more about the stages and the phases of maturity. So, I gave them a handout that laid out the five stages of evolution:

Stage 1 goal: Deliver a feasible plan. The first S&OP process originated with a goal of developing a feasible plan. Early evolution of the planning enabled organizations to develop a forecast, visualize operational requirements, and align metrics. The introduction of the Theory of Constraints (TOC) in 1984 and the evolution of the concepts into manufacturing planning applications enhanced this capability. It allowed organizations to identify constraints and build a feasible, or realistic, plan.

Each of these supply chain planning models is very industry specific. A conglomerate composed of process, discrete, and apparel manufacturing found that it needed multiple systems to model operations. Approximately 25 percent of companies are functioning at this level. Joe's company was one of them.

Stage 2 goal: Match demand with supply. As organizations mature, and after building capabilities to have a feasible plan, teams need a solution with more advanced capabilities to model the trade-offs of volume and product mix. The issues with the impact of changing product mix are not trivial. These trade-offs can be very complex. Through the use of technologies, companies are able to visualize and balance customer service, assess network strategies, and build inventory plans to best match demand with supply. To meet this requirement, companies have invested in "what-if" modeling environments. Over the past 10 years, these processes were augmented by management technologies to evaluate multitier inventory analysis and postponement. Approximately 45 percent of companies today are at this stage. It was the opinion of Joe's team that this would be an aspirational goal to reach in the next two years.

Stage 3 goal: Drive the most profitable response. While stage 1 is supply-driven and stage 2 is sales-/marketing-driven, stage 3 is business-planning-driven. This is commonly dubbed by many as *integrated business planning* (IBP). The question of the right name for the process is often a heated argument in the organization. When a company defines the term *supply chain* as a function within operations, the organization often will feel that the S&OP process must be renamed to achieve sufficient status to enable the process evolution. The belief is that the renaming is needed to gain permission to cross over and align the functions of finance, sales, and marketing. To drive the quickest returns, it is important to not get hung up in this argument. Instead, the focus should be the definition of a clear value network or supply chain strategy and a well-defined definition of supply chain excellence. For most, this is a gating factor for success.

The process basics and the technology requirements are deeper in stage 3.

Approximately 12 percent of organizations are focused on driving the "most profitable" response.

Stage 4 goal: Build demand-driven supply chain capabilities. At this stage of S&OP, the process is designed from the outside in. It is focused on product sell-through in the channel, whereas the earlier stages are focused on selling *into* the channel. This stage requires redefining the forecasting processes to sense market conditions based on channel demand signals and then shaping demand to increase lift. Demand sensing reduces the latency to see true channel demand, while demand shaping combines the techniques of price, promotion, sales, and marketing incentives, and new-product launch to increase demand lift.

The definition of demand-driven value networks, for the purpose of this book, is processes that sense shifts in channel demand with zero latency to enable the organization to shape and translate demand across the functions of sell, deliver, make, and sourcing operations.

Stage 5 goal: Orchestrate through market-driven value networks. The horizontal processes in stages 3 and 4 are foundational in building market-driven value networks. This technology portfolio helps companies to sense and shape demand and supply bidirectionally between sell- and buy-side markets. This process of bidirectional trade-offs between demand and a supply market is termed "demand orchestration." This capability allows companies to win in this new world of changing opportunities and supply constraints. It is especially relevant with the tightening of commodity markets.

The dialogue continued with a discussion of market-driven processes, where I explained, "In market-driven orchestration, the demand-shaping levers are traded-off against market-driven orchestration levers to ensure that a company can maximize opportunity and mitigate risk."

I then handed out what is shown here as Table 4.3.

Joe then passed around an article that I had written earlier on the potholes and pitfalls of S&OP and asked for the group to read it overnight so that we could build on the discussion in our next session together.

TABLE 4.3 Orchestration: Trading Off Demand Shaping for Market-Driven Orchestration Levers

Demand-Shaping Levers	Market-Driven Orchestration Levers
New Product Launch	Price-to-Price Orchestration
Marketing	Alternate Bill of Materials
Sales Incentives	Alternate Sourcing
Trade Promotions	Change in Assortment
Distributor Incentives	Orchestration of Product Mix (incent products with less commodity variability)
Assortment	
Price	Changes in Demand-Shaping Strategies
Run Out of Obsolescence of Mark-Down Strategies	Commodity Hedging

Potholes and Pitfalls of S&OP

S&OP is a popular topic today. There are many consulting organizations and technology providers touting S&OP best practices and technologies. Before starting on the journey to drive balance and alignment through S&OP, Joe's team felt that there were nine potholes to avoid:

1. *The role of the executive team.* The largest barrier to S&OP performance is the executive team's understanding of supply chain as a complex system. The most mature S&OP teams have worked on the education and alignment of the executive teams. Before starting the engagement in S&OP, ask the question, "What is the best way to educate and bring onboard the executive team?" Do not ask for executive involvement without education and alignment of the team on the supply chain as a complex system.

2. *Agility and alignment improve with S&OP maturity,* but only if you build with the goal in mind. Consciously craft the organizational map for improvement with a clear definition of process impacts and technology evolution as the goal changes. Each step requires a redefinition of process and technology. The greatest impact for organizational alignment happens when there is movement from a focus on volume to profitability, while the greatest improvement in agility happens when the organization moves from inside-out to outside-in thinking. Both are important.

3. *Manage the supply chain as a complex system.* Work cross-functionally with a consistent set of metrics that includes forecast accuracy, customer service, inventory levels (days of inventory or inventory turns), profitability, and revenue growth/market share. Focus on helping the organization gain an understanding of systems.

4. *Avoid spreadsheets. Eliminate spreadsheet ghettos.* The trade-offs of the supply chain cannot be adequately modeled in a spreadsheet. The trade-offs of the complex time-series data elements are just too difficult. Encourage planners and participants to move off of Excel spreadsheets by improving the usability of S&OP applications.

5. *Don't manage metrics in isolation.* One of the great benefits of an effective S&OP process is the management of organizational trade-offs. However, as you train the members of the team, help them to understand the trade-offs between metrics for your organization and to never manage metrics as single entities in the absence of a total system approach.

6. *Avoid religious arguments.* Stay focused. The discussion of S&OP maturity has become a political, sometimes almost a religious, war

(continued)

(continued)

within organizations. Avoid this pothole. The political issues revolve around the definition of supply chain as a function versus focusing on the supply chain as an end-to-end process, and the evolution of S&OP as integrated business planning (IBP). Sidestep these issues, use the best-accepted name, and focus on business results. Do not get mired in the politics.

7. *Be sure the organization knows the quarterback.* Connect S&OP planning to S&OP execution. Use "what-if" capabilities in today's technology solutions to build organizational playbooks and orchestrate the S&OP process from planning to execution. Ensure that the "plays" are well-understood and there is alignment of the organization to the calls of a single, universally recognized quarterback for action.

8. *Define clear regional/global governance.* S&OP processes have become more complex. Spend time educating the organization on S&OP maturity and evolution, and work to clearly define governance. This may not be trivial. For one multibillion-dollar manufacturer, the definition of global/regional governance took two years.

9. *Avoid cookbook approaches.* There is no technological silver bullet, but the most mature S&OP processes have focused on visualization and what-if analysis.

As we worked through the options for Joe's organization to become market-driven, the interest in S&OP grew. They understood how this 30-year-old process was experiencing a renaissance. Technology advancement makes greater capabilities available, but industry progress is inching along. They were clear that a major barrier was clarity of operational strategy and the goals of the company on the Effective Frontier. They were ready to build organizational potential.

MOVING TO THE NEXT LEVEL OF THE EFFECTIVE FRONTIER

As an outcome of the workshop, the team decided to build a project plan to drive a market-driven transformation. The goal was to try to move to the next level of the Effective Frontier. The group also agreed that they needed to build a dashboard to measure weekly progress on sales growth, operating margin, inventory levels, return on invested capital, and levels of carbon used in their processes. They felt that this was a balanced scorecard.

Everyone thanked Joe for arranging the workshop, and they predicted what their new level of performance could be. Frank started a contest and allowed them to place bets with odds. They even plotted what they thought their orbit charts would look like for the period of 2015–2020.

The team then formed subteams to work on the implementation of plans to improve the metrics that matter through horizontal processes. The working group decided to bring the workgroups of risk management, corporate social responsibility, and sales and operations planning together for a training session on market-driven value networks. The focus of the training was on how to improve the potential of the system to drive to the next frontier through changing the mental model.

The Notes from Joe's Journal

As companies begin their journey on the Metrics That Matter, the terms *alignment, agility, balance,* and *resiliency* seem straightforward and easy to achieve, but as a group evolves, we gain a deeper level of appreciation of what these terms mean. It helps us to:

1. Use orbit charts to plot divisional data to understand the progress and potential on the Effective Frontier. It is easy to see the gaps and identify the progress when we plot the intersections for customer service, inventory, costs, and complexity. Look for patterns and try to understand root-cause issues.
2. Understand "oops" moments. Form a cross-functional team and plot all of the "oops" moments of over- and underperformance to customer service goals. After this activity, look for patterns and ask the group the questions, "Are there data sources that could give the organization faster and more reliable signals? Is this data being used? Does the use of this data require new forms of analytics? Are new processes needed?"
3. Use horizontal processes to drive alignment and balance in corporate performance. The lack of alignment cross-functionally is a barrier to maximizing performance on the Effective Frontier. Use horizontal processes to drive cross-functional alignment and improve corporate performance. To maximize success, ensure that all the horizontal processes have the same goals. Ensure that they are clear on the operating strategy and there is alignment between corporate objectives and the Metrics That Matter.

CONCLUSION

My mind was racing at the end of the day. I firmly believed that achieving balance, strength, and resiliency on the Effective Frontier requires the adoption of market-driven processes. Conducting the strategy day was hard work because adopting these processes was a difficult change management journey. Some in the group, like Frank, had struggled. At the end of the day, it was crystal clear to me that the easiest way to drive the right behavior was to build horizontal processes to drive alignment against common goals. I also firmly believed that the fastest progress could be made when groups have access to market data that is daily data, daily, with no latency. I cracked a grin as I reflected on the day. I loved Frank's antics. I also adored Joe's sincerity and applauded Edgar's leadership. The team had made a lot of progress, yet there was more to do.

We were now ready to take these concepts and apply them. In the structure of the upcoming days of the workshop, we would first evaluate the consumer value chain, and then reflect on these insights overnight before we tackled the evolution of the health-care value chain. On the last day we would wrap up the session by evaluating operations improvements in the industrial value chain. It was a lot of material, and I knew that the team faced some long days, but I was up to the challenge.

As I closed the door to the conference room to leave for the day, I smiled, realizing that Joe's team would first find that there is no single leader that has done everything right. Instead, the path forward for Joe's team would be piecing together insights from multiple companies across industries. I looked forward to helping them in that journey.

 Notes

1. The PDQ Company case study is from six months of work with an actual consumer products company. They have requested that their name be withheld from this book. As a result, the story has been made generic and some of the numbers have been altered, but the issues discussed are both company specific and prevalent in the industry.
2. "Can You Afford the Risk?" *Supply Chain Insights* (April 22, 2014).

CHAPTER FIVE

What Drives Value in the Value Network?

Industry Progress in Consumer Value Chains

T HE BRISK SPRING BREEZE made me grab my coat as I left my car. The team had come a long way on Project Orbit since our last meeting. Progress on the project was in full swing. The groups running the horizontal processes were maturing, and Edgar was feeling good about their progress. I had been in touch by phone with most of the team during the past three months, but today was our first face-to-face meeting since the strategy session in the winter.

It had now been 14 months since I first met Joe. I grinned as I thought about his efforts to unveil his big hairy audacious goal (BHAG) on inventory at his kick-off meeting last year. Joe would often laugh with me about how much he had learned on the journey of championing Project Orbit. He was a bit embarrassed when thinking of his naivety a year ago, but he was also proud of how far he had come in his understanding of the Metrics That Matter.

The goal of the meeting on this beautiful spring day was to understand how other companies had progressed over the course of the past decade on improving value in their value chains. The team wanted to know what was possible. They also wanted to understand how quickly they could drive progress. They understood that leaders focused disciplined efforts on small, incremental improvements over many years.

189

THE QUESTIONS

We were meeting together to work on Project Orbit for the first time in three months. As we started the session, there were many questions. I opened with a check-in. The energy was high and the discussion was frenetic. It seemed that all of the members of the team wanted to talk all at once. I was having a hard time facilitating the session, but I let the discussion roll.

Filipe started. He said, "Let me share what is in my head. I've really been thinking about the work we've been doing together. Here is where I am struggling. I have been asking my group to drive value-chain mapping to improve results; and we all know that it is a well-known Lean technique. However, in the work, I have not been clear on the definition of value. Instead, we have been focused on costs. So, I had a thought. Do the metrics that we defined in our last strategy session serve as the right definition of "value" for this effort? Should the group now switch from looking at costs and return on assets (ROA) to make a change? Should they now drive new levels of value based on return on invested capital (ROIC) and the orbit chart progress at the intersection of inventory turns and operating margin?"

"My thoughts run along the same lines. We have spoken for years about having a balanced scorecard," Lou added, "but we have never defined balance. Do the metrics that we selected in our last session represent balance?"

"Yes, exactly. In the past five years, I have driven continuous improvement programs for the corporation," Joe said, then paused and looked at Filipe. "However, today I realize that we have been trying to drive better performance on a few metrics using old definitions of processes powered by old technologies. I like the concept of the Effective Frontier. Should we redefine the continuous improvement programs to now focus on market-driven processes to power us to a new level on the Effective Frontier?"

Edgar smiled. He spoke in a droll, thoughtful way. "I have been asking teams to align for years, but I have not been successful in driving the hard choices of aligning functional results to the larger goal within the organization." He then looked at Joe. "Part of the difficulty is getting to the right information, but the rest is just me. I don't know when to ask a team to drive a lower level of results so that we can drive higher levels of corporate performance. For example, I have let the work we have been doing on transportation costs degrade our work on customer service. Our focus on trying to ship full-truckload orders has undermined our efforts to ship what our customers really want, when they want it. As a leader, how do I get the right information to ask groups to drive the right level of results so that we can stay in balance?"

It was Angela's turn to chime in. "I am mapping the key metrics that we discussed at our last meeting into metrics hierarchies for the operations teams, and I want to get them right. Can we spend some time on mapping the metrics of growth, operating margin, days of inventory (DOI), case fill rates, return on invested capital, and carbon footprint into a metrics hierarchy to ensure that it is actionable and aligned with incentives? My goal is to align metrics to incentives to ensure that we are working together. For me that means we would be aligned from the team that runs the packaging-line filler on the factory floor to the person sitting on Edgar's team. I like the idea of doing it in a way so that we can have continual alignment market-to-market so when things change in the market we are all still working together against the same goals."

Jeff liked what Angela said, but then added, "I think that our journey has been both good and bad. Ever since we started looking at orbit charts, we have been learning how the shifts in corporate performance relate to each other. This has been good." Jeff caught Lou's eye and then gave him a nod and a smile. "Yes, I am now realizing that these relationships between metrics are not ones that can easily be represented in a spreadsheet. However, I find all of these metrics confusing." Over the weekend, he had spent some time mapping them and trying to understand the impact of metric shifts on the profit and loss statement. He then looked at me and asked, "For simplicity, could we focus on a narrower time range?" He found the period of time 2000–2013 to be too broad, and asked if we could narrow the focus to 2006–2013.

Frank was furiously typing on his keyboard. Without missing a keystroke, he commented, "I have been thinking that if we want to be truly market-driven, we need to change our sales incentives from a reward system in which we reward when we ship the case, to rewards earned by the sales team when the cases are sold to the end user. I want to know how to do this. I would like to reward the sales team to manage the inventory in the channel. So, how do sales groups manage this transition? I have to keep the team motivated and I would love some insight."

Jeff laughed at Frank, and threw one of Lou's pistachio shells at him. "Don't you ever stop working? Get your nose out of your laptop and join the group!" he implored. He then turned to me and asked, "As we learn about the impact on sales incentives, I would love to know of the effects of the collaboration efforts of the companies on the consumer value chain. Did the efforts between retailers and consumer manufacturers improve value?"

After a decade of retailers and consumer products companies collaborating by using vendor-managed inventory (VMI) efforts and retail scorecards, Jeff wanted to know the impact of these efforts on the balance sheet.

I quickly wrote the questions on the board as they spoke, and then asked the group what they thought. "Have I captured them all?" I questioned.

The responses came fast and fervently. The group quickly told Filipe that they were comfortable with switching the goals on value-stream mapping. They also affirmed to Lou that they thought the goals selected for Project Orbit represented balance and alignment for their scorecard. They then suggested to Edgar that they let the corporate strategy team run monthly models to help him understand the impact of the trade-offs so that he could become more conscious about the interrelationships of metrics in his decision processes.

The team was now confident and aligned. It was very different from the atmosphere at the beginning of our meeting. They were also more supportive. Joe shared that they had invested in a new modeling technology that he thought could help. They also congratulated Frank on his idea of shifting sales incentives to focus on sales through the channel. Angela agreed to help Jeff track these shifts.

They unanimously agreed with Jeff that a narrower focus on 2006–2013 would be a good idea. Frank laughed, shut his laptop, and looked over his reading glasses to comment that his kids were in diapers in 2000, and he certainly did not want to go back that far! The group laughed at the thought of Frank changing diapers.

Filipe settled it. He thought that it just seemed like it was too far back in history to be relevant. I agreed. I needed to quickly change my presentation during the break to reflect the new time frame.

As for Angela's question on mapping the metrics, the group thought that this was too much to cover in this strategy session. As a result, they put this item on the "parking lot" for the group session at the end of the three-day workshop. They asked if we could first go through companies' progress during 2006–2013 to understand progress, and then come back and map the metrics and build an incentive system using a metrics hierarchy. We all agreed that this would be a good plan.

Edgar then chimed in, "I want to call my admin to clear my calendar for the afternoon. If you are going to review some case studies, I want to stay for as many as possible. If I can learn from other companies' successes and failures, maybe I can use the insights to leapfrog the competition." And so it began. I started to tell the group about the journey of industries within value networks. We would spend the first day studying consumer-value networks; the second day focusing on the health-care value network; and the discussions on the third and final day would enable an understanding of industrial value networks. At the end of the session we would be able to map the metrics hierarchies to enable adoption of Project Orbit for the company. We then paused for a coffee break.

LEVELING THE PLAYING FIELD

As we got started again, Jeff spoke up. He said, "When you talk about the metrics on the Effective Frontier, my mind goes into a spin. There are so many metrics and I find the definitions complex. Could we look at the analysis a bit differently?"

I was all ears. Jeff was always very insightful. He continued, "I have been thinking. I am currently training for a triathlon." He looked at the group and laughed and said, "Don't worry, I haven't gone too crazy. It isn't an Ironman or a long-distance race, but I have learned through my training that a triathlon is a measure of strength, balance, and flexibility. I think that it is similar to the discussion of a balanced portfolio of metrics driving balance, strength, and resiliency to corporate performance."

He stood up and started drawing a table on the board. He continued, "What we are doing reminds me of a triathlon, so I was wondering if we could use a methodology of stack-ranking companies on the Effective Frontier, much like I am measured in running a triathlon."

He then drew a number of columns on the board. "My thought is that we could rank the companies for the period of 2006–2013 based on the progress that they made on balance, strength, and resiliency and then give them a rank. My thought is that those that did the best would get a value of 1 and the next best a value of 2, and so on, until we have ranked all the companies. I then thought that we could compare them using a table like the one that I just drew on the board."

As we thought about the table that Jeff had just drawn, which is represented in Table 5.1, the group agreed that it could have promise as a way to compare companies by industry peer group and to judge relative progress on the Effective Frontier.

Frank commented, "I like it. It was a rough night. Simple, simple, simple works for me today. I need to talk about the numbers without so much gobbledygook."

Jeff then continued, "My thought is that we could give balance, strength, and resiliency equal rankings and see which companies outperformed. There is just one 'Watch out!' We will have to remember that the bigger the number for balance and strength, the better the score, while we want the pattern on

TABLE 5.1   Methodology to Compare Companies on the Effective Frontier

			Supply Chain Index				
NAICS Code	Balance	Balance Ranking	Strength	Strength Ranking	Resiliency	Resiliency Ranking	Overall Ranking

Source: Supply Chain Insights, LLC.

resiliency to be small and tight, so this will need to be rewarded with a smaller number."

At that point, Edgar spoke up. "Jeff, I think this is a brilliant idea. I would like to use the metrics that we discussed yesterday in the analysis. I would like to define balance as a company's progress at the intersection of year-over-year sales growth and return on invested capital (ROIC). And, how about defining strength as the company's progress at the intersection of operating margin and inventory turns? And, I think that if a company is resilient that they would have a tight pattern at that intersection. What do you think? Could we make this work?" The group nodded in agreement. There was energy in the room. They liked it.

Edgar then turned to me, and said, "Is there a way to calculate the pattern at these intersections? The orbit charts, while valuable, are a bit confusing. I like the fact that they show patterns over time, but it is hard to compare the progress of companies. When I look at them, I struggle to know if one company is doing better than another. Is there a way that we could measure company progress based on the orbit patterns using a numeric, calculated value?"

I beamed and then shared some research that I had been working on. My research team had been working together with an operations research team at Arizona State University (ASU) for the past three months to apply mathematical techniques to quantify the patterns in the orbit charts.

As I passed out the methodology and started to explain it, Frank's eyes rolled back in his head. He stated, "This seems rather complex. I know the team at Arizona State University. They are very smart. Can we just take their word on how they determined the best method?" The group agreed and we were then ready to move on to discuss the progress of the industries. They had no energy to go through the details of the math, but were happy to have a methodology that would allow them to quantify the differences between the orbit charts.[1]

To improve the understanding of the industry trends, Edgar asked that I allow enough time to share interviews and insights from industry leaders in each of the industry peer groups. He wanted to be sure that the group got a complete understanding of the rhythms and cycles and market drivers of each of the industries. He thought that spending time gleaning the insights was important for them to decide on their next steps for Project Orbit.

THE SUPPLY CHAIN INDEX

My team and I have worked for two years to understand the orbit chart trends. My goal was what every CEO tries to do: Develop metrics to run the organization that will maximize shareholder value. It sounds simple, but the research project has been more difficult than I ever imagined. While our approach isn't a recipe for instant success, it does clear out a lot of distractions in the data to get a team to the core operating principles quickly.

The work began as I hired a small team to mine data from online annual reports, by industry, to construct spreadsheets of common financial metrics. The spreadsheets quickly became cumbersome and complex. We had experimented with a multitude of ways to turn a spreadsheet into a story. After much fine-tuning and experimentation, we settled on the use of orbit charts and had hired ASU to help us quantify the trend lines. I was glad that Edgar's team liked the approach. It was great to see Joe talking with his team in a relaxed and confident way about the metrics.

Over the past two years, I built these charts for over 100 business leaders for free. This allowed us to learn with them. As we plotted the metrics that they thought were important against the peer groups that they valued, we got to hear their stories and interpretation of the data.

As we shared our findings with educated business leaders about finance ratios, they helped us to better understand the data. "What caused this downswing in inventory in 2007?" we would ask. The company would then share that it was the result of a six-month laser-focus brought on by a new manager. When we asked, "What caused these cash-to-cash cycle gyrations in the period of 2002–2004?" they told us the story of a difficult merger, or about a strategic consultant giving them bad advice on an inventory target.

Through these discussions, we found that this was a new way of looking at data, and while it took adjustment and training, it provided a new and fresh perspective at most organizations. Why? Progress in operations happens over time, not in months or quarters but in years. And the interrelationships between the metrics are real. The data cannot properly be assessed in a spreadsheet.

In January 2014, we began work on applying the pattern detection to the orbit charts. This was my first opportunity to share it with a group. I was excited to see what they thought. During a break, I built a series of charts using Jeff's concepts on a ranking system to share with the group.

I was eager to use the new methodology with this group. It was a good test. Edgar's team was now aligned, motivated, and energized. Frank had shut his laptop, and the team was engaged. They had leadership support, a clear mission, and a compelling event ahead of them.

I felt that the next three days would be exciting. My plan was to share the insights of the results and progress of three value networks—consumer, health care, and industrial—and then facilitate a group discussion on which metrics mattered and why. We would then build Angela's hierarchies.

THE CONSUMER VALUE CHAIN JOURNEY

After lunch, I started the session with a simple definition. "The consumer value chain is a chain, or network, of companies that work together to ultimately serve the consumer in the store to purchase a product. The value network is composed of the retail, apparel, consumer products, food and beverage, and chemical companies. At each level of the value network, the demand signal becomes more distorted. Today, I am going to share insights on how each of these industry segments has performed on the Effective Frontier. We will see trends both within the value network and also in industry peer group analysis for the period 2006–2013."

I continued. "In the past decade, companies have deployed many technologies and the world has become more connected. This has enabled the global economy. However, each company has defined global differently. While retail companies are regionally focused, consumer packaged goods and chemical companies are global. The food and beverage companies are multinational in their product portfolios. This is driven largely by the differences in the consumer palate. The focus is different. While the energies of a retail company are on cycles—inventory, seasons, markdowns, promotions—the drivers of the manufacturing operations team are on the cost of conversion.

"Of all the value chains, the relationships of companies within the consumer value chain are the most mature for collaboration. While the companies within the value chain have not been able to build win-win relationships to reduce costs and improve the inventory levels, they are more mature on data sharing, scorecarding, and the management of joint inventories through VMI relationships."

At that point Frank commented, "Walmart's rise in power in the late 1990s changed this value chain. They became a power broker dictating new policies to the suppliers. It changed the game and the nature of the relationship." Lou rolled his eyes as Frank recounted story after story of his sales calls on Walmart when he was at P&G.

At that moment, the conference room door opened. We had a delivery. As Filipe signed for it, he commented, "The game was changed again with the rise of Amazon. For example, take this part that we ordered and received today for the whiteboard. A decade ago, we would have ordered it from the manufacturer and it would have taken weeks, not days, to receive."

"Yes," said Angela. "I now order almost everything from Amazon. I love that I can order the shipment on my phone and the trucks are there the next day delivering to my high-rise apartment, without me having to lug heavy bags down the street. Last night I ordered curry sauce, and the day before it was toilet paper. In fact, I just placed an order for new ballet tights this morning. I can get almost anything that I want now from Amazon. How has this changed the consumer value chain?"

Shift in Power

This was a good preamble for the discussion. I then asked the group to open their deck of slides, and began the workshop.

In the 1990s, the power was with consumer brands. Advertising and promotional programs gave the power of the value network to the consumer products company. Companies made their money being good at marketing. Their processes became very marketing-driven.

However, with the disintermediation of media and the rise of the modern retailer at the end of the 1990s, the power shifted to the retailer. Consumer products companies attempted to fight back and aggregate power through mergers and acquisitions. However, it did not change the course of history. In the last decade, the retailers have had the power in this value chain.

With the evolution of e-commerce, the power in the value chain shifted to the consumer. With this shift, the manufacturers are now free to sell and ship directly to their consumers, but they have been slow to mobilize. Today, less than 5 percent of products are directly sold to consumers by manufacturers.

A Review of Progress on the Effective Frontier

Along with the power shifts toward the shopper, there was consolidation of companies within the value chain. To aggregate power, and try to wield strength against the retailers, over 100 manufacturers consolidated in the past decade. The product portfolios were more complex, and as a result, as seen in Table 5.2, the average consumer packaged goods company saw an increase in operating margin.

The size of a company matters. The consumer packaged goods and chemical companies tend to be larger than the retailers. They have more complex operations and are attempting to manage global supply chain operations while accommodating regional differences.

All companies within the consumer value chain increased efficiency, but as shown in Table 5.2, not all improved the effectiveness of the value network to

TABLE 5.2 Value Chain Shifts within the Consumer Value Network

	Consumer Value Chain (2006–2013)					
Industry	Year-over-Year Revenue Growth	Operating Margin	Inventory Turns	Cash-to-Cash Cycle	Revenue per Employee (K$)	SG&A Ratio
Retail (n = 19)	7.6%	0.06	10.1	23.5	418.0	16.8%
	↓93.3%	↓4%	↑7.5%	↓30.4%	↑34.6%*	↓0.9%*
Apparel (n = 11)	11.1%	0.11	3.6	109.5	318.0	31.1%
	↓103.2%	↓12.1%	↓5.0%	↓12.4%	↑26.2%*	↑8.7%
Food & Beverage (n = 21)	5.0%	0.16	6.5	43.7	413.6	22.8%
	↑29.2%	↑25.7%	↑14.8%	↓233.1%	↑71.3%	↓13.5%^
Consumer Packaged Goods (n = 17)	5.9%	0.16	5.1	52.9	575.6	27.3%
	↓56.9%	↑10.0%	↑10.3%	↓3.2%	↑21.4%*	↓5.3%*
Chemical (n = 18)	7.4%	0.11	5.0	80.8	632.4	14.4%
	↓12.2%	↑34.7%	↓5.7%	↑2.2%	↑35.9%*	↓6.4%^

Industry Average comprised of public companies (beverage: NAICS 312111), (consumer packaged goods: NAICS 3256%, where % is any number from 0 to 9), (cereal food industry: NAICS 3112%, where % is any number from 0 to 9), (food conglomerate industry: NAICS 311821 and 312111), (agricultural food: NAICS 311520 311941), (mass retail: NAICS452%, where % is any number from 0 to 9) reporting in One Source with 2012 annual sales greater than $5 billion.
*Calculated from 2002 to 2012 due to data availability; ^Calculated from 2003 to 2012 due to data availability; NC = no change.
Source: Supply Chain Insights LLC, Corporate Annual Reports 2006–2013.
Peergroups based upon September 2014 Supply Chains to Admire research report.

TABLE 5.3 Year-over-Year Growth in the Consumer Value Network

Retail Industry—Year-over-Year Sales Growth								
Industry	2000–2004	2005	2006	2007	2008	2009	2010	2011	2012
E-Commerce	15.7%	3.0%	17.9%	28.2%	24.1%	6.8%	27.9%	25.2%	N/A
Drugs	14.8%	26.0%	11.3%	13.1%	−1.0%	13.0%	12.4%	6.6%	N/A
Grocery	9.6%	14.5%	12.9%	15.1%	17.3%	−0.9%	8.2%	6.9%	15.3%
Mass	15.7%	16.0%	10.1%	14.3%	11.0%	−3.2%	9.7%	9.3%	8.4%
Specialty	11.0%	16.3%	14.7%	14.2%	8.2%	0.0%	0.0%	4.6%	4.4%

Mean values utilized excluding outlier data greater than 100%.
Retailers with 2011 total sales exceeding USD$5 billion.
Source: Supply Chain Index Analysis from Annual Reports 1990–2012 as of June 16, 2012.

manage costs and decrease inventory levels while increasing inventory turns. In addition, as shown in Table 5.3, growth slowed, putting more pressure on the value chain.

Retail

Today, times are tough for retail. As the financial numbers are posted, it looks bleaker and bleaker. The shift to e-commerce is making it more difficult for a store to compete with the e-commerce endless aisle. The impact is pervasive: The concept of the shopping mall is becoming obsolete. The team shook their heads, as I shared these recent headlines:

- In the spring of 2014, 1 billion square feet of retail space is sitting vacant in the United States.
- In April 2014, Radio Shack announced they were going to close more than 1,000 of their stores.
- In February 2014, Staples announced they were going to close 225 of their stores. For 13 quarters in a row, same-store sales at Office Depot have declined.
- This year, JCPenney, which has been slowly dying for years, announced plans to close 33 more stores. The company lost $586 million during the second quarter in 2013 alone, and while much was being written about the choices of their CEO, their sales were continuing in a downward trend.
- Since 2010, Sears has closed down approximately 300 stores, and CNN has been reporting that Sears is expected to shutter another 500 Sears and Kmart locations soon. For 27 quarters in a row now, overall sales numbers have declined at Sears.
- Target has recently announced that it plans to eliminate 475 jobs and will refrain from filling 700 empty positions.

- A fast-food chain giant, McDonald's, reported that sales at established U.S. locations dropped, down 3.3 percent in January.
- Macy's announced that it will be shutting down five stores, as well as eliminating 2,500 jobs.
- By 2016, the Children's Place will be closing down 125 of its "weakest" stores.
- In Canada, Best Buy recently closed approximately 50 of its stores.
- Blockbuster, a video rental giant, completely shut down every one of its stores.
- U.S. supermarket sales are projected to drop by 1.7 percent this year as the overall population increases.
- There are projections that up to at least half of all shopping malls in the United States might shut down within the next 15 to 20 years.[2]

As we discussed these startling facts, Angela asked, "Why haven't the retailers been more active in redefining their stores to be more competitive?"

The team was in disbelief as I shared how the evolution of the e-commerce model was first adopted by the retailer as a profit center. This definition as a profit center made the company slow to move to an omni-channel product delivery method. While the shopper wanted a product anytime, anywhere, the retailer had two distinctly different teams that were each focused on competing for the shopper's attention. They were each profit centers. Even today, omni-channel concepts are talked about everywhere and implemented at only a few retailers.

Frank commented, "Here it is again. Alignment, alignment, alignment. It's a consistent theme. Alignment issues are pervasive in organizations." He turned to Lou, and said, "Remember when you and I were talking about setting up profit centers, and we axed the idea when you mentioned that each profit center makes alignment, over time, more difficult? This is a good example of your point."

Lou nodded his head in agreement.

Our gears turn faster in e-commerce. The rhythms and channels are very different. We have to learn and evolve processes to manage the each (the selling of individual items versus selling cases or pallets).

Today, we are picking and managing cases at a case level, not for an each. Our systems are not set up to manage the individual unit very well. In this regard, we are a long way from omni-channel capabilities.

Additionally, retail can think only in terms of push. Pull is a foreign topic for a retailer. For decades, retail has been in the process of getting the forecast right, and if we miss, then we just merchandise it and send it to a deep discounter. These techniques no longer work.

The omni-channel disrupts this. We just do not have enough room to have inventory and people want low prices all the time, so traditional merchandising does not work well. It cannot be enabled by push concepts. It requires the definition of push/pull logic."

Leader in Omni-channel Retailing

As shown in Figure 5.1, the adoption of e-commerce models over the past decade put more pressure on the stores to improve store effectiveness. The cost of labor in a store, compared with the lower cost of operating an e-commerce channel, put the stores at a disadvantage.

These challenges varied by retail segment. The group could clearly see that the mass merchant and specialty store formats were hit the hardest. The impact was quick, and the results were pervasive. The adoption of e-commerce by grocery retail is a more recent phenomenon.

As seen in Table 5.4, the challenges were extensive. As a result, for the retailer managing performance on the Effective Frontier, there was growing urgency to manage results at the intersection of growth and ROIC.

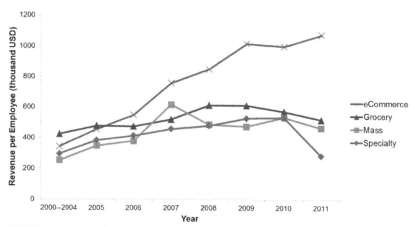

FIGURE 5.1   Rise of e-Commerce over the Past Decade
Averages calculated for retail companies with net sales exceeding USD$5 billion in FY 2011.
Source: Supply Chain Insights LLC, Corporate Annual Reports (2000–2011).

TABLE 5.4   Retail Barriers by Segment

Top Three Challenges Regarding Physical Store Performance			
	Grocery	Mass Merchant	Specialty
Consistency in store operations	59%	55%	39%
Rising cost of store labor and turnover of employees	50%	61%	45%
Price management	66%	36%	42%
Doing different better: a unique banner strategy that can be executed effectively against a targeted demographic	38%	30%	24%
Show-rooming: consumers coming to the store to compare prices and see items but not buying	3%	24%	33%
Changing needs of store format requirements based on cross-channel competition	19%	30%	18%
Defining the right store formats based on demand insight data	13%	21%	18%
Changing trip types and the design of the store to meet these changing needs	13%	9%	12%
Determining the right metrics for the store based on channel convergence	13%	18%	6%

Base: Retailers and have physical stores and know how many—Grocery (*n* = 32), Mass Merchants (*n* = 33), Specialty (*n* = 33). *Note:* Base too small to show "Other" industries. Q15: What are your company's top three challenges when it comes to physical store performance? Please select no more than three.
Source: Supply Chain Insights LLC, Role of the Store Study (August 2012–May 2013).

When we applied Jeff's methodology to the retail sector in Table 5.5, we find that very few companies were able to make improvements in strength or balance over the period. Retailers struggled over the past decade to be resilient. The push was on suppliers to close the margin gaps, infuse excitement into the store, and improve inventory turns.

At this point, Angela summarized her evaluation, "The most successful retailers adopted new formats. At the beginning of the decade there was very little emphasis on the club or the dollar format stores but, looking at the rankings, almost all of the successful retailers had adopted new format stores." The group agreed.

As Jeff reached for his coffee, he also commented, "Look at the shifts in the drug channel. I love what these stores have done. When my kids are sick, and I need to get a few items, I can easily get what I need while I am waiting for a prescription, and their loyalty programs reward me for my shopping, unlike the traditional supermarket."

TABLE 5.5 The Index: Retail

Company	2013 Revenue (billions USD)	Balance	Balance Ranking	Strength	Strength Ranking	Resiliency	Resiliency Ranking	Index (0.3B + 0.3S + 0.3R)	Ranking
Dollar General Corp.	16.0	−0.06	5	0.10	3	0.51	5	3.9	1
Costco Wholesale Corporation	105.2	−0.04	4	0.01	6	0.46	4	4.2	2
J Sainsbury PLC	36.9	0.75	1	0.22	1	3.23	13	4.5	3
Walmart Stores, Inc.	469.2	0.00	3	0.01	7	0.70	6	4.8	4
The Kroger Co.	96.8	0.01	2	0.04	4	1.87	10	4.8	4
Target Corporation	73.3	−0.07	6	0.01	8	0.24	3	5.1	6
Kphl' Corporation	19.3	−0.13	7	−0.03	9	0.20	2	5.4	7
CVS Caremark Corporation	126.8	−0.13	9	0.17	2	1.73	9	6.0	8
Walgreen Company	72.2	−0.17	10	0.04	5	0.84	7	6.6	9
Sears Holdings Corporation	39.9	−0.43	13	−0.22	14	0.19	1	8.4	10
Canadian Tire Corporation Limited	11.5	−0.13	8	−0.06	11	2.78	12	9.3	11
Safeway Inc.	36.1	−0.81	14	−0.05	10	1.05	8	9.6	12
Marks and Spencer Group PLC	15.8	−0.20	11	−0.06	12	2.12	11	10.2	13
Tesco PLC	102.9	−0.22	12	−0.11	13	3.63	14	11.7	14

Source: Supply Chain Insights LLC, Corporate Annual Reports 2006–2013.

"Yes," I commented. "As e-commerce channels grew, companies struggled to redefine the role of the store." The group continued the discussion on formats, loyalty programs, and in-store programs. Everyone in the group could relate to the shifts in the retail sector, and the concentration and energy in the room was becoming palpable.

Angela then asked, "Was the retail industry able to improve the economies of scale by adding stores or consolidating?" We then took a closer look at the industry trends.

Examining the Economies of Scale for the Retailer

I nodded my head in affirmation and showed Angela the data in Figures 5.2 and 5.3. Large retailers, greater than $5 billion in revenue, were more successful than smaller retailers. Larger retailers had higher margins and greater resiliency, but they were not able to achieve the same level of inventory turns.

As we will see in most industries, the larger the size of a company, the greater the advantages gained from the economies of scale. As a result, the average values for margin and revenue per employee become more favorable.

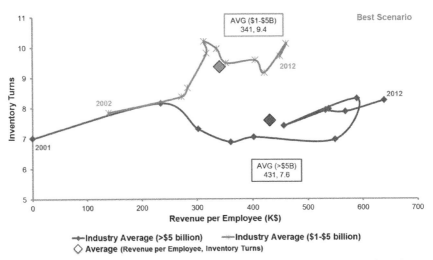

FIGURE 5.2 Retail: Inventory Turns versus Operating Margin: 2000–2012 (Comparison of Companies Greater Than $5 Billion in Revenue and $1–$5 Billion in Revenue)
Industry Average composed of public companies (NAICS code 452%, where % is any number from 0 to 9) reporting in One Source with 2012 annual sales greater than $5 billion and $1–$5 billion, excluding outliers.
Source: Supply Chain Insights LLC, Corporate Annual Reports 2001–2012.

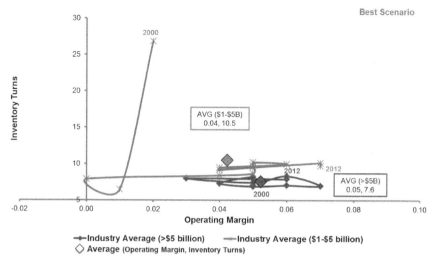

FIGURE 5.3 Retail: Inventory Turns versus Revenue per Employee: 2001–2012 (Comparison of Companies Greater Than $5 Billion in Revenue and $1–$5 Billion in Revenue)
Industry Average composed of public companies (NAICS code 452%, where % is any number from 0 to 9) reporting in One Source with 2012 annual sales greater than $5 billion and $1–$5 billion.
Source: Supply Chain Insights LLC, Corporate Annual Reports 2000–2012.

However, as we will see in the evaluation of the index, the ability to drive balance on inventory is often easier for a small company versus a larger one. While the ability to make progress on the Effective Frontier is more difficult for a larger company, requiring a greater focus and leadership.

Edgar spoke, "In my experience, the larger the company, the more difficult it is to achieve balance and alignment. The functional silos are difficult to penetrate. I have found out the hard way that it is even more important in a larger organization to do some of the things that we spoke about at our last session, like clarifying the operating strategy and building strong horizontal processes." He then motioned to Frank, "The larger the company, the more important it is for the organization to be clear about who is the customer and align sales with the channel. I think that this was one of the issues with retail. They became confused, thinking the store was the customer instead of the shopper filling the basket."

When I put up the next slide (Figure 5.2), Lou groaned. He said, "Look at that see-saw line between operating margin and inventory turns for these smaller companies in retail. I would have hated to manage those earnings calls."

"Yes," said Filipe. "Their processes were just not as mature as the larger companies."

The group then engaged in a great discussion on resiliency and efficiency. They noted that all mass merchant retailers were able to improve efficiency, but that they were not able to power the same level of improvement on inventory turns.

Lou commented, "These companies would like for their corporate performance on margin and inventory turns to look like their progress on revenue per employee on the second chart. Isn't it strange that all of the business magazines would lead you to believe that we have made linear progress on these metrics when we have not?" Everyone agreed with Lou.

As Frank finished texting a message to one of his star performers on a team that was closing a contract, he commented, "Yes, if you believed all of the signs in the airports, you would see a very different picture. The retailers really put the squeeze on me when I was a supplier. Their standards got tougher and tougher throughout the decade. They killed me if I missed an on-time delivery. They really stressed reliability in performance. I would never have known that they were struggling with reliability issues of their own."

"Yes, and I am sure that you put the squeeze on the guys in operations as well. Right, Frank?" Joe said with a wink.

As voiced by Mike Laflamme, from Vermont Country Store, on-time delivery is the most important metric for a supplier to drive improvement in the retailer relationship.

Interview with Mike Laflamme, Vermont Country Store

Today "The Vermont Country Store," is a United-States-based catalog, retail, and e-commerce business based in Vermont. There are physical stores in Weston and Rockingham, Vermont, a company headquarters in Manchester, and a distribution facility and customer service center in North Clarendon.

The Vermont Country Store is family-owned by seventh- and eighth-generation Vermonters, and fourth- and fifth-generation storekeepers, who still adhere to old-fashioned values. They pride themselves in being the "Purveyors of the Practical and Hard-to-Find." They go to great lengths to find goods that are not sold in other places. And each and every item is backed up with a no-hassle, no-fuss 100 percent guarantee to deliver quality products.

Mike, tell us about you.

I manage a small supply chain team in Vermont in the northern part of the United States. We manage the supply network for the Vermont Country Store. Previously, I managed Manufacturing, Commercialization, and Global Quality at L.L. Bean. I have enjoyed working in manufacturing and as a part of the retail supply chain for almost 40 years.

Which metrics do you think matter and why?

Many metrics should be considered disposable. Organizations that keep the same metrics tend to come to a standstill. Most people have a hard time connecting how their performance ties to the bottom line. Profit and process should be very fluid as the situation evolves.

The hardest part of determining metrics is to choose 10 to 12 metrics that fit their business and serve to align the organization's efforts toward the company's strategic goals. People who try to go with generic metrics that do not represent your business fail. I prefer very industry-specific metrics.

For example, 50 percent of returned items in apparel come back for fit. I track the ratio of fit returns for too large and too small. Getting this to a one-to-one ratio means that the fit is consistent. At this point we can begin to refine measurement specifications to lower returns and improve the customer's experience with the product. For a company like L.L. Bean, the returns are worth millions of dollars. Managing a retail supply chain can mean managing hundreds of vendors. I built a vendor scorecard to more effectively communicate a vendor's performance and align the vendor and the retailer to a performance improvement plan.

For my suppliers, I focus on measuring:

- *Productivity.* It is as simple as dollars produced/dollars spent.
- *Customer satisfaction.* I try to align the metrics around how customers see value.
- *Net sales.* I adjust for the returns.

How have the metrics changed over time?

Financial metrics do not move that much. Process metrics are the ones that are going to drive all of the work in metrics systems. Let me give you an example. Sometimes a simple, but useful, process metric is the pounds of waste that leave a facility each day.

I can tell if a factory is good or not by walking through it. I manage a large amount of vendors, so therefore the measurements have to be simple and clearly understood by all.

(continued)

(*continued*)

I don't believe in metrics encyclopedias. Instead, I think that you pick them carefully and well. Which is harder, picking the right metrics or being patient? I think that it is about persevering. If you own the metric, you can be more patient.

Impact of Collaboration in the Consumer Value Network

"VMI programs were developed in the 1980s as a collaborative program between retailers and suppliers," I told the team. "The first work was by Walmart in the 1980s through the use of Walmart's Retail Link. I was a participant in some of the original pilots. At that time, the focus was just to get started. We had high hopes to reduce total costs and improve inventories.

"However, we lost focus on our original goals. Many used it as a way to shift costs. In time, other retailers followed suit and asked their suppliers to participate in a VMI program. Over many years, major retailers reduced their reliance on the program, but smaller retailers increased participation, primarily to shift the cost of labor from the retailer to the supplier."

"These programs were hard to implement," Frank added. "We had to get the data and establish the programs. They drove us hard to comply. For many, it was a condition of doing business. It was as hard to get it started in my own organization as in the retailer that I was selling to. As a result, we implemented the programs in the sales organization. We operated as an island. We didn't care if it connected to our enterprise systems. We just needed to get the program started."

Angela said, "Are you surprised that it didn't improve inventory turns?"

"Yes," said Frank. "For all the trouble that these programs were, you would have hoped that we would have seen greater improvement."

I then continued, "In parallel, to improve customer service and on-time delivery, retailers started measuring performance. The first scorecard was operational in nature with a laser-focus on improving on-time shipments. Over time, additional scorecards were added. Today, the average supplier to retailer has three scorecards, and few of the scorecards tie performance to buying behavior.

"Today, these collaborative efforts are in their third decade. Most of the processes have been inherited. Despite the evolution of new forms of technologies, they have not been redesigned."

The research I shared with the group is in the following feature.

Impact of Scorecards

True collaboration is about the right balance of the carrot and the stick. Progress happens when companies measure progress in relationships over many years. Improvements happen faster when there is more carrot than stick. Over the past decade, scorecards have become more of a stick than a carrot.

Consumer value networks are now in their second decade of scorecard automation. The most common one is a scorecard for supply chain. Today the focus is on physical movement. As shown in Figure 5.4 and Table 5.6, most of the improvements are better labeling, improved performance with on-time shipments, and the use of Advanced Shipment Notification (ASN) documentation. Each element of the value network has improved through the use of scorecards. However, it has not reduced the cost of shipments.

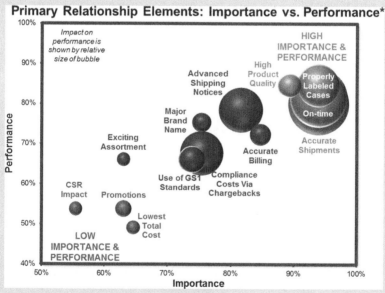

FIGURE 5.4 Benefit of Retail Scorecards
Base: Manufacturers and Retailers Who Work with Retail Scorecards (where retailer evaluates supplier) (*n* = 58).
Q16. When you think about your primary [supplier]-[retailer] relationship, how important is each of the elements listed? SCALE: 1 = Not at all important, 7 = Extremely important (Rated 5–7 on 7-point scale).

(continued)

(continued)

Q17. How would you rate your primary [supplier]-[retailer] relationship on each of these same areas? SCALE: 1 = Poor, 7 = Excellent (Rated 5–7 on 7-point scale).

Q18. Please pick the three areas where scorecards have had the greatest positive impact on your primary [supplier's][retailer's] performance. Please pick no more than three.

Source: Supply Chain Insights LLC, Retail Scorecards Study (January–June 2014).

TABLE 5.6 Impact of Retail Scorecards

Primary Supplier/Retailer Relationship Elements			
	Importance*	Performance*	Top 3 Impact
On-time performance	93%	82%	63%
Accurate shipments	93%	82%	58%
Properly labeled cases	93%	86%	33%
High product quality	90%	88%	11%
Accurate billing with no deductions	86%	72%	9%
Advanced shipment notifications	79%	77%	33%
Management of compliance costs via chargebacks	76%	67%	32%
Major brand name	74%	75%	7%
Use of GS1 or other standards	71%	63%	12%
Lowest total cost	66%	49%	2%
Excitement in assortment	62%	67%	4%
Promotions to stimulate demand	60%	53%	5%
CSR impact	53%	54%	4%

Base: Manufacturers and Retailers Who Work with Retail Scorecards (where retailer evaluates supplier) (*n* = 58).

*Importance and Performance = Rated 5–7 on 7-point scale.

Q16: When you think about your primary [supplier][retailer] relationship, how important is each of the elements listed? SCALE: 1 = Not at all important, 7 = Extremely important.

Q17: How would you rate your primary [supplier][retailer] relationship on each of these same areas? SCALE: 1 = Poor, 7 = Excellent.

Q18: Please pick the three areas where scorecards have had the greatest positive impact on the your primary [supplier's][retailer's] performance.

Source: Supply Chain Insights LLC, Retail Scorecards Study (January–April 2014).

Not only have they not improved costs, but they also have not improved corporate social responsibility (CSR), merchandising, or cost-to-serve. Today, they are anything but balanced.

The barrier to driving greater improvements is functional alignment within both the retailer and the manufacturing organization. The gaps in the retailer are between merchandising and operations, and the gaps for consumer products are between sales and operations.

Frank chewed on his pen. He winced. It was hard for him to accept that retail scorecards had improved on-time delivery, but not total cost. We had a great discussion about why this had happened. Frank then asked me to share the research on the VMI programs that he had helped to pilot while at P&G. Frank had difficulty accepting that there was no lasting impact on operating margins or inventory turns.

I then shifted to share the VMI research. We discussed the impact of VMI on the consumer value network.

The consumer value chain is the most mature in the use of VMI programs. They have been adopted by many industries to shift inventories from buyer to seller. At this point, Filipe was very interested. To him, VMI was an extension of Lean thinking—a virtual kanban—connecting two parties driving a pull-based form of replenishment. He was sure that the VMI programs and improved data sharing had improved value, but was surprised when I shared the following research.

The concepts of vendor managed inventory were defined in the 1980s. At the beginning of the pilots, there was a strong focus on the building of end-to-end supply chains (E2E).

At that time, the conference circuit in the consumer value chain was buzzing. The terms *collaboration, efficient consumer response (ECR), VMI,* and *collaborative planning, forecasting, and replenishment (CPFR)* filled the air. There was a flurry of promises. The concepts were en vogue. The models were right, but the execution was flawed. The processes were overhyped and companies rushed head-over-heels to join the throng.

The missing gap? They were implemented between a buyer and a seller as part of the transfer of goods. The relationships were not redefined to sense demand. As a result, many well-intentioned sales teams adopted the VMI programs.

Today, the average consumer packaged goods (CPG) company has 11 VMI relationships and six VMI planners. The programs are not growing.

(continued)

(continued)

They are not contracting. Instead, they are caught between sales-driven and supply-driven processes. In the value chain today, we have stasis.

While initial programs focused on large accounts, today's VMI programs focus on the drug and dollar retail channels. There are few VMI programs left with the major players of Publix, Safeway, Target, and Walmart. As a result, today companies are shipping fewer and fewer cases using VMI processes.

The VMI programs operate as on an island. Few companies are actively working on the building of E2E processes, outside-in, connecting the flows of VMI. Ironically, while it is connected to the outside world, it isn't well-connected to the manufacturer's enterprise systems. Most companies' demand-planning systems do not allow easy integration of retail data, and the connection to the planning systems requires an unwanted redesign that most companies try to avoid.

Reflections

We are now entering our fourth decade of managing VMI processes. Most of the programs have been inherited. The teams that were running them were not part of the overhyped exuberance.

The teams now running them are heads-down working and in management mode. Most of the VMI processes report through customer service. The technologies are fixed and the processes are tried-and-true. These teams are not actively trying to design end-to-end flows or synchronize the VMI programs with other demand signals. VMI has become a reliable part of the order flow.

A Head-Scratcher

In the research we completed, the average company using VMI reduced the costs of transportation by 3 percent and reduced the order cycle time by at least a day. And, as shown in Figure 5.5, the orders are cleaner and more reliable. Customer service levels improve. So why, if the process reduces costs and improves order cycle times and order reliability, are we not driving greater adoption? The answer lies in the fact that the program is juxtaposed between the opposing forces of sales and supply. When companies become market-driven and understand the differences between a sales-driven approach and a market-driven value chain, the processes take on greater value. The mapping of flows outside-in and horizontally across the company enables greater value.

FIGURE 5.5 VMI Performance
Base: Those in consumer packaged goods or food & beverage industry, familiar with VMI processes at company.
*VMI relationship most familiar with.
Q9. How would you rate the VMI relationship you are most familiar with on each of these supply chain components, compared to your non-VMI relationships? Is the VMI relationship better, the same, or worse than the non-VMI relationships? SCALE: 1 = VMI is much worse, 7 = VMI is much better.
Source: Supply Chain Insights LLC, Vendor Managed Inventory Study (December 2013–April 2014).

Frank hung his head, and said, "I get it. I implemented the VMI and scorecard programs to work to the advantage of sales, not to serve the larger organization. I, like many well-intentioned sales teams, implemented the programs to be very sales-driven."

Summary

The team wrote a summary of their key insights on the board. The goal was to do this for each industry that we studied. At the end of the workshop, the team was going to use all of these insights to build the roadmap for their 'future state' of Project Orbit. They listed the following on the board:

Seize new opportunities. As technologies evolve, new opportunities arise. The retailers that were the most aggressive in adapting to new formats performed the best on the Effective Frontier.

Break down silos. E-commerce was a fundamental shift. Functional silos can be an obstacle to adaptation. Leadership is essential to break them down.

Redesign relationships. The collaborative practices of VMI and scorecards could have been used to radically improve the value network. Instead, they became embedded into sales-driven practices with minimal positive impact. Retailers were slow to adopt their practices.

We then moved on to discuss consumer packaged goods (CPG) and food and beverage companies. I opened by stating, "While both CPG and food companies are suppliers to retail, their performance on the Effective Frontier is quite different."

Consumer Packaged Goods

Consumer products companies want to grow. Today, progress is stalled. Companies can either grow though expansion into new markets, the launch of new products, or merger and acquisition (M&A). At a corporate growth rate slightly higher than the gross domestic product (GDP), the cost of new products is escalating. The R&D investment to bring a new product to market is roughly four times the cost that it was five years ago.

New Product Launch

Success in new product launch and trade promotions is critical to accomplish this goal. Sales of new products represent 17 percent of total cases shipped. New product shipments increased 10 percent over the past three years. Along with the increase in new products, seasonality and promoted item volume escalated. There was a major impact on forecast accuracy. How? New products and promoted items have four to five times the bias of turn volume. Products in the long tail of the supply chain have an average error of 70 percent mean absolute percent error (MAPE) and a 15 percent bias.[3]

The challenges are also greater. Product innovation is becoming more targeted while supply chain complexity is rising. Let's examine the challenges more closely, starting with some definitions. A New Product Pacesetter is a measure published by IRI/Symphony group for the United States market. IRI is a syndicated data provider to the consumer products industry. The company defines a New Product Pacesetter as a product that is able to reach $7.5 million in sales during the first year of introduction in U.S. grocery stores.

In 2012, based on the IRI reporting, 1,900 new products hit the shelves. Of them, 77 products achieved New Product Pacesetter status. The average net new revenue of a New Product Pacesetter in the first year was $39.5 million. But, what was the cost? When we take the R&D budgets of companies for 2012 and divide them by the number of new products reaching New Product Pacesetter status, we find that the average cost of a New Product Pacesetter for the average CPG company in 2012 was $71 million.

As shown in Figure 5.6, when you compare R&D annual spending to the number of New Product Pacesetters brought to market, there is a wide range of corporate performance. Revlon, over the period of 1997–2012, has the best performance and Kimberly-Clark has the worst. While it isn't prudent to compare a global competitor like P&G, Unilever, or Nestlé to a more regional player like General Mills or Kellogg, when you compare the companies based on geographic reach, there are clear patterns. For all, bringing a new product to market is more expensive (and this does not include the marketing and advertising spend or the extra sales support).

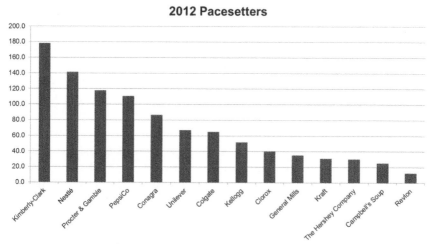

FIGURE 5.6 Cost of a New Product

2012 Pacesetter Performance: Number of New Pacesetters in 2012/R&O Spend for 2012.

Source of Pacesetter Data: Symphony IRI Group. *Source of R&D Data:* Corporate balance sheets.

The expense to bring a new product to market (R&D/Number of New Product Pacesetter Products) for the period of 1997–2010 was $15 million.

Supply Chain Costs Are Rising

Supply chain costs to bring a new product to market are also climbing: Progress on operating margin is stalled in 9 out of 10 industry sectors. One of the issues is rising complexity. In the period of 2011–2012, nearly 1,900 new consumer brands hit retail shelves in North America representing $1 trillion in net new annual sales. The average sales of a new product, over the past four years, have a downward trend. New products are becoming more targeted.[4]

It is harder to forecast a new product than a stable product. A forecast error for a new product is often 70–80%. As a result, it becomes more important to sense channel sales, and to build demand networks.

Review of Progress of Consumer Packaged Goods Companies

When I paused, Frank grinned mischievously. He said, "Okay, you may think that I am slow and even a bit obstinate, but I am getting the picture. So, there are now more products in consumer value chains, and growth is slower and tougher. We talked about collaboration, but it is questionable if the companies that worked together drove value."

He continued, "VMI and retail scorecards helped us improve shipments to our customers, but were not a panacea. Each of these programs could have had even greater impact if we had been smarter to not be *so* sales-driven and if we had connected them to market-driven initiatives." Then he asked me, "Can you share how the companies in Consumer Products performed in the same period? I want to show the group how well P&G did against competitors. I am quite proud of the work that we did there."

I prepared the group to view the progress of the consumer value network for the period of 2006–2013 as shown in Table 5.7. I reminded them that this chart reflected positive change on the three criteria. The CPG group made the greatest progress on growth and ROIC. They were also the most resilient.

We then had a long discussion about the list in Table 5.7. While P&G had made progress on Unilever and other competitors at the beginning of the decade, in the latter part of the decade the relationships reversed. As complexity increased, it became more difficult for the company to maintain balance at the intersection of operating margin and inventory turns. As a result, the company experienced a degradation on operating margin during the five-year period 2008–2013. With the retirement of the supply chain leadership team in 2009, the new leadership group at P&G had a more singular focus on inventory. This threw the supply chain out of balance, enabling other companies to

TABLE 5.7 Supply Chain Index: Consumer Packaged Goods

Company	2013 Revenue (billions USD)	Balance	Balance Ranking	Strength	Strength Ranking	Resiliency	Resiliency Ranking	Index (0.3B + 0.3S + 0.3R)	Ranking
Estèe Lauder Companies Inc.	10.2	0.17	1	0.05	6	0.21	5	3.6	1
Beiersdorf AG	8.2	−0.04	4	0.06	5	0.19	3	3.6	1
L'orèal S.A.	30.5	−0.05	5	0.00	12	0.19	2	5.7	3
Colgate-Palmolive Company	17.4	−0.09	8	0.02	8	0.20	4	6.0	4
Church & Dwight Co., Inc.	3.2	−0.08	7	0.09	2	0.66	12	6.3	5
Scotts Miracle–Gro Co.	2.8	−0.10	10	0.07	4	0.61	11	7.5	6
The Clorox Co.	5.6	−0.01	3	0.00	13	0.59	10	7.8	7
Unilever N.V.	66.1	−0.12	11	0.07	3	1.00	14	8.4	8
British American Tobacco PLC	23.9	−0.10	9	−0.01	14	0.30	6	8.7	9
Kimberly Clark Corp	21.2	−0.17	15	0.04	7	0.48	8	9.0	10
Reckitt Benckiser Group PLC	15.7	−0.14	12	0.01	10	0.56	9	9.3	11
Imperial Tobacco Group PLC	44.1	−0.45	17	0.28	1	1.09	15	9.9	12
The Valspar Corporation	4.1	−0.08	6	0.00	11	1.12	16	9.9	12
Avon Rubber PLC	10.0	−0.38	16	−0.08	16	0.18	1	9.9	12
Kao Corporation	13.5	−0.16	13	−0.02	15	0.40	7	10.5	15
Lorillard, Inc.	7.0	−0.06	2	−0.10	17	3.56	17	10.8	16
The Procter & Gamble Company	84.2	−0.16	14	0.01	9	0.68	13	10.8	16

Source: Supply Chain Insights LLC, Corporate Annual Reports 2006–2013.

outpace their progress. As a result, in the peer group, P&G ends up next to last. In contrast, Unilever made progress in both growth and strength, but wasn't resilient. A quieter, and less mentioned, competitor is Colgate. The more balanced approach for Colgate, supported by a strong finance team in operations, helped the company to outpace competitors. Another interesting example is Beiersdorf. A company rich in cash reached balance by collaborating with the sales team to improve customer service. The operational leader convinced the company that a reduction in inventory would improve customer service. His belief was that excess inventory insulated the company from the channel and made them less responsive. He was right. The reduction in inventory improved customer service while reducing costs.

Filipe commented that it was now becoming clearer to him why companies needed to work holistically to drive balance. He was amazed at the impact of product complexity on P&G's progress. Frank hung his head. He had been part of the group that had pushed for greater product proliferation in the regions.

Angela then asked if there was the same economy of scale of larger companies driving better performance in CPG. I answered, "Yes. We see some of the greatest economies of scale in consumer products companies." Then I showed her Figures 5.7 and 5.8.

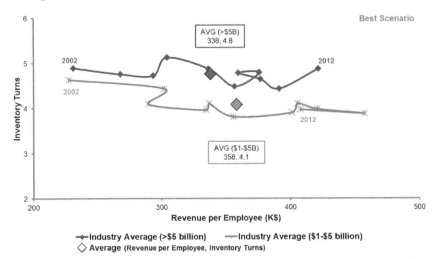

FIGURE 5.7 Consumer Packaged Goods: Inventory Turns versus Operating Margin: 2002–2012 (Comparison of Companies Greater Than $5 Billion in Revenue and $1–$5 Billion in Revenue)

Industry Average composed of public companies (NAICS code 3256%, w % is any number from 0 to 9) reporting in One Source with 2012 annual sales greater than $5 billion, $1–$5 billion, $500 million–$1 billion.

Source: Supply Chain Insights LLC, Corporate Annual Reports 2002–2012.

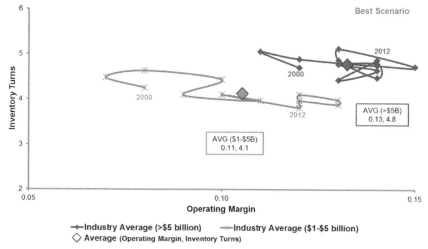

FIGURE 5.8 Consumer Packaged Goods: Inventory Turns versus Revenue per Employee: 2000–2012 (Comparison of Companies Greater Than $5 Billion in Revenue and $1–$5 Billion in Revenue)

Industry Average composed of public companies (NAICS code 3256%, where % is any number from 0 to 9) reporting in One Source with 2012 annual sales greater than $5 billion and $1–$5 billion.

Source: Supply Chain Insights LLC, Corporate Annual Reports 2000–2012.

Filipe and Joe then started the discussion of how larger companies have driven better performance on the Effective Frontier, but with a slower rate of change. They also commented about the lack of resiliency in the past three years. The reversal of the operating margin gains surprised them.

As a large company with many initiatives, they talked quite a bit about the slippage of P&G in driving improvement. The group wanted to understand more. They were eager to see how Kraft, Nestlé, BASF, and Dow Chemical performed.

Edgar wanted more. He asked if I had any case studies from operations leaders that had managed the value chain in this period. I then shared these two case studies: first, a small, scrappy start-up, Seventh Generation, and a case study and interview with Rick Sather, vice president of Customer Supply Chain for Kimberly-Clark.

I shared that I thought both companies were leaders, but in different ways. Seventh Generation was doing some great work with supplier scorecards to improve the carbon footprint of the product while Kimberly-Clark is a leader in building outside-in processes to drive growth through the channel. The following features show the two case studies that I shared.

Interview with John Replogle, President and CEO at Seventh Generation

Seventh Generation is a consumer products company focused on the manufacturing of socially responsible cleaning products. Established in 1988, the privately held, independent company distributes to natural food stores, supermarkets, mass merchants, and through e-commerce channels.

John, tell us about Seventh Generation.

We manufacture socially responsible solutions for your home, your family, and your environment that protect and nurture your well-being today. By doing this, we want to open the door to a more sustainable world for generations yet to come. By making conscious choices, we believe the earth will return the favor and continue to care for us, too. We want to care for the seven generations of tomorrow. How do we do this? It's really quite simple. In caring for the future, we believe we are creating brighter solutions for right now.

When you think about operations excellence, which metrics matter to you?

I think that it is a balance across four elements: corporate sustainability, quality, cost, and people.

What does corporate sustainability mean to Seventh Generation?

For us, corporate sustainability is at the core of what we do. We think about the impact of the supply chain on our core carbon footprint in everything we do. We are always thinking about our impact on the environment.

To improve our performance, we do a detailed scorecard for each supplier. We evaluate their operations and the carbon footprint of their manufacturing processes. We also evaluate their impact on corporate social responsibility, based on miles traveled in transportation. We measure their operations and efficiency and evaluate their employment practices. We set joint goals with them.

It takes patience. We have worked closely with them over the years. We now talk a common language and we drive incentives for doing the right thing versus leveraging penalties for doing the wrong thing. What the suppliers have come to realize is that a metrics-based management approach creates value. We jointly drive costs out of the system with a sustainability impact. We have had lots of fits and starts over the years, but I think that we now have it right.

It starts with a top-to-top relationship. You have to have a shared belief with your supplier base. If you start there, you can make the metrics work. If this isn't the initial predisposition, nothing will really drive the outcome that you want. So, we have to drive what we want and define the core values.

Quality

When it comes to quality, we ask ourselves a couple of questions. Have we improved the quality of the products? And are we delivering quality service to our customers? We want all of our shipments to be on time and shipped in full.

Cost

When it comes to cost, we are continuously seeking ways to improve. The method is to drive cost/unit price down through operational programs. It is important to measure all of the cost drivers and continuously refine the processes to drive improvement.

People

A core metric for us is safety. We want to continuously improve the growth and capabilities of the team. Our focus is on culture and coaching to move us forward.

Consistency matters. As much as a team might be tempted to play with the metrics, I have learned that it is important to be consistent. Consistency drives clarity. We are attending to the long view and drive the connection between metrics back to our operations. We believe that it is summed up by a triple bottom-line: people, planet, and profit.

Transforming Kimberly-Clark and Improving the Metrics That Matter

Interview with Rick Sather, Vice President of Customer Supply Chain, Kimberly-Clark

Kimberly-Clark has 58,000 employees working in manufacturing facilities in 37 countries. The focus is on the selling of consumer products like

(continued)

(continued)

Huggies, Kleenex, Kotex, Pull-ups, and Scott Paper Towels to consumers in more than 175 countries. The company had over $21 billion in sales in 2012 and ranked first in the personal care category of the Dow Jones Sustainability Index World (DJSI World) for five consecutive years.

Rick, let's start with which metrics you think matter and why.

I would like to start with the basics up front. It is all about the management of the product in the channel. The in-stock position at the shelf at the point of purchase is a key measurement. Then it is a measurement of cost through the supply network, and the third metric that is important is inventory, or the cash-conversion cycle for both you and your customers. We have been focused on driving these three outcomes for our customers in the network. It means that you have to go beyond the traditional cost/unit, inventory, and customer service metric that is defined by you, and set joint goals with your customers.

How has your perspective changed?

It is an evolution. First, it takes time. Some customers still measure us on fill-rate or on-time delivery, and have difficulty focusing on in-stock at the shelf. We are working together to improve that outcome, but it is a shift.

Second, it is a balancing act. You cannot focus on one metric at the expense of another. It needs to be about sales growth, operating profit, and gross margin. If you do not balance these correctly, it will cause a decline in performance of the metrics that really matter.

In the past, there were periods where we pressed inventory beyond the potential of the network and it adversely affected service. So, it made us ask the question, "How do we build the potential of the business to drive it in the right direction?" As a result, our focus has been a forward-looking vision with strong business planning based on business outcomes.

Within the company, we have a strong sales and operations planning (S&OP) process that is based on a broad view of measures across the business that can connect the outcome. It evolved over time. Our focus has been to create metrics underneath the process to connect functions. First our focus was on us. Then it changed to focus on the customer and joint planning.

There is still opportunity for consumer products companies and retailers to align. It takes strong discipline. And, asking ourselves constantly, "Are we doing what we said that we would do?"

How do you feel about your performance as compared to your peer group?

When we look at financial reports, we can see sales growth and cash conversion, but we cannot see a comparison on service. On the service side, when we compare results at the retailers, we find that we are in the top quartile.

Our progress with inventory and costs is tougher. If you look at inventory efficiency, we are similar to our peer group. And we have made progress on the cash conversion cycle.

What have you learned?

We are treating flows in a differentiated way. Should you focus on output metrics or the input metrics that drive it? We have found that it needs to be on the measurement of inputs. In this process, we need to be forward-looking with a focus on root-cause analysis or the trail gets cold very quickly.

The personal lesson I have learned is to start small and learn fast. I want to get information every day to drive a different type of conversation. For example, we had a damage rate of three cases per 1,000 cases handled. No matter what we did, the difference did not change much. However, when we went from a monthly view of the data to a weekly view to a daily view, we saw change. Last month, we had our record lowest damage rate. We have cut it by 50 percent and now we have cut it another 33 percent.

So, my insight is that it isn't just about the metrics. It is about the frequency and consistency of your attention on what you measure that makes a difference. It is about how frequently I can look at data and hone it down to the root cause. I think that the secret of leaders is driving the power of people to get engaged in the process. I look at my distribution metrics daily. I get one scorecard, and then I delete it. It frees me up to think strategically. I have empowered the employees to act on the scorecard.

Summary

When I asked the team to summarize their insights, Frank spoke first. He said, "Never assume that a company is a leader. Analyze, analyze, analyze the data before assuming." I then handed Frank the marker so he could write down the insights from the group on this part of the session. He wrote:

> When CPG companies lost power over the last decade, they pursued an aggressive M&A strategy, built global product strategies, and launched a set of new product launch initiatives.

The industry peer group has some of the highest margins and the lowest inventory turns of the value network.

They have not been less aggressive in the adoption of e-commerce strategies and adapting to new retail formats. The focus on traditional marketing and sales programs has been a barrier to building effective demand networks and powering greater channel growth.

The focus on new product introduction and the added complexity from item proliferation has been detrimental to the metrics that matter.

Joe smiled. He was enjoying the session. He felt that the team was now getting a much clearer picture of how to benchmark corporate performance and align the metrics that matter.

Food and Beverage

The food and beverage company is smaller, more regional, and more susceptible to commodity variations than the consumer packaged goods company. While many companies will group CPG with food and beverage, they are distinctly different industry players.

While we spoke about the positive progress made by Beiersdorf, Colgate, and Unilever, when it came to the food and beverage industry, I spoke in great detail with the group about the work at Campbell's Soup and Hershey Foods. Both are great examples of successful implementations of market-driven initiatives. I shared how Campbell's had just completed a program to standardize their raw materials. Angela laughed when I told her that they used to have 33 different cuts of carrots, and how the leader of supply chain had worked with R&D to simplify the product portfolio to reduce the number of raw materials. This was important in a commodity-based business.

I also spoke about the great work at Hershey on improving operating margin and inventory turns. I shared that if they wanted to see the impact of successful planning, they should consider adopting the practices from Hershey. While the pressures from the board earlier in the decade created a compelling event for the Hershey team to come together and redefine processes, they were successful because of the culture that focuses on getting things done.

I cautioned the team that this was a partial list because it was difficult to fit all of the companies in the industry together onto one slide, since there are just too many.

I handed them the list of 33 companies. Edgar smiled; he loved getting this data and talking about real case studies. It also made him believe in the progress that his team could make with this new focus. He was friends with David Lyon from Wells, and was glad that I selected this as a case study. He loved the work that Wells had done with their suppliers to create a more sustainable product.

Angela spoke clearly, "The largest companies performed the worst. Kraft was resilient, but not balanced or strong, while Coca-Cola performed below average in all three categories." She wanted to know more about what drove the improvement at Hershey and Campbell's Soup. When I answered "no-nonsense discipline and leadership," Felipe smiled. The team was beginning to see the greater need for leadership to drive improvement in larger companies.

I then shared the case study and interview I had with David Lyons.

Orchestrating Market-to-Market at Wells Blue Bunny

Interview with David Lyons, Senior Vice President of Operations and Supply Chain at Wells Blue Bunny Ice Cream

Wells Enterprises, Inc. is the largest privately held, family-owned ice cream and frozen treat manufacturer in the United States. The company was founded in 1913 and is headquartered in Le Mars, Iowa. The company produces more than 150 million gallons of ice cream a year, including its signature brand, Blue Bunny, super-premium brand 2nd St. Creamery, and the iconic Bomb Pop. Wells also manufactures licensed frozen treat brands including Yoplait frozen yogurt and Weight Watchers frozen novelties. Products are sold at grocery, convenience, and club stores, on mobile vending trucks, and in foodservice settings (such as educational institutions, hospitals, and restaurants). The company's corporate office and two ice cream plants are located in Le Mars. Wells also operates an ice cream plant in St. George, Utah.

David, which metrics do you think matter and why?

I believe that the metrics that matter are the perfect order, the cash-to-cash cycle, and in the inbound sourcing scorecard. I have found that it is important to connect the operations performance to corporate performance outcomes.

I often see functions operating in silos because they are focused on functional, or siloed, metrics. I see metrics systems as a pyramid. At the bottom of the metrics hierarchy are the fundamentals and beliefs of the organization. It includes metrics like safety and quality, which are

(continued)

(*continued*)

nonnegotiable. At the top of the metrics hierarchy are the metrics that drive distinctive performance. All of the metrics have to be well documented and understood as you move up the pyramid. You also have to build capabilities in employees. It is easy to say that someone attended a course, but in my view, it is how they lead, the actions they take, that makes a difference.

What have you learned?

Our incentive programs were in constant flux. There is a balance between the metrics and among the metrics. When the company is performing well, the metrics systems work better. When the company isn't performing well, there is a tendency to put pressure on metrics that are at a suboptimal level. We have to resist this temptation.

Instead, the focus needs to be on coordination and balance. It is about alignment. My advice is to always avoid too many metrics. A company cannot focus on more than five to eight. So, in supply chain, I roll up what is important into five metrics that everyone understands.

Angela loved the fact that Seventh Generation, Wells, and Unilever had made progress faster than their peer groups while improving their carbon footprints. She also appreciated the supplier scorecard examples that I shared in the session.

Lou was mesmerized by the lack of resiliency of smaller food companies in Table 5.8. For him it was a strong wake-up call to implement market-driven orchestration in Sales and Operations Planning (S&OP). He was so inspired that he started a side conversation with Frank on the cost of sales and the effectiveness of promotions.

When we reviewed the charts that are shown here as Table 5.8, Figure 5.9, and Figure 5.10, Angela was intrigued that this was one industry where size had not translated into a competitive advantage. We began a discussion on how the mix and pack operations of food were less affected by economies of scale.

Summary

I asked the group if they could quickly summarize their key insights about the food value network before they went to break. They listed the following:

The more mature that you are on the Effective Frontier, the tougher it is to make progress. They noted that the food industry was a fast-follower to CPG.

The larger the company, the greater the need for leadership.

TABLE 5.8 Supply Chain Index: Food and Beverage

Company	2013 Revenue (billions USD)	Balance	Balance Ranking	Strength	Strength Ranking	Resiliency	Resiliency Ranking	Index (0.3B + 0.3S + 0.3R)	Ranking
Hershey Co.	7.1	0.28	2	0.02	11	0.54	7	6.0	1
Diageo PLC	17.9	0.05	6	0.00	14	0.08	1	6.3	2
Kraft Foods Group, Inc.	18.2	−0.20	17	0.19	3	0.27	2	6.6	3
Hillshire Brands Co.	3.9	5.82	1	0.52	7	2.36	20	6.6	3
H.J. Heinz Company	11.5	−0.13	13	0.05	8	0.51	6	8.1	5
The J.M. Smucker Company	5.9	0.06	5	0.03	9	0.73	13	8.1	5
Coca-Cola Enterprises, Inc.	8.2	0.09	4	0.24	2	4.98	21	8.1	5
General Mills, Inc.	17.8	0.15	3	0.00	15	0.65	10	8.4	8
Nestle SA	99.4	−0.14	14	0.03	10	0.36	5	8.7	9
Anheuser Busch inbev SA	43.2	0.00	8	0.18	4	1.51	18	9.0	10
Molson Coors Brewing Company	4.2	0.04	7	0.15	5	2.06	19	9.3	11
Mead Johnson Nutrition CO	4.2	−0.04	10	−0.05	20	0.32	3	9.9	12
Carlsberg A/S	11.8	−0.10	12	0.12	6	1.15	16	10.2	13
Kellogg Company	14.8	−0.05	11	0.02	12	0.73	12	10.5	14
The Coca-Cola Company	46.9	−0.29	18	0.00	13	0.61	9	12.0	15
PepsiCo	66.4	−0.18	16	−0.01	17	0.55	8	12.3	16
ConAgra Foods, Inc.	15.5	−0.41	20	0.09	7	0.77	14	12.3	16
SABMiller PLC	23.2	−0.14	15	−0.01	16	0.69	11	12.6	18
Campbell Soup Company	8.1	−0.86	21	−0.02	18	0.33	4	12.9	19
Maple Leaf Foods, Inc.	4.3	−0.01	9	−0.16	21	1.28	17	14.1	20
Danone SA	28.3	−0.31	19	−0.05	19	1.05	15	15.9	21

Source: Supply Chain Insights LLC, Corporate Annual Reports 2006–2013.

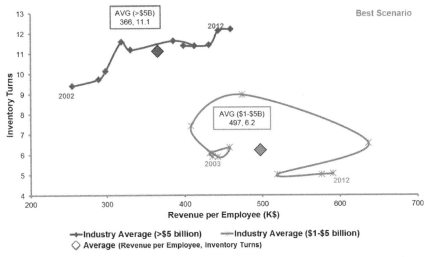

FIGURE 5.9 Food and Beverage Subset, Inventory Turns versus Operating Margin: 2002–2012 (Comparison of Companies Greater Than $5 Billion in Revenue and $1–$5 Billion in Revenue)
Industry Average composed of public companies (NAICS codes 311520 & 311941) reporting in One Source with 2012 annual sales greater than $5 billion and $1–$5 billion.
Source: Supply Chain Insights LLC, Corporate Annual Reports 2002–2012.

When commodity volatility is high, the need is greater for market-driven value network strategies.

Food and beverage companies had 30 percent less margin, but twice the inventory turns of CPG. The combination of commodity pressures and short life cycles made the management of inventory more important.

Joe cleared his throat to make a point. Before the group left for break, he mentioned that he was looking forward to hearing about the chemical industry. He had a lot of respect for BASF, and he was sure that they had made a lot of progress.

Chemical

After the break, the team's energy was still high. It was time for us to begin the discussion on chemical value chains.

The chemical companies are large, global, and asset-intensive. This process-driven industry sits three to five steps back in the value network. The companies are dependent on the sharing of demand signals from their

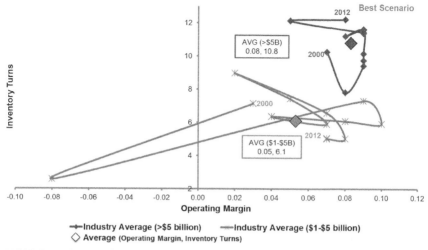

FIGURE 5.10   Food and Beverage Subset, Inventory Turns versus Revenue per Employee: 2000–2012 (Comparison of Companies Greater Than $5 Billion in Revenue and $1–$5 Billion in Revenue)
Industry Average composed of public companies (NAICS codes 311520 & 311941) reporting in One Source with 2012 annual sales greater than $5 billion and $1–$5 billion.
Source: Supply Chain Insights LLC, Corporate Annual Reports 2000–2012.

downstream partners in CPG and food and beverage. As companies recovered from the recession, they struggled with resiliency. As shown in Figure 5.11, the chemical industry is less resilient than any other in the consumer value chain.

Over the decade, chemical companies were squeezed for margin. No company in the consumer value network traded demand data and offered channel transparency of flows to help the chemical companies establish greater balance.

Lou coughed and then said, "What do you do in the case like this where the returns oscillate so much between operating margin and inventory turns?" I answered, "The further back in the value network that you are the more difficult it is to maintain resiliency. As a result, it becomes even more important to implement an operations strategy focused on improving agility, further focused on form and function of inventory, and building strong horizontal processes."

As we talked through Table 5.9, we had Lou's attention. He had always admired Dow. His question: Why was the Dow Corporation last on the list

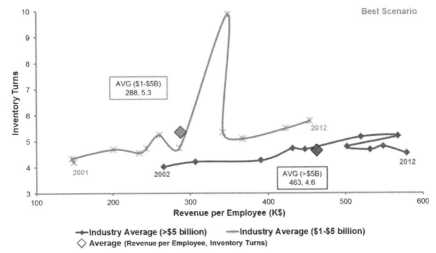

FIGURE 5.11   Chemical: Inventory Turns versus Operating Margin: 2001–2012 (Comparison of Companies Greater Than $5 Billion in Revenue and $1–$5 Billion in Revenue)
Industry Average composed of public companies (NAICS code 325188 & 325998) reporting in One Source with 2012 annual sales greater than $5 billion and $1–$5 billion.
Source: Supply Chain Insights LLC, Corporate Annual Reports 2001–2012.

while BASF, a much larger company, ranked so much higher? My answer was leadership. While BASF had consistency of leadership, the Dow Corporation had gone through many twists and turns through the Rohm and Haas acquisition and a number of large projects. The group's question was, "In an asset-intensive industry like the chemical peer group, was there a factor for economies of scale?" Lou's question was, "Does scale matter?"

I assured him that it did and showed him the next set of slides.

Chemical Company Economy of Scale

We then turned to Figure 5.12. It clearly shows the economy of scale. I assured him that the chemical industry had economy of scale like what we saw in the CPG industry. Angela said, "I get it. These companies struggle for resiliency, and the market-driven processes matter more than in other industries, but when they get it right, they have a scale advantage."

Joe was anxious to hear the BASF story. Robert Blackburn had spoken at a recent conference, and Joe was a fan. He smiled as I shared the story of BASF from the interview that I had done recently with Robert Blackburn.

TABLE 5.9 The Index: Chemical

Company	2013 Revenue (billions USD)	Balance	Balance Ranking	Strength	Strength Ranking	Resiliency	Resiliency Ranking	Index (0.3B + 0.3S + 0.3R)	Ranking
Monsanto Company	14.9	0.10	3	0.10	4	0.28	2	2.7	1
Celanese Corporation	6.5	0.04	5	0.16	2	1.06	11	5.4	2
Westlake Chemical Corporation	3.8	0.37	1	0.20	1	1.98	17	5.7	3
Givaudan S.A.	4.7	0.00	8	0.02	10	0.35	3	6.3	4
Henkel AG & Co. KGaA	21.7	−0.08	12	0.08	5	0.43	6	6.9	5
Eastman Chemical Company	9.4	0.37	2	0.10	3	2.01	18	6.9	5
Asian Paints Ltd.	2.0	0.00	7	0.03	9	0.50	8	7.2	7
Lanxess AG	11.0	0.10	4	−0.17	17	0.40	5	7.8	8
Syngenta AG	14.7	−0.74	18	0.03	8	0.15	1	8.1	9
FMC Corp	3.9	0.03	6	0.05	7	1.60	16	8.7	10
Air Liquide	20.2	−0.07	11	0.05	6	1.07	13	9.0	11
E I Du Pont De Nemours and Co.	35.9	−0.06	10	−0.06	16	0.55	9	10.5	12
BASF SE	98.2	−0.15	13	−0.03	12	0.69	10	10.5	12
Huntsman Corporation	11.1	−0.26	16	−0.04	14	0.50	7	11.1	14
Dow Chemical Company	57.1	−0.15	14	0.00	11	1.07	12	11.1	14
Ecolab, Inc.	13.3	−0.01	9	−0.03	13	1.17	15	11.1	14
Chemtura Corp.	2.2	−0.53	17	−0.28	18	0.36	4	11.7	17
Sasol Limited	20.5	−0.18	15	−0.06	15	1.09	14	13.2	18

Source: Supply Chain Insights LLC, Corporate Annual Reports 2006–2013.

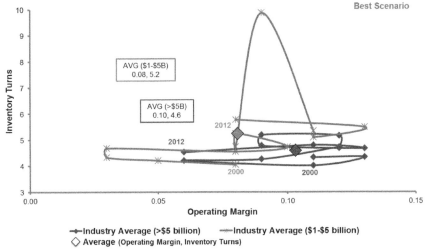

FIGURE 5.12 Chemical: Inventory Turns versus Revenue per Employee: 2001–2012 (Comparison of Companies Greater Than $5 Billion in Revenue and $1–$5 Billion in Revenue)

Industry Average composed of public companies (NAICS code 325188 & 325998) reporting in One Source with 2012 annual sales greater than $5 billion and $1–$5 billion.

Source: Supply Chain Insights LLC, Corporate Annual Reports 2000–2012.

Metrics That Matter at BASF

In May 2014, we interviewed Robert Blackburn of BASF on the metrics that he thinks matter to manage global operations. Since 2007, Robert Blackburn has been Senior Vice President of Global Supply Chain & Process Innovation. He is located in Ludwigshafen, Germany.

BASF is the world's leading chemical company. In 2013, BASF posted annual sales of €74.0 billion with income (before special items) of approximately €7.2 billion. With more than 112,000 employees, six Verbund[5] sites and 376 additional production sites worldwide, BASF is a global company serving customers and partners in almost all countries of the world.

Robert, tell us about your mission.

By 2020, BASF has a goal of €115 billion in sales. These products must be manufactured and delivered sustainably and reliably.

In your role as a leader of one of the world's largest value chains, what have you learned about metrics and measuring a supply chain?

Coming from a sales and P&L leadership role, I was accustomed to sales, EBIT, and net profit targets in an environment where creativity in marketing was king. When I joined the supply chain division I quickly learned that all along the value chain, from procurement through production and logistics, supply chainers are deep analytic thinkers, but they lack the insights into how to apply a profit-and-loss mentality to operations. While extremely good at managing complexity, adapting flexibly to volatile markets in a differentiated way was simply a new skill to be learned for much of the team. To support our team, we decided to do wide-ranging agreements with MIT and KIT to build a program that combined the classroom learning with on-the-job projects. It was a stroke of luck that the timing of this training coincided with two crises: the economic downturn and subsequent upturn of 2008–2009. We gained experience that we could immediately apply, thereby further enabling our positive performance.

When I think about supply chain leadership, I think about the companies in high-tech and fast moving consumer goods in which excellent supply chains are required for business survival. We have merged practices from companies as diverse as IBM Semiconductors, Cisco Systems, and Nestlé with existing BASF best practices. This has enabled BASF's performance and made us a case from which others can learn.

Our metrics have adapted based on these integrated practices. In parts of our portfolio, we are similar to fast-moving consumer goods companies. We want smaller and more agile factories in our markets, close to the customer, and to have higher numbers of articles combined with smaller-sized "packaging." To reduce waste in other parts of our portfolio, for example, in exploration and production and petrochemicals, we connect factories by pipelines. In many of our businesses, we are moving even closer toward our end consumer. For example, we manufacture paints that are available in the do-it-yourself retail stores in Brazil.

We live in a world where the management of risk, systemic risk in particular, and reliability are fundamental to success. Today, I feel that supply chain leadership is about delivering sustained reliability in this context. Based on what we measure, we have made major progress against this goal. As a result BASF did not falter, as other companies did, in the recent crisis in Japan. A lot of this success can be attributed to what we measure, although I am not able to share all of this.

What do you measure?

Daily, I view a dashboard of 11 metrics, five of which are proprietary. They are part of our secret sauce. We have built them with a focus on sensing

(continued)

(continued)

and resilience. Risk mitigation is built in and we are constantly analyzing flows across our supply network. I can tell you about our work on cash, cost, and service.

First of all, let me give you a disclaimer. BASF carries a lot of inventory, much of which is customer-based VMI. To ensure that we measure value, we measure on-hand inventory valued along the value chain. We are constantly analyzing the impact of the market; for example, we measure valuation specific to customer industry as the value of the inventory at the time that it was produced versus the value of the inventory at the time that it was sold. It helps us to understand how effectively we are doing product costing from inbound raw material through final delivered product.

When it comes to service, we measure service in the way that a specific customer needs it to be measured in that industry. We have a large oil business and petrochemicals supply chain; however, our portfolio is moving toward very customer-centric material requirements. As such, our business looks ever more like a consumer goods supply network.

For example, we are sensing the tighter windows for pharmaceutical ingredients two to three times a day, whereas in the case of bulk chemicals there is lower frequency. An important factor for us to measure in the bulk chemical business is cycle time in and out of a site or port. We measure the time to the site or port, turnaround time in site or port, and the remaining time to the customer. Our goal so far is to do this far faster and more efficiently than competitors. In the chemicals business, the turnaround time in ocean ports is deeply important. It is a measurement of excellence.

Customer complaints and returns are measured daily. For me, they are a leading indicator for quality improvement. We seek to understand root causes in each case.

Like everyone else, we are also constantly analyzing costs. We bring suppliers into the value chain analyses, and engage them in network-wide discussions regarding competitiveness of supply networks. We work to help them reduce costs and improve inbound services. This is a good example of a best practice that we adopted from extended supply chains in the high-tech and electronics industries.

Summary

It was almost the end of the day. It had been a long session. I asked the team to summarize their key insights. Angela volunteered to be the scribe. The participants began to speak all at once. I was pleased that there was still a lot of energy in the group. Angela quickly wrote:

- It is easy to throw a company out of balance. Frank remembered that Dow Chemical Company was a positive outlier on revenue per employee.
- Again, the group learned that when a company focuses on being the most efficient, that will often throw a company out of balance.
- Consistency of leadership matters. The group liked the interview with Robert and agreed that the continuous focus on the metrics that matter by a single leader through this period made a difference.
- The greater the issues with resiliency, the more important it is to be market-driven.

WRAPPING UP THE STRATEGY WORKSHOP

At the end of the day, I asked the team to make a list of what they had learned about value chains, and the lessons that they would like to apply to Project Orbit. This is the list that they created:

- Embrace new technologies and power shifts. Don't be like retail and let old perspectives slow the progress of adopting new business models.
- Use corporate social responsibility as part of the balanced scorecard. The inclusion can drive new progress with suppliers.
- The power structures and design of the value network are an important concern. The further back in the value chain that a company is, the greater the importance to read channel signals and become market-driven.
- Balance, strength, and resiliency metrics make a difference in corporate performance. The group felt that they were making progress in understanding the balanced scorecard.
- When implementing scorecards and VMI programs, it is important to tie the collaborative initiatives to the metrics that matter and develop a win/win value proposition with trading partners.
- Some industries have economies of scale and some do not. It is important to understand the impact of economies of scale in the planning of mergers and acquisitions.

Even though the energy was still high, the group was tiring. The information was overwhelming. While they were glad to gain these insights, it had been hard work. They were glad to get a break before tackling the health-care value chain, and we agreed to meet again the next day.

TABLE 5.10 Supply Chain Index: Consumer Value Chain

Industry	Number of Companies	Average Balance	Average Strength	Average Resiliency
Retail	14	−0.12	0.01	1.40
Consumer Packaged Goods	17	−0.11	0.03	0.71
Food & Beverage	21	0.17	0.06	1.03
Chemical	18	−0.07	0.01	0.85

Source: Supply Chain Insights LLC, Corporate Annual Reports 2006–2013.

In closing, Angela pointed out that there were stark differences in how the industries performed in the period of 2006–2012 on the Effective Frontier. Like a well-tuned machine, she quickly wrote this final table of the averages on the board (see Table 5.10).

I then asked the group, "What do you see in the data?" After a minute of pregnant silence that seemed like an hour, Joe broke the ice.

He said, "During the period, the CPG industry had the highest operating margin, but made little progress on the Effective Frontier. The companies in the CPG peer group focused on growth and they executed many programs; but as they pushed the growth agenda, progress slipped on operating margin and inventory turns." The group agreed that when it came to understanding best practices they needed to learn from CPG. They were the most impressed with the recent improvement in performance of Colgate, Beiersdorf, and L'Oreal, but agreed that P&G and Unilever were early leaders.

After another minute, Lou spoke. He said, "The poorest performance for the period was a toss-up between the retail and chemical groups. Retail struggled with both resiliency and improving strength and balance. They were slow to adopt new ways of doing business. I think that this needs to be a clear signal to us that we need to constantly ask ourselves the question, "Is there a better way to accomplish their goal?" And then work to break down our silos to embrace new ways of doing business." Lou turned to the group and stated the obvious. "This is hard for us, but I think that we really need to try." Edgar put his hand on Lou's shoulder and agreed, and spoke next.

In a deep, resounding voice, Edgar stated, "The food and beverage industry had started a lower level of performance in both inventory turns and operating margin than CPG. During 2006–2012, they learned from the practices of CPG and propelled progress forward on the Effective Frontier. They had made progress, but there was an increasing need to adopt market-driven processes to improve resiliency. For me, this was a clear lesson. I think that we could have made more progress in our business during the recession if we had orchestrated our processes market-to-market."

The group also commented that they could see the impact of pushing costs and waste backward in the supply chain, and the lack of true collaboration. The lack of progress in both balance and strength by the chemical industry was a strong wake-up call for the group. They agreed that they needed to review their practices to see how they could help the chemical companies that were important to them to be more resilient.

Resiliency, and the lack of reliability, in retail and chemical industry sectors was a key insight for the group. It was a new way of looking at corporate performance. They found it interesting that the companies with the best results on resiliency were more active in owning their value chains, adopting innovation, sharing data, and owning the channel. They were also better in the design of their value networks and orchestrating the response from market-to-market.

Angela then spoke of how in the old days there was a surplus of chemical products, but now that capacity was tighter, she thought that the lack of progress of the chemical companies was a factor to be considered in their risk management programs. Lou agreed, and Joe spoke up, "I think that it is important for us to own our value chain. We can't thrive and drive competitive advantage by always focusing on buy/sell relationships. The writing is on the wall. The question now is, What to do about it?"

 ## CONCLUSION

Each value chain has different drivers and flows. As a result, companies should be compared within their own peer group. In the process, it is important to understand several factors: progress on the Effective Frontier, economies of scale, and lessons learned by leaders.

As we will see in later chapters, the consumer value chain has done many things right. They are further ahead in their ability to drive progress on the Effective Frontier and drive balance than those in the health-care or the industrial value chains.

 ### Notes

1. The methodology developed by Arizona State University to calculate the patterns of the orbit charts is defined in the Appendix of this book.

2. Michael Snyder, "Twenty Facts about the Great U.S. Retail Apocalypse That Will Blow Your Mind," *The Economic Collapse*, March 9, 2004, http://theeconomiccollapseblog.com/archives/20-facts-about-the-great-u-s-retail-apocalypse-that-will-blow-your-mind (accessed May 17, 2014).
3. 2013 Forecasting Benchmarking Study, Terra Technology (2013).
4. "New Product Pacesetters: The Fuel to Accelerate Growth," Information Resources, Inc. (IRI), Chicago, IL.
5. A *verbund site* is a BASF term that links the output from one factory as the input to another. Many of these verbund factories are interconnected by pipeline to minimize the costs and waste associated with the transportation of raw materials.

6

What Drives Value in the Value Network?

Industry Progress in the Health-Care Value Chain

R AIN PELTED THE window. Gale force winds hurled the sheets of rain against the walls of the conference center where we were meeting. The winds were so strong that it was difficult for Jeff to pull the door shut as we met on the second day. As Jeff wiped the rain from his forehead, Frank quipped that he'd always suspected that Jeff was all wet, but now he knew it was true. The group laughed. He loved to chide Jeff in a fatherly, but friendly way. In his own way, Jeff liked it, too.

The meeting sprang to order when Edgar countered, "Frank, we were thinking before Jeff came in that it was you that was all wet. Will you be able to join us today and shut your laptop? I know that it's hard for you to disconnect from the day-to-day to focus on the important work that we need to do together, but, I need for you to be with us today. It is hard for us as a group to move forward with you jumping in and out of the session."

Frank shoved his briefcase under the conference table, but kept his phone by his side, as he reluctantly got ready for the meeting to begin. Edgar then turned to me and said, "I enjoyed our discussion yesterday. I got a lot out of it, but I have a request. Could we spend some time as a group reflecting on what we learned yesterday before we begin the discussion of the next value chain?"

The group agreed but rolled their eyes when Frank stood up and walked to the front of the room and added, "You know we worked hard yesterday, but this isn't brain surgery. All we really want to know is how we can get better at customer service and drive improvement on the balance sheet." He glanced at Filipe and Angela and continued, "I know that some of you really like to measure every little detail and get into the nitty-gritty, but I just don't have time to go down every little rabbit hole. I am a simple guy with a clear agenda. I just want to find out how we can drive more sales and make more money. You guys all know that I am all about making more money. If we're able to improve margin, drive down inventories, and improve sales, we all get our bonuses. And, you know that this is my goal. Filipe and Joe, I just don't understand why you can't continue to improve our profitability and ship things on time. Sometimes I just feel like you're complaining. I'm tired of the whining. I think that it's time to get to work and fix operations so we can be more successful in sales." Frank then sat down and returned to texting on his phone.

Edgar frowned, and reached over and gently placed his hand on Frank's shoulder and said, "Yes, alignment is so important. Thanks for bringing us back to the meeting at hand but we need your help. Can you rejoin the group in a positive way? I need for you to be part of the solution. I want to be clear. It isn't just about driving sales. It is about us winning together."

I smiled. It was always tough to get the group started, but after yesterday's workshop their energy was still high. So, I took Edgar's suggestion and asked that they work together to come up with their primary take-aways from yesterday's strategy session. To reduce the tension in the room, I grouped Edgar with Frank, Filipe with Jeff, and let Lou and Joe work with Angela. Before they got started, I asked them to discuss the findings from the prior day for 30 minutes. At the end of the time, each group was to share their primary insights.

As I got a cup a coffee, I noticed some heated debates. They were getting into the discussion, and were still actively sharing what they had learned when I called time. Begrudgingly, they agreed to stop. Here is what they wrote on their flipcharts:

Edgar/Frank

Procter & Gamble started the decade as the company making the most improvement and ended the decade making the slowest progress in their peer group. Large companies like Dow Chemical, Coca-Cola, PepsiCo, and

Kraft also struggled to keep pace with their peer groups. Why is it so hard for a big company to drive progress?

Filipe/Jeff

A buy/sell arrangement isn't a relationship. The lack of true relationships hindered value creation in the consumer value chain. A true relationship is built on a sustainable win/win business agreement. (Frank and Jeff commented that they were surprised that there was not more progress for the value chain after a decade of collaborative initiatives.)

Angela/Joe/Lou

We do not know how to define best practices until we understand the impact of these practices on corporate performance. Companies have used the term "best practices" too loosely. We need to be more thoughtful about the use of the term "best practices" and relate the processes to actual results.

As we debriefed, Filipe said, "Overall, we're surprised that so many companies that we consider leaders stalled in their ability to drive performance improvements in both inventory and operating margin during 2006–2012. We had assumed that more companies were making progress. This has been enlightening." He turned to the group and asked, "What do you think?"

"It makes me think harder about what I am doing," said Edgar. "I've been moving forward on decisions with confidence. I shouldn't have. It isn't that easy. I believe that I need to be more careful. There's more to the management of the operations side of our business than I originally thought. We cannot drink the Kool-Aid of all of the advertisements in the airports, or the many consultant presentations. Instead, I need to be more deliberate in what I advocate as the path forward."

Joe was smiling, nodding his head in agreement. We were making progress. I was now ready to start the discussion on the progress on the health-care value network.

I wrote the following on the whiteboard:

In the development of the strategy for a value network, companies must first determine:
- What is value?
- Who is the customer?
- Where are they headed?

I asked the group if we could apply this methodology to better understand the health-care value chain.

"I think so," Frank quipped. "How can a company not be clear on the answers to these questions? I just can't imagine a sales team that isn't clear on their customer. Or a company that isn't clear on where they are headed. Isn't this fundamental?"

"Yes," I answered. "As you will see, the answers to these questions sound simple, but they aren't. And yes, they are fundamental to growth and driving progress."

Edgar then quietly remarked, "Let's see where this goes. I am not clear on the definition of value. I have many unanswered questions from our discussion yesterday."

I then turned on the projector and we got into the materials.

WHAT IS VALUE?

The plan for the day was to review the progress of hospitals, pharmaceutical, and medical device companies on the Effective Frontier. These industries compose the health-care value network. Each has very different drivers and cycles, but they need to work together to improve patient-based outcomes.

I began by explaining, "Over the past decade, the two value networks—consumer and health care—experienced growing complexity, but it looked very different. In the course of the past decade, the pace of change for the consumer value network was much slower than that of health care.

"Today, in health care, the focus is shifting from efficient sickness to improving health and wellness, but the path forward isn't clear. The impact is pervasive and the processes are in flux. In the process, many companies have resisted change and dragged their feet. Traditionally, they have enjoyed high margins and have protected the status quo. As a result, governmental regulation is now forcing change."

I continued, "Let's look at the challenges by industry. The complexity for retail was in omni-channels and the changes in store formats; for consumer products companies it was in the expansion of the product portfolio; in food and beverage it was in the management of 'fresh and short' life cycle products. Each industry experienced complexity in a different form.

"Complexity in the health-care value network also comes in a very different state. For the health-care industry, it is about the changing dynamics of affordable treatment. For pharmaceutical and medical device companies, compliance is increasing—with each country exerting new and varying regulations. In parallel, the pace of innovation in medicine is accelerating.

"Historically," I continued, "the medical device and pharmaceutical companies have had the luxury of high margins. As a result, optimizing performance on the Effective Frontier was not as important as it is now.

"Let me tell you a story about business drivers." I then told them of a major health and nutrition company that I had worked with the previous week.

Case Study on Business Drivers in Over-the-Counter Drug Products

Recently, we had a discussion with the chief operations officer of a major health and nutrition company on market drivers. They had just implemented a number of changes, and they were proud of their progress. The following are some excerpts from the interview.

My path into managing operations is different from most. I had a degree in chemistry. The path I took came through R&D. I had many different roles like R&D management and quality assurance. When my boss retired, I took over R&D and supply chain operations. You don't often see R&D and operations together, but for me it is a perfect fit. . . .

I think that my expertise is in pattern recognition. Operations is a numbers-based business. I use my skills to look at patterns to construct business models to deliver on both efficiency and effectiveness.

Before I took my new job, I had a whole series of ideas that I thought that we should be doing. When I started the new position, I had the list in my back pocket. I said to my team, "Here is a list of ideas." I was wrong.

It wasn't that easy. In researching the ideas, like moving a nutritional business to the point of sale, we discovered that the base numbers of the business drove the strategy. Today, transportation and duties are five times a greater expense than labor and overhead. This is a very different mix of inputs from the garment industry where labor would be a major driver. The opportunity was in reducing the transportation and duty cost, not in moving to low-cost labor markets.

In prestige beauty and nutritional supplements, the cost to make the product is minuscule. However, home care, where an item is mostly water, is a different story. As a result we had to analyze what the drivers were of the supply chain cost. And what opportunities were presented by each business line that were unique to our model.

We found that each country has nuances. For example, people want prestige beauty from the United States, Europe, or Japan. Customers aren't looking for prestige beauty from the emerging economies of India or China. Take another example: Few people know where their TV was made,

(continued)

(continued)

but the buyer cares greatly about the reliability of that product. Product reliability, in the case of consumer durables, is the driving factor for product satisfaction. So when you are designing for value, it is important to analyze distribution costs, material variability, and the costs of labor along with the degrees of freedom you have with what the buyer wants. Through this analysis, you are able to develop an effective and efficient supply chain.

It took six to nine months to look at the numbers. Great modeling is critical. It is only accurate if you have the right data going in. For example, we produce in Vietnam and China. We produce there because the regulations say that you have to manufacture there to sell there. Vietnam is a low-cost market in which to produce. Our factory is efficient, yet it costs us more to manufacture the product in Vietnam and ship to North America than to manufacture it in the United States. It is about total costs. You have to have a model that helps you to see the interrelationships. Free trade agreements also matter. In our business, there isn't one lever, there are 20 levers.

Our operations serve the globe. We're in 100 countries and territories around the world. Our activities are broad. We were engaged in everything from raising crops to making home deliveries.

Service level is my most important metric. If someone is building a health-care facility and they are focused on water treatment systems, but we do not have them, then we're out of business. We must be responsive to demand and be diligent to reduce demand interruptions. We must also have a consistent supply of quality product. As a result, our focus is to make it right the first time. Reliability in both of these two metrics is critical.

Most companies inherit supply chains. To a great extent, we inherited the supply chain that we had. When we got into it some things did not make sense. If you aren't going to add value, why do it yourself? My question was always, "Why?" For example, we made our own corrugated packaging. The equipment was 20 years old. It did not make sense, so we outsourced it and focused our efforts on what we're good at."

We invested where it made sense. We grow our own crops. Our focus shifted to getting the right seeds, controlling the planting, and ensuring quality conversion all the way through finished products. We have three large-scale farms heavily invested in the production of biologics."

"Communication to the work teams is critical. Go slow and be clear. Don't expect that something that took you nine months to figure out is going to be effectively communicated in one meeting. It has to be communicated in the right way. Our restructuring of operations meant a lot of communication. We believe in transparency, and we told people why we were making the decision and shared the drivers. We were going to invest where it made sense.

My second suggestion is to seek to understand your model and the fundamental drivers of your supply chain. Find out what it is. Is it labor? Is it duties, or is it transportation? Actively define both efficiency and effectiveness.

We started with consultants, but we kicked them out. I trusted my team to know the business. Collecting the data isn't easy. I suspect that there are many companies that have great capabilities to get data, but we did not. We spent the time to overcome our data challenges. I think that we made better decisions doing it ourselves. We were not impatient. We asked ourselves hard questions. I think that our results are better because of it.

Chief Operations Officer of a major health and nutrition company

Edgar laughed. He liked the story and lightheartedly said, "I am guilty of working on a project for months and then asking employees to understand it in a 30-minute presentation. The relationship between metrics and market drivers is heady stuff. We need to think about how we communicate the results of Project Orbit as we go forward."

"I get it," stated Lou. "For every value network, there are different drivers. The key to building the strategy is to understand the drivers and the impact on the value chain. In parallel, as business leaders, we have to knock down the barriers to adopt new technologies and processes so that we're not forced to do the right thing by government. It reminds me of a story that I was reading last night. Did you know that Kodak had some of the first patents for the digital camera? Instead of embracing a new way of delivering photography to the consumer, they shelved the patents and tried to delay the innovation. I tried to buy black-and-white film for my old camera last week: It is now tough to find. People just aren't taking pictures using film the way they used to. Kodak had the opportunity to be a leader. Look at Kodak now. If only they had seized the opportunity versus fighting it. Think of what we discussed about the retail industry yesterday. The companies that did the best adopted new formats. I think that we should put *drive innovation through the adoption of new business models* on our action list. I want your support to create a new team and commit funding to have them think about shifts in technology and actively redesign value networks in front of, not behind, the disruption cycle." The group then asked me to put this action item on the follow-up list for the end of the meeting.

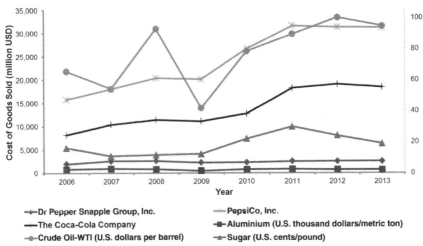

FIGURE 6.1   Impact of Market Drivers on the Carbonated Beverage Manufacturers

Source: Supply Chain Insights LLC, Corporate Annual Reports 2006–2013, Index Mund.

Edgar then reiterated the importance of market drivers and how to design networks to increase value. At that point, Jeff showed the group the chart in Figure 6.1. Jeff had taken the corporate balance sheet data for three carbonated beverage companies and plotted the increase of cost of goods sold against market drivers.

As he handed out his chart, Jeff explained, "Yesterday, I was looking at the positioning of PepsiCo and Coca-Cola and the progress that they made on the Effective Frontier versus their peer groups. So I was curious about how the shifts in the cost of goods sold compared to the shifts in commodity prices. You know that I like data, and enjoy graphing relationships. I am goofy like that." The group laughed. Frank retorted that there was no one goofier. The group then began to discuss the work that Jeff had done.

"Yes, I found it interesting that the companies that sold products that had more water, and were therefore heavy, struggled more to make progress," said Joe. "Remember how well the beauty products did compared to the rest of the consumer packaged goods peer group? These products have high margin and a low cost of transportation. They did well on the Effective Frontier as a group. What I found interesting was the comparison of peer groups where there was a spread. I think that we can learn from the spread between General Mills and Kellogg, and between PepsiCo and Coca-Cola. The companies with heavier products are getting hammered right now on the costs of transportation. They have not been able to redesign to raise the potential to reverse the impact of rising oil prices." I nodded.

> People consume more soup when it is a cold winter. However, the same things that drive demand—cold and wet weather—are the barriers to transportation to move the product to market.
>
> We have trouble getting transportation carriers to move our product during the biggest demand peaks. As a result, we cannot select transportation carriers based on the lowest cost. When the times are tough, and it is difficult to move freight in adverse weather, the loads that don't move are the ones that have the lowest negotiated price. We need to buy transportation based on reliability.
>
> *Business Leader at Campbell's Soup*

Frank put down his phone and looked up. "So, let me understand. If we were one of these carbonated beverage companies, and we applied the market-driven methodology that we learned yesterday, we would be thinking about how to redesign the physics of what we do to minimize these impacts. We might ask my sales team to not overload the trucks with a 5-for-$10 promotion during a holiday, investigate the design of a pallet, or ask a retailer to let us deliver in a period of time when it is more efficient to get to the stores. Am I on the right track?" asked Frank.

"Yes," said Lou. "If we were driving a market-driven response, that is exactly the type of discussion we would be having in sales and operations planning. We would be pressuring you to maximize opportunities based on both growth and profitability. That is very different from today's discussion that only focuses on volume, and rewards you only on cases. We would also change your bonus structure so that the sales team is held accountable for both cost and volume."

Filipe walked across the room, got a cup of coffee, put his hand on Frank's shoulder and said, "How would you like that?"

Angela quipped, "It would certainly be a very different discussion!"

"Perhaps we should try it," said Edgar.

The team asked me to put a note on our follow-up list in our parking lot to come back later and discuss the use of market-drivers to make decisions in S&OP. (A *parking lot* is a term used in group meetings to "park" important, unsolved issues.)

I then returned to the agenda to focus on the task at hand. We were now ready to discuss the health-care value network and compare and contrast it to the insights that we gained from discussing the consumer value network.

WHO IS THE CUSTOMER?

In the consumer value network, it is clear who the customer is. This isn't the case in the health-care value chain.

When a value chain can align, and become customer-centric, progress happens more quickly. Without a clear definition of the customer, it is tougher to make progress. It is incumbent upon leadership to define value-based outcomes for the customer. Clarity on this goal is critical for alignment.

In the consumer value chain, the customer is the person checking out and paying for the product. While the consumer products companies and food and beverage manufacturers sell to retailers, their focus is on the shopper. The focus is clear.

Shopper. Consumer. Retailer. The roles are well-defined. Companies realize that the person who uses the product is the consumer, the person who buys the product is the shopper, and the company that sells the product is the retailer. For the operations teams in the consumer value network, the focus is on delivering value to maximize the experience for the shopper. They work with the retailer to improve this customer experience while maximizing the value for the retailer. This includes having the correct product on the shelf when the shopper wants to buy it while ensuring product quality at the point of delivery. They are now in their third decade of refining the processes.

In the health-care value chain, the role of the customer is not as clear. The roles of who does what to whom are confused. They are changing. Whom is the supplier serving? Is it the physician? The hospital? The patient? The insurer? In this value network, each party has a slightly different focus, and the payment system is more bifurcated than in other value networks (split payments to multiple parties). As a result, it is hard for the industries within the network to align on clear metrics that define customer-centric excellence.

Traditionally, the health-care value chain sold products to physicians. Over the past decade, the focus has changed. Today the customer is the hospital or the payor. This shift continues to be difficult for manufacturers since their sales and marketing organizations were aligned to sell to the doctor. As more and more suppliers to hospitals are asked to focus on value-based outcomes for patients, it is a change management issue redefining the entire value chain.

At that point, Jeff spoke. "I am currently working on getting some help for my wife. She runs a lot and has knee problems. The physician has scheduled her for surgery. The doctor has contacted a medical device supplier to get a knee replacement. In the dialogue with the salesperson at the medical device company, they talked about 'trunk stock.' Can you believe that the suppliers for this type of operation are rolling inventory in the back of the salesperson's car? And that we needed to call the sales guy to be sure that it could be secured for the operation?" The group rolled their eyes and contributed their own stories about scheduling an operation. Jeff continued, "I then had to call the health-care insurer and get authorization, and then schedule the operation with the hospital. It appears that I even need to schedule the *salesperson* from the medical device company to be in the operating room for the procedure. It used to be much easier."

"And, if that was not enough," Jeff continued, "the doctor suggested to me that I write down the serial numbers of the knee and save them in a secure place. I am thinking about placing the data in my safety deposit box."

"Evidently, the ability to recall and track products in the health-care value chain isn't at the level that he would like," Jeff said as he gestured with his hands. "My doctor spoke about the adoption of GDSN and GS1 numbers and the evolution of standards. Quite frankly, much of the discussion went over my head, but I find the lack of standards and the informality of inventory control on knee implants to be disconcerting. Especially since these things are going into my wife's body. She is just 35 with her entire life ahead of her. The thought of having a recall on her implant scares me. I am shocked."

When I get a recall notice, I hope that it is for peanut butter in the kitchen. I have more luck tracking these codes than the knee replacement in the operating room.

Hospital Supply Chain Leader

Jeff had hit a nerve. The group recounted a number of stories about hospitals, operating rooms, and medical implants. Lou had a bill in his well-worn bag that he carries back and forth to work. It was from his recent hospital stay. The group had a field day looking at the cost of everyday items like cotton swabs and cotton balls on his bill.

Angela then spoke of the rising costs of health care for the corporation. Lou slammed his fist down on the table and asked, "When will the escalating costs of health care end? How can pharmaceutical and medical device companies make such high margins and not take a more active role in redefining the value network to drive more affordable health care?"

This was a good introduction to the topic at hand.

WHERE ARE WE HEADED?

"The health-care industry is on a slow and winding road to improve patient-based outcomes, but the path is convoluted. Companies are slow to adopt standards and compliance requirements are mounting," I stated.

Edgar asked, "Has anyone done it well? I would like an example of a company that was forward-looking and drove success." I responded, "One of the best examples of principle-based leadership in the health-care value network is the Johnson & Johnson Credo."

Johnson & Johnson Credo

Robert Wood Johnson, former chairman of Johnson & Johnson from 1932 to 1963, and a member of the company's founding family, crafted the J&J Credo himself in 1943, just before Johnson & Johnson became a publicly traded company.

This was long before anyone ever heard the term *corporate social responsibility*. At J&J, the Credo is more than just a moral compass. The Company believes that it's a recipe for business success. The J&J Credo is:

> We believe our first responsibility is to the doctors, nurses and patients, to mothers and fathers and all others *who use our products* and services. In meeting their needs everything we do must be of high quality. We must constantly strive to reduce our costs in order to maintain reasonable prices. Customers' orders must be serviced promptly and accurately. Our suppliers and distributors must have an opportunity to make a fair profit.
>
> We're responsible to *our employees*, the men and women who work with us throughout the world. Everyone must be considered as an individual. We must respect their dignity and recognize their merit. They must have a sense of security in their jobs. Compensation must be fair and adequate, and working conditions clean, orderly and safe. We must be mindful of ways to help our employees fulfill their family obligations. Employees must feel free to make suggestions and complaints. There must be equal opportunity for employment, development and advancement for those qualified. We must provide competent management, and their actions must be just and ethical.
>
> We're responsible to the communities in which we live and work and to the world community as well. We must be good citizens—support good works and charities and pay our fair share of taxes. We must encourage civic improvements and better health and education. We must maintain in good order the property we're privileged to use, protecting the environment and natural resources.

Our final responsibility is to our stockholders. Business must make a sound profit. We must experiment with new ideas. Research must be carried on, innovative programs developed and mistakes paid for. New equipment must be purchased, new facilities provided and new products launched. Reserves must be created to provide for adverse times. When we operate according to these principles, the stockholders should realize a fair return.[1]

Edgar and Lou talked about the beauty of the Credo and the clarity of purpose. Angela's best friend worked at J&J and she spoke of how well it aligned the organization to be more purposeful on focusing on the patient. Unlike other organizations that have changed their mission frequently, the beauty of the Credo at J&J lived in the ethical processes, and in the minds and hearts of the employees for 70 years.

"Stryker is an early adopter of standards," I continued. "Let me share a case study."

Stryker Health Care Adopts GS1 Standards ahead of Industry

Stryker Corporation is a medical device supplier to the health-care industry. The products include implants for joint replacement; surgical equipment for patient handling; emergency medical equipment; neurosurgical, neurovascular, and spinal devices; as well as other medical device products used in a variety of medical specialties.

The products are sold in over 100 countries through company-owned sales subsidiaries and branches as well as third-party dealers and distributors. The company has three business segments: Reconstructive, Medical, and Surgical; Neurotechnology; and Spine.

The spokesperson who gave us the following information has asked that he remain nameless:

Four years ago we began the journey to become more customer-centric. It was our burning platform. At that time we had quality issues including FDA warning letters and recalls. Previously, we had driven high straight-line sales growth, but it started to flatten. It went from 10–20 percent growth rates to 3 percent in the past couple of years. We had cash on the books. We had recently acquired 10 companies, but we had a high cost structure.

(continued)

(continued)

In the beginning, we served the surgeon. The surgeon isn't aware, nor does he care, about the issues of inventory. Now that we're selling directly to hospitals, the model has changed. About eight years ago, we began to talk about vendor managed inventory (VMI). However, it was really about reassigning the responsibility for inventory. It was about consignment, not about a true VMI program with data sharing. Today, I cannot see the data on usage at the hospital.

When I came to Stryker, I was one of the few people who was ever a supply chain professional in a hospital. Today, in medical device organizations, there is a huge gap. Too few people at suppliers understand the world of operations in a clinical setting.

Salespeople do not like supply chain concepts. Their primary requirement is to support the clinical needs. They do not understand the basics. What is an item file? How do we improve three-way match? Improve order-to-cash process? There is no requirement for our sales team to understand the business side of our process flows.

There was so much low-hanging fruit to drive improvement that we were like a kid in a candy store trying to decide what to do first. We had 59,000 products and 10 sales representatives calling on the same hospital. Thirty-one factories operated globally to sell 90 percent of our products. We were trying to be a more services-based company without well-defined processes. New competition was coming at us, and we were trying to be more competitive. We were awesome at selling to the physician, but we were not good at selling to the hospital administrator.

Customers told us, "You are too difficult to do business with. You need to drive better communication on orders, case management, and product changes." We agreed. There was a need for a change. There was a gap in a lot of the basics.

It was a great culture. It was like nothing that I have ever experienced before. It took us three years to set up a distribution network and five years to adopt GS1 standards. Previously every division shipped directly. We had 42 points of shipment into an average hospital like the Mayo Clinic. We had 13 instances, or separate implementations running in parallel, of enterprise resource planning (ERP). Due to the complexity, it took us five years to adopt the standards, but it was the right thing to do.

In the health-care industry, inventory is being pushed back on suppliers. The hospitals are trying to increase my obligation by driving consigned inventory practices. We're in conflict. I need to reduce inventory. As I try to work through the issue to drive resolution, I struggle with the lack of a common data standard for an item. I have been at Stryker for over three years. You would think by now that we would have developed sophisticated systems and ability to use hospital data. We have not. Standard adoption was our first step.

World-class products make patients' lives better. The profile of our sales professionals is very clinical.

The most successful relationship with a hospital professional is when we're talking about customer service. How do you flip the switch to discuss value?

I have a couple of lessons that I learned the hard way:

- *Drive alignment from the top down.* This has been a problem. We think we have alignment at the C-level, but then it falls apart as we start to execute.
- *Get real customer insights.* Previously it has been all about pushing product and hoping that customers catch in the right way. We need to take responsibility for the product through the channel.
- *Change management is hard.* Get some success under your belt, but don't try to do it all at one time.

The J&J and Stryker case studies spoke to the group. It prompted Edgar to turn to them and ask, "What is our Credo? And how do our customers feel about us?" The group agreed that these were open issues that needed clarification. As a result, they put them in the parking lot to work on at the end of the session.

It was time for a break. As the group filed out, I glanced out the window and noticed that the rain torrents were dissipating. The warm mug of coffee in my hand felt good on this cold and damp day. As I stood at the window looking at the puddles in the parking lot, and the clearing skies, Joe came over and said, "I like how this meeting is progressing. They are slowly beginning to understand the concepts. Even though no company that we have discussed is just like us or has all the answers, we're learning, and aligning. It feels good."

I smiled. Joe and the team had come a long way.

 ## THE HEALTH-CARE VALUE CHAIN

After the group returned from break and took their chairs, I started, "The health-care value chain is ever-changing. While the power has been traditionally with the health-care suppliers, with the shift of focus to affordable health care, power has shifted to the provider and the payor. In the consumer value network, there were power brokers—large retailers like Amazon, Target, and Walmart—that orchestrated the shifts in the channel. In the health-care value chain, the health-care providers (a combination of hospitals and insurers) are small and fragmented. As a result, there was no channel master relationship that evolved to build demand and supply chain sharing. Additionally, no supplier stepped up to the plate to build a demand or supply chain B2B network to facilitate data sharing for the value network.

"Instead, companies automated buy/sell transactions," I continued. "This happened through electronic data interchange (EDI) and the formation of a consortium, or a many-to-many data exchange play, in the building of the Global Healthcare Exchange (GHX) in 2000. The investors in GHX were Abbott Laboratories, Baxter International, Johnson & Johnson, GE Healthcare, and Medtronic."

Frank was yawning, and I knew that I had to speed up to keep his attention so I briefly skimmed over the history. "The effort was significant, but insufficient. GHX currently connects 400,000 unique trading partner connections made up of 6,500 health-care delivery organizations and 700 suppliers in North America and Western Europe. GHX connects more than 70 percent of acute care hospitals in the United States with the suppliers. However, the progress is slow. It cannot compare to something like Walmart's Retail Link."

Frank looked up from his laptop and said, "Why was this not sufficient?"

"While GHX automated the processes of buying and selling, it did not provide data sharing on channel usage; and even if they had, no supplier was ready to use the data. There is no demand sensing. This is a missed opportunity," I stated.

Lou nodded his head in agreement, and said, "Sounds like us. Before these sessions, we were focused on automation of buy- and sell-side transactions, but missed the opportunity to automate the channel and drive greater data visibility to improve demand processes. If someone laid channel data at our doorstep, I am not sure that we would know how to use it, either."

I smiled. The group was getting it. Frank peered over his new red-framed glasses and said, "I understand, but was it the power structure? Who had power? We don't have any power. It isn't sufficient to have data unless you have the power to make a change. Right? Isn't that what we learned yesterday?"

Joe and Filipe commented that this was one of their key insights from the day before. They had a lot of thoughts about data sharing and how channel relationships change with shifts in the power structures between trading partners. The group had an intense discussion on how this had changed within their value network, and how they could adopt new practices to drive these shifts to their advantage.

"Hospitals are regional," I said. "They are small and fragmented. There is no entity large enough to drive data sharing. There are no power brokers. In certain regions of the world there are a few distributors, but they did not step up to the plate to drive data sharing. Instead, they made the demand signal lumpier and insulated the suppliers from the market. Over the course of the last decade, no channel master emerged.

"In addition, due to the slow usage rates, data latency was high and the demand signal was lumpy," I continued. "The suppliers enjoyed high margins. They carried three times the levels of inventory, as compared to the suppliers, to the consumer value chain, but companies did not see the reduction of inventory as a priority. No supplier in the value network took the bull by the horns to drive down the cost of health care. The insurers tried, but they were too fragmented. The situation was at a standstill until the United States government intervened with compliance standards termed *unique device identifier* (UDI). A UDI is a unique numeric or alphanumeric code that consists of two parts: identification of the part and specifics about usage.[2] This new level of compliance mandated new product standards and identification for product tracking for medical device manufacturers. This work is ongoing. Companies could no longer drag their feet.

"However, it has been tougher for both hospitals and medical device companies to improve margins and while pharmaceutical companies enjoyed high margins in the early part of the past decade, this has also changed. The entire value chain is feeling squeezed," I continued as I showed them the data in Table 6.1.

Edgar shook his head, "These are tough times for these industries. It makes me wonder, why didn't anyone inside the value network drive a redesign of health care to stem the tide of rising costs? It is so obvious that they needed to work together to improve margins and reduce inventory. Why didn't they work together to drive change? Look at the shifts in the health-care value chain."

The group then began a discussion of the dynamics of the health-care value chain. Lou was scratching his head as he said, "Let's look at the math. It tells a story. The margins of the medical device and pharmaceutical companies are two to three times the margin of the hospital. These suppliers are also three to four times larger in size than the care provider. The health-care providers lack scale, and the suppliers did not work to improve the value network. This explains a lot."

"Yes," I said. "In the past decade, the hospitals had the power, but they were too fragmented to drive change. The suppliers talked about change, but couldn't mobilize fast enough. This was largely motivated by a sales-driven culture that could not adapt quick enough from the shift of selling to the physician to selling to the service provider. The defense by the suppliers is that much of this profit is pumped back into the development of new life-saving drugs and

TABLE 6.1 Overview of the Health-Care Value Chain for the Period of 2000–2012

	Medical Value Chain (2000–2012)				
Industry	Operating Margin	Inventory Turns	Cash-to-Cash Cycle	Revenue per Employee (K$)	SG&A Ratio
Hospital Industry	0.07	11	−84	165	12%
(n = 6)	↓11%″	↑53%″	↓3215%″	↑68%*	↓ −54%*
Medical Device	0.16	3	141	270	28%
Industry (n = 6)	↓56%	↑2%	↓4%	↑59%*	↓3%^
Pharmaceutical	0.19	3	139	462	27%
Industry (n = 24)	↑12%	↓8%	↓1%	↑98%*	↑24%*

Industry Average comprised of public companies (hospital: NAICS62211), (medical device: NAICS 339112), (pharmaceutical: NAICS 325412) reporting in One Source with 2012 annual sales greater than $5 billion.
″Calculated from 2001 to 2012 due to data availability;
*Calculated from 2002 to 2012 due to data availability;
^Calculated from 2003 to 2012 due to data availability.
Source: Supply Chain Insights LLC, Corporate Annual Reports 2000–2012.

medical devices. R&D costs are rising. The products are becoming more specialized, but no company mobilized to drive more value in the value chain."

Building Effective Relationships in Health-Care Value Chains

Frank was trying. His phone kept buzzing and he continued to push it aside. Edgar grinned. His plan was working. Lou and Angela were deeply engaged in the discussion on health-care costs and Joe and Jeff were busy calculating what the value of improvement could have been if the parties had worked better together.

I cleared my throat and continued, "Driving more value in the value chain requires a major shift in buy/sell interactions. It must move from a transactional focus on buy and sell contracts to joint alignment on patient-based outcomes. While all three entities were able to improve cash-to-cash cycles, primarily through the automation of transactions, over the past decade the hospital shifted the cost of inventory to the suppliers and, like many sales-driven organizations, the suppliers did not push back. While they should have bargained to be sure that they were getting better data sharing on hospital usage in return for accepting the inventory burden, they did not. They just blindly accepted the VMI programs."

I turned to Frank, and said, "Make sense? Can you see the important role that sales plays in defining a win/win relationship?" His arms were folded. As I spoke, he nodded his head in agreement and motioned for me to move on.

"As Frank rightly pointed out in our discussion of building the consumer value chain, scorecards help to build the right behavior in driving new relationships. In the health-care value network, there are no well-established scorecards. They lag the consumer value chain in this area. The collaborative efforts in this value chain are stalled. The focus has been on efficiency. While there are more hands-free and touchless orders moving through the health-care value chain than the consumer value network, they are not aligned to joint goals and value-based relationships to drive greater value. Again, this is a case where we have become more efficient, but not more effective."

I looked at Frank and continued to speak to the larger group, "It is much like the issues that Frank mentions when we talk about channel automation and the needed changes in sales compensation. Over the past year, I facilitated a number of sessions between medical device manufacturers, distributors, and hospitals, and time and time again the discussions stalled. The groups were often gridlocked. The stumbling block was supplier compensation systems. No sales team is going to volunteer to change its incentives if they run the risk they are going to lose compensation. There was a need for leadership to transform old processes and move the sales organizations past buy/sell behaviors. It did not happen. This value chain experienced a leadership vacuum. No supplier stepped up to the plate to drive change.

"It cannot happen from the hospital back. The health-care provider network is fragmented and it is hard for anyone in the service organizations to get traction. While over 70 percent of health-care providers now have value analysis programs to evaluate new products and services, and 67 percent of that group rates the programs as effective in meeting the goals of managing costs, determining physician preferences, and reducing infection rates, progress is stuck.[3] While hospitals have improved inventory turns by pushing the responsibility backward onto the supplier, in the past decade there has been no improvement in cash-to-cash and inventory cycles for the value network in its entirety. In short, they're not aligned," I continued and showed the group some research.

"When we asked companies to assess what they were good at, as shown in Figure 6.2, both the supplier and the provider rate themselves high in the management of regulatory compliance. Much of the energies of both organizations have been focused on meeting the ever-changing set of regulations;

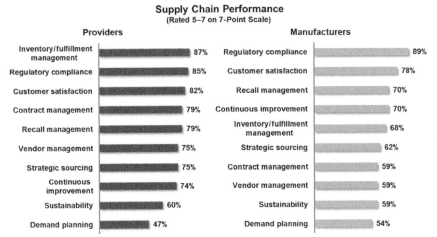

FIGURE 6.2 Focus of Organizations in Health-Care Value Chains
Base: Health-care providers (*n* = 68), Health-care manufacturers (*n* = 37).
Q35: How would you rate the performance of your organization's supply chain on each of these items? SCALE: 1 = Poor, 7 = Excellent.
Source: Supply Chain Insights LLC, Healthcare Study (February–September 2013).

however, the principles of planning and working together are still in their infancy. Note that for both the provider and supplier, the processes of demand planning ranks at the bottom of the list. As a result, the value chain operates blind. It is reactive and there is very little data sharing," I continued.

"While the manufacturer's organization was formed in the mid-1990s and the hospital's supply chain organization is newer, as shown in Figure 6.3, hospital providers feel far more familiar with their own supply chain than do manufacturers," I stated. I then stepped back and waited for all of the research to sink into the minds of the participants to stimulate a discussion.

Filipe spoke first, and said, "Let me see if I get it. The suppliers' organization is now three decades old. The hospitals' efforts are considerably newer—I am going to guess less than a decade old. Ironically, despite the larger size and maturity of the supplier's organization and the higher margins, the manufacturer rates itself significantly worse in their ability to deliver on their goals to drive value than the provider. A major factor is the lack of alignment between operations and commercial functions within the manufacturer's organization. Am I close?" he asked.

"Yes," I said. "The health-care value chain is in a gridlock. Suppliers, with higher margins and larger size, could step up and define new business models to

Success in Delivering on Supply Chain Goals

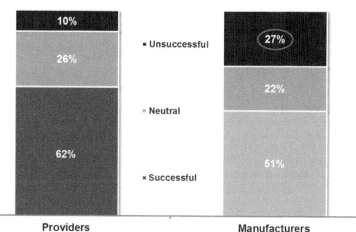

FIGURE 6.3 Capability Self-Assessment in the Health-Care Value Network
Base: Health-care providers (*n* = 68), Health-care manufacturers (*n* = 37).
Q7: Overall, how successful is your organization's supply chain today in delivering on these goals? SCALE: 1 = Not at all successful, 7 = Extremely successful; *Note:* Summary % may not match sum of parts due to rounding.
Source: Supply Chain Insights LLC, Health-Care Study (February–September 2013).

improve patient outcomes, but no supplier has taken this initiative. In a similar fashion, hospitals, smaller and more fragmented, have more limited options; but they could actively participate in data-sharing programs, and work to change the legacy programs of suppliers to align supply chain to supply chain to make improvements. The industry is in a standoff of unequal partners."

I then turned on the laptop to show some research slides, and the group grabbed a quick snack. Lou was still shaking his head. He could not believe that no one in the industry had worked harder to drive value.

 HOSPITALS

I waited for a moment for the group to take their seats, and continued, "Today, the hospital administrator faces many challenges. Growth is slowing and compliance pressures are increasing. The question is how to balance patient outcomes with better cost management. In solving this problem, the hospital

TABLE 6.2 Hospital Performance 2000–2012

	Hospital Industry (n = 6)				
Year	Operating Margin	Inventory Turns	Cash-to-Cash Cycle	Revenue per Employee (K$)	SG&A Ratio
2000–2003	0.09	10	−37	140	14%
2004–2007	0.05	10	−106	145	13%
2008–2011	0.07	12	−90	176	11%
2012	0.08	12	−85	245	6%

Industry Average composed of public companies (NAICS62211) reporting in One Source with 2012 annual sales greater than $5 billion.
Source: Supply Chain Insights LLC, Corporate Annual Reports 2000–2012.

board isn't clear. How does a hospital move forward with an uncertain future? And, what will be the impact of health-care reform? Historically, there was no design of the value chain to place expensive assets in the right places. As a result, the system is facing the issue of having medical diagnostic equipment in the wrong places.

"The rules of health care are ever-changing, and the industry is consolidating. Each country is experiencing increasing legislation and the rate of change is deafening," I said as I showed the group Table 6.2. "In this table, we summarize top-line growth over the past 13 years for hospitals. While there are ups and downs, the general trend is improving due to mergers and acquisitions.

"With rising regulation, hospitals are looking for new ways to drive value. Improved supply chain management, and redesigning the supply chain from patient back to hospital, represents a significant opportunity for the industry. The imperative is to better align with patient outcomes. For all this is an opportunity," I stated. As I presented what is shown here as Figure 6.4, I continued, "There is a focus on costs, but there is a gap in the ability to collect and analyze data to drive decisions. The hospital faces dueling challenges: health and wellness versus improving costs. Balancing the two is difficult."

N HS estimates that €950 million is tied up in consigned stock within the NHS system. This plus lost and out-of-stock inventory is simply written off each year.

John Warrington, Deputy Director of Policy and Research at the UK's National Health Service (NHS)[4]

Expected Top Three Business Challenges for 2013

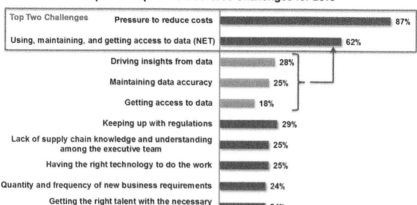

FIGURE 6.4 Business Challenges for the Hospital
Base: Health-care providers (*n* = 68).
Q5: What do you expect will be your organization's top three business challenges in 2013? Please select no more than three.
Source: Supply Chain Insights LLC, Health-Care Study (February–April 2013).

Rethinking the Value of Procurement in Hospitals

"The procurement function in the hospital historically focused on the lowest cost. They were not able to understand total costs," I continued. "Inventory and supply costs are estimated to be between 30 and 40 percent of a hospital's budget, and minimizing those costs has been the top priority for decades.[5] In addition, procurement has existed in a departmental silo, separated from other functions of the hospital, and often even separated from other procurement departments within the same organization. The effect has been a very inefficient ordering processes.

"This is changing. Hospital organizations are currently in the middle of a procurement redesign. In the future, we expect procurement to no longer act as a cost center, but instead, focus on driving value-based outcomes. By integrating horizontally the procurement transactions of a single hospital, or several hospitals, and across the continuum of care, there is great opportunity for clarity on processes and cost savings," I continued as we reviewed the research shown in Figure 6.5.

"Centralized procurement has happened in the hospitals. As a result, the gaps in purchasing are small while the gaps in other areas like standardizing

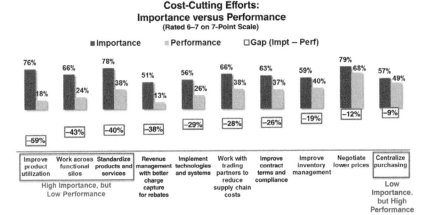

Cost-Cutting Efforts:
Importance versus Performance
(Rated 6–7 on 7-Point Scale)

■ Importance ▪ Performance ▢ Gap (Impt – Perf)

| Improve product utilization | Work across functional silos | Standardize products and services | Revenue management with better charge capture for rebates | Implement technologies and systems | Work with trading partners to reduce supply chain costs | Improve contract terms and compliance | Improve inventory management | Negotiate lower prices | Centralize purchasing |

High Importance, but Low Performance

Low Importance, but High Performance

FIGURE 6.5 Hospital Focus on Reducing Costs
Base: Health-care providers (*n* = 68).
Q9: How would you rate the importance of each of these items when it comes to lowering overall costs of your organization? SCALE: 1 = Not at all important, 7 = Extremely important.
Q10: How well does your organization perform on these same cost-cutting efforts? SCALE: 1 = Poor, 7 = Excellent.
Source: Supply Chain Insights LLC, Health-Care Study (February–April 2013).

products, and improving the utilization of equipment, are large. Additionally, the gap in alignment, as shown in the gap of working across functional silos, is also a major issue," I continued.

Lou asked, "What do we do now? This seems grim. I can clearly see the impact of a focus on procurement for the sake of procurement, and how this type of focus can throw an organization out of balance, but help me. What happens now?"

I nodded, and continued, "The hospital operating environment is changing. The space is getting more expensive and companies are realizing that patient care and cost control do not need to be conflicting objectives. Hospitals are in the middle of a redesign for value. In the past five years, over 50 percent of hospitals have introduced cross-functional teams to analyze value. These teams rationalize the addition of new equipment, changes in procedures, and redesign. While the definition of value isn't consistent, it is evolving and maturing. While there are no scorecards and little data sharing, today we have a good first step. The key is to transform value into reimbursements in

How Health-Care Providers Measure Value

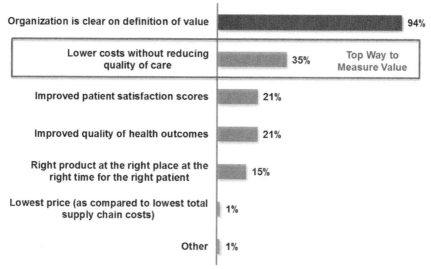

Organization is clear on definition of value	94%
Lower costs without reducing quality of care	35% — Top Way to Measure Value
Improved patient satisfaction scores	21%
Improved quality of health outcomes	21%
Right product at the right place at the right time for the right patient	15%
Lowest price (as compared to lowest total supply chain costs)	1%
Other	1%

FIGURE 6.6 Definition of Value in Value Analysis Groups
Base: Health-care providers (*n* = 68).
Q8. How does your organization measure "value" today, at a company level? Please pick the one that best applies.
Source: Supply Chain Insights LLC, Health-Care Study (February–April 2013).

billing and to better align for patient outcomes," I said, and showed the group Figure 6.6.

Progress on the Effective Frontier

The group was anxious to apply the Index methodology to these groups. Jeff asked, "Are any of the health-care providers making progress? I can't believe that they are all stuck. . . ."

Filipe nodded, and said, "Yes, I think that we will be able to see some of the progress of lean and value analysis programs on operational improvement."

"There has been some small improvement. Let's look at the hospital's progress on the Effective Frontier," I said as I handed out Table 6.3 for the group's review. "The hospital has been less balanced and less resilient than their trading partners. However, through the shifting of costs and inventory in the value chain, hospitals posted greater results at the intersection of operating

TABLE 6.3 Supply Chain Index: Hospitals

Company	2013 Revenue (billions USD)	Balance	Balance Ranking	Strength	Strength Ranking	Resiliency	Resiliency Ranking	Index (0.3B + 0.3S + 0.3R)	Ranking
HCA Holdings Inc	34.2	0.09	1	0.10	2	0.72	2	1.5	1
Primary Health Care Limited	1.5	−0.17	2	0.31	1	2.03	3	1.8	2
Cummunity Health Systems	13.0	−0.18	3	−0.01	3	0.71	1	2.1	3
KPJ Healthcare Berhad	0.7	−0.20	4	−0.01	4	4.10	4	3.6	4
Tenet Healthcare Corporation	11.1	−0.79	5	−0.29	5	10.30	5	4.5	5

Source: Supply Chain Insights LLC, Corporate Annual Reports 2006–2013.

margin and inventory turns for the period of 2006–2013. This is largely due to the efforts to consolidate purchasing and shift inventory costs to suppliers. However, the total costs of inventory in this value chain did not decline in the period.

Lou, leaning back in his chair, scratched his head, and commented, "This seems like a consistent theme. There are very few instances that we are seeing where companies have been able to work together to improve costs or outcomes. I would have expected that we would be further along in the automation of costs and the management of inventories between trading partners. This time together is making me rethink some of my practices. Filipe, we also have been guilty of forcing our suppliers into VMI programs and shifting inventory without giving them better data to run operations. I think that this is an area of opportunity for us as well."

The group was in agreement, as Joe stood up and stated, "Lou, too bad that we did not have this workshop a year ago when you were harping on me to be more aggressive with these programs." He grinned as he continued, "Those were some tough discussions. Let's go forward. I don't want to go back." As he concluded and sat down, the group laughed. Previously, the work on VMI within the organization had been intense and Lou had pushed it hard.

Economies of Scale

"One of the issues was that there was no economy of scale in the hospital industry. Companies less than $5 billion in revenue outperformed companies greater than $5 billion. This is due to the lack of process maturity and industry fragmentation," I continued as I showed the group Figure 6.7.

"However, like most industries, there is economy of scale in efficiency as measured by revenue per employee," I continued as we reviewed the data in Figure 6.8.

"Oh, my," said Angela. "Another industry, where industry scale does not improve the potential. This is making me think harder about our merger and acquisition strategy. Lou, I don't think that we can automatically assume that a larger company is more effective. For me, this is an important insight." Lou agreed with Angela, and I mentioned that this might be a good time for lunch.

The aroma of minestrone soup permeated the room as the catering staff set up lunch, but the group wanted to wrap up their thoughts on this industry before taking a much needed break. Frank commented, "There is so much rich data here, that if I don't do it now, I will forget." The group agreed, so I asked them to quickly summarize their thoughts.

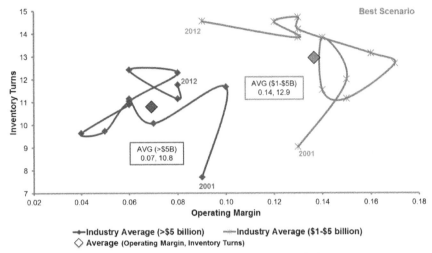

FIGURE 6.7   Evaluation of Economy of Scale of Hospitals for Operating Margin and Inventory Turns
Industry Average comprised of public companies (NAICS codes 62211) reporting in One Source with 2012 annual sales greater than $5 billion and $1–$5 billion.
Source: Supply Chain Insights LLC, Corporate Annual Reports 2001–2012.

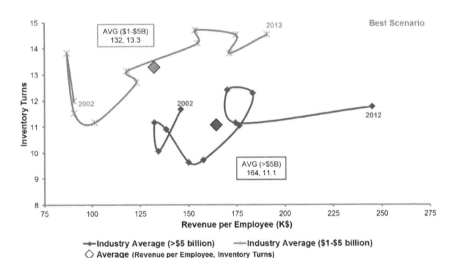

FIGURE 6.8   Economies of Scale: Evaluating the Progress of Hospitals by Annual Revenue
Industry Average comprised of public companies (NAICS codes 62211) reporting in One Source with 2012 annual sales greater than $5 billion and $1–$5 billion.
Source: Supply Chain Insights LLC, Corporate Annual Reports 2002–2012.

Summary

The group wrote the following statements on the board.

The lack of true relationships, and the definition of value, in the health-care value chain has been a barrier to building an effective value network.

The hospital value network needs a redesign from the outside-in to enable data sharing and flow of materials. As regulation increases, this will become more important.

The focus needs to be on patient-based outcomes. The industry is a leader in buy/sell transactional processing, but these are not tied to outcomes.

At this point, Lou commented that, "I still do not understand why no company stepped up to the plate to drive the redesign of health care and design processes from the patient back." This was the million-dollar question, but we agreed that we would tackle this after the lunch break. As the participants rushed to answer their phones and emails, we agreed that we would start the discussion again at the top of the hour with the review of the pharmaceutical industry.

 ## PHARMACEUTICAL INDUSTRY

As the team regrouped, Edgar commented that he was anxious to understand the progress of big pharmaceutical companies. His business strategy hinged on molecular development of new products. For him, growth was the primary mission.

So, as we began, I looked at Edgar and said, "In the face of declining growth, the pharmaceutical industry has consolidated. Over the past five years, few pharmaceutical companies have not completed a major merger or acquisition activity. It is ongoing.

"The industry is characterized by high margins, low inventory turns, and global reach. Over time, the industry has improved efficiency as measured by revenue per employee, but they lag other industries in improving operational excellence."

Felipe's brow furrowed, and he blurted, "With these margins, how could they not reinvest in operations? How can they sit on cash?" I smiled and showed him Table 6.4.

I said, "In short, you have identified the problem. Not a lot has changed within the company, but a lot has changed outside the company. The company is insular, but the market is very dynamic.

What Drives Value in the Value Network?

TABLE 6.4 Average Results for the Pharmaceutical Companies on the Effective Frontier

	Pharmaceutical Industry (n = 24)				
Year	Operating Margin	Inventory Turns	Cash-to-Cash Cycle	Revenue per Employee (K$)	SG&A Ratio
2000–2003	0.18	3	141	320	28%
2004–2007	0.19	3	144	426	28%
2008–2011	0.19	3	135	557	27%
2012	0.19	3	131	545	26%

Industry Average comprised of public companies (NAICS 325412) reporting in One Source with 2012 annual sales greater than $5 billion.
Source: Supply Chain Insights LLC, Corporate Annual Reports 2000–2012.

"This has created a sense of instability within the industry. With high margins and the ability to fund large inventory stockpiles, there has been little need to balance costs, inventory, and customer service. However, this picture is now changing." I then wrote the four primary drivers of the pharmaceutical operating environment on the whiteboard:

1. **Channel redefinition.** The first decade (1990–2000) of the pharmaceutical supply chain was based on molecule discovery. The historical focus of the pharmaceutical supply chain was building a strong personalized relationship with the doctor and improving time to market for new drugs. Over the past decade, the requirements and restrictions for the pharmaceutical supply chain have become a more complex system of hospital, provider, and physician networks. As a result, the channel through which pharmaceutical sales occur has become more complex with an increasing need to develop improved supply chain capabilities.

2. **Globalization.** The evolution of global operations, with distinctly different regional regulations and compliance rules, also increases the need for more advanced supply chain capabilities. Globalization is increasing the need for more well-defined governance structures, as well as the need for technology to streamline the order-to-cash process from manufacturer to consumer.

3. **Commoditization.** With fewer new products successfully navigating the drug approval process, and more drugs leaving "patent protection," the pharmaceutical companies' market is becoming more competitive. There is a greater need for supply chain practices to help companies become more

competitive against generic drugs. As a result, there is no question that supply chain is becoming more and more important in the pharmaceutical industry.

4. **New requirements.** Pharmaceutical delivery systems need to be rethought and redesigned to enable traceability. This system-level thinking and redesign will enable drug serialization and the management of new drugs requiring specialized handling in cold-chain conditions. Serialization and cold-chain requirements are driving the need for redesign of physical distribution systems.

State of the Industry

I continued, "While companies in other supply chains have struggled with low margins as a result of their operating environment, and focused on improving efficiency and driving improvements in supply-chain excellence, the large operating margin values in the pharmaceutical industry have had the opposite effect. It has driven more of a laissez faire attitude toward improving operations.

"Remember yesterday, and the margins for consumer packaged goods. These margins are much higher than in other process industries. Well, times are changing. Faced with a changing operating environment fueled by globalization, commoditization, and increasing complexity, there is a need to improve baseline capabilities."

Angela said, "Yes, if we don't manage our industry, then we're subject to more and more legislation. With the rising costs of health care, I think that we're headed for a showdown."

"Absolutely," said Felipe. "I would hate to be managing an operations team in the pharmaceutical industry. That would be a tough spot to be in."

Effectiveness of R&D Spending

"This industry has been about new products and growth. As growth slows, a major factor in the pharmaceutical supply chain is the upcoming drug patent cliff," I stated. Since some in the group looked confused, I explained, "In essence, a patent cliff is when there are more drugs expiring from patent protection than are gaining regulatory approval. While the absolute value of the cliff is debated and lacks agreement, all parties realize that it is a significant event," I continued.

"The impact is transformative," I stated. "Experts like Pricewaterhouse-Coopers and Evaluate Pharma estimate that from 2012 to 2018, nearly $150 billion of profit will be lost to generic drugs.[6] Additionally, recent studies support that there is a $50 billion opportunity for major drug providers with drug prescriptions that are written and not filled. They are definitely squeezed."

At that point Frank stated that the only thing that he thought was being squeezed was his wallet. He pulled out a recent receipt from his pocket, and said, "I give my pharmacy more than I give my ex-wife." He then grinned and looked around the room, and said, "You know that this is a lot."

Edgar laughed and said, "Let's not go there."

The group laughed, and I continued. "With this impending loss of revenue, pharmaceutical companies face a challenge. Not only must business leaders make their companies more effective, they must also improve the impact of research and development (R&D) spending. Improved effectiveness of R&D spending has the power to act as a differentiator in a commoditized market."

> This is the fourth time I've been through a patent cliff in my career and the objective of this is to avoid a fifth one.
>
> *Christopher Viehbacher, CEO of Sanofi[4]*

"Effective R&D spending has always been a critical part of a successful pharmaceutical company, but the cost to bring a new drug to market is high and getting higher. The cost of a new molecule ranges between $75 million to $4 billion, according to the same PricewaterhouseCoopers report." I then switched the projector image to show Figure 6.9, and said, "This image illustrates pharmaceutical companies' performance on R&D margin, a measure of R&D effectiveness over the preceding decade."

Edgar then asked, "How do you define R&D margin?" "Good question," I said. I went to the board and wrote the equation:

$$R\&D\, Margin = \frac{Revenue - R\&D\, Budget}{Revenue}$$

At that point, Jeff, looking up from the report that I had given him, chimed in, "Here is how I read this report. The winner is clearly Abbott Laboratories. Merck's declining performance was a major factor in its decision to merge with Schering Plough. While Eli Lilly shows consistency in past performance, the future looks bleak with Eli Lilly losing patent protection on 66 percent of its 2010 pharmaceutical sales by 2013.[7] Other pharmaceutical companies face similarly steep patent cliffs.[8] Is this how you see it?"

"Yes," I stated. "As companies try to reverse this trend, the design of the clinical trial supply chain, to ensure effective deployment of drugs and trials, is

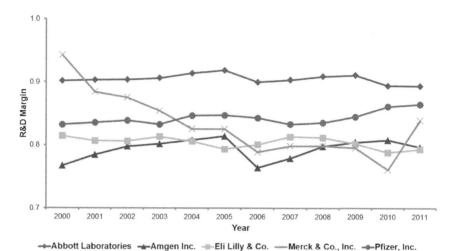

FIGURE 6.9 Effectiveness of R&D Spending
Source: Supply Chain Insights LLC, Corporate Annual Reports 2000–2011.

critical. In addition, effective commercialization of supply chains early in the new drug stage-gate processes is vital. Due to the fact that pharmaceutical companies are closely regulated, and manufacturing sites aren't interchangeable, it is very important for companies to design the whole supply chain early in the process of a new product launch. This issue is of more importance to pharmaceutical companies than any other industry due to the level of regulation."

Progress on the Effective Frontier

Edgar was ready. He was sitting on the edge of his seat as he said, "Okay, let's see the results. How did this industry perform on the Index? What can we learn about their progress on the Effective Frontier?"

I rubbed my hands and smiled, and continued, "The pharmaceutical companies, as a whole, are resilient but have made little progress on the Effective Frontier. The progress on operating margin and inventory turns is small. It is not as great as the impact we saw in the consumer products and food and beverage industries." The group intently discussed the results by reviewing what is shown in Table 6.5.

Edgar said inquisitively, "How did Biogen drive improvements? What did they do?" To help answer his question, I shared a recent case study that I had worked on with the group.

TABLE 6.5 Supply Chain Index: Pharmaceutical

Company	2013 Revenue (billions USD)	Balance	Balance Ranking	Strength	Strength Ranking	Resiliency	Resiliency Ranking	Index (0.3B + 0.3S + 0.3R)	Ranking
Biogen Idec Inc	6.9	1.66	1	0.18	1	0.18	2	1.2	1
Novo Nordisk A/S	14.9	0.15	4	0.13	3	0.23	4	3.3	2
Bayer AG	53.3	0.01	6	0.06	5	0.25	5	4.8	3
Gulf Pharmaceutical Industries PSC	0.4	0.31	3	0.01	11	0.20	3	5.1	4
Shire PLC	4.9	0.52	2	0.03	8	0.58	12	6.6	5
Bristol-Myers Squibb Co	16.4	0.03	5	0.07	4	0.89	15	7.2	6
Alliance Pharma PLC	0.1	-0.02	7	0.16	2	1.25	16	7.5	7
Eli Lilly & Co.	23.1	-0.09	9	0.02	9	0.29	7	7.5	7
GlaxoSmithKline PLC	41.5	-0.24	12	-0.03	12	0.18	1	7.5	7
Johnson & Johnson	71.3	-0.03	8	-0.04	13	0.38	8	8.7	10
Novartis AG	58.8	-0.15	11	0.02	10	0.52	9	9.0	11
Teva Pharmaceutical Industries Limited	20.3	-0.13	10	-0.04	14	0.26	6	9.0	11
Pfizer Inc.	51.6	-1.06	15	0.05	7	0.53	10	9.6	13
Abbott Laboratories	21.8	-10.50	16	0.05	6	0.55	11	9.9	14
AstraZeneca PLC	25.7	-0.35	13	-0.06	15	0.62	13	12.3	15
Merck & Co.	44.0	-0.49	14	-0.10	16	0.80	14	13.2	16

Source: Supply Chain Insights LLC, Corporate Annual Reports 2006–2013.

Interview with Robert Cantow, Biogen

B iogen Idec's products treat multiple sclerosis, Crohn's disease, non-Hodgkin's lymphoma, and rheumatoid arthritis. Founded in 1978, Biogen is the world's oldest independent biotechnology company. Their corporate offices are in Massachusetts.

We interviewed Robert Cantow, leader of the operations team driving excellence to understand which metrics he thinks matter and why. Here is our interview:

Robert, which metrics do you think matter?

It is a portfolio. We have to manage the metrics together. The metrics are connected, with finite trade-offs. To manage the corporation and judge success, I look at:

* Forecast accuracy
* Service level in case fill
* Cost-to-serve clients
* Inventory turns and obsolescence

Some of these metrics are straightforward and some are not. The relative importance is dependent on the strategy. For example, we are executing a growth strategy. Part of our challenge is that we are making decisions on how to make investments in new products that may take two to five years to launch, but five years to build the supply chain to deliver it. As a result, we are modeling the probability of product success based on the product pipeline.

How do you achieve balance in a metrics portfolio?

It needs to be modeled. You don't know until you measure the potential. For example, inventory is reflective (on inventory) of supply chain design. Inventory is also a part of total cost. Consider if I offshore production and lead times increase 20 days. I know that this will increase in-transit inventories and safety stock. My group will understand this cost increase and weigh the impact against sourcing alternatives for tax efficiency or better customer service. These are trade-offs that need to be modeled and agreed upon.

To help us, I created a team to do this type of analysis. It is a small team, and I measure the success by "pull" by the business. The usage is

(continued)

(continued)

increasing. I did it successfully when I was at Boston Scientific, and I am just starting the journey at Biogen, but it makes a difference.

What have you learned about using metrics, and driving a data-driven discussion?

The first is that metrics have to be aligned up and down and across the organization. I work with the business to define what metrics mean to each individual within the company.

The second thing I have learned is that in the analysis we often uncover a performance problem. When we do, it is critical that we focus on the problem and not assign blame. How you manage the process is as important as the discovery of the issue itself.

And, third and most important, you cannot have balance without doing the analysis and understanding the trade-offs.

The discussion on the Biogen case study led to a heated discussion on modeling organizational potential. At this point in the dialogue, Lou asked, "I wonder how this compares with Angela's models? I would put her work up against anyone's in the industry." Angela smiled and thanked Lou for the compliment.

At this point, Joe spoke. "There is an important point here that I did not understand until I started working with the Effective Frontier framework. Financial ratios are nonlinear relationships that *cannot* be modeled in a spreadsheet. They are interrelated. No matter how good Angela is, we will not be successful modeling them in a spreadsheet." His voice trailed off and he looked at Angela. "This is not about having great Excel skills. You know how impressed I am with your skills. Instead I think that this is about understanding and modeling the Effective Frontier using more advanced modeling techniques. I, too, used to think that we did a good job. I now sadly know that I was wrong."

"Joe, I appreciate the honesty," said Edgar. "We all have a lot to learn here. I have been thinking about the group that I want to fund to examine new business models. I would like to emulate Robert's work at Biogen and create a center of excellence to do regular modeling of the Effective Frontier." Edgar turned to Angela and Lou, and said, "Would this be good input into the monthly S&OP processes?"

Filipe then spoke. "Edgar, I think that this is a great idea. I have been wanting to do this modeling to understand volume cost trade-offs for a long time and it certainly seems to be working for Biogen." There seemed to be a consensus, but then Frank spoke, "I am in agreement, but let's get one thing clear. I don't have the resources to spend any more time getting ready or executing the S&OP processes. If this is something that you want to support, I can get there, but don't ask anything else from me. I need to have all of my salespeople concentrating on selling."

"Frank, what happened?" said Filipe. "I thought that you were committed to the process yesterday. Did you have a bad morning? How can we move you past these objections?"

The air seemed to go out of Frank. "Oh, boy," he said. "It is hard to break old habits. I am sorry. You are right. I am just feeling a lot of pressure right now to make our numbers for the quarter. Bear with me. I need to be the leader in sales to share and drive insights market-to-market."

Impact of Mergers and Acquisitions

I changed the focus to mergers and acquisitions (M&A) and stated, "Just as in the chemical industry, M&As have played a large role within the pharmaceutical industry over the past decade. Although there is the potential for M&A activity to create a lot of instability and shifting conditions, the pharmaceutical industry has done a remarkable job of weathering the storm. Pfizer's acquisition of Wyeth, and Merck's acquisition of Schering-Plough are two examples of the level of consolidation and activity occurring within the industry. This turbulence creates a difficult environment to drive year-over-year improvements, yet the pharmaceutical industry as a whole has demonstrated a level of stability in regard to M&A activity that signifies a higher level of maturity than we had expected. As a result, larger companies today are more resilient with larger margins. However, their inventory turns are significantly worse than the smaller pharmaceutical companies. Some of this is due to the issues with M&A execution."

After passing out the figures, shown here as Figures 6.10 and 6.11, to the group, I then turned to Angela and stated, "While the pharmaceutical companies did not achieve the revenue per employee efficiencies of other global process companies like CPG and the chemical companies, there is a small, but not a major difference on the efficiency achieved based on the economy of scale factors. Today, companies sit on cash, and progress on cash-to-cash cycles is stagnant. The future of the pharmaceutical industry will be tightly woven with stories of globalization and declining margins, increased regulation, and heightened delivery requirements for drug safety. There will be more and

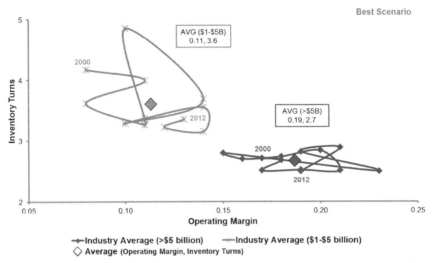

FIGURE 6.10 Pharmaceutical Companies: Inventory Turns versus Operating Margin for 2006–2012

Industry Average comprised of public companies (NAICS code 325412) reporting in One Source with 2012 annual sales greater than $5 billion, $1–$5 billion, $500 million–$1 billion, excluding outliers in operating margin > 1 and < –1.

Source: Supply Chain Insights LLC, Corporate Annual Reports 2000–2012.

---

more pressure for custom drugs in the face of intense legislation. While the pharmaceutical industry does operate globally, the design of their operations is regional or multinational. They lack the sophistication in global/regional governance of chemical or consumer packaged goods companies. As a result, an opportunity exists in the design of that governance to enable companies to maximize economies of scale while obeying increasing regulations."

At this point in the presentation, Filipe spoke, "Why would an industry with this much margin to invest not have made more progress on the Effective Frontier? Or taken more leadership to improve value in the value chain?"

I answered, "I think that this is the million-dollar question that most CEOs in the pharmaceutical industry need to answer. However, it will not be for me to give an opinion. It should be their board of directors. As we will see through our three days together, there is an inverse relationship between margin and success on the Effective Frontier. Companies that have the largest margins typically make the slowest progress. There is a lot of room for the pharmaceutical companies to make progress in the next decade. But, to do this, they will have to learn from other industries."

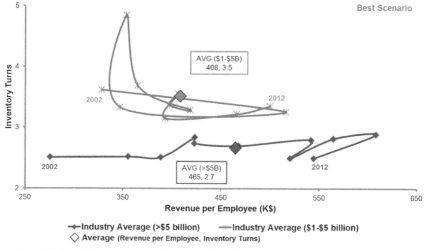

FIGURE 6.11 Pharmaceutical Companies: Inventory Turns versus Revenue per Employee for 2006–2012
Industry Average comprised of public companies (NAICS code 325412) reporting in One Source with 2012 annual sales greater than $5 billion and $1–$5 billion.
Source: Supply Chain Insights LLC, Corporate Annual Reports 2002–2012.

Before break, we summarized our key insights on the pharmaceutical industry.

Summary

The group then hastily wrote the following on the board.

▪ High margins can be a barrier for success. (Lou chuckled and cracked a joke, but the group readily agreed.)
▪ If you are a leader in the industry, you need to act like a leader.
▪ The longer the lead times for R&D launch, the more critical it is to model operations.

I then summarized the group's discussion. "For many years the pharmaceutical industry was insulated by high gross margins and patent protection. Those years are now ending. Not only to survive, but to be profitable moving forward, companies need to reconsider the traditional approach and build both innovation and stability into the company culture. Today, both are lagging. By doing this, we believe pharmaceutical companies will not only weather the upcoming challenges, but also drive operational excellence and approach a new level of maturity for the industry."

MEDICAL DEVICE MANUFACTURERS

The day was almost over. The group energy was still high, but I could tell that they were anxious to get back to their desks and take care of pressing issues. So, I started early and tried to condense the materials to wrap up the day a bit early. To stimulate the discussion, I started with some quick data. "Many medical device companies are enamored with the 'good old days.' These are gone. Operating margin has declined precipitously in the period of 2000–2013. This rapid drop in margin hurt." A group discussion on Table 6.6 ensued.

"As hospitals adopted consignment planning programs, inventory progress slowed. The turns of the medical device company are the lowest of any industry and, despite investments in technologies and processes, inventory turns have only improved 3 percent, and cash-to-cash (C2C) cycles have declined 4 percent. Companies are feeling pain."

"Just to be sure that we're grounded, let me see if I can give you some comparisons," said Lou with a furrowed brow. "The operating margin for the medical device industry is four times that of the food and beverage manufacturer and two times the margin of the hospital. The business operating environment has changed. The pressures of affordable care and global regulation are transforming the market, but they are not redefining operations fast enough. Am I close?" I nodded my head in agreement.

"Why are these companies not being more aggressive in driving balance and resiliency?" asked Edgar. "I just don't understand why they are not more aggressive."

"I know that it is hard to understand, but there are a lot of changes, and it is not clear for many companies how to drive effective change," I stated. "It is

TABLE 6.6   Progress in the Medical Device Industry

Medical Device Industry (n = 6)				
Year	Operating Margin	Inventory Turns	Cash-to-Cash Cycle	Revenue per Employee (K$)	SG&A Ratio
2000–2003	0.17	3	145	205	29%
2004–2007	0.16	3	132	259	28%
2008–2011	0.16	3	145	298	28%
2012	0.08	3	151	308	28%

Industry Average composed of public companies (NAICS 339112) reporting in One Source with 2012 annual sales greater than $5 billion.
Source: Supply Chain Insights LLC, Corporate Annual Reports 2000–2012.

hard for industries to sense changes in the value network and then orchestrate changes. We can see this by examining the progress on the Effective Frontier."

Progress on the Effective Frontier

"As we have seen, companies with lower margins tend to do better on the Effective Frontier. Why? It matters more. In these industries, the adoption of new technologies and processes becomes essential to doing business. In industries with high margins, change happens slowly and the leaders tend to be insular. This is the case in the medical device industry. Their results have been resilient, but they are not strong and they are not balanced," I said. "Let's examine the results." I then showed them the results in Table 6.7.

At this point, Edgar stated, "This is serious stuff. I think that this industry is in trouble. What recommendations would you have for them?"

I then told the group that I had four recommendations, which included a focus on patient-based outcomes, measurement of effectiveness through scorecards, aggressive adoption of scorecards, and a determination to get and use channel data in outside-in processes.

Build Economies of Scale in Medical Device Companies

I then stated, "Unlike the pharmaceutical companies, we do not see the economy of scale benefits in the medical device industry that we saw in the pharmaceutical industry. The larger companies have slightly better margins but worse inventory turns, and negligible effects on revenue per employee. Smaller companies are slightly more resilient. They just do not have the levels of global complexity." I then turned to Angela, and stated, "Again, we have an industry that is not benefiting from M&A." I could tell that she was thinking intently as she traced the pattern on Figures 6.12 and 6.13.

Summary

In our wrap-up, Angela stated, "Wow! What a difference in the progress of both the industries and the value chains. As you have been talking, I have been working with Jeff to look at the average results of all industries on the Effective Frontier. Let me just tell you guys, these are huge differences." She then turned to Jeff and said, "Jeff, let's put our results on the board."

As Jeff went to the board, she continued, "As we look at these numbers we need to remember that the bigger the value of the balance factor means that the industry has made more progress at the intersection of growth and ROIC; and

TABLE 6.7 Medical Device Progress on the Effective Frontier

Company	2013 Revenue (billions USD)	Balance	Balance Ranking	Strength	Strength Ranking	Resiliency	Resiliency Ranking	Index (0.3B + 0.3S + 0.3R)	Ranking
Smith & Nephew PLC	4.4	0.17	1	-0.02	3	0.11	2	1.8	1
Getinge AB	3.9	-0.07	4	-0.01	2	0.20	6	3.6	2
Zimmer Holdings, Inc.	4.6	-0.12	7	-0.05	7	0.10	1	4.5	3
Medtronic	16.6	-0.14	8	-0.01	1	0.21	7	4.8	4
Baxter International Inc.	15.3	0.03	2	-0.03	6	0.28	9	5.1	5
Covidien PLC	10.2	0.00	3	-0.03	4	0.45	11	5.4	6
Becton, Dickinson and Co.	8.1	-0.10	5	-0.05	8	0.17	5	5.4	6
Stryker Corporation	9.0	-0.16	9	-0.06	12	0.13	3	7.2	8
Fresenius SE & Co. KGaA	27.3	-0.11	6	-0.03	5	1.00	13	7.2	8
Terumo Corp	4.8	-0.29	12	-0.06	11	0.14	4	8.1	10
DENTSPLY International Inc.	3.0	-0.17	10	-0.05	9	0.26	8	8.1	10
Fisher & Paykel Healthcare Corp Ltd	0.5	-0.17	11	-0.09	13	0.45	12	10.8	12
Boston Scientific Corporation	7.1	-0.31	13	-0.18	15	0.44	10	11.4	13
Cardinal Health Inc	101.1	-0.33	14	-0.06	10	1.90	15	11.7	14
Olympus Corp	9.0	-0.43	15	-0.13	14	1.15	14	12.9	15

Source: Supply Chain Insights LLC, Corporate Annual Reports 2006–2013.

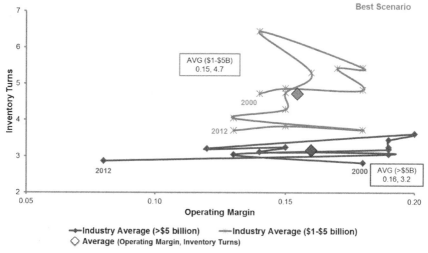

FIGURE 6.12 Contrast of Company Size on Operating Margin and Inventory Turns for Medical Device Companies

Industry Average composed of public companies (NAICS codes 339112) reporting in One Source with 2012 annual sales greater than $5 billion and $1–$5 billion.
Source: Supply Chain Insights LLC, Corporate Annual Reports 2000–2012.

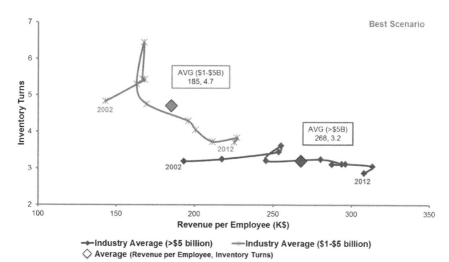

FIGURE 6.13 Contrast of Company Size on Operating Margin and Revenue per Employee for Medical Device Companies

Industry Average composed of public companies (NAICS codes 339112) reporting in One Source with 2012 annual sales greater than $5 billion and $1–$5 billion.
Source: Supply Chain Insights LLC, Corporate Annual Reports 2002–2012.

TABLE 6.8   Industry Comparison on the Effective Frontier

Industry	Number of Companies	Average Balance	Average Strength	Average Resiliency
Retail	14	−0.12	0.01	1.40
Consumer Packaged Goods	17	−0.11	0.03	0.71
Food & Beverage	21	0.17	0.06	1.03
Chemical	18	−0.07	0.01	0.85
Hospital	5	−0.25	0.02	3.57
Pharmaceutical	16	−0.65	0.03	0.48
Medical Device	15	−0.15	−0.06	0.47

Source: Supply Chain Insights LLC, Corporate Annual Reports 2006–2013.

the larger the strength factor, the larger the improvement at the intersection of inventory turns and operating margin, and the greater the progress. This is our measure of strength. However, when it comes to resiliency, the smaller numbers are better. Let's take a closer look at the numbers." With that, Jeff turned the board around to show the results to the group (see Table 6.8).

"Yowza!" said Joe. "Look at the large resiliency numbers for retail, hospitals, and food and beverage. Lou, how would you like to be managing those businesses?" Lou shook his head.

"And, it looks like the manufacturers are making more progress on the strength factor than hospitals and retailers," continued Joe.

"Yes," Angela continued, "it is late. I have been working with Jeff to summarize the data, and we have come up with the following conclusions. Can we put them on the board and get your feedback? It might make it quicker to end the day."

With that Frank clapped his hands. He wanted to go. He was in a hurry. The sun was out and he wanted to show Jeff his new red Porsche. The chrome on the car shone brightly in the parking lot and as he pointed to it out the window, he asked the group if we could wrap up our meeting quickly.

Edgar nodded and thanked Angela for her proactivity, and then agreed to make it a short summary.

Jeff and Angela wrote on the whiteboard:

Overall, in the period of 2006–2012, the health-care value chain has not made as much progress as the consumer value chain. In many ways it is weak and needs to be redefined.

While there were leaders in the consumer value chain, we do not see the same leadership at an individual company level in this industry.

Instead, companies continued with the status quo. They were often sitting on large amounts of capital that they could be using to improve the effectiveness of health-care processes, but no company drove process innovation in value-chain relationships.

While the consumer value chain attempted to partner with their trading partners and improve value, this has not happened in the health-care industry. They are at least 10 years behind in scorecards and the use of channel data.

It was time for one of Edgar's leadership moments. As he cleared his throat, Frank sat back down in his chair. He knew that he needed to stay for Edgar's summary. As Edgar sat back in his chair, he said, "Thank you. I have learned a lot. Leaders need to lead. It is not enough for us to do well within our organization; we need to take responsibility for our value chain. Without doing so, we are vulnerable to risk and cannot maximize opportunity. Today has been a wake-up call for me." He then looked at Filipe and Joe, and continued, "We, like the companies that we have studied today, have focused on improving efficiency within the four walls of our organization. I think that it is time for us to go to the next level and drive leadership in the value network."

With that we called it a day, and agreed to meet the next day to review the industrial value chain. Frank quickly zipped up his briefcase, jingled his keys, and laughed. He demonstrated for the group how he could put the top down on his car remotely from the conference room.

As I packed my things, I reflected. It was good to see the sun shining and have the group end a tough day with lots of data and with so much positive energy.

 ## CONCLUSION

Progress on the Effective Frontier happens slowly over many years. The greatest progress happens when there is a redefinition of relationships, the adoption of new business models, and the consistent leadership that understands that managing metrics within operations must be approached as a complex system with increasing complexity. On these points, I thought that the group was making progress.

As I closed the door, I reflected. The lack of leadership at first creates stasis, which can follow with bankruptcy. Companies need to own their value networks and win with partners. I looked forward to sharing these insights from the industrial value networks with the team, on the next day.

Notes

1. Johnson & Johnson, "Our Credo," www.jnj.com/sites/default/files/pdf/jnj_ourcredo_english_us_8.5x11_cmyk.pdf (accessed May 2014).
2. U.S. Food and Drug Administration, "Unique Device Identification (UDI)," www.fda.gov/MedicalDevices/DeviceRegulationandGuidance/UniqueDeviceIdentification/default.htm?utm_source=Members-Only%20Updates (accessed June 1, 2014).
3. Supply Chain Insights Report, "Insights on the Building an Effective Healthcare Value Network" (October 2013).
4. Supply Chain Movement, "Overhaul of Supply Chain Will Save Millions on Health Care," www.supplychainmovement.com/overhaul-of-supply-chain-will-save-millions-on-health-care/?goback=%2Egde_100178_member_192421138.
5. *Science Daily*, "Prescription for Healthier Hospital Supply Chains," www.sciencedaily.com/releases/2011/06/110620103856.htm.
6. PricewaterhouseCoopers, "From Vision to Decision: Pharma 2020," www.pwc.com/en_GX/gx/pharma-life-sciences/pharma2020/assets/pwc-pharma-success-strategies.pdf.
7. *Seeking Alpha*, "4 Pharmaceutical Companies Facing Huge Patent Cliff Hurdles," seekingalpha.com/article/322020-4-pharmaceutical-companies-facing-huge-patent-cliff-hurdles.
8. *Harvard Business Review*, "The CEO of Novartis on Growing after a Patent Cliff," http://hbr.org/2012/12/the-ceo-of-novartis-on-growing-after-a-patent-cliff/ar/1.

CHAPTER SEVEN

What Drives Value in the Value Network?

Industry Progress in the Industrial Value Chain

T WAS OUR LAST day together. Normally, I show up early and set up for a session, but not today. I was late.

I grimaced as I entered the room. I like to be punctual. However, to my surprise and delight, the group had started the session without me. So I just sat down and listened as the dialogue evolved.

It had been a rough morning for Frank. Last night, he drove Jeff to dinner. A man with a heavy foot, he was eager to demonstrate the capabilities of his new, red Porsche. On the way to dinner, Frank put the top down and floored the gas to show Jeff the rapid acceleration. As he hurtled through a stop sign, police lights flashed blue. Red-faced, Frank was forced to pull over.

The policeman was a neighbor of Jeff's, so Frank got off with only a warning. However, it was a rallying point for the group to harass Frank that morning. Filipe piped up, "See, Frank, you may want to go fast, but we all have rules that we need to follow. Someday, you won't have Jeff to bail you out."

Frank shook his head ruefully and asked, "I know you are having fun, but when is enough really enough? Seriously, haven't I paid my dues . . . ? Just working with you guys is tough enough."

Lou peered over his glasses, and smiled. He was having fun, but wanted to get the meeting back on track. He said, "Okay, we've had fun with Frank, but I think that it's time to move on." He looked at Edgar and said, "I wonder if we will ever learn this basic, and hard, lesson?"

As Lou made this comment, he got up and poured himself another cup of coffee. While in mid-sentence, he slowly stirred it. He said. "My takeaway from our work so far is that it takes a team to conquer the Effective Frontier. I wonder if we have what it takes?

"I have also learned a lot from these sessions," Lou continued. "For me, there is an overarching theme. If we want to be successful in our mission, we need to build organizational potential slowly. It needs to happen gradually based on a clear vision, but we need to exercise strong discipline. I think that we have a disconnect. This will be hard for us."

As he sat down, and furrowed his eyebrows, he leaned over and touched Edgar on the arm, looking him in the eyes. He said, "Edgar, you are guilty of the 'program of the month.' It seems like you change our goals and the metrics every month. After you read an article or listen to some speaker, it seems like you have a new goal for us. This is the opposite of what we learned in the past two days. Do you really think that we can make this *new* approach stick?"

"Yes," said Edgar, "I've been thinking about this as well. I think that it's as much about what we do *not* do versus what we do. It is about conscious choice. Today, we measure too many things. And our focus is scattered. I admit I'm guilty of initiating the program of the month. I have a better understanding of the impact of this now on the organization."

Edgar then turned and looked at Frank. "Frank, do you think that we're pushing volume into the channel no matter what the cost? I know that I'm guilty of changing programs and throwing the organization into a tailspin, but, Frank, I think you are guilty of pushing cases and not taking time to build strong channel relationships. I think we need to rethink our channel strategies to build stronger relationships.

"Before I went to bed last night, I was thinking about what we learned yesterday in our session about the health-care value chain," Edgar continued. "Can you believe that not *one* supplier seized the opportunity to build its infrastructure? No one invested to implement a new business strategy. I was contrasting this view of history to the lessons we learned earlier from Joe." He then looked at me and said, "I think that you shared the case study of Taiwan Semiconductor (TSMC) with Joe last year." I agreed.

Edgar continued, "What if there had been a TSMC in the health-care value chain that would have provided the infrastructure for collaborating companies?

Or what if the distributors like Cardinal or McKesson had created something like the IBM iBAT system? Would we be at a better place today? I think so."

Joe joined the discussion. "The adoption of new business models was also an issue. Remember our discussion about who is the customer in the health-care value chain? This lack of clarity made these models less effective. The transition to sell directly to the hospital, while servicing the physician, was a tough evolution," said Joe. "When I contrast the insights from the past two days about the two different value chains, I see one thing very clearly. When you win with customers, you all win. Remember the presentation that we saw from General Mills last week at the Business Leaders Conference?" Filipe nodded his head yes.

Angela said, "No, I didn't see it. What did you learn?"

"As part of their market strategy, General Mills built core capability to help their customers optimize their effectiveness on return on invested capital, margin, and inventory. In fact, they built a whole team to do this kind of work. Frank, I think that we should consider adding this type of value network thinking into our sales processes. I think that it could improve our channel relationships."

Jeff looked at Joe, and asked, "How would this work? Tell me more."

Joe was eager to share. He leaned forward and placed his elbows on the table, dangling his glasses from one hand. He looked Jeff directly in the eye. "The focus is to design the value network from the customer back. Our goal would be to help our customers better serve their customers with our products. At General Mills, they have a team of over 20 people who work with their sales organization to design the value network to be sure that the flows of products and services are aligned to maximize profitability while minimizing inventory and returns. I was impressed that their customers value the service. In 2014, their retailers rated them as the most improved supplier for the past two years."

Lou then entered the conversation, "Is this something that they charge for? I know that industry well. The margins are razor-thin, and you're talking about adding costs and infrastructure. How do they justify it?"

Joe smiled, and continued, "They try to make it a win/win. As they identify opportunities, they share in the savings or use it to barter for services. It might be a better rate on a promotion, or placement in the store, or perhaps a reduction in fee for slotting allowances. In short, they work with the sales team to make it part of the negotiation." Joe then looked at Frank, and said, "Do you think that we could make this work?"

"I don't know. You know there are many times when we just don't work well together. Joe, your team really doesn't understand the pressures that we are under every week to drive sales. It would require a lot of work," said Frank. He then turned to Jeff, and asked, "What do you think?"

Jeff said, "I think that it's worth a shot. I think that it would improve the 'stickiness' of the relationship in our major accounts. Most of our customers are also struggling with their ability to drive margins and manage inventories. In many ways, the work that Filipe and Joe have done on lean and network design could be used to our advantage." He then quickly stated, as he sat back in his chair, "It would also give the sales team something more to talk about when they are visiting the customer. We need more conversation starters. I think that this could add value.

"So, yes, I would like to do it, Frank," said Jeff. "I think that it is time for us to be more of a part of this team. Improving value in Project Orbit is about more than driving sales and reducing costs."

Frank took a deep breath as Angela took over the conversation. "I agree with Lou. Let's look at the lessons from health care. Yesterday we saw that no supplier stepped up to do this in the health-care value chain. I think that this is one of our problems today with the escalating cost of health care. As regulations got tougher, companies focused on themselves and maximizing their own profitability; but no one took ownership for the value chain. I am not sure what our customers and suppliers have to say about us, but I doubt that it would be good. Getting clear on how we serve the customer in Joe's emerging market opportunity in Brazil would help us to drive alignment, and ultimately improve balance.

"Remember the quote from Hau Lee that I have on my desk?" she continued. "It was great that Lou sponsored my efforts to go back to graduate school last year. I also appreciate your support to let me have this experience." Lou smiled as he briefly met Angela's eyes.

She continued, "Dr. Lee was one of my professors. I love hearing him talk about operations and finance. Edgar, remember the article that defines Triple-A supply chains?" She then reached into her red briefcase and passed around copies. "I think that it explains why we haven't been more successful in defining and executing value network strategies."

> The best supply chains are not just fast and cost effective. They are also agile and adaptable, and they ensure that all their company's interests are strong and aligned.[1]
>
> Hau L. Lee, "Triple-A Supply Chains," *Harvard Business Review*, October 2004

I had watched the dialogue from the back of the room, and thought that this would be the right time to jump in and start the day's discussions. "Angela, do you think that it's because your current set of metrics reward efficiency over effectiveness?"

"Yes," she said. "This is one of my key insights from the work that we are doing together. If you notice in the presentation that you did yesterday, industry by industry, companies have improved their own efficiency, but have not had any qualms about pushing costs and waste upstream to their suppliers. It is ironic, because very few companies have used their brand power and their ability to get capital to power an advantage."

I was enjoying the exchange, and used it as an opportunity to come to the front and start to facilitate the session. "Angela, you will see this very clearly in the definition of the industrial value network."

"Great," said Angela. "But, I have a request. I would like to share some of the work that Jeff and I did together last night." She then looked at the group, and continued, "Would this be okay with the team?"

> We live in a world where supply chains, not companies, compete for market dominance. But companies often have diverging incentives and interests from their supply chain partners, so when they independently strive to optimize their individual objectives, the expected result can be compromised.
>
> Hau L. Lee, "Triple-A Supply Chains," *Harvard Business Review*, October 2004

They all nodded their heads in agreement, and Angela plugged her laptop into the digital projector. She continued, "Jeff and I were struggling with some of the slides that you showed yesterday. It's hard to absorb this material all at once. It's a very deep topic. My mind was spinning at times. You gave us a lot of material, and in some cases the scale used on the orbit charts was different." She then looked back at me, and continued, "Please don't take this wrong, I know that you've changed the scale to show the story, but it seems to me that unless you can view the companies together in the value network in an orbit chart framework, you can't really get the entire picture."

Jeff then spoke up, "Last night after dinner, Angela and I put all of the companies in a value network on the same orbit chart and made the scale the same so that we could compare them. We found that the slides got too confusing if we showed all the companies in an industry, so we just picked the companies at the top of the Index. We thought that it would be interesting to look at the patterns of the companies that were driving the highest level of improvement, and contrast their improvement within the value chain." He then turned to the group and said, "Make sense?"

Animated, Lou chimed in, "I think that this is a great idea! It should help us to get grounded for the work for Project Orbit."

Edgar approved and stated. "I love the proactivity. Let's see what you've built."

Angela then showed the slide for the consumer value network (as depicted in Figure 7.1) on the screen at the front of the conference room. She began to explain the orbit chart of the value network that they developed, "We placed the financial results of Walmart, BASF, VF Corporation, Hershey, and Colgate on the same chart. What we see is that each of the companies operates in its own space, or Effective Frontier."

"Yes," said Jeff as he continued. "What I find fascinating is that we see the entire value network is not improving. Even when we map the companies with the greatest progress, we don't see an overall trend of continuous improvement in the value network. Most companies are stuck. The road taken had tough turns. So, we are wondering if we could use some of Joe's ideas to define a new

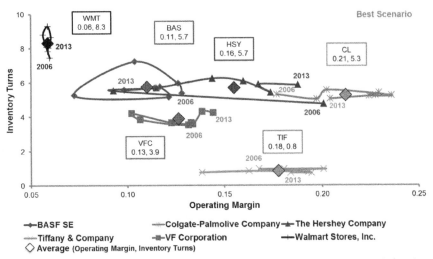

FIGURE 7.1 Orbit Chart of Companies in the Consumer Value Network for the Period of 2006–2012
Source: Supply Chain Insights LLC, Corporate Annual Reports 2006–2013

model for our business sector that could help to drive value not only for us but for our customers and our suppliers to break this paradigm."

Angela then turned to Frank, and said, "I know when you were at P&G you were heavily invested in driving improvements through collaboration. We also saw your face when you saw how Procter & Gamble performed on the index. We had always used P&G as a reference point for our benchmarking activities. We saw a different story when we did the Index. So we wanted to contrast the two value chains to see if we could see a different pattern." She then pressed the switch to move to the next slide, which is shown here as Figure 7.2.

"Again, we find that while companies have talked about collaboration across value chains and creating value in value networks, this has not really happened," Angela said. "In the case of the health-care value network, the hospitals pushed back the responsibility of inventory onto their trading partners without sharing data, and the health-care suppliers have moved backward on operating margin and not made any improvements in inventory. We just find it interesting that while we've gone to many conferences where we have talked about collaboration and creating value, we still struggle to see it in the corporate performance numbers," Angela concluded. As she sat down, Lou let out a low whistle.

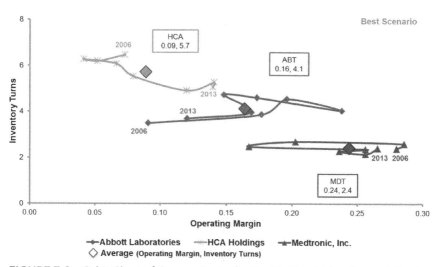

FIGURE 7.2   Orbit Chart of Companies in the Health-Care Value Network for the Period of 2006–2013
Source: Supply Chain Insights LLC, Corporate Annual Reports 2006–2013

"Bravo," Lou said. "I love the initiative. These slides portray the discussion that Edgar and I had last night. We believe that each company is operating within its own plane, or performance zone. When you are in this zone, companies have a defined potential. This is the concept of the Effective Frontier that we are struggling to understand. On these charts, you can clearly see that each company is performing in a different zone, or facing a different Effective Frontier." He looked at Edgar, and the quiet leader concurred.

Lou continued, "I also think that it is useful to see companies within a value chain grouped together on an orbit chart. It helps us to better understand the impact of technology and process improvements across the value chain. When grouped this way, you can see that each company is carving out their own path, but that the industry, as a whole, is not getting better. This surprises me a bit. Does it surprise you?" The group agreed. Lou then turned to Filipe and asked, "Why do you think that this is so?"

Filipe thought awhile, and then countered, "I was struck by one of the slides that Joe shared with me when we first started Project Orbit last year. It was a research study on supply-chain visibility and risk management." He turned to me and asked, "Remember that research that you shared with Joe a year ago?" Joe answered, "Yes." "Joe, if you still have it, I think that it would be good to show it to the group. I found it valuable.

"Let me tell you why," Filipe stated with authority, "I have listened quietly to this discussion, but I have been thinking deeply about the concepts. I think that many companies, like ours, are struggling with the same thing. We are driving continuous improvement programs and thinking that we can make linear progress against the goals. But we are managing the metrics in isolation. Sometimes it's a focus on cost, sometimes it's customer service, and then on a whim we'll change it to inventory. As we do this, we move backward and forward on the plane of performance that we call the Effective Frontier. As the markets shift, even that can be a struggle."

He continued, "We have also not built potential to enable us to be more agile or nimble on this frontier. We have not made the building of value networks and developing systems to connect trading partners a priority. Our second, and perhaps bigger barrier, is our traditional thinking about how we buy and sell. It's just hard for us to get out of our way to move past a traditional buy/sell relationship to create value. And finally, we have let complexity creep into the organization without rationalizing good and bad complexity."

"What does that mean? Good and bad complexity?" said Edgar.

"For me, a good analogy is how your doctor talks to you about cholesterol," Frank said. "You know how you have good and bad cholesterol? And, that you want to reduce, and even eliminate, bad cholesterol? Complexity is the same. You want to increase the complexity that drives profitable sales, but you want to eliminate the complexity that does not add value to customers. As a result, many leading companies look at item rationalization quarterly to try to reduce bad complexity. In the past, we have worked on platform rationalization; that was good complexity. To reduce complexity, we have also cut slow-selling products from our portfolio. Make sense?"

"However, the more powerful concept for me is the concept of moving to a new frontier," said Filipe. "When we do this, we put ourselves on a new plane. I am interested in raising our potential."

Edgar said, "I am still struggling with the gnarly patterns of these charts. I've been naïve, I thought that the pattern would have been more linear; and I thought that companies were making more progress." It was settled. For the group, the value of the index methodology was clear to measure improvement.

"I also thought that, as an industry, we were making more progress," Edgar exclaimed. "When I go to conferences and I hear the stories of how companies have invested in technologies and driven improvement, I have believed that aggregate progress was higher. I now think that we are treading water.

"When I reflect on our journey, Edgar continued, "I believe that our singular focus on productivity and efficiency hurt us, and I think it harmed the industry. I now have much better insights into why the most efficient operation may not be the most effective. This concept of balance and alignment and the creation of value networks is a deep topic. I think that it will take us a while to learn how to master the concepts and drive it into action, but it has been a valuable discussion."

Edgar then turned to me and asked, "To ensure that we have the concepts right, can we spend a minute outlining the differences between what helps us to build potential on the Effective Frontier and what moves could take us to a new frontier? I am also interested in understanding when you know that you have maximized the opportunity on the frontier and recognizing that it's time to move to the next."

The group then spent time brainstorming the answers to Edgar's probing. As they discussed the thought-provoking questions, they built the simple chart that is shown in Table 7.1.

"Thanks," Edgar said. "This helps. I think this is a good start." He then looked at his watch and said, "Unfortunately, I have to meet with some auditors in a couple of minutes. Before I go, I think that it would be great if we could capture the high-level thoughts from yesterday. I also like these charts and this approach. It helps us to be more grounded. Would it be possible to

TABLE 7.1 Understanding the Effective Frontier

How Do We Drive Improvements on the Frontier?	When Is It Time to Move to the Next Frontier?	How Do You Know That You Have Maximized the Possible improvements on the Frontier?
1. Continues Improvement Programs	1. New Opportunities in Either the Product Platform, Business Operating Models, or Technologies	1. Performance at the Intersection of Operating Margin and Inventory Turns or Growth and ROIC Is Difficult and Cannot Be Sustained
2. Investment in Technologies to Optimize Outcomes		
3. Lean Improvement Programs to Reduce Waste	2. Major Shift in the Market	2. Pattern of Stalled Performance in Both the Balance and Strength Factors of the Index Is Present for All Major Competitors
4. Investment in People to Work More Effectively Together	3. Merger and Acquisition Activity	
5. Focus on Effective Horizontal Processes	4. Competitive Activity That Dramatically Changes the Market	
6. Managing a Balanced Set of Metrics	5. Change in Strategy	
7. Use Channel Data and Sense Market Changes	6. Significant Shift in Business Complexity	
	7. Major Shifts in the Network Changing the Balance of Power of Trading Partners	

quickly assemble a similar chart on the industrial value network? I think sharing it up front before we get into each industry will jumpstart the discussion." I acquiesced, knowing in the pit of my stomach that there would be a lot of work to get done during the coffee break.

Angela then said, "I've been processing all of this information and there are several notes that I want to share to see if I have this right." The group asked her to continue. "My first insight is that we should not always assume that a bigger company has a competitive advantage on the Effective Frontier. Over the course of the past two days we are clearly seeing that in some industries, like food and beverage, a smaller company may have an advantage on the frontier."

"Yes," Lou said. "I think that this has relevance to our current thoughts on executing our merger and acquisition targets."

Angela then continued, "My other insight is we talk about complexity, but we don't manage it. I like Frank's analogy of good and bad cholesterol. When we operate in functional silos, we cannot see the impact or the effect of complexity on our ability to drive performance on the Effective Frontier. I think that we should consider inserting the processes to analyze complexity and the impact on the business into our group's efforts when we focus on risk management and sales and operations planning."

Jeff then raised his hand. "Angela, I like these. I just want to add a story from my personal experience that may help the group. As you know, I have been riding my bicycle to work for the past five years. I started doing this to save money, but now I do it for peace of mind. I enjoy it. What I have found is that it has slowly improved my resting heart rate and my heart's recovery rate. In essence, I am improving my body's potential. My body is getting stronger. It is not happening quickly; instead, it is happening very slowly. I liken this to the work that we need to be doing as a group on building organizational potential to conquer the Effective Frontier. Slowly building the right competencies speaks to me.

"So, when I think about moving to the next level or stage of the frontier, an analogy that works for me is my recent decision to upgrade my bike. My body is stronger and I can improve my times on the road, but my bike is old and the frame is heavy. I expect to post much better times with my new carbon frame triathlon bike. While Frank has a Porsche, I've spent my sales bonus money on a spiffy new bike." The group laughed at the thought of tightwad Jeff shelling out thousands of dollars for a new bike.

Jeff continued, "I would be embarrassed to tell you how much it cost, but I do believe that my performance on this new bike will propel me to a new level. In my mind, this is analogous to what we are talking about. We raise the potential of our processes and people while minimizing complexity at this level, and then we need to make conscious choices to move to the next frontier. There are two lessons for me that I think fit our situation. First, we are not patient. Improving performance takes time. It took me a couple of years to build peak performance on my bike. The leaders in the index moved slowly, not quickly."

Frank looked down his glasses, stared at Edgar, and said, "I think what Jeff is trying to tell you is that you are going to need to temper your expectations. Jeff is just too nice to tell you this, but you change our goals too frequently. It is a barrier to alignment."

Turning to Jeff, Frank said, "Sorry to interrupt, Jeff, but I think this is an important point. Please continue. . . ."

Jeff swallowed hard, and looked down and said, "In addition, we are not good at making conscious choices. I have to be very careful about when I train and when I rest."

Frank piped up and stated, "Edgar, what Jeff is trying to say is that we do an awful lot of what I would call 'knee-jerking' and flailing." He looked at others, and said, "And I know that much of it is caused by me talking to Edgar on the sidelines and nagging him about what we could do."

"Thank you, Jeff, and thank you, Angela," said Edgar. "Frank, I am not sure what I would do without you; and then some days, I am not sure what to do with you, but I do agree that those are great insights." He then turned to me and asked if we could wrap up the morning session so that he could get to his meeting with the auditor. The morning had been long, and Edgar was eagerly looking at his watch, so, I quickly divided the group into dyads and triads to reflect on the insights from our second day together. Here are the three insights they shared before going to break:

1. **Frank/Lou:** Be clear on who your customer is. When your customer shifts, realign your value network and your sales strategy. Actively communicate this shift to the entire organization so they can identify the impact and change their processes.
2. **Joe/Angela/Jeff:** Actively work to create value within the network. When you create joint value, the impact is exponential. To do this, we must build outside-in processes. (This group questioned why the suppliers to the health-care value network had not seized the opportunity to collaboratively work together to drive value in the redefinition of the value network for affordable health care.)
3. **Edgar/Filipe:** Markets change faster than companies can. As a result, one of our greatest competitive threats is start-up companies that we can't know about today. How can we embrace new models quickly? Biogen and Amazon are new companies. How can we be more adaptive to market changes? We want to be like Apple, not Kodak.

At the end of the exercise, the group took a break. Angela, Jeff, and I then worked together to build the composite orbit chart for the industrial value chain. The coffee mug was warm in my hand, and the caffeine was as stimulating as the conversation, as I quickly dug deep into the data in my laptop to create the files for the next part of the day.

UNDERSTANDING THE INDUSTRIAL VALUE NETWORK

During the break, Frank was still the recipient of some lighthearted teasing. Jeff had framed his ticket from the prior evening and the group had signed it. Angela had taken a picture of Jeff giving Frank his framed ticket and she quickly posted it on the company intranet. While all in good fun, Frank acknowledged that it was a good reminder that everyone has to play by a set of rules.

The team returned to their seats to share insights into the industrial value network. I looked at the group and reflected on how far they had come in their understanding of metrics, metrics potential on the Effective Frontier, and how to apply it to their own value network thinking. I was pleased. The sun was shining and I was looking forward to wrapping up the strategy session and enabling them to construct their next steps on Project Orbit. I like to help teams.

Edgar was pleased. He could see how Project Orbit was taking shape. It was already helping to improve corporate performance. The discussions were helpful in not only defining goals, but driving alignment. He could see the impact from work that the team sponsored to improve horizontal business processes. The shift in focus from functional silos to driving continuous improvement was building the potential of the organization. Angela was tracking the improvements on her balanced scorecard of growth, ROIC, operating margin, and inventory turns, and she was seeing improvements. Excitement was building, especially among Jeff, Angela, and Joe. Filipe, Lou, and Frank could see it in the numbers, but they had reserved their judgment, waiting to see if the improvements could be sustained. One thing had changed. Everyone was now speaking the same language about metrics.

Overview of the Industrial Value Network

I took a deep breath and looked at the group. With the help of my research assistant, Abby, I had completed the new charts. They were hot off the printer.

When Frank laid down his phone, I began the dialogue, "The industrial value network is composed of manufacturers with a focus on discrete processes. While the companies in the value chains we just studied had more of a focus on make-to-stock processes, inventorying products for promotions, seasonality, and market-shaping activities, the discrete industry sits further back from the customer (tightly integrated into second- and third-tier manufacturers), operating more design- and material-intensive processes. Today, we will review the progress of the high-tech manufacturers and their semiconductor suppliers, automotive manufacturers and their suppliers, and the evolution of a new industry—contract manufacturing—that supports manufacturing processes across the industry."

At this point, Filipe showed great excitement. "This is what I've waited for. I want to understand how lean has improved companies within this industry.

I'm eagerly waiting to see the results of Toyota on the index we've created. Lean thinking is the Toyota Way. I want to show you how everyone else stacks up against them."

At this point, I projected Table 7.2 for the group to review. Then I continued the discussion, "While the automotive industry results show improvement—posting progress in all of our major areas of the Effective Frontier—the industry struggled through the recession due to a lack of market sensing. In contrast, the high-tech value chain composed of consumer electronics and the semiconductor industry fought margin pressure as the price of consumer goods plummeted. To survive, they sensed market demand. As a result, the high-tech industries developed some of the best supply chain planning and inventory management processes across manufacturing. Inventory in this industry is like bananas."

"Like bananas?" asked Lou. "How so? Help me with this one."

"Sure," I said. "When you buy apples, you might buy a bag because they age slowly, but not so with bananas. They age quickly. You only buy the ones you need. Now let's think about high-tech. How many cell phones have you

TABLE 7.2 Industrial Value Network Summary

Industry	Industrial Value Chain (2000–2012)				
	Operating Margin	Inventory Turns	Cash-to-Cash Cycle	Revenue per Employee (K$)	SG&A Ratio
Automotive Industry	0.04	15	44	616	8%
(n = 39)	↑67%	↑5%	↓37%	↑199%*	↓30%*
Automotive Supplier	0.05	9	52	283	7%
Industry (n = 24)	↑40%	↑8%	↓42%	↑118%*	↓18%*
Consumer Electronics	0.03	6	57	525	14%
Industry (n = 12)	↓71%	↑34%	↓38%	↓7%*$	↓23%*
Semiconductor	0.04	6	63	367	10%
Industry (n = 13)	↓53%	↓16%	↑38%	↑57%*	↑13%*
Contract	0.05	8	53	356	8%
Manufacturing	↓60%	↑23%	↓34%R	↑87%*$	↑17 %*
Industry (n = 11)					

Industry Average composed of public companies (automotive industry: NAICS 336112), (automotive supplier industry: NAICS 336312& 336412), (consumer electronics industry: NAICS 33431 %where % is any number from 0 to 9), (contract manufacturing industry: NAICS 33441 %, where % is any number from 0 to 2, 4 to 9), (semiconductor industry NAICS 334413) reporting in One Source with 2012 annual sales greater than $5 billion
*Calculated from 2002 to 2012 due to data availability; $ = excluding outliers
Source: Supply Chain Insights LLC, Corporate Annual Reports 2000–2012

used in your lifetime? The life cycles get shorter and shorter. It's an issue of inventory aging. When a high-tech manufacturer puts an item into inventory, the inventory loses value due to the shortening of the product life cycle. Let's say that Apple releases a new phone. At first release, the phone sells for a dollar value of Y, but overtime, the market potential for that product declines and the effective price of that product becomes half of Y. At the beginning of the decade, in 2000, the life cycles of these products were years. Today, many are three to four months. As a result, the value of the inventory quickly declines. Companies in this industry must be extremely good at the management of inventory processes. Make sense?"

"Yes," said Lou. "Thanks, I was having a hard time with the banana analogy, but it makes total sense now. I often liken our inventory that doesn't move to rotten apples."

Edgar stood up and walked to the chart and stared at the precipitous drop in margins of the high-tech sector. "I have a new respect for this industry. This makes our challenges look simple." "Absolutely," said Joe and Filipe in unison. At this point, Frank was scribbling aimlessly on his pad. He had a hard time sitting still in a chair.

When I showed them the composite orbit chart (Figure 7.3), the group became very animated.

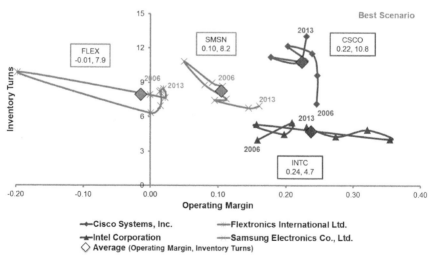

FIGURE 7.3 Orbit Chart of Companies in the Industrial Value Network for the Period of 2006–2012

Source: Supply Chain Insights LLC, Corporate Annual Reports 2006–2013

Lou asked me, "How did you select these companies for this chart?" I replied, "These companies rank at the top of the index charts that we are going to review today."

Filipe then asked, "How can the operating margin pattern of Samsung and Intel buck the trend of their industry? These are serious thought leaders. I'm looking forward to understanding how the industry sector can show such negative trends on operating margins; yet, these two companies can outperform in this area. I am also impressed that Intel made progress at this intersection based on what is happening in the continual evolution and rapid pace of the semiconductor industry."

Lou then commented, "Isn't it interesting that in all three of our value chain views, there is no company at the top of the Index that is making linear improvement toward the goal of improved operating margin and inventory turns? I didn't realize how hard this is until I started studying the charts."

He then began peering at the prior charts, and comparing the results, and continued, "The closest was the movement of HCA Holdings, but we know that the hospitals all shifted inventories to their suppliers. I also think that the inclusion of VF Corporation into the consumer value chain shows a company that is making progress for the period of 2006–2012. However, look at how low the margins and inventory turns are for the apparel industry. But, like Angela so wisely says, progress happens in small increments. Hershey and BASF did incredible mid-course corrections and Colgate and P&G are stalled. Wow, I would never have known this. Fascinating to see. . . ."

Angela jumped in and said, "Look at Flextronics. Oh my, what a tough ride! Look at the loss of operating margin through the recession. While they have regained their operating margin in a tough industry, they are now at the same position that they were in 2006. These composite industry orbit charts help me to get a better view of the industry." She turned to me and said, "Thanks for doing these new charts. I know you had a tough morning, and Jeff and I popped this on you, but I think seeing the companies together in a chart like this really helps. Especially since we now have Jeff's methodology to make sense of the orbit charts and see which companies are making the most progress on the Effective Frontier."

HIGH-TECH AND ELECTRONICS

"Let's start then with the high-tech industry, and then follow up with an understanding of the automotive industry. Does this sound good to the group?" I asked. They were ready to continue the discussion.

TABLE 7.3 Comparison of Revenue per Employee Performance across Industries (1990–2012)

Revenue per Employee (K$)	1990–1999	2000–2009	2010–2012
Chemical	328	627	825
Consumer Electronics	530	597	720
Consumer Packaged Goods	226	345	464
Food	394	357	423

Chemical: BASF SE, E. I. du Pont de Nemours and Co., The Dow Chemical Co. Consumer Electronics: Apple, Inc., Dell, Inc., Intel Corp., Motorola, Inc. (now Motorola Solutions, Inc.). Consumer Packaged Goods: Colgate-Palmolive Co., Procter & Gamble Co., Unilever NV/PLC. Food: Campbell Soup Co., General Mills, Inc., Kellogg Co., Kraft Foods, Inc. (now Kraft Foods Group, Inc.). Revenue per Employee = Revenue/Employee Count.
Source: Supply Chain Insights LLC, Corporate Annual Reports 1990–2012

"Revenue per employee for consumer electronics companies (as shown in Table 7.3) outpaced other industries by a significant margin," I said. "There were several drivers: greater dependency on supply chain outsourcing, effective management of global operations, and improvements in productivity. These companies were early adopters of technologies.

"Leadership from the consumer electronics sector led to the definition of new business process models that was fundamental to their success," I continued. "These companies were some of the first to use supply chain processes as a core differentiator. The examples are many and include Dell's direct-ship model, IBM's remanufacturing program, HP's reclamation of printer cartridges, and Apple's utilization of data sent daily from retail stores to better understand and model demand. These companies invented remanufacturing processes (breaking down a product at the end of its life cycle into subcomponents for socially responsible recycling) to ensure that they could reclaim critical metals and machine parts to meet zero-waste goals and accelerate aftermarket service. In short, they have done a better job of using the supply chain as a business model to drive growth. They have a history of driving leadership in new business models."

Today, the life cycle of the product in the market is 30 percent shorter than the time that it takes us to bring a new product to market, which is 35 percent shorter than the length of our supply chain to supply a finished unit to the market. Shortening cycles and alignment of cross-functional processes was critical to drive revenue; we needed to redesign the value network outside-in and rethink conventional processes.

Direct quote from a high-tech manufacturer

"Cisco Systems, Inc. is especially interesting to me," I continued. "I consider the company a leader. They have done one of the best jobs of building resiliency into enterprise processes.

"In 2001, the company encountered major write-offs due to the recession. Yet, in 2007, they survived the recession without a hiccup. They applied the lessons learned from the first downturn and they were ready for the second. Today, their processes on market sensing are world-class. Look at some of the press articles that appeared when they posted the write-off in 2001 . . . "

On Tuesday, the network-equipment giant provided the grisly details behind its astonishing $2.25 billion inventory write-off in the third quarter, essentially admitting that it, too, was caught up in the Internet hype that, at its peak, gave the company the highest market capitalization in Wall Street history.

Shares in the company were down $1.25, or 6 percent, to $19.13 by market close.

Lou commented, "There are some lessons for us to be learned here. We were definitely surprised in the recession of 2007. Joe, remember how we had to shut down some of our production facilities? If Cisco has adapted their processes to sense and adapt to market shifts, we should see if there is something that we can emulate here in our business." Joe and Filipe were smiling and agreeing with Lou.

"Yes," I said, "2001 was a painful lesson for Cisco. Contrast the tone in their two annual reports. You can see the maturity in both financial and operations processes."

Cisco Systems Annual Reports on Inventory Management

These are the excerpts from the Cisco Annual report that I shared with the team.

2001: "On April 16, 2001, due to macroeconomic and capital spending issues affecting the networking industry, we announced a restructuring program to prioritize our initiatives around high-growth areas of our business, focus on profit contribution, reduce expenses, and improve efficiency. This restructuring program includes a worldwide workforce reduction, consolidation of excess facilities, and restructuring of certain business functions.

As a result of the restructuring program and decline in forecasted revenue, we recorded restructuring costs and other special charges of $1.17 billion classified as operating expenses and an additional excess inventory charge classified as cost of sales. The excess inventory charge recorded in the third quarter of fiscal 2001 was $2.25 billion. This excess inventory charge was subsequently reduced in the fourth quarter of fiscal 2001 by a $187 million benefit primarily related to lower settlement charges for purchase commitments. As a result of the restructuring program, we expect pretax savings in operating expenses will be slightly more than $1 billion on an annualized basis."[2]

2012: "Our provision for inventory was $115 million, $196 million, and $94 million for fiscal 2012, 2011, and 2010, respectively. The provision for the liability related to purchase commitments with contract manufacturers and suppliers was $151 million, $114 million, and $8 million in fiscal 2012, 2011, and 2010, respectively. On a combined basis, the $44 million decline in our provisions for inventory and purchase commitments with contract manufacturers and suppliers for fiscal 2012 was primarily due to the absence in the current fiscal year of charges we recorded in connection with the restructuring and realignment of our consumer business during fiscal 2011. If there were to be a sudden and significant decrease in demand for our products, or if there were a higher incidence of inventory obsolescence because of rapidly changing technology and customer requirements, we could be required to increase our inventory write-downs, and our liability for purchase commitments with contract manufacturers and suppliers, and accordingly our profitability could be adversely affected. We regularly evaluate our exposure for inventory write-downs and the adequacy of our liability for purchase commitments. Inventory and supply chain management remain areas of focus as we balance the need to maintain supply chain flexibility to help ensure competitive lead times with the risk of inventory obsolescence, particularly in light of current macroeconomic uncertainties and conditions and the resulting potential for changes in future demand forecast."[3]

"It's a story of boom and bust," I continued. "Not all companies performed equally. As shown in Table 7.4, Apple, LG Electronics, Research in Motion (RIM), and Samsung outperformed competitors. No longer is this a story of Japanese supremacy. There has been a shift in leadership from Japanese to Korean global conglomerates. Motorola, Nokia, and RIM underperformed in the market.

TABLE 7.4 Growth Rates in the Consumer Electronics Industry

Consumer Electronics Year-over-Year Sales Growth (2000–2013)					
Company	Average	2000–2003	2004–2007	2008–2011	2012–2013
Apple, Inc.	30%	−6%	42%	46%	27%
BlackBerry Ltd.	56%	66%	80%	63%	−24%
Dell, Inc.	5%	6%	13%	2%	−4%
LG Electronics	9%	17%	18%	−3%	5%
Motorola Solutions Inc.	−3%	−10%	−3%	1%	3%
Samsung Electronics Co., Ltd.	14%	13%	18%	9%	18%

Source: Supply Chain Insights LLC, Corporate Annual Reports 2000–2013

Profitability: Building Resilient Supply Chains

At the dawn of the century, in 2000, growth was high, but margins were stalled and inventory write-offs were more common. These were the go-go years," I continued. "Over the course of the past decade, no industry has done better at maximizing margin than consumer electronics." (See Table 7.5 for the results shared with the team.)

"Wow!" exclaimed Lou. "Look at the decline of Motorola. What happened there?"

I responded, "The reasons were many, but the most fundamental was the lack of innovation. Motorola's products just were not as attractive to their client base. The second was the shift in product requirements in their government sector. They were slow to respond. And a third, which I think is a lesson for everyone, is the concept of product platform."

TABLE 7.5 Operating Margin in the Consumer Electronics Industry

Consumer Electronics Operating Margin (2000–2013)					
Company	Average	2000–2003	2004–2007	2008–2011	2012–2013
Apple, Inc.	0.16	0.00	0.12	0.27	0.32
BlackBerry, Ltd.	0.06	−0.15	0.14	0.25	−0.02
Dell, Inc.	0.07	0.08	0.8	0.05	0.06
LG Electronics	0.04	0.05	0.04	0.03	0.02
Motorola Solutions, Inc.	0.05	−0.04	0.09	0.04	0.14
Samsung Electronics Co., Ltd.	0.12	0.13	0.11	0.08	0.15

Source: Supply Chain Insights LLC, Corporate Annual Reports 2000–2013

Jeff then said, "What does that mean? I have never heard of the concept of product platforms."

I continued, "Product platform rationalization is a concept where the base design of the product is rationalized against the products in the platform. For example, the Motorola Razr was a totally different platform from their other phones. In 2002, the engineering group in Motorola's computer group tried to develop 120 products, but their resources were spread so thin that they produced no products at all. The next year, they reduced the number of projects to 22 and they were able to introduce 8 products in 24 months. In 2004, they focused on only 20 products and launched 14 products in 12 months. As a result, they were able to triple manufacturing productivity, improve revenue by 2.4 times, and increase operating margins from a negative 6 percent to a positive 7 percent in just three years. This work continued. In April 2011, the number of phones introduced by Motorola to carriers declined by 40 percent with no decline in sales. However, the rate of innovation by Apple outpaced Motorola."[4]

"2002 seems so long ago," said Filipe. "But I think that the concept of product rationalization equally applies to us now. It may even be more important today than it was a year ago." He then turned to the group, "Would you agree?"

Frank said, "All of those products that we are getting from marketing? Some are laughable. When we get a few of the right products, then we are golden. We can really put the pedal to the metal then . . . " (the group laughed, knowing that he still had the picture of his speeding ticket in front of him). Frank laughed with them and said, "But now I can really see how proliferating new products can create havoc if we don't have a common platform."

"Yes," said Joe. "The secret is to sense market response quickly. When a product is doing well we need to blow it out at the shelves, and when it's not, we need to quickly kill it. Product rationalization and the management of complexity needs to be a core piece of our business strategy. We need to get the signal quickly to know what to do."

He then looked directly at Frank, "Good news travels quickly here, but bad news travels slowly. Frank, you are quick to whip off an email and tell us about record sales, but we never hear about the bad news. This is a problem because it is even more important to know about the products that are *not* selling. It is easier to speed up than to put on the brakes.

"Our networks are complex. Turning down the faucet for product inventories can often be more difficult than ramping up. It is for this reason that we need to see channel inventories directly. Daily channel inventory needs to be a core capability of Project Orbit. Have I convinced you yet?" Joe asked. Frank shook his head dismissively.

"I know you think that I am slow, but I get it," Frank said with a wink to Joe. "I now just have the challenge of helping our customers to get it. Maybe you can help me with this one." With this remark, Joe smiled. He knew that Frank was saying in his own way that he was ready to change the work that they did together with the channel.

Index for High-Tech and Electronics

"Okay, the suspense is mounting. Let's get on with it," says Jeff. "Let's look at the index. Who made the most progress in the high-tech industry for the period of 2006–2013?"

I then presented the high-tech index that is shown in Table 7.6.

"Oh, boy," said Edgar, as he rubbed his hands together. "That is quite a chart! I was expecting to see Apple at the top of this index." He stepped to the front of the room and peered at the numbers. "We have another surprise. Look at the progress of LG Electronics and Seagate. Both are driving progress in balance and strength, but struggling in resiliency. Any insights into why?"

"It is a tough industry," I continued. "Companies that have driven the fastest innovation supported by a strong supply chain have outperformed. Notice how Motorola, Ericson, Canon, Nokia, and Sanyo fall to the bottom of the list. It is hard to buck falling demand. This market is unforgiving. When consumers like products, the velocity is high. When they don't, it happens quickly. Cycle times are critical in this industry to adapt to changing market conditions."

Filipe then spoke, "I like this methodology. It is agnostic. It's a very powerful way to look at which companies are driving improvement. It's not about their marketing campaign, their stock price, or whom they know. It's objective and data-driven. I find it helpful."

High-Tech Orbit Charts

"Economy of scale is not always a good thing," I told the group. "We can see this pattern again in this industry: Both sectors, those greater than $5 billion in revenue and those less than $5 billion, have tough trends." (I showed them Figure 7.4.)

"Wow," said Angela. "That chart is incredible. It makes my head hurt. This definitely is a much tougher industry than ours. I wouldn't want to manage treasury in one of these companies. It's just too volatile."

"Yes," says Edgar. "I guess that I should be happy that it makes our problems look easy in comparison."

TABLE 7.6 The Index: Consumer Electronics

Company	2013 Revenue (billions USD)	Balance	Balance Ranking	Strength	Strength Ranking	Resiliency	Resiliency Ranking	Index (0.3B + 0.3S + 0.3R)	Ranking
Alcatel Lucent SA	19.2	1.21	3	0.51	3	0.69	7	3.9	1
LG Electronics Inc.	53.1	24.06	1	28.55	1	1.07	13	4.5	2
Lexmark International Inc	3.7	0.04	6	0.05	10	0.60	6	6.6	3
EMC Corporation	23.2	-0.03	9	0.10	7	0.83	9	7.5	4
Cabot Microelectronics Corporation	0.4	-0.08	11	0.01	12	0.57	4	8.1	5
Seagate Technology PLC	14.4	0.08	4	0.15	5	2.09	19	8.4	6
Emerson Electric Co.	24.7	-0.15	15	0.06	9	0.77	8	9.6	7
Samsung Electronics Co Ltd	208.9	0.06	5	0.04	11	1.56	17	9.9	8
LG Corp	8.9	0.03	7	0.93	2	8.12	24	9.9	8
Seiko Epson Corporation	10.3	1.68	2	-0.19	22	1.04	12	10.8	10
Apple, Inc.	170.9	0.02	8	0.21	4	26.38	25	11.1	11
Cisco Systems	48.6	-0.09	14	0.11	6	2.03	18	11.4	12
Kyocera Corporation	15.4	-0.23	17	-0.07	19	0.54	2	11.4	12
Bosch Ltd	1.5	-0.26	18	-0.04	18	0.54	3	11.7	14
Ericsson	34.9	-0.21	16	-0.03	17	0.92	10	12.9	15
Vtech Holdings Ltd	1.9	-0.08	12	-0.02	16	1.38	15	12.9	15
Applied Micro Circuits Corporation	0.2	-0.51	21	0.06	8	1.55	16	13.5	17
Bang &Olufsen A/s	0.5	-0.60	22	-0.27	23	0.49	1	13.8	18
LSI Corp	2.4	-0.39	19	0.00	13	1.09	14	13.8	18
Logitech International SA	2.1	-0.50	20	-0.32	24	0.59	5	14.7	20
Motorola Solutions Inc	8.7	-0.09	13	0.00	14	3.27	22	14.7	20
Western Digital Corp	15.4	-0.06	10	-0.07	20	4.34	23	15.9	22
Sanyo Eletric Co Ltd	17.8*	-1.12	24	-0.99	25	0.95	11	18.0	23
Canon Electronics Inc.	1.0	-1.31	25	-0.01	15	3.13	21	18.3	24
Nokia Oyj	16.9	-0.65	23	-0.17	21	2.95	20	19.2	25

*2010 revenue.
Source: Supply Chain Insights LLC, Corporate Annual Reports 2006–2013

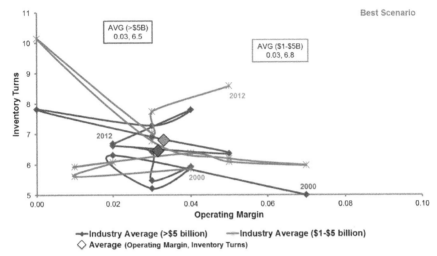

FIGURE 7.4 Inventory Turns and Operating Margin for the Consumer Electronics Industry for 2006–2012
Industry Average comprised of public companies (NAICS code 33431%, where % is any number from 0 to 9) in One Source with 2012 annual sales greater than $5 billion and $1–$5 billion, excluding outliers.
Source: Supply Chain Insights LLC, Corporate Annual Reports 2000–2012

"Yet," I continued, "If you contrast the two sizes of companies (less than $5B in revenue and those greater than $5B in annual revenue) in this industry on revenue per employee and inventory turns, you get quite a different pattern. It is more linear." I then looked at Angela, and said, "This chart doesn't make my head hurt. It clearly shows that companies have economy of scale on employee productivity, but the majority of the cost in this industry is in sourcing materials. However, if you looked only at this view, you would get the wrong impression that this is a very controlled, predictable industry. That's anything but the case."

I continued, "Over the past decade, the high-tech companies have built longer supply chains. These stretch across many geographies, which leads to a rise in transit times. This also increases the number of links in the supply chain, creating interdependencies. There is less resilience. It also creates a domino effect—an industry that can be easy to topple and hard to restore. The Thailand flooding in the fall of 2011 was a prime example of these challenges. The effects of the natural disaster rippled through large consumer-facing businesses like Dell and Apple. It was disastrous. Seagate Technology PLC summarized the situation the following way in their 2013 annual report."

In early October 2011, floodwaters north of Bangkok, Thailand, inundated many manufacturing industrial parks that contained a number of the factories supporting the HDD industry's supply chain. The HDD industry had concentrated a large portion of its supply chain participants within these industrial parks in an effort to reduce cost and improve logistics. As a result, the inundation of floodwaters into these industrial parks had caused the closure or suspension of production by a number of participants within the HDD supply chain. During the supply chain disruption in fiscal year 2012, we believe demand exceeded supply due to the impact from the flooding in Thailand, resulting in an increase in the average selling price ("ASP").[5]

"Yes," said Angela. "I find these charts fascinating. I can see the lack of resilience. Clearly the challenge is in managing margin independent of company size. I also see some of the impacts of the recessionary cycles in the second chart, but the first chart is so chaotic that it is impossible to understand the patterns. I think that this explains what we are seeing in the evolution of risk management practices. This industry just has to be good at planning and sensing to survive." We then spent time reviewing the trends in the chart shown in Figure 7.5.

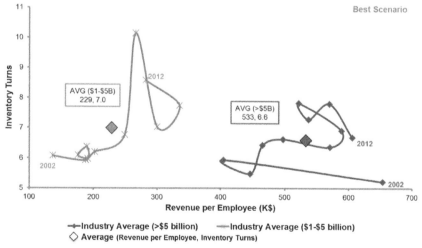

FIGURE 7.5   Inventory Turns and Revenue per Employee for the Consumer Electronics Industry for 2006–2012

Industry Average comprised of public companies (NAICS code 33431%, where % is any number from 0 to 9) in One Source with 2012 annual sales greater than $5 billion and $1–$5 billion, excluding outliers.

Source: Supply Chain Insights LLC, Corporate Annual Reports 2002–2012

I then switched off the projector and asked the group to give me some feedback. "What have we learned from the high-tech industry?"

The group quickly assembled their thoughts. The process of assimilating orbit chart information was coming much more quickly to them at this point, and their insights rolled off of their tongues:

Rationalize product portfolios and look for ways to create common platforms.
In volatile market conditions, sensing true market demand becomes essential. Create mechanisms to understand market drivers early, so that you don't get stuck with inventory.
Due to the stress placed on the high-tech industry, there is a lot to learn from networking with industry leaders who created leading-edge practices. This industry is at the forefront of dealing with change and mitigating risk.

SEMICONDUCTOR INDUSTRY

The discussion then shifted to the semiconductor industry. "While every industry has a unique set of challenges and opportunities when it comes to maximizing potential and creating better functioning operations, the semiconductor sector has a special challenge: the management of cycles. No industry has to manage cycles to the same degree.

"Demand is unpredictable. Semiconductor manufacturers are four or five steps back in the value chain with no predictable signal from their customers. They are dependent on reading market signals and consumer adoption of the parts that they supply to the upstream manufacturers. It takes a long time to build a new factory, called a 'fab,' so they have to invest in front of demand. The overriding and primary cycle is the rate of change that comes from the shifts in capabilities to increase the number of transistors in a circuit. This is termed Moore's Law and is named after Gordon E. Moore, founder of Intel. After the launch of a new product, the industry then needs to manage the launch of overlapping product lifecycles." I then showed the group the data outlined in Table 7.7.

Angela then commented, "Look at the impacts of the first recession in their numbers! There is a similar pattern here that we see in the Intel case study. The entire industry has declined in inventory turns as they have stabilized margins, but they are getting clobbered on cash-to-cash cycles. Can I assume that their upstream customers are lengthening payables?" "Yes," I said.

TABLE 7.7 Semiconductor Industry Overview

	Semiconductor Industry ($n = 13$)				
Year	Operating Margin	Inventory Turns	Cash-to-Cash Cycle	Revenue per Employee (K$)	SG&A Ratio
2000–2003	−0.10	7	57	280	10%
2004–2007	0.12	6	59	366	10%
2008–2011	0.09	6	69	400	9%
2012	0.07	5	72	392	9%

Industry Average comprised of public companies (NAICS code 334413) reporting in One Source with 201 2 annual sales greater than $5 billion.
Source: Supply Chain Insights LLC, Corporate Annual Reports 2000–2012

"Their average revenue per employee is much lower than in other industries despite the investment in technologies," Angela said. "Can I assume that this is because they are so asset intensive?" Angela was an asset to the group. She was eager to learn and quickly saw the patterns.

I continued, "The simplified version of Moore's law states that processor speeds, or overall processing power for computers will double every two years. More specifically, it states that the number of transistors on an affordable central processing unit (CPU) will double every two years. In 2000 the number of transistors in the CPU numbered 37.5 million while in 2009 the number went up to an outstanding 904 million. The limitation that exists is that once transistors can be created that are as small as atomic particles, then there will be no more room for growth in the CPU market as far as speed of computing is concerned. However, we don't know when that will be, and at that time the industry will be totally transformed.

"The second cycle that dominates the semiconductor industry is the ebb and flow of demand and supply," I said. "The integrated circuit that's made by the semiconductor firm is a component of other subassemblies or final products. As a result, it must pass through the hands of other companies within the semiconductor network."

Frank was yawning and looking at his watch, but the rest of the team was engrossed in the discussion as I continued, "The manufacturing cycle times, despite automation, in the semiconductor industry are very long. While design can be measured in weeks, the manufacture of integrated circuits takes months and testing is measured in days. To speed the manufacturing process, many of the manufacturers will postpone in the die banks offering generic wafer products that can be configured prior to test. This type of process innovation has been critical to align the product demand cycle to the supply cycle," I explained.

"Because the production of semiconductors is asset-intensive, based on foundries, and is produced through an elaborate network of fab and fabless companies, the forecasting and management of demand and supply through the ups and downs of the life cycle are critical." My work was getting easier; the group easily saw the connection.

> The "semiconductor cycle" is an important concept that refers to the ebb and flow of supply and demand. The semiconductor market historically has been characterized by periods of tight supply caused by strengthening demand and/or insufficient manufacturing capacity, followed by periods of surplus inventory caused by weakening demand and/or excess manufacturing capacity. These are typically referred to as upturns and downturns in the semiconductor cycle. The semiconductor cycle is affected by the significant time and money required to build and maintain semiconductor manufacturing facilities.[6]
>
> Texas Instruments Annual Report, 2012

"Let there be no mistake," I said, "product innovation is the lifeblood of this industry. The growing demand for consumer electronics devices, and the proliferation of mobile and tablet products, drove a strong market for semiconductors over the past decade. The number of active cell phones is expected to top 7.3 billion by the end of 2014, according to the International Telecommunications Union.[7] In short, the number of cell phones will exceed the global population at some point this year. The average person has more phones than toothbrushes."

Semiconductor Index

Filipe stood up to stretch his back. It had been a long session; however, the group came to life when they saw the progress of Intel. I smiled and continued. "When we look at the Index, we can see that Intel has outperformed," I said. "There is not a better example in any industry of a company that has built strong potential to attack the Effective Frontier than Intel."

Edgar said, "Tell us more. What did they do?"

"Their efforts are legendary. They tackled what seemed impossible in process innovation and new business models. Like I said before, when speed became an obstacle to bringing new products to market, they postponed products in the die bank."

"Okay, you are losing me now," said Lou. "Tell me more about the die bank. Go easy; you know that we've never seen a semiconductor manufacturing operation."

I smiled and said, "Thanks for slowing me down. All manufacturing processes have their unique terms. In the long manufacturing process, the individual chips are placed onto fabbed wafers. These are also called *die*. The inventory of die is termed the "die bank." The die are tested by connecting to the contact points on the die of the wafer and performing electrical tests. Results from these tests are used to continually improve the fab yield of good die by evaluating patterns of malfunctioning chips on the wafer and other process parameters. Optional production steps in the sort process include grinding to reduce wafer thickness and power consumption and applying gold to the back of the wafer for better package adhesion. To postpone inventory in the die bank, the customers are offered a variety of prepackaged options that can be configured prior to test and assembly. Intel has been a leader in rethinking these processes. Does this help?"

The team was sitting back in their chairs as if I had just placed them in a wind tunnel. Their eyes were glazed over, so I started again. "Sometimes high-tech jargon gets overwhelming. What they do is they start with a standard version and then offer it to their customers as options that can be configured versus starting with a finished product specification at the beginning.

"They are a leader in the design of the value network. While many companies inherit their value networks, they actively design them. They have a team of operations research experts that is continually modeling and redesigning their networks. They have also built a super-model for skill acquisition and retaining employees in this group. They believe that the design and execution of a network model is essential to driving great results. I interviewed an Intel executive, Tony Romero, for my recent book. Would you like to hear it directly from him?" I continued. Edgar moved his head in agreement.

"Let me contrast two interviews from two leaders in this industry for you to consider on the metrics that matter. Let me first share the transcript from my interview with Intel, and then we'll contrast it another interview, with Xilinx. Okay?" I asked.

Edgar then commented that he got a lot of value from the case studies. He liked hearing the stories from the business leaders. It made it real for him. The team spent an hour discussing Table 7.8. Their interest was high in understanding how Intel had made so much progress.

TABLE 7.8 The Index: Semiconductor Industry

Company	2013 Revenue (billions USD)	Balance	Balance Ranking	Strength	Strength Ranking	Resiliency	Resiliency Ranking	Index (0.3B + 0.3S + 0.3R)	Ranking
Intel Corporation	52.7	−0.07	2	0.11	1	0.72	4	2.1	1
Maxim Integrated Products, Inc.	2.4	−0.10	3	0.00	4	0.55	2	2.7	2
Xilinx	2.2	−0.17	5	0.04	2	1.14	6	3.9	3
Taiwan Semiconductor Mfg. Co. Ltd.	20.1	−0.04	1	0.00	3	2.25	10	4.2	4
Fairchild Semiconductor Intl., Inc.	1.4	−0.27	7	−0.13	7	0.37	1	4.5	5
Texas Instruments Incorporated	12.2	−0.23	6	−0.05	6	0.62	3	4.5	5
Broadcom Corporation	8.3	−0.16	4	−0.04	5	1.50	8	5.1	7
TriQuint Semiconductor	0.9	−0.44	9	−0.25	9	0.86	5	6.9	8
Freescale Semiconductor Limited	4.6*	−0.43	8	−0.21	8	1.20	7	6.9	8
Advanced Micro Devices, Inc.	5.3	−1.21	10	−1.04	10	1.87	9	8.7	10

*2011 revenue.
Source: Supply Chain Insights LLC, Corporate Annual Reports 2006–2013.

314

Interview with Tony Romero, Intel

Tony Romero is the general manager of the Customer Fulfillment, Planning, and Logistics Group (CPLG) for the Intel Corporation. CPLG is responsible for the supply chain business management and logistics functions for Intel products.

He joined Intel in 1990 and has held numerous positions across Intel's supply chain. He spent his first nine years working in fab manufacturing and then moved to industrial engineering. He has held a variety of roles including his current position where he leads the worldwide organization of 650 employees that own and execute Intel's supply chain strategy in partnership with Intel's other supply chain groups.

I interviewed him in the fall of 2013.

Which metrics matter and why?

The metrics that are important for Intel include:

- *Cycle time:* We measure the full supply-chain cycle time. This is not only our manufacturing cycle time (manufacturing cycle times are very long), but our full cycle to get products to market. As we continue our development, we face longer cycle times. The 14-nanometer technologies have more manufacturing steps with longer manufacturing time. It takes a long time. It can be four months before you do a wafer from start to shipment, and with the newer technologies, it can be even longer. I measure the cycle time as the time that it takes to get the signals from the customers, which can be three to four months, plus the execution horizon and execution of what we build. Cycle time is a challenge.
- *Inventory time:* We want to be sure that we are building the right units. We first build the wafer and then assemble the unit and then finally test the assembly. We are constantly testing our processes here. This includes die bank postponement and modifying and testing. We are constantly assessing how good our inventory is at this point in the value network.
- *Responsiveness* is another important measurement. We question, Are we delivering the product for the perfect order measures? This includes the delivery with the right quality. To do this we use our forward-stage locations. For all of our original equipment manufacturers (OEMs), we directly service all of their major items with direct replenishment. To do this, we put in the standard products and service multiple customers for most, but not all, of their items through close monitoring. This allows us to get a downstream signal.

(continued)

(continued)

Tell me more about the management of inventory.

In the beginning we saw some of the opportunity in what the customers were pulling and negotiated with all of them to get inventory in this type of program. We have been able to take the information gathered from customers over the past couple of years and redesign the supply chain. To do this, I reorganized parts of the organization to combine several efforts. I now have a team that is managing all of our finished goods inventory through one organization. They manage where it goes. Inventory is an area where I think central control is mandatory.

We take the time to reach out to customers and say, "We think that you have too much of our inventory in your location and we will make sure that your service levels are right, but we want to manage it directly." As a result, we have seen some strong partnership with a couple of companies who are also interested in evolving the supply chain. I am trying to get the group to see: If we are engaging the sales teams, it creates "stickiness." It lowers their requirements and the demand that they are selling and tightens the relationship with them.

Do you have anyone responsible for the end-to-end supply chain?

We have folks who are engaged with the sales teams and the geographic teams to analyze how we best service our customers. Today, when I hire someone, I want to be more strategic. I want to see more of this evolution of looking at end-to-end and articulate it. We look end-to-end, but can we articulate it into action? We need to get better at it. It is difficult. We are constantly analyzing where we are spending our money and analyzing new customer requirements.

We take a current set of requirements and question ourselves. "How do we think about this more strategically?" Today, we do not articulate it enough, but we are trying....

At the executive level there is tremendous energy and effort. How do we shrink our time to launch new products and take them to market? We have a lot of focus and energy in this space. Our CEO understands this very well. He fully gets the capabilities that we need to have. What he is asking us to focus on is faster and better collaboration with customers. Our goal is to get products to market faster. His guidance to me is, "At no time let the supply chain become a limiting factor. We are evolving, but this is still a challenge."

Edgar and Frank enjoyed this interview. Edgar winced when he heard that there were 650 employees on Tony's planning team, and commented, "They definitely reward what is important and give their planners time to plan. This is quite different from how we are wired organizationally. This is a strong contrast to automotive."

"Yes," said Frank. "And I hear something else. I like Tony's advice about working with customers on inventory strategies and using it as a demand signal. Joe, I think this was what you were advocating earlier in the day. Right?" And Joe leaned forward in agreement. "However, I think we also have a long way to go until the supply chain is not a limiting factor to sales. Both have to work together. Do you agree?" And to that, Joe shook his head yes.

"So, Joe, if I help you to get the downstream data daily, do you commit to me to make the supply chain less of an issue for my sales team? If you can do this, then I think that we have a much better deal," continued Frank. "Who knows, maybe these efforts will even increase sales!"

Edgar then commented that he would like to contrast the guidance from Intel with what I got from Xilinx.

"Sure," I replied. "Just let me find that interview," I said, rummaging in my folder for the transcript from the leaders at Xilinx. I then passed it to the group.

Xilinx Case Study

I would like to remain anonymous. I run the supply chain at Xilinx, and while I manage supply chain planning, I don't have the responsibility for the logistics network or the warehousing component. I am a veteran. I've been at Xilinx for 11 years.

When you think about delivering operational excellence, which metrics do you measure and why?

The primary ones are inventory, on-time to the first order commit date, and the number of orders with a lead time of less than six weeks. We would like to have 85 percent of orders greater than a six-week lead time. It just makes it easier for us.

For inventory we measure net inventory. This is both inventory at Xilinx and also in our distributor network. We do not own the inventories in our distributor network, but we do measure it. We term it gross reserves.

We measure our first time to commit based on the time that the customer originally wanted the order. We try to be over 98 percent. This

(continued)

(continued)

is something that we are proud of and we have been at this level for over a year.

We used to not have good performance on our first commit date. The most important thing we have learned in improving this metric is ensuring process reliability.

We have to forecast long-lead-time subcomponents. We push a couple of hundred parts to a die bank and it then fans out from there. It takes us six weeks to get the product to the die bank and then to configure it for our customers. The process used to range from four weeks to nine months. Six weeks is best in class.

Over the years, we have learned to be really disciplined in measuring the metrics constantly in the same way over time.

After the discussion, the room was silent.

Frank was the first to speak. "Such long lead times! And we think that we have problems. If they can drive reliability in these processes without a good demand signal, then what we have to do pales in comparison. I definitely need to network more with the guys I know at Intel to understand how they have driven these results."

Edgar agreed, "Frank, see how important it was for the semiconductor industry to have distributor data? Maybe your friends in that industry can give you some insights into how they approached the problem of getting cooperation from their downstream partners."

He then turned to Filipe and Joe and said, "I love the discussions in this industry about cycles and late-stage postponement. I still think that we could be more aggressive in these areas to ensure greater reliability in what we do. I would like to adopt Intel's philosophy of never letting the supply chain be an obstacle. Your thoughts?"

Filipe said, "I agree that these were great insights, but one of the things that we need from you, Edgar, is consistency. I liked the closing statement by the executive from Xilinx about measuring the metrics consistently over time."

Progress of the Semiconductor Industry by Company Size

I looked at my watch and said, "We're almost ready for lunch. How about 15 more minutes to finish discussing this industry?" The group was getting into the material, so I continued, "There are few companies greater than

$5 billion in revenue, but as you can see, in the semiconductor industry, like the high-tech industry, the inventory turns/operating margin orbit charts are chaotic, and the revenue per employee and inventory turn charts show a pattern that is easier to see. Note, however, we do not see the same economy of scale in this industry that we see in high-tech and electronics. In this industry, the smaller guys have actually outpaced the larger ones." (We then studied the wavy lines of the orbit charts for the semiconductor industry in Figures 7.6 and 7.7.)

"This is fascinating," Angela said. "Do you think that it is more difficult for the larger companies to manage global operations?"

I nodded my head yes. "The semiconductor industry enjoyed high demand with the rise of personal computing and now mobile and tablet products. The results have been steady double-digit sales growth and wide margins. They have bucked a trend. The industry has rebounded from the recession stronger in margin. This is rare given their downstream location within many consumer electronics supply chains. However, rising complexity and outsourcing bring new supply chain challenges. The good news is that the process capabilities within this industry are strong and ready to meet the challenge."

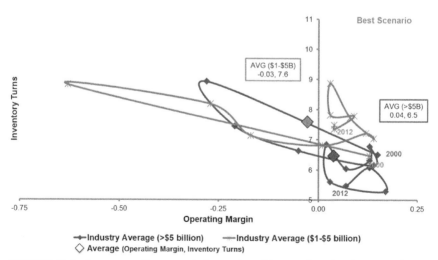

FIGURE 7.6 Inventory Turns and Operating Margin for the Semiconductor Industry for 2006–2012

Industry Average comprised of public companies (NAICS code 334413) in One Source with 2012 annual sales greater than $5 billion and $1–5 billion.

Source: Supply Chain Insights LLC, Corporate Annual Reports 2000–2012

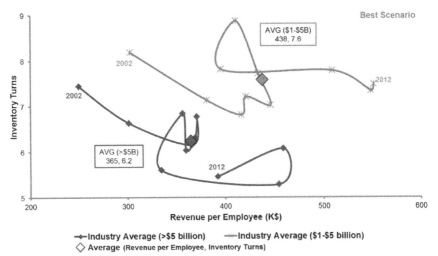

Revenue per Employee (K$)

→ Industry Average (>$5 billion)   — Industry Average ($1-$5 billion)
◇ Average (Revenue per Employee, Inventory Turns)

FIGURE 7.7   Inventory Turns and Revenue per Employee for the Semiconductor Industry for 2006–2012
Industry Average comprised of public companies (NAICS code 334413) in One Source with 2012 annual sales greater than $5 billion and $1–5 billion.
Source: Supply Chain Insights LLC, Corporate Annual Reports 2002–2012

CONCLUSION

The team did a quick wrap-up on what they learned from the discussion on the semiconductor industry and wrote the following on their whiteboard:

Reliability is critical to improving cycles. Cycles are decreasing due to the proliferation of data. We need to get better at driving data-driven discussions.
We have learned from the Intel case study that there should be no excuses. A company with long cycles and no demand visibility has successfully climbed the Effective Frontier.
The supply chain should never be an excuse for not delivering on customer promises.

The team then took a badly needed break, and continued the discussion over lunch. Earlier that morning, Frank had made a special picture for Joe. It was an elaborate presentation. Neatly wrapped was a collage of Joe sitting in a car with his supply chain at his back and his foot on the accelerator. Frank had written below the image, "I know that you have it in you. Put your foot on the gas and drive down the cycles of the supply chain." The group laughed. Edgar looked over his glasses and clapped his hands. "Good one, Frank." He then turned to Joe and said, "I know that you are the man to get this done."

Joe was quiet. He remembered that awkward moment when he wrote "77" on the flipchart and initiated the discussion on his BHAG. It was a humbling moment.

Notes

1. Hau L. Lee, "The Triple-A Supply Chain," *Harvard Business Review* (October 2004)/ftp://ftp.software.ibm.com/software/emea/dk/frontlines/Tripple_supply_chain_Havard.pdf (accessed June 4, 2014).
2. Cisco Systems, Inc., 2001 Annual Report, pp. 17 and 18.
3. Cisco Systems, Inc., 2012 Annual Report, p. 45.
4. "Good Strategy, Bad Strategy," by Richard E. Rumelt, UCLA Professor of Strategy at the Anderson School of Business, 2011.
5. Seagate Technology PLC, 2013 Annual Report, p. 44.
6. Texas Instruments, Inc., 2012 Annual Report, p. 42.
7. *Silicon India Magazine*, "World to Have More Cell Phone Accounts Than People by 2014," www.siliconindia.com/magazine_articles/World_to_have_more_cell_phone_accounts_than_people_by_2014-DASD767476836.html.

CHAPTER EIGHT

What Drives Value in the Value Network?

Industry Progress in the Automotive Value Chain

A FTER LUNCH WE continued the discussion by focusing on the auto industry. It seemed that cars had dominated a large portion of our strategy session on prior days, so it only seemed fitting that the session end with a focus on the automotive value network.

When the team returned to their seats, I started the discussion by saying, "The auto industry is back. The demand for cars is strong and increasing. In August 2013, the Detroit Three—Chrysler, Ford, and General Motors—sold over 600,000 vehicles domestically. Total U.S. auto sales were estimated at 1.48 million units. The industry is on track to match or exceed 2008 annual sales (16.1 million units) by the end of 2014.[1] Let the good times roll, right?"

At that point Frank smiled, and quipped, "I hope you're right. You know I love my cars. I even have a picture to prove it." As he held it up and moved it sideways in front of him, Joe said, "Don't forget, I now have one, too! We're joined at the hip, you and I."

Laughter rippled through the room as Frank and Joe went back and forth with their car jabs, but for Filipe this was the moment he had been waiting for.

"Come on guys. I've waited three days for this. I'm excited to see the results for the automotive industry," said Filipe. "It was great to see Intel pull forward on the index in semiconductor. I'm sure that we will see Toyota outperform as well. They did such great work on lean in their work on the Toyota Way.[2] We've tried to adopt these processes here. We've made great strides, but we are not Toyota. It's my goal to prove to you that we need to ratchet-up our work on lean."

Filipe continued, taking the book *The Toyota Way* out of his briefcase and holding it where everyone could see the cover, "This has been my bible. It's the backbone of what we have focused on in our redefinition of operations excellence. For some, it may be boring, but I find it very exciting. I am proud of the progress that we've made. I would love to see us embark upon an effort to help the entire organization embrace lean." He then looked at me, and said, "I look forward to seeing these results."

I smiled. Not wanting to burst Filipe's bubble of preconceived ideas about supply chain leaders, I moved slowly into the next slide, shown in Figure 8.1. "Edgar, I appreciate the discussion on the composite orbit charts, and I applaud the work that Angela and Jeff started. I thought there was so much value in the review of the work in high-tech that I also built a composite orbit chart for the automotive industry. On this chart, we have graphed the aggregate performance of Volkswagen, Honeywell, and Intel. As you know, the integration

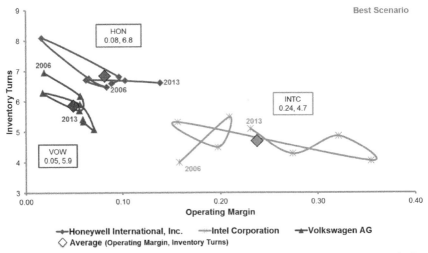

FIGURE 8.1 Composite Orbit Chart for the Automotive Value Network for 2006–2012
Source: Supply Chain Insights LLC, Corporate Annual Reports 2006–2013.

of software and electrical components into the automotive industry has vastly changed the product development and maintenance cycles.

"Volkswagen," I said, "has had the most consistent growth in the industry, and some of the best results. As you can see in the chart before you, they are making progress on operating margin, but not inventory turns. The pattern of Honeywell is similar. Note that they are almost at the same levels of performance today as when they started the automation of their value chains in the mid-part of the decade. Contrast the performance of these two companies with the steady progression of Intel. It is quite a difference."

Lou agreed. "Yes, I'd rather be like Intel than anyone else I've seen so far in this industry." Joe nodded his head in agreement as Filipe said, "Just wait until we see the rankings of Toyota on the index chart."

AUTOMOTIVE PROGRESS ON THE INDEX

"Okay, Filipe," I said, "normally I talk about the industry first and then show the index charts, but you have so much interest in the performance of the automotive industry, and Toyota specifically, why don't we review this now?" Filipe leaned back in his chair and stretched his arms, and then said with an air of arrogance, "Show us the numbers. I want to show the group how Toyota outperformed in their industry!"

I smiled, knowing that this was going to get Filipe's attention, "In the automotive industry, the company that rises to the top of the list in delivering operational performance is Volkswagen. Filipe, most people are surprised when I show them this chart. As you can see, Toyota sits midway in the rankings. The biggest barrier for Toyota was market sensing and the adoption of market preferences into design, and then they were hit with quality issues and write-offs." I then showed the team Table 8.1.

Frank whistled. "First it was P&G, then it was Amazon, and now we find out that Toyota is not leading on the index of their peer group. Why do you think that the companies we thought were doing well are not outperforming their peers?" asked Frank.

"As we discussed this morning, the measurement of operational excellence is easier said than done. Both Toyota and P&G were early leaders in the design of process improvement. They were early adopters of technologies and leaders in building new processes," I said, taking a seat at the table next to Filipe.

With arms crossed, Filipe sat red-faced, quietly trying to figure it all out. There was a puzzled look on his face. It was a paradigm change that he was not ready for.

TABLE 8.1 Automotive Index

Company	2013 Revenue (billions USD)	Balance	Balance Ranking	Strength	Strength Ranking	Resiliency	Resiliency Ranking	Index (0.3B + 0.3S + 0.3R)	Ranking
Volkswagen AG	261.5	0.01	2	0.27	2	0.73	2	1.8	1
Bayerische Motoren Werke AG	101.0	−0.12	5	0.02	5	0.62	1	3.3	2
Toyota Motor Corp	265.9	0.04	1	−0.03	6	1.06	4	3.3	2
Hyundai Motor Co	79.7	0.00	3	0.47	1	2.70	8	3.6	4
Audi AG	66.2	−0.08	4	0.04	4	1.25	5	3.9	5
Oshkosh Corporation	7.7	−0.23	6	0.05	3	1.90	7	4.8	6
Mitsubishi Motors Corporation	21.9	−0.24	7	−0.25	8	1.43	6	6.3	7
Navistar International Corp	10.8	−0.61	10	−0.55	10	0.96	3	6.9	8
Ford Motor Company	146.9	−0.51	8	−0.19	7	2.89	10	7.5	9
Kia Motors Corporation	43.5	−0.53	9	−0.50	9	2.77	9	8.1	10

Source: Supply Chain Insights LLC, Corporate Annual Reports 2006–2013.

I was sensitive to the fact that Filipe felt deflated. "It is hard for most industry leaders to continue the kind of momentum that we saw with Intel. P&G has struggled with complexity. In a similar vein, Toyota is lagging in its ability to read market signals. I looked at Filipe and continued, "My take is that lean processes are useful for improving waste and reducing cycles, but they're not sufficient to conquer the Effective Frontier. Lean processes need to be coupled with demand sensing and shaping techniques that we've been talking to Joe and Frank about. Companies need to sense channel demand and actively listen to customer sentiment. It's like tuning a car. As you know, it's not enough to have it in great operating condition. You need to step on the gas and accelerate. In my opinion, most people who implement lean processes don't take it far enough. They focus within their four walls, but do not take the work into the channel."

Filipe was crestfallen. Empathetically, Joe spoke up and said, "This is why we're doing this workshop. We want to know which companies have been able to power the greatest improvement on the Effective Frontier to improve corporate performance. I think that we need to judge a company by their results and then translate what this means to our operations strategy. I think that this is a good topic for us to develop further. I can understand fully how the implementation of lean practices doesn't go far enough."

"I see that Ford is at the bottom of the list and I know that you couldn't list Chrysler and General Motors due to their recent bankruptcies and restatements," Lou said. "But, isn't it interesting that the European automotive companies are outperforming the industry. Why do you believe this is so?"

I turned to Lou. "I think it has to do with the management of the product development cycle, and the building of an effective network with the supplier base to not only deliver the parts, but also help in the innovation cycle. European buyers are often more willing to order a vehicle and wait for it to be manufactured. In North America, customers expect to buy it off the lot. The signal of what customers really want helps them to better understand their customer; and as a result, they are building designs that better meet the needs of their buyer."

Toyota had " . . . net income of 291 billion yen in the quarter that ended Mar. 31, equivalent to $2.89 billion, down 5.3 percent from a year ago partly due to the $1.2 billion fine the car company paid the U.S. government for covering up unintended acceleration problems."[3]

James R. Healey, "U.S. 'Coverup' Fine Barely Slows Toyota Earnings," USA Today

TABLE 8.2   Growth of Companies within the Automotive Industry

	Automotive Year-over-Year Sales Growth (2000–2013)				
Company	Average	2000–2003	2004–2007	2008–2011	2012–2013
Daimler AG	2%	1%	0%	3%	3%
Ford Motor Company	−1%	−1%	1%	−4%	4%
General Motors Company	−1%	N/A	N/A	−2%	2%
Honda Motor Company Limited	6%	6%	10%	3%	7%
Toyota Motor Corporation	7%	3%	13%	2%	10%
Volkswagen AG	10%	8%	12%	12%	9%

Source: Supply Chain Insights LLC, Corporate Annual Reports 2000–2013.

"Let's take a closer look," I continued while showing them the data in Table 8.2. "Note that Volkswagen's growth is constant, but look at the ups and downs of General Motors and Ford. Toyota's inconsistencies hurt them in the index ranking. Some of this was caused by the issue that they had with their braking systems and the unintended acceleration issue in some of their models like Prius. They were slow to recognize the problem, and even slower to build customer loyalty after this issue was acknowledged. Who wants to buy a car when they are unsure if it is safe?" Filipe agreed, but he was still in shock.

"Now let's focus on margin. No doubt about it, it's been a tough ride for the automaker. With slowing growth, and tight margins of only 3 percent, Toyota Motor Corporation, with its legacy of lean thinking, led profitability at the beginning of the decade, but could not sustain it. As growth slowed, and quality problems mounted, it was hard for them to compete. The write-offs were material.

"Also, note the overall volatility of the companies in this industry. Automotive value networks, with trade-ins and model releases, are cyclical with lots of downs and a few ups. I also find it interesting that the profitability for European and U.S. car manufacturers is a stark contrast. Note the difference. While the U.S. automakers have focused on efficiency, the Europeans have focused on design of the vehicle from the customer back. I think that it is for this reason that Volkswagen has delivered consistent growth and operating margin over the last decade," I said. With that statement, I showed them Table 8.3.

Lou shook his head and said, "My head is swimming. I had no idea that other companies had these ups and downs. I thought it was only us. With this discussion, resiliency takes on a whole new dimension. As we get ready for

TABLE 8.3 Company Profitability in the Automotive Industry

| | Automotive Operative Margin (2000–2013) | | | | |
Company	Average	2000–2003	2004–2007	2008–2011	2012–2013
Daimler AG	0.04	0.01	0.05	0.05	0.07
Ford Motor Company	0.00	0.01	−0.03	0.01	0.04
General Motors Company	0.11	N/A	−0.02	0.24	−0.08
Honda Motor Company Limited	0.07	0.08	0.08	0.05	0.04
Toyota Motor Corporation	0.06	0.07	0.09	0.02	0.04
Volkswagen AG	0.04	0.05	0.03	0.05	0.06

Source: Supply Chain Insights LLC, Corporate Annual Reports 2000–2013.

Project Orbit, I think that we need to agree on the peer groups and companies that we want to emulate instead of just relying on tribal lore or hearsay."

Almost simultaneously, Edgar and Angela both piped up in agreement. Edgar then said, "I love the fact that the methodology can be used to have a data-based discussion. I like the fact that it puts all companies on an even playing field without emotions or commentary."

REVIEW OF THE AUTOMOTIVE INDUSTRY

"Can you wrap your mind around why Volkswagen is at the top of the index?" I said. Filipe nodded reluctantly. I then cautioned the group, "Our research indicates that the auto industry remains vulnerable. I don't believe that they've learned the lessons of the past decade. Unlike Cisco, which failed and then rethought the approach to not fail again, the shortcomings in the auto value network remain problematic.

"The current situation is one of high demand. Executives in the industry are flying high on exuberance. The supply chain is ramping up. Companies throughout the supply chain, from manufacturers to third-tier suppliers, are struggling to meet high demand levels. In fact, many domestic auto plants shortened summer shutdowns in 2013 to meet demand levels. The traditional two-week break at the beginning of July, to perform maintenance tasks and retool for the upcoming model year, was shortened or completely eliminated for many plants, including some run by Ford and Chrysler.[4] Due to the government bailouts, the U.S. automakers are getting a lot of press that the good times are ready to roll.

"Business is good. Demand is high. But is the rebounding automotive supply chain flexible, agile, and resilient?" I waited for the group to think this over. They were unsure how to answer. "And furthermore, is this industry ready to withstand the inevitable downturn coming in the economy moving forward? I think not. This downturn may not occur tomorrow, but it will happen. The results of our analysis of supply chain financial ratios indicate that the boom-and-bust cycle of the automotive industry remains the dangerous status quo. The automotive manufacturer has not learned how to sense channel data and read market signals.

"We have emerged from a long and deep recession in which people delayed big purchases like automobiles. Now that they've purchased a new one, do you think that they'll go back to buying a new car very two years? We don't know," I said. "And, when the next recession hits, do you think that the automotive companies and their suppliers are now ready to withstand the next crisis? I don't think so," I concluded.

With that, Lou furrowed his brow. "What do you mean by that?"

As I handed out what is shown here as Table 8.4 to the group, I continued, "Note the decline in cash cycles and the decrease in inventory turns. Like the hospitals in the health-care value network, automotive manufacturers have worked very hard to push costs and waste backward onto their suppliers. This makes them less resilient because these critical links in their value network have no flexibility. Unlike Intel, they have been slow to actively design the value network and improve flows. Instead, their focus is on cycles without giving the suppliers the right information to plan. Short cycles define excellence in this industry, but if it is with the wrong data, then we are just doing the wrong things quicker. As a result, the automotive company is reactive. With their current high growth rates, if they had been successful in the design of the

TABLE 8.4   Effectiveness of the Automotive Industry on the Effective Frontier

Automotive Industry (n = 39)					
Year	Operating Margin	Inventory Turns	Cash-to-Cash Cycle	Revenue per Employee (K$)	SG&A Ratio
2000–2003	0.03	13	52	374	9%
2004–2007	0.05	15	46	481	8%
2008–2011	0.05	18	37	753	8%
2012	0.05	12	33	997	7%

Industry Average composed of public companies (NAICS code 336112) reporting in One Source with 2012 annual sales greater than $5 billion.
Source: Supply Chain Insights LLC, Corporate Annual Reports 2000–2012.

supply chain and managing channel data, their turns would be much higher. Instead, they are not, which means that they are highly vulnerable once a downturn happens.

"Conquering the Effective Frontier requires companies to get good at both flows and cycles. Make sense?" I stated as I looked Filipe squarely in the eyes. He squirmed a bit uncomfortably as I continued, "While lean reduces waste and improves cycles, I believe that what most companies in the automotive industry have missed is the need to continually redesign the value chain based on market shifts outside-in. Instead, the automotive industry has historically focused on saving costs. This was to such an extreme that they almost put their suppliers out of business. A good example was Delphi. General Motors was Delphi's sole customer, and they were forced into bankruptcy. In short, I think that the leaders in the automotive industry have pinched pennies and lost dollars. You can't simply push the problem back onto the suppliers and expect it to go away. This had an impact on quality. As you will see, the number of write-offs due to quality impacts, like Toyota's, has been material."

At this point, Frank pulled out a newspaper article detailing the current issue with GM ignition switches, and said, "To this extreme?"

I sadly had to say, "Yes."

Frank commented, "Can you guys believe that GM could produce cars for an entire decade with a faulty ignition switch? How does this happen?"

Frank then read the article, "Engineer's Switch from Hell Begins GM's Woes" to the group. Slowly, he shared the narrative while making animated faces during the reading. The article bordered on the ridiculous, but it sadly reflected the reality of the dialogue that we were having.

Engineer's Switch from Hell Begins GM's Woes

The ignition switch on the steering column of the Chevrolet Cobalt and other small cars was so poorly designed that it easily slipped out of the run position, causing engines to stall. Engineers knew it as early as 2004. By GM's admission, the defective switches caused over 50 crashes and at least 13 deaths.

Yet inside the auto giant, no one saw it as a safety problem. For 11 years.

CBS News (June 6, 2014), www.cbsnews.com/news/engineers-switch-from-hell-began-gm-recall-woes (accessed August 15, 2014).

Frank shook his head, and said, "How could this happen at a company like GM? First it was the Jeep tires, and then Toyota acceleration, and now it's the GM ignition switch. Isn't safety the first thing that an automotive company should guarantee? The group nodded their heads in agreement. Their collective question was, "How could this happen?"

My answer wasn't pretty, but it was honest. "When there is a singular focus on cost, bad things happen. The automotive industry has focused on driving efficiency in its processes while whipping its suppliers for costs for a decade. As you will see, this almost crippled the automotive industry, but the dogmatic procurement practices have added to the quality issues."

"Yes," said Edgar. "I bet GM has as many people in procurement trying to cut costs and take money out of the pockets of their suppliers as Intel has designers and planners trying to drive value. This is an industry that has been ruthless in cutting costs and squeezing suppliers. I get it. You cannot *save* your way to value. A lesson for us all."

I then told the story of Fiat. This is a case study from a book that I was writing, and due to the sensitive nature of the material, the speaker asked to remain anonymous.

Fiat in the Recession

"The start of the recession at Fiat hit us hard. While our models were not selling off the dealer lots, we continued to make cars. Why, you might ask? Simply put, we valued full manufacturing utilization and wanted to keep the factories humming. We were tightly coupled to our suppliers, and they were also busy making parts.

Despite the fact that we were not selling cars, we kept running our factories. After a couple of months, we had a real cash-flow issue. We had to shut down our factories and we could not pay our suppliers. I padlocked the gates so that the suppliers could not have access to our factories and put my phone into 'out- of-office mode.' I remember the suppliers lining up outside the locked gates trying to deliver parts that we no longer needed and were not going to pay for. This was a stark realization for me that companies cannot just focus on minimizing cycles and squeezing suppliers. Instead, we needed to manage both cycles and flows from the outside in. What good is an efficient cycle if it is out of step with the market?"

"In addition," I said, as I shifted my tired feet in my shoes, "as we can see from the Fiat case study, the Lean processes did not focus equally on cycles and flows. The automotive industry has been effective in improving manufacturing and procurement efficiency, but they are not good at capturing and translating dealer signals into the value chain to modulate supply. When a downturn happens, it is the supplier left at the gate holding the parts with no payment. As a result, suppliers either go out of business or they shift their focus to other industries.

"Compare the investment and organizational focus of Intel to that of an automotive company. Intel has over 600 professionals focused on nothing but maximizing the effectiveness of the value chain and building strong relationships with suppliers. If you asked the same question of an automotive company, they'd give you the staffing levels for their purchasing organization. The automotive company does not understand the difference between purchasing, and squeezing costs from suppliers, and building effective supplier relationships. At Intel it is about supply chain resiliency, whereas at an automotive company, it is about cost cutting," I stated.

Edgar laughed and said, "Well, that is clear. We have a bit of that kind of mentality here as well."

"I get it," said Filipe. "I have a much clearer picture of what I need to do. Taking responsibility for the demand signal throughout the nodes of the value network matters. We are not good at this, and I think we need to get better. Would you agree, Joe?" And with that the group began a deep discussion on the definition of demand and how to build an organization to sense and shape the demand signal to become more market-driven. Lou and Edgar were disappointed that Sam, their chief procurement officer, had not made it to the meeting. They made a follow-up note on the board to share the notes with Sam and work with him on a strategy to improve supplier resiliency. Joe agreed to help drive the change to get suppliers a better signal.

Progress in the Automotive Industry on the Effective Frontier

It was now late in the afternoon. My throat was parched and the blister on my left foot was as painful as the discussion on this industry had been for Filipe. It had been a long three days. The group was anxious to move on, so I quickly showed the team the charts on the automotive industry's economy of scale and continued, "It is hard to be competitive in the automotive industry without scale, as you can see in the charts (Figures 8.2 and 8.3)."

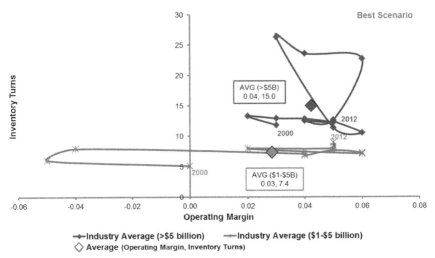

FIGURE 8.2 Comparison of Automotive Companies Greater Than $5B and $1–$5 Billion at the Intersection of Operating Margin and Inventory Turns
Industry Average comprised of public companies (NAICS code 336112) reporting in One Source with 2012 annual sales greater than $5 billion and $1–$5 billion, excluding outliers.
Source: Supply Chain Insights LLC, Corporate Annual Reports 2006–2012.

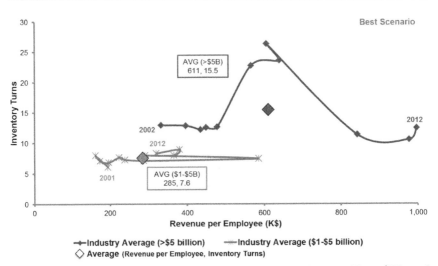

FIGURE 8.3 Comparison of Automotive Companies Greater Than $5B and $1–$5 Billion at the Intersection of Inventory Turns and Revenue/Employee
Industry Average comprised of public companies (NAICS code 336112) reporting in One Source with 2012 annual sales greater than $5 billion and $1–$5 billion, excluding outliers.
Source: Supply Chain Insights LLC, Corporate Annual Reports 2002–2012.

"Isn't it amazing how the revenue-per-employee charts are so much more predictable than the operating margin views," Angela commented. "This is true for all industries." "Companies are so much more reliable at driving the efficient response than a more effective one."

Edgar then added to the conversation, "It is just tough to know, without doing a session like this, how to define what *good* looks like. Our ability to have this conversation is so much greater now than it was a couple of days ago."

Summary

It was break time, so the group agreed to quickly write down their insights from the discussion on the automotive industry. At the end of the discussion, they wrote on the board:

A singular focus on cost can throw an organization out of balance. Bad things happen with a narrow focus.

The dogmatic procurement practices of the automotive industry stalled the growth for the U.S. automotive industry. The focus on cost stalled innovation. Incorporating procurement into the team was going to be important for Project Orbit.

It is essential to separate historic perception from the current reality. When looking at measuring progress on the Effective Frontier, it is important to use a data-driven approach.

Companies need to be good at design, planning, and supply chain execution. They go together like hand in glove. Organizations need to actively design to improve resiliency, use channel data in planning, and ensure that they are executing according to the plan. Building strength in horizontal processes helps us to keep this all together.

Auto Suppliers and Contract Manufacturers

I had decided to tackle the auto suppliers and contract manufacturers last, because it would help the team gain valuable perspective on what it is like to manage operations in an extremely challenging environment where it is almost impossible to predict the future. It was a nice way to wind up our discussions because it was a cautionary tale of what happens when you don't get your demand signals right.

The story was also important to understand because a company's success, especially if you have a lot of suppliers, is highly dependent upon keeping that group of suppliers healthy and responsive. The group was interested, but was also anxious to wrap up the day, so I prepared summary information for the group's review.

TABLE 8.5 Progress of Automotive Suppliers on the Effective Frontier

	Automotive Supplier Industry (n = 24)				
Year	Operating Margin	Inventory Turns	Cash-to-Cash Cycle	Revenue per Employee (K$)	SG&A Ratio
2000–2003	0.04	9	57	176	8%
2004–2007	0.05	10	56	266	7%
2008–2011	0.05	9	49	321	6%
2012	0.07	9	34	365	6%

Industry Average comprised of public companies (NAICS codes 336312 & 336412) reporting in One Source with 2012 annual sales greater than $5 billion.
Source: Supply Chain Insights LLC, Corporate Annual Reports 2000–2012.

As I handed out Table 8.5, I engaged the group in thinking about their favorite automotive supplier. They had a hard time identifying a supplier that only sold into the automotive industry. In the discussion, they learned that most automakers were now conglomerates. To survive the economic downturns, companies had to serve multiple industries, not just one. As a result, they had improved their margins and reduced their cash-to-cash cycle.

I was in agreement and continued, "Most of these suppliers to automotive are now conglomerates supporting many different industries. They have diversified. Part of their strategy is to use the different divisions within the conglomerate to trade-off the cyclical swings of their upstream customers. They are also, through their sales cycles, attempting to teach automotive buyers better procurement practices." With this, Frank smiled. In his own way, he let me know that he got the message.

"After the recession, and the horrific issues that the suppliers experienced in the downturn, they changed their business model to focus on more attractive industrial sectors like Aerospace and Defense and Industrial Equipment. They realized that they needed to change their strategy to be more profitable. As a result, these conglomerates were able to make great improvement on the index." I then showed them Table 8.6.

"It may have been a healthy thing for the automotive suppliers as well, because keeping suppliers healthy is critical to having a resilient automotive supply chain. The downside for the automotive suppliers is that they now have less leverage in negotiating pricing than they did when they were the sole industry that these companies served. However, all is not lost for the automotive purchaser because they still represent a high percentage of revenue for the supplier," I continued while discussing the index results.

TABLE 8.6 Automotive Index: Progress of Automotive on the Effective Frontier for 2006–2012

Company	2013 Revenue (billions USD)	Balance	Balance Ranking	Strength	Strength Ranking	Resiliency	Resiliency Ranking	Index (0.3B + 0.3S + 0.3R)	Ranking
Valeo SA	16.1	0.23	3	0.16	1	0.98	4	2.4	1
Honeywell International SA	39.1	−0.06	6	0.08	2	0.47	2	3.0	2
TRW Automotive Holdings Corp.	17.4	0.28	2	0.08	3	1.72	6	3.3	3
Magna International Inc.	34.8	0.29	1	0.04	5	2.13	7	3.9	4
United Technologies Corporation	62.6	−0.07	7	0.00	7	0.39	1	4.5	5
Johnson Controls Inc	42.7	−0.17	8	0.06	4	0.66	3	4.5	5
Continental AG	44.2	−0.05	5	0.03	6	1.46	5	4.8	7
Lear Corporation	16.2	−0.04	4	−0.36	8	4.34	8	6.0	8

Source: Supply Chain Insights LLC, Corporate Annual Reports 2006–2013.

Contract Manufacturer

I looked quickly at my watch. The days had gone very fast, and our time was almost over. I asked if the group needed a break, and they said no. Instead, they asked me to move quickly through contract manufacturing. They also wanted to wrap up and compare their notes on all the industries. It was important to them to forge ahead. I had whetted their appetites and they wanted to finish the task at hand.

I shifted my feet in my shoes and took back the projector clicker to continue. "Contract manufacturing is now two decades old. Today, contract manufacturers run their businesses in a different business model than when they started. Ever so slowly, they morphed into their new form to serve their upstream brand owners. Today, it is a very cutthroat business. Brand owners are squeezing the contract manufacturers on cost. While contract manufacturing companies have tried to differentiate based on capabilities, not costs, the results have been disappointing. It is a commodity business."

"The management of the industry sector is relatively new. Each company started with very different roots," I said. "For example, Kimball International initially began producing electronic components for electric organs. In contrast, Celestica operated as a manufacturing unit of IBM for 75 years before 1993, when it became a contract manufacturer." I then showed them the timeline in Figure 8.4.

At this point, Lou raised his hand. "What is a contract manufacturer? I am sorry, but I am unfamiliar with the term. Can you explain?"

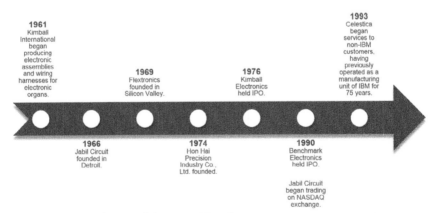

FIGURE 8.4 Evolution of Contract Manufacturers
Source: Supply Chain Insights, Corporate Annual Reports.

I loved Lou's honesty and openness in asking for clarity within the group. So I stopped and shared a definition, "As brand owners in the high-tech sector distanced themselves from ownership of manufacturing assets, the industry and relationships between the brand and contract manufacturers evolved. Essentially, they redefined the value chain. In the new definition, brand owners designed and sold products, and the contract manufacturers produced them, but it is not yet clear whether the business model is viable long-term.

"I feel that the lack of resiliency in this industry should be a stay-awake issue for companies. Sadly it is not. Global supply chains will only get more complex in the next decade. This lack of resiliency should not only be a problem for contract manufacturers, themselves, but should also concern the brand owners that contract for these services in industries as diverse as medical device and automotive manufacturers, as well as consumer electronics companies. These industries have increased their dependency on contract manufacturing to deliver products on time and on budget. The lack of resiliency demonstrated in the financial results can endanger the future success of these downstream companies. It is a ticking time bomb," I continued.

"The contract manufacturing industry operates purely on buy-and-sell transactions based somewhat on capabilities, but primarily on cost. As a result, capturing and retaining market share is critical for success among contract manufacturers. The year-over-year sales growth for the companies is a dismal story." With that, I showed the group Table 8.7.

As the group looked at the handout, I continued, "Note the level of volatility seen here. It is not present to these extremes in any other industry we have discussed. Several companies show negative growth levels, and negative operating margin, and you know that's no way to run a business.

TABLE 8.7 Year-over-Year Sales Growth of Contract Manufacturers for the Period of 2000–2013

Contract Manufacturing Year-over-Year Sales Growth (2000–2013)					
Company	Average	2000–2003	2004–2007	2008–2011	2012–2013
Benchmark Electronics, Inc.	4%	5%	13%	−5%	6%
Celestica, Inc.	−3%	−11%	6%	−2%	−10%
Flextronics International Ltd.	12%	28%	9%	14%	−8%
Hon Hai Precision Industry Co., Ltd.	36%	55%	46%	25%	7%
Jabil Circuit, Inc.	15%	12%	27%	8%	5%
Kimball International, Inc.	0%	−3%	4%	−1%	0%

Source: Supply Chain Insights LLC, Corporate Annual Reports 2000–2013.

"There are many root issues. In general, contract manufacturers operate on short-term contracts, always competing to get the next piece of work. This creates instability within the industry. Celestica explains the issue in their 2012 annual report," I said and showed the group the quote from Celestica:

> Although the industry is characterized by a large revenue base and new business opportunities, the revenue is volatile on a quarterly basis, the business environment is highly competitive, and aggressive pricing is a common business dynamic.
>
> —*Celestica, Inc., 2012 Annual Report (10K), pp. 34–35*

"In addition, most contract manufacturers have a small list of clients who are responsible for a large percentage of their sales. Brand owners pit the contract manufacturers against each other. With their shorter life cycles, and plunging market values, they have to. Celestica received 68 percent of total revenue from their top 10 customers in 2012. The combination of short-term contract work with a concentrated list of clients creates a challenging environment for stable growth. The loss of any contract could be disastrous for any of the contract manufacturers," I said and showed them the quote from Benchmark Electronics:

> Sales to our ten largest customers represented 56%, 53% and 48% of our sales in 2012, 2011 and 2010, respectively. In 2012, sales to International Business Machines Corporation represented 21% of our sales. The loss of a major customer, if not replaced, would adversely affect us.
>
> —*Benchmark Electronics, Inc., 2012 Annual Report (10K), p. 8*

"It is tough to run a company with small growth and tight margins. This is, unfortunately, getting to be the norm. Two of the six companies demonstrate an average operating margin over the past 13 years that is negative; and the highest average operating margin, reported by Foxconn, is only 0.06. Compare this to the margin levels that we discussed this morning of the high-tech brand owners, especially those companies operating in the consumer electronics industry," I continued as I handed out Table 8.8 to the group to support the discussion.

"Now imagine what happens when digital printing becomes mainstream, and instead of pouring plastics into molds and hand-assembling platforms, we

TABLE 8.8 Year-over-Year Operating Margins of Contract Manufacturers for the Period of 2000–2013

Contract Manufacturing Operating Margin (2000–2013)					
Company	Average	2000–2003	2004–2007	2008–2011	2012–2013
Benchmark Electronics, Inc.	0.02	0.02	0.04	0.00	0.04
Celestica, Inc.	−0.01	−0.02	−0.02	−0.01	0.02
Flextronics International, Ltd.	−0.01	−0.01	0.01	−0.04	0.02
Hon Hai Precision Industry Co., Ltd.	0.05	0.08	0.06	0.03	0.03
Jabil Circuit, Inc.	0.02	0.03	0.03	0.00	0.03
Kimball International, Inc.	0.02	0.03	0.02	0.01	0.02

Source: Supply Chain Insights LLC, Corporate Annual Reports 2000–2013.

print them. This industry is vulnerable, and as a result, their brand owners upstream are vulnerable as well. Not many recognized the problem," I said.

At this point, Edgar let out a sigh, leaned over to Lou, put a firm hand on his shoulder and said, "Aren't you glad that we're not operating in this environment?" He then looked around the room, "We think that we have it tough, but our Effective Frontier looks far different than it does for contract manufacturing companies. But this makes me think. Joe, don't we have contract manufacturing relationships?"

Joe shook his head yes, and said, "Edgar, right now it's about 32 percent of what we make. Many of these contract manufacturers are also vulnerable because we are not good at giving them good demand signals. We would be better served if we took more responsibility for the entire value chain."

At that point, Angela chimed in, "Edgar, this also is very important for the work that we have just kicked off for corporate social responsibility. I think that it is much harder for a company that is operating without a good demand signal to minimize waste and operate CSR programs effectively. I also think that it is critical for us to build supplier scorecards to ensure that we can make progress on improvement on our entire value chain, not just what we do within our own four walls. Would you agree?"

"Absolutely," Joe said as he leaned into the discussion. "I am hoping that one of our take-aways from this session is that we have to own our entire value chain. If we do not, we are vulnerable. The contract manufacturing business model evolved over several decades into its current form. What began as a brilliant business model now needs to be questioned and reexamined for viability. With decreasing volume, increasing instability, and the ongoing variability in demand and supply, the contract manufacturing model may now pose greater

TABLE 8.9 Performance of the Contract Manufacturing Industry on the Effective Frontier for the Period of 2000–2012

	Contract Manufacturing Industry (n = 11)				
Year	Operating Margin	Inventory Turns	Cash-to-Cash Cycle	Revenue per Employee (K$)	SG&A Ratio
2000–2003	0.05	8	60	520	8%
2004–2007	0.06	8	48	328	8%
2008–2011	0.03	8	50	333	7%
2012	0.04	8	53	317	7%

Industry Average comprised of public companies (NAICS code 33441%, where % is any number from 0 to 2, 4 to 9) reporting in One Source with 2012 annual sales greater than $5 billion.
Source: Supply Chain Insights LLC, Corporate Annual Reports 2000 2012.

risk than opportunity for brand owners. I think that we should tread carefully. We can outsource our supply chain, but not the risk."

With that, I showed the group the contract manufacturing industry's progress on the Effective Frontier in Tables 8.9 and 8.10. As I turned off the projector and passed out a file folder with all of the industry data we had reviewed and the group started studying and comparing them. The room was buzzing with energy even though it was late in the day.

"No doubt about it, this is an industry with low turns, low margins, and low growth. Why would major brands risk their future on a model that is so risky?" asked Filipe.

"Good question," I said. "My view is that it comes from not looking at the industry holistically. Few companies are doing the tough work to look at value chains and asking themselves these hard questions. For example, let's take a look at the industry orbit charts."

I then turned the page to show Figures 8.5 and 8.6. "If they understood the impact of orbit charts, this random pattern should be a red flag." My throat was dry as I continued, "Even the revenue/employee charts show randomness. These orbit charts are the most random of any industry that we have studied. They make my head hurt."

I sat down, and we began to look at the chart of all of the industries and their progress on the Effective Frontier as shown in Table 8.11. It was a summary chart of all of the industries that we had reviewed together. Frank was tapping his foot. His patience was wearing thin. It had been a long day.

Angela started the conversation by saying, "I would much rather be a consumer packaged goods company than a supplier to them. I also would much

TABLE 8.10 The Contract Manufacturing Index for the Period of 2006–2012

Company	2013 Revenue (billions USD)	Balance	Balance Ranking	Strength	Strength Ranking	Resiliency	Resiliency Ranking	Index (0.3B + 0.3S + 0.3R)	Ranking
Benchmark Electronics	2.5	−0.15	4	0.00	2	0.86	2	2.4	1
Flextronics International Ltd.	23.6	0.95	1	−0.02	3	1.23	4	2.4	1
Jabil Circuit, Inc.	18.3	−0.03	2	0.06	1	1.23	5	2.4	1
Kimball International Inc	1.2	−0.05	3	−0.04	5	0.68	1	2.7	4
Hon Hai Precision Industry Co.	133.1	−0.24	5	−0.04	4	1.18	3	3.6	5
Celestica Inc.	5.8	−1.02	6	−0.55	6	1.28	6	5.4	6

Source: Supply Chain Insights LLC, Corporate Annual Reports 2006–2013.

343

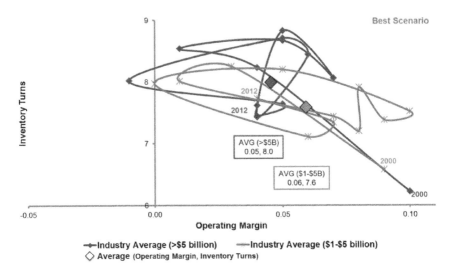

FIGURE 8.5 Orbit Chart of the Contract Manufacturing Industry Contrasting Inventory Turns and Operating Margin

Industry Average comprised of public companies (NAICS code 33441% where % is any number from 0 to 2, 4 to 9) in One Source with 2012 annual sales greater than $5 billion and $1–$5 billion.

Source: Supply Chain Insights LLC, Corporate Annual Reports 2000–2012.

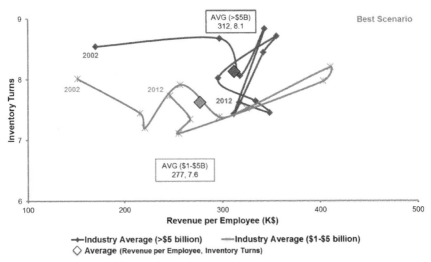

FIGURE 8.6 Orbit Chart of the Contract Manufacturing Industry Contrasting Inventory Turns and Revenue per Employee

Industry Average comprised of public companies (NAICS code 33441% where % is any number from 0 to 2, 4 to 9) in One Source with 2012 annual sales greater than $5 billion and $1–$5 billion, excluding outliers.

Source: Supply Chain Insights LLC, Corporate Annual Reports 2002–2012.

TABLE 8.11 Progress of Industries on the Effective Frontier for the Period of 2006–2012

Industry	Number of Companies	Average Balance	Average Strength	Average Resiliency
Retail	14	−0.12	0.01	1.40
Consumer Packaged Goods	17	−0.11	0.03	0.71
Food & Beverage	21	0.17	0.06	1.03
Chemical	18	−0.07	0.01	0.85
Hospital	5	−0.25	0.02	3.57
Pharmaceutical	16	−0.65	0.03	0.48
Medical Device	15	−0.15	−0.06	0.47
Automotive	10	−0.22	−0.07	1.63
Automotive Suppliers	8	0.05	0.01	1.52
Consumer Electronics	25	0.83	1.14	2.70
Semiconductors	10	−0.31	−0.16	1.11
Contract Manufacturing	6	−0.09	−0.10	1.08

Source: Supply Chain Insights LLC, Corporate Annual Reports 2006–2013.

rather run a company that's a brand owner in the industrial markets than be a contract manufacturer in their value chain." The group laughed.

Lou then added, "I am struck by the lack of resiliency of most industries. I can clearly see the impact of demand and supply volatility. It is clear to me now that this is a risk factor that most companies do not understand."

"While the consumer value network may not have reduced total costs and total inventories, I have to think that the better results on this chart represent a start of improvement through collaborative practices," Frank said. "Note how the industries within this value chain did better than the rest in aggregate. I think that there is something there. I think that it needs time and, yes," he said with a grin, "it requires the adaptation of sales processes." He flippantly said to Joe, "I get it now. I am a convert."

Edgar then spoke, "Notice the importance of a brand. In all cases, companies with strong brands are performing at a very different level on the frontier. What this says to me is that investing in our brand improves our potential, and we need to ensure that we protect our brand with everything we do. We cannot afford to have Toyota or GM's quality issues. Filipe, it reminds me of how important the work is that you're doing on improving product quality and customer satisfaction."

MOVING FORWARD WITH PROJECT ORBIT

The three-day session was completed, but the work on Project Orbit lay ahead. The challenge for the group was now what to do with all the insights from the intense discussions from the past three days. As follow-up, Angela and Jeff agreed to assemble all of the take-aways into a workbook for the team.

Previously in the day, Angela and I had constructed a diagram of interconnecting functional metrics that tie to the Effective Frontier. She asked if this work could be quickly shared before we continued. Lou beamed and said, "We always have time for your good work, Angela." As he said this, he placed his hands on Frank's shoulders to keep him in his chair. Angela stood up nervously and in faltering a voice stated, "I think that we need to optimize corporate performance. Consequently, I feel that it is important to hold the leaders in the business functions—marketing, sales, customer service, distribution, manufacturing, and procurement—responsible for reliability. In parallel, I think that it is important to align corporate metrics to the metrics that matter for all employees of the organization. At the highest level, are we in agreement that the metrics that matter are year-over-year growth, return on invested capital, operating margin, inventory turns, and customer service?" She then unveiled a drawing that is captured here as Figure 8.7.

Frank whistled as he looked at Angela's drawing. It made so much sense, but it was difficult to conceive that the group was going to streamline the hundreds of functional metrics that they religiously reported on weekly into this simple metrics reporting structure. He thought for a moment, and then without missing a beat said, "So, Joe, would this mean that I would be able to sell more product?" The group laughed, but Joe looked at Frank and replied in a serious voice, "Yes, Frank, I think accelerated sales would be one of the outcomes. I also think that we will be able to make substantial progress on the rest of the metrics." He turned to Angela and said, "I don't know about you guys, but I like this model. I think that Angela has done a powerful job of capturing how we as a team can improve all of the metrics that matter. I think that this drawing is the outcome that we were searching for when we first started Project Orbit."

We were an hour behind our agenda, and I was sensitive to the time pressure, so I took Edgar aside and asked for advice. He suggested that they order in pizza and continue the discussion. He wanted to be sure that they did not minimize the time to reflect and to build a guiding coalition for Project Orbit.

At a Corporate Level, Focus on Balance, Strength and Resiliency ➡	Corporate Bonus for all Functions: 60% Based Equally on Goals in Revenue Growth, Operating Margin, Inventory Turns, On-Time Orders, Safety and ROIC				
	Stretch Objectives for CSR: Carbon and Electricity Usage				
	Marketing	Sales	Customer Service	Manufacturing	Procurement
At a functional level, focus on reliability (each function to be rewarded 40% of bonus on reliability metrics.) ➡	Market share	Deductions from orders	Orders shipped complete	Overall equipment effectiveness (OEE)	Delivered costs of direct materials
	Profit/case	Returns	Hands-free orders	First pass yield	Prevention of outages
	Good/bad complexity ratio of product portfolio	Customer scorecard ratings	Returns	Product quality	Material quality

FIGURE 8.7 Metrics That Matter for Project Orbit

So, after a short break, and receiving and signing for pizza delivery, I asked the team to think about what they had learned from our three-day session and then project how it applied to Project Orbit. We started with a five-minute quiet period for reflection, and then slowly went around the room to share. After consideration, Edgar volunteered to speak first, cavalierly dangling a piece of pepperoni pizza in his hand, trying to not get it on his white shirt.

"I have gone to many conferences and heard business leaders speak eloquently about improving business performance. However, what I learned through this workshop is that a new form of leadership is needed to conquer the Effective Frontier. Let me give you an analogy. I sail, and when things are going well it is because I have a firm hand on my rudder. This is especially true at night when I have my running lights on and I am carefully navigating my boat into the slip. Only I can steer the boat, and when I do it, I need to have a firm, but gentle hand. I have to know where I am going, but I must read the wind and current and stay constantly aware of my surroundings. I have been a better ship captain than I have been a leader of this team. I need to make sure that I stay focused and disciplined while keeping you aligned as a team," said Edgar. He then turned to Joe, and continued, "All the best to you and your work with Project Orbit in Brazil. You have my blessing." With a twinkle in his eye, he said, "We look forward to plotting your orbit charts as you build an organization to tackle a new Effective Frontier. It is my hope that you can drive a steady and successful project for us in this new venture." He laughed as he continued, "I now know to watch out for wild gyrations at the intersections of the metrics."

Next was Filipe. He wiped his mouth, crumpled his napkin, and said, "I came to this session thinking that I knew which companies I wanted to emulate in my drive for operations excellence. As you know, I am a competitive guy. I want to be known for doing things well. In fact, I want to be the best. For years, I have embraced the concepts of Lean operations. My efforts have been steadfast to reduce waste. My take-away is that while Lean is important, it is not sufficient. Our focus needs to be on the design for value from the customer back. We must sense, and manage, our metrics together on the Effective Frontier." He then turned to Edgar and said, "I like your sailing analogy. I am never patient enough. I am afraid that I probably would not be able to get my boat into the slip."

Lou then raised his hand, and began to speak intensely, "My world is about accuracy in transactions. Let's face it. That is why we are called bean counters. Angela and I have gotten very good at looking backward with high accuracy. But, in our finance world, we discuss very different concepts than where we have focused in this workshop. Moving forward in the face of volatility and uncertainty, based on flows, is not something that I am good at. I have to say, for a finance guy, making this transition is tough. This just is not how our brains are wired. As an organization, we want to control; and this is something that cannot be controlled." He looked first at Joe, then Angela, and finally rested his gaze on Jeff. "I think the work that you three are doing in the building of strong horizontal processes is essential. I also think that we need to rework the bonus and incentive systems so that all employees understand these concepts, and it aligns with Angela's diagram of the metrics reward system that she showed before the pizza arrived. I like the thought of us all having shared metrics, and a clear understanding of how each function works together, to maximize the frontier by the end of the next quarter. We need to start our new fiscal year off on the right foot." Jeff looked him in the eye and agreed with his comments.

Next it was Angela's turn. She pushed her fork aimlessly through her salad, and looked at the group and said, "I feel lucky to have been a part of these sessions. It has made me think very differently about operations strategy. We have blindly been pursuing a pattern of mergers and acquisitions that I think we need to revisit. Based on what we have studied together, we cannot assume that a larger company gives us scale. We serve regional markets with unique product portfolios. I also firmly believe that we can't continue to pursue functional metrics without a more holistic framework, like the one that I showed, to help employees. Filipe, I have also had some good insights into lean techniques and how to balance both cycles and flows. A real key for me is the design of processes from the outside-in. I am now a strong believer in market-driven concepts."

"Yes," said Jeff. "I have been reflecting on the concept of building human potential to conquer the Effective Frontier. Like an athlete trains, I think that we need to get more serious about building agility, resiliency, and responsiveness in the hearts and minds of our employees. Through these sessions, I have a much better idea of how my work in sales operations ties to the greater whole, but I think that others would benefit from this training. We need to very clearly define these concepts to make them actionable. I would like to lead our efforts in this area." Edgar smiled, and patted Jeff on the arm when he said, "I think that would be a great idea. Let's work together to make this happen."

Frank then put his hand on Joe's shoulder and stated, "Joe, we are better, as a team, for doing this work. I thank you for initiating this effort. I know that sometimes people think that I am tough to work with."

With that comment smiles flashed across the room and Joe retorted sarcastically, "Really, I would never have known that . . ."

Frank continued, "Seriously, Joe, I have learned that I must understand before I judge, and that I need to rethink how I approach customers. Sales is quite different today from how it was ten years ago. You're right; my customers are facing the same challenges that we see. I think a team-based approach to build value chains makes sense, but can we just be sure that we sell a lot of cases in the process?" With that statement, the group laughed.

Joe spoke last. There was a pregnant pause in the room, as he cleared his throat. "I leave here feeling that we are aligned. Do you know how good this feels? It is one thing to talk about operations excellence, and another to have a shared, and a common, vision. This is the first time that I am clear on what *good* looks like. It will help me as a leader going forward. Thank you for allowing me to lead this new initiative."

With that, the group slowly left the room. While it was late, it was almost as if they didn't want to leave. They lingered on and on . . . they talked for hours in groups of twos and threes, and continued the dialogue while they walked out to the parking lot. The air was crisp, and the quarter-moon shone brightly in the night sky as I turned the key in my ignition to leave. I backed the car out of the marked lines on the pavement; but as I turned the wheel to leave the parking lot, my phone buzzed on my dash. A short text on the screen summed up the experience for me:

Thx for a couple of great days! Let's catch up in a couple of months.
I am busy packing for Brazil. See u soon. Joe.

I smiled and put the phone back on the dash. As I turned into the exit, I reflected on just how much I would miss working with this team. I was saddened to see the workshop come to a close. The busy days of Joe scribbling in his notebook had come to an end, but his new adventure was just beginning. I wished him well.

 ## Notes

1. Angelo Young, "August 2013 U.S. Auto Sales: Detroit Three Sold 662,669 Vehicles in U.S. Last Month; General Motors (GM) up 15%, Ford (F) and Chrysler Both Up 12%," *International Business Times* (September 4, 2013), www.ibtimes.com/august-2013-us-auto-sales-detroit-three-sold-662669-vehicles-us-last-month-general-motors-gm-15-ford (accessed September 26, 2013).
2. Jeffrey K. Liker, *The Toyota Way: 14 Management Principles from the World's Greatest Manufacturer* (New York: McGraw-Hill, 2003).
3. James R. Healey, "U.S. 'Coverup' Fine Barely Slows Toyota Earnings," *USA Today* (May 8, 2014), www.usatoday.com/story/money/cars/2014/05/08/toyota-earnings-record-fine-coverup-acceleration/8841829 (accessed May 8, 2014).
4. Chris Isidore, "Auto Plants Skipping Summer Shutdowns," *CNN Money* (May 22, 2013), http://money.cnn.com/2013/05/22/news/companies/auto-plants-summer/index.html (accessed September 26, 2013).

CHAPTER NINE

9

The Smoke Clears

T HE ROOM WAS packed and stuffy. Cigar smoke filled the air as the paddles of the ceiling fans slowly turned. The applause went on and on. . . .
At times, it was to the point that Joe felt overwhelmed and a bit awkward sitting alone on the hard wooden chair in the center of the stage at the U.S. embassy. As he looked at the faces in the audience, memories of Project Orbit flashed in his mind. It took five years of planning and two years of hard work in Brazil to launch the new program. Today, he had the opportunity to celebrate success; but, as a humble guy, Joe struggled with accolades. Being in the limelight was hard for him, as he was more comfortable doing the work than telling others about it. At this moment, he was looking forward to the event being over, and getting home to see his son's ballgame. He was only here today at Filipe's urging.

As he waited for the applause to subside, he smiled and glanced at his well-worn brown briefcase, shoved hastily into the corner of the stage behind the black drapery. The handle was frayed, and the mottled leather now sported a badly stained patina finish. Over the course of the past two years, the briefcase traveled many miles as Joe defined the new operations in Brazil. He had trained a new team and started up a series of manufacturing centers and distribution hubs. The work with the Brazilian distributors and the use of daily channel data on a daily frequency underpinned his success.

Tucked inside the briefcase was a new *Forbes* magazine. On the front cover was Frank sporting a bespoke Scottish tweed suit from his personal tailor on Bond Street. Coming out of Project Orbit, Frank had hit his stride while opening up new opportunities. The sensing of market channel inventory as part of Project Orbit enabled Frank to post double-digit sales, and he took full advantage of the windfall to place himself in the spotlight. The record sales year landed him on the front page of the *Wall Street Journal*, and he reveled in the acclaim. This press opened up a new opportunity for Frank to become the CEO of an obscure manufacturer of penknives in New Jersey, and he savored the power of his new position. It was a leveraged buyout, and the new management team tapped Frank to transform the company into a worldwide powerhouse of security products and tailored services. On the cover, Frank was working his magic.

Joe laughed when he picked up the magazine at the corner grocer. Frank's portrait was one that Joe knew all too well. Despite their differences, the two were now close. The picture showing Frank leaning forward on the cover, conspicuously sporting a new gold watch while flashing a big smile, was the essence of Frank in action. Joe was happy to see Frank actualize his goals.

When they had met for lunch in New York the previous month, Frank spoke of the power of outside-in processes, and the importance of using channel data to drive organizational alignment. In this dicey dialogue, Joe teased him by saying, "Until now I didn't know a leopard could change his spots so easily." After a deep laugh by Joe and a sheepish grin by Frank, they both spoke openly and fluidly about Frank learning to work with others, and gaining an understanding that sales-driven processes were not market-driven, and that market-driven processes were more effective. At the core of the conversation was the realization that building effective relationships with the distributors in the channel, and the sharing of daily channel data with the larger organization, had been fundamental to the success of both their careers.

In the past two years, much had changed in Joe's organization. Lou had retired and Angela had taken his place. She had become a fierce compatriot with Joe. Sitting on the chair in the middle of the stage, his mind flashed back to the day when Greenpeace picketed their Park Avenue offices. It was Angela who found herself sitting in the center of the conference room in the middle of the angry activists on that spring day. Her quiet demeanor, along with the tracking on the corporate social responsibility scorecards, served her well. Because of the meticulous reporting, the Greenpeace representatives dropped their threats. They liked the company's deep approach, and the focus on principle-based supplier scorecards.

Recently, Edgar died quietly in his sleep. This was a great loss for Joe. He could not forget his tight grip on his shoulders in his day-to-day interactions with his team, and constantly felt Edgar's presence as he built the operations in Brazil. Edgar's legacy still permeated the organization, and his coaching to Joe on principle-based leadership was central to the speech that Joe had prepared to present today.

Felipe was Edgar's replacement, and Joe had been recently promoted to the role of chief operations officer. Over the years of working together, they had bonded. Felipe had become more holistic, and Joe was more confident. The launch of Project Orbit to determine the right pace and set points for the metrics that matter seemed like yesterday, but it happened slowly. Joe spent five years working on building metrics that matter before he was able to launch the new team in Brazil. Along the way, the steps seemed awkward at first, but slowly the global team found their way. Joe even got to the point that he enjoyed the global strategy meetings and today missed Frank's antics. At the end of this speech, Joe would take a plane home to start his new job.

It had been seven years since we first met and kicked off the project. In our ongoing conversations, Joe would often laugh about his misguided efforts to launch his big hairy audacious goal. He would often comment, "As I stumbled in building the project, I fell forward into a larger opportunity." He was thankful for the experience.

What was clear for Joe, sitting on this stage in Brazil, was that the journey of building the metrics that matter to drive operational excellence, and the design of supporting processes, is a journey that is never done. As he stood up to face the audience, he smiled. While he was normally a quiet and unassuming guy, Joe found teaching others these principles fulfilling. While he hated presentations, he loved sharing. His mind flashed back through the stages of the project.

 ## REFLECTIONS

Today, Joe cannot pass by a sycamore tree without thinking about the adoption of orbit charts. The team's learning as they defined operations excellence together was about improving patterns of corporate performance over time. He fondly remembered that crisp fall day when we first met in his office. Joe often remarked, "You see what you understand." The journey of learning what was possible and how quickly an organization can drive performance was now etched in his mind, and his well-worn notebooks from our many dialogues were still on his bookshelf in his office.

For Joe now, the bark of the sycamore tree that stood in the parking lot next to his office when he started Project Orbit is now a symbol of the many patterns that are possible in defining corporate performance. While initially surprised to learn that a company's progress on operational excellence after a decade of technology, and process investment, was not a linear line of continuous improvement, Joe now understood that progress happens in small, incremental steps based on balanced and aligned metrics. As a result, he was now a much more capable leader.

As the seasons progressed, the icicles cascading from the roof and the flowers of spring also ignited images of thawing frozen concepts to breathe new energies into the organization. Joe remembers how immobile the company was in their functional silos. He hated the infighting and lack of alignment on what was important. It was so tough to work in an organization where metrics were not clear and the metrics targets were not actionable. While leaders always spoke of balance, Joe was proud that his team had actually accomplished this goal while delivering strength, balance, and resiliency.

JOE'S STORY

The applause quickly stopped as the U.S. ambassador and the president of Brazil moved to the center of the stage to give Joe an award. They were grateful and their presentations overflowed with accolades for Joe and his team. Together they thanked Joe for his efforts in stemming the outbreak of a deadly plant virus attacking the forests in the Amazon. The new product that Joe manufactured was uniquely tailored to thwart the spread of the disease, which had decimated large regions of what had once been dense jungle. Through Joe's efforts to work with the local government, his organization had quickly sensed the crisis and mobilized manufacturing for the increased demand. The outbreak was far worse than anyone had expected, and they were amazed that Joe's team could respond. As the U.S. ambassador and Brazilian president presented their congratulatory speeches, Joe began to have flashbacks. When the outbreak happened, the alignment of suppliers and materials was assimilated at a blistering pace in response to the danger. He was proud that his new organization could orchestrate processes outside-in from market-to-market. Because of this core competency, Joe's new product was successful in stopping the horrific outbreak and saving vast tracts of valuable jungle. It had been a whirlwind of activity, and a very tumultuous time for this team, but they responded with excellence.

After receiving the award and posing for a brief picture, it was Joe's turn to give a speech. The embassy had asked Joe to speak on leadership to an audience of 850 attendees. As Joe cleared his throat and moved toward the podium, he stood up straight. He moved his shoulders back until they touched the seams in his suit jacket and stood tall in his shoes. Today, he was proud. Standing in front of the audience with his signature stance, wearing a crumpled tie and nondescript suit, Joe told his story to an admiring audience of Brazilian manufacturers.

"Two years ago, we started a new venture here in Brazil with a focus on creating new molecules to stop the eradication of the Amazon forests," Joe passionately stated in his opening remarks. With a twinkle in his eye, he held the gaze of the front row, and then continued his speech with an energized voice, "To accomplish this mission, we built a new team in a new country to launch a new product. It was my dream job. I'm a builder. I love people and I am passionate about the environment. Doing the two together was a wonderful opportunity that I'm excited to share."

Joe pushed the button, and flashed a picture of his start-up team on the screen in center stage. In the picture, the audience could see a diverse team with big smiles. Joe continued with a paternal tone in his voice, "We started small. In this picture, the team was breaking ground at the new plant that we built two years ago. Ours was a start-up with all of the issues that you would expect to find in a new operation. My first focus was on delivering manufacturing reliability. I firmly believe that you need a foundation to build from, and that if you have to choose between fast and reliable, reliable should always win. As a team, we defined reliability as making products right the first time with no waste, and in a reliable manner." At that point, Joe beamed one of his infectious smiles and paused before going forward.

He stepped away from the podium, and stared hard at the audience and stated, "One of things I would like for everyone to learn from my journey is that it is important to overcommunicate to employees. I cannot emphasize this enough. I know that you might think it a bit ridiculous as I define all the terms that we used in the execution of the operating strategy, but I learned the hard way that it's important." He rubbed the beads of sweat from his head, and continued, "It seems in life that I don't learn things easily. This was one of my tough lessons. I used words like *reliable, agile, responsive,* and *efficient* in the definition of the operations strategy; and while I thought that everyone understood the meaning of these words, we found that we had different working definitions in our minds. This was a barrier to our success. While it may seem simple to expect that people would know what I meant, it's almost a given that every word you will use could have as many definitions as you have employees. And I don't need to tell you guys how tough this is to navigate." The audience laughed.

Joe let the laughter subside and continued, "My next goal was to create a culture where teams were incented to produce-to-demand. Based on years of training with my management team in the United States, I firmly believe that market-driven concepts where demand and supply is managed from channel to supplier and orchestrated across functional silos are critical to ensure that we're able to deliver on our objectives to deliver operations excellence. In this journey, the relationship between volume and value needs to be constantly optimized and redefined through a focus on horizontal processes. As leaders, we cannot allow people to get lost in self-directed missions within functional silos. This is an opportunity cost to all of our operations.

"As a business leader, I believe that I am the steward of a complex system with intricate relationships." Joe flashed the image of the Effective Frontier on the screen (shown in Figure 9.1). "This is my guiding principle. The relationships between growth, profitability, cycles, and complexity have to be managed holistically, and there is no substitute for leadership. Throughout the startup, I used the model shown here to help all of my employees to understand that metrics cannot be measured in isolation. I kept coming back to this model to ground discussions. As a leader, it is a constant battle to manage complexity and keep this in balance with business goals. The relationships between these metrics are not obvious when you start, and it's difficult to build organizational potential to maximize corporate performance."

"I liken it to my journey as an athlete. First, let me state for the record that I'm not a great athlete, and you'll never find me on the cover of *Sports Illustrated*," Joe said with a chuckle and a twinkle in his eye. "But, I find the process of training and athletic conditioning fascinating. I like tracking my progress over time." He held up his arm to show his heart rate monitor, and continued, "It is amazing what happens when you can track real-time data. By logging my workouts on my mobile application, I can train smarter.

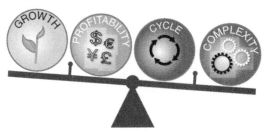

FIGURE 9.1   The Effective Frontier

"However, I'm no spring chicken. I'm older, and I find that when I train harder that I get stronger, but I lose flexibility. I never used to get stiff as a teenager, but I do now. As a result, I have to consciously train every day to improve my capabilities for strength, flexibility, and balance. There are different exercises for each, and the progress happens ever so slowly over time. It is so slow that sometimes I wonder if I'm making progress, but we have to keep many things like stress, age, and base-level capabilities in perspective. In the end, I can only compare my progress to my results. Joe needs to be compared to Joe; and I have to hold myself accountable. It's my personal journey."

He took a drink of water, and continued, "In short, we've got to make time to exercise. It's easy to put it off. Tying my shoes every morning for a 5:00 A.M. run takes discipline, but over time my body responds. Believe me, I realize that it's much easier to walk downstairs and get coffee and linger in front of a TV channel than to push myself out the door in nasty weather. Conditioning the body takes focused discipline and hard work. You cannot rush it, and you cannot forget about it. In the process, the body tears down muscles and then repairs them. It is easier if you track your progress on a device like this because it happens ever so slowly. I find the building of organizational muscle to be a similar process. It is a good analogy for what I experienced in building this team.

"I believe that building operations excellence is a pillared approach requiring clear leadership and aligned matrixed teams. It is analogous to my athletic training. In my prior roles, the manufacturing plants didn't work together with the larger organization, so I wanted to build a balanced and aligned organization as part of our Greenfield startup here in Brazil. We also wanted to build a community, or network, of distributors and suppliers to help us become successful," Joe stated as he displayed a map with the multitude of suppliers that contributed to the startup's success.

"When we started the factory, we asked our suppliers to work with us so that we could win together. Due to the nature of our product, we knew we needed a responsive network: one that could flex as the market shifted. To accomplish this, we put skin in the game. I changed the incentive systems by agreeing to pay the supplier based on the accuracy of our forecast. As a result, if we were good at transmitting accurate demand signals to the supplier, the price was lower, but if our forecast was lousy, they could price higher. We built a sliding scale. It gave us an incentive to get good at translating demand to our critical supply base. We also built scorecards and paid based on performance. The suppliers responded, and it defined effective supplier relationships."

With his hands on his hips, Joe stated, "I don't know how it works in your organization, but I think we spend way too much time building PowerPoint decks and talking about what we're going to do. I like just doing it." Joe motioned and rolled his eyes as he stated, "You know those strategy decks that are massive. Some in our organization are over 80 slides: I wanted to change the game. To accomplish this goal, I built a one-page strategy for the team that laid out our primary goal areas. The five that we chose were:

1. Transform the organization to become market driven.
2. Support growth and innovation while achieving flat to declining total delivered costs.
3. Improve or maintain the business fundamentals of safety, customer service, and corporate social responsibility.
4. Deliver on the metrics that matter.
5. Drive strength, balance and resiliency into performance.

"We call this our winning strategy. It was our goal to win in three ways. First, we wanted to win versus the competition, and we wanted to win with our employees. And, finally, we also wanted to win with our community. Our intention was to maintain purpose and continuity with all constituencies. To do this, we had to get very structured at balancing cost and continuous improvement programs. It requires an end-to-end system approach to the initiatives. It's not easy," said Joe as he flashed his infectious grin. "In this slide I share the story of our journey." He then moved the image shown in Figure 9.2 onto the screen.

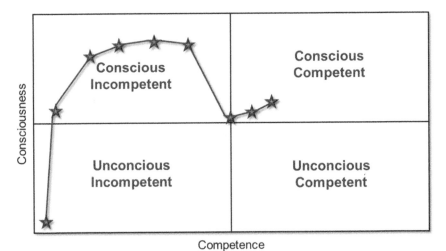

FIGURE 9.2   Joe's Journey on Project Orbit
Key: Each star represents one year of Joe's personal journey.

The paddle fans were humming and the stage lights shone through the patterns of the smoke as Joe continued, "Let me tell you a story. I have been working in Brazil on this startup for two years. This slide represents my journey. Five years prior, I worked with my global leadership to determine which metrics matter and what defines excellence. At first, we were unconsciously incompetent." As Joe spoke these words, a nervous laugh cascaded through the audience. "However, we did not realize it. We thought we were doing well and everyone on the team was happily driving continuous improvement programs in vertical silos, but as a team we weren't going anywhere."

He stepped away from the podium and stated, "We were good at it, and stuck in our ways. But as time went on, we could see that while we were improving the metrics within the function, we weren't able to drive the improvements on the corporate balance sheet. This is why I say that we were unconsciously incompetent." Joe spoke from his heart as he shared the stories of the many functional projects that were well intended, and how he had personally committed to many projects based on return on investment that never seemed to drive the expected value. He continued, "The gap was the lack of an operating strategy and clarity of how and when to invest based on the operating strategy." He quoted Angela as saying, "If they had half the money that was promised in the project scoping, then they would all be rich." Joe continued, "The reality was quite different: The project approach just didn't work. We were stuck; and let me assure you, we were not stuck in a good way. It was like having the organization's feet embedded in concrete. We had not delivered on the first set of promises, and we couldn't get new monies for the new projects because we had not produced the expected results on the first set of projects. It was a vicious cycle.

"When we were unconsciously incompetent, the gap between the promises that were made and reality of what was delivered was large. I'm embarrassed just how large the gap was. . . ." His voice trailed off and then he asked others to raise their hands if they were facing similar issues. He asked the stage crew to raise the lights so that he could see the hands raised. When the lights went up in the audience, there were few attendees who did not have their hands in the air.

He then spoke about the ensuing confusion and bewilderment. "Corporate performance improvement happens through small, focused efforts driven by leadership. The scorecards have to be balanced and teams do not know what balance is until it's defined. We've spent years trying to make our organization the most efficient, and we had to learn that the efficient organization is not the most effective. All of this required constant education. When new team members join, you cannot sidestep the need for onboarding and training. It may seem awkward, because everyone comes into an organization feeling very confident, and you want to embrace new ideas, but it's essential. It requires patience for everyone on the leadership team to talk through all the terms and get aligned.

"Slowly as an executive leadership team, we embraced the principles of the Effective Frontier and started managing the business as a system. At first it felt awkward, sort of like what new shoes feel like on your feet. We struggled to manage a cascading set of metrics and help functional leaders focus on corporate metrics, sometimes at the expense of functional excellence. Luckily, we learned quickly, by studying the progress of others, that progress happens slowly over time, and that we needed to closely study the progress of other companies to understand what's possible. While we've had many expensive consultants come and tell us that we were moving too slowly and we could drive progress faster, we stuck to our guns because we could see in the performance of other companies that when metrics are managed in isolation, or there's a focus on a singular metric with an aggressive target, the system gets out of balance. That's when we all lose. I call this our period of being conscious, but still being incompetent in how to bring these concepts into day-to-day business management.

"After extensive work together, the leadership team became consciously competent over the course of about four years. I was lucky to have this experience before I started the operation in Brazil. Through this journey, I learned that business leaders must define the operational strategy. While there's much time spent on the business strategy, it's often defined at too high a level to be actionable. We also find that there's not enough time spent translating the operational strategy into process design. In the journey, one can never assume that there are 'best practices.' Instead, the processes need to be fit for purpose.

"As I have moved through this journey, I've also learned there's no substitute for leadership, or for effective relationships. Value networks need to be built based on meaningful relationships. I wouldn't have been successful in this project if I hadn't focused on building a value network. There should be many suppliers and distributors on stage with me today accepting this award. We did it together. This kind of result cannot be effectively built on buy/sell transactions and pushing cost and waste backward on suppliers. Instead, we need to create an environment where we win together. To showcase that this is true, I would like for everyone that was a supplier to me in this critical time to stand." Joe took another drink of water as about 20 suppliers proudly stood in the audience and the group gave them a warm round of applause.

"Over the past decade, it has become tougher to manage global operations. Global corporations have invested in procurement systems, and elongated payables, and have become more difficult to do business with. I knew that it was critical to my success to be easy to do business with. I wanted to change the dynamics with suppliers. It's for that reason that we built a value network for data sharing and we continuously align metrics top-to-top. I believe that when my suppliers win, I have a higher probability of being successful." Joe stopped and backed away from the podium.

"I would encourage all of you to try to do business with yourself. You will find that it's not easy. Use your portals and interact with your outsourced procurement organizations, and see how easy it is to do business with your own organization. I laugh all the time that money today flows more quickly than ever. Think about it. We can wire funds, use credit cards globally, and process funds electronically minute-by-minute; yet we have lengthened payables and asked our suppliers to do more with less. It just didn't make sense to me.

"No doubt about it, making this leap in building this startup required education. Finance and accounting are backward-focused on transactions while the processes of managing operations are forward-looking based on flows. The finance team is happy improving cash-to-cash by lengthening payables, and I had to work hard to help them to see that our cost of capital was better than our suppliers', and that we needed to use this to leverage to build new relationships. These were tough talks," Joe said with a wry smile. "But, in the end, I won. This project would not have been successful without the work with the suppliers, and the suppliers wouldn't have jumped through hoops for me when I needed them if they were not connected and incented to do so. It is not about moving money from one hand to another to starve the supplier; instead, it needs to be about the creation of value. What seems so obvious in this statement often gets lost in discussions with corporate treasury." Joe stated. From the nods of the people in the audience, he could see that these remarks were resonating with the audience.

"To do this, I kept returning the discussion to focus on value. I told the team that if they would allow me to build value networks the right way, I'd deliver on growth, operating margin, inventory turns, and return on invested capital. The success in focusing on these key corporate performance metrics, and delivering on operations improvement, earned me the right to do this my way. If I had not worked long and hard with the executive team to understand the metrics that matter, I could not have accomplished the goal."

He looked at his watch, and said, "Sorry to get so long-winded. As you can see, I get passionate about this stuff. I've run out of time. Let me quickly finish. In summary, to drive excellence and become consciously competent, you have to know your culture, and define the processes from the outside in, market-to-market, based on the business strategy. In this process, everyone on the team has to become equal partners, but most important, you have to manage yourself. This was the hardest part of the journey for me. I would get excited and tempted to overcommit and try to drive progress faster than was possible; and then when it didn't happen like I wanted, I would lose enthusiasm. Keeping yourself moving on the journey requires will. The team depends on you, and only you can manage yourself through the journey.

"One day on a sheet of paper, I mapped my emotions through this journey," Joe said as he flashed up the slide shown in Figure 9.3. "Can you see how rocky this was for me? It was full of ups and downs. When I was consciously incompetent, I had a lot of self-doubts. I was my own worst enemy. In the end, let me reiterate, it comes down to you. Your team depends on it, your suppliers count on it, and it matters to the health and welfare of the community. We all know operations excellence matters. For me, this award is a testimonial to just how much a small team working on a new project can make a difference. It takes concerted efforts within a value network. Thank you for giving me this award today. I accept it for my team, and I am honored. I wish you well in your journey."

With that Joe cradled the award in his arm to leave the stage, but was stopped in his tracks as the audience rose to give him a standing ovation. He was alone on the stage, but he smiled, thinking back on his journey. His mind

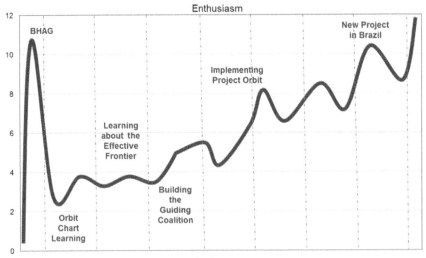

FIGURE 9.3   Joe's Emotions through the Journey

flashed back, remembering the discussions, the people, and the arguments that now seemed so unimportant. While he was alone now, he had not been alone on his journey.

REFLECTIONS

As Joe picked up his briefcase to amble down the stairs from the stage, he realized that the journey for operations excellence is about people, working with people, and that the metrics that matter become the glue to align efforts for success. He had learned the hard lesson that improvement happens gradually through focus and discipline; and for it to be valuable, the efforts need to be measured based on a disciplined approach of peer group comparison. Charting the path was about driving slow and measured change. This perspective made him a more valuable leader.

When he walked down the crowded hallway, shaking hands and sharing stories, Joe was invigorated. The crisp night air felt good on his face as he opened the door. He was ready for a new day.

Appendix: The Methodology

I N THIS SECTION, we describe the methodologies used in the book to define the Metrics That Matter. Here we first define the financial ratios used to determine corporate performance, and then detail the math used to calculate the supply chain index used in Chapters 4–9.

UNDERSTANDING THE FINANCIAL CHAIN RATIOS

Throughout the book, we reference a number of commonly used financial ratios. These ratios are based on the most common metrics that we find used by teams to measure corporate performance.

Each company has a unique potential. The size of the company matters as does the industry. Both have a major impact on the company's potential on the Effective Frontier. As a result, in the development of the tables in Chapters 4–8, we focused on companies with annual revenues greater than $1 billion in 2012.

The definitions of the most commonly used ratios in the analysis of corporate performance are listed here:

Cash-to-cash cycle = Days of inventory + Days of receivables − Days of payables

Current ratio = Total current assets/Total current liabilities

Days of inventory = (Days of inventory × 365)/Cost of goods sold

Days of receivables (Days of sales outstanding) = (Accounts receivable × 365)/Total sales

Days of payables = (Accounts payable * 365)/Cost of goods sold

Gross margin = Gross profit/Total sales

Inventory turns = Cost of goods sold/inventory

Operating margin = Operating income/Total sales

Return on assets = Net operating profit/Total assets

Return on invested capital = Net income/(Total liabilities + Shareholder's equity)

Return on net assets = Net income/(Property, plant, equipment + Total current assets – Total current liabilities)

Revenue per employee (K$) = Revenue/Employee count

SG&A ratio = SG&A expense/Total sales

Working capital ratio = (Total current assets – Total current liabilities)/Total sales

Year-over-year revenue growth = (Total sales (year 1) – Total sales (year 0))/Total sales (year 0)

INDEX METHODOLOGY

To measure performance, companies need to compare and benchmark. To make this easier, we developed the supply chain index. In the building of the index, we used financial ratios rather than absolute numbers. The use of ratios allowed us to compare companies regardless of size, and also compare companies across currencies.

The math behind the index is defined next. This methodology was built with the help of a research team from the School of Computing, Informatics, and Decision Systems Engineering at Arizona State University during the spring of 2014.

Balance

To develop the balance factor used in the index, we evaluated a scatter plot of revenue growth and return on invested capital (ROIC) for a specific company. The balance factor (B) is the proportional difference of points on an orbit chart for the period of 2006–2012 at the intersection of revenue growth and return on invested capital. To calculate the balance factor, let REV_i denote the revenue growth of the ith time period, $ROIC_i$ denote the return on invested capital of the ith time period, and n denote the total number of periods under consideration. Thus the balance factor is defined as:

$$B = \frac{1}{n-1}\left(\frac{REV_n - REV_1}{REV_1} + \frac{ROIC_n - ROIC_1}{ROIC_1}\right).$$

Strength

Strength factor is a similar calculation to balance factor, but with a focus on the intersection of operating margin and inventory turns. For this analysis, we used a scatter plot of operating margin and inventory turns on an orbit chart for a specific company. Let OM_i denote the operating margin of the ith time period (e.g., ith year), IT_i denote the inventory turns of the ith time period, and n denote the total number of periods under consideration. The strength measure (S) is defined as:

$$S = \frac{1}{n-1} \left(\frac{OM_n - OM_1}{OM_1} + \frac{IT_n - IT_1}{IT_1} \right)$$

The denominator reflects that there are $n - 1$ differences between n time periods. Figure A.1 depicts the intersection of operating margin and inventory turns for an example company. The difference in operating margin and inventory turns between the first and last time period is shown.

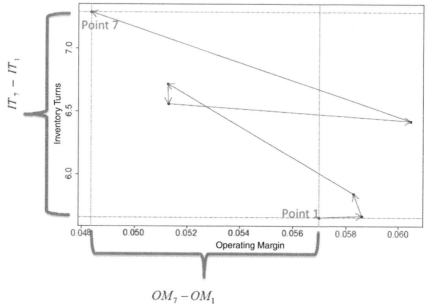

FIGURE A.1 Inventory Turns and Operating Margin Intersection for an Example Company

Resiliency

The resiliency factor is a measurement of the tightness of the pattern at the intersection of operating margin and inventory turns for a given company. For companies that did well, and had a tight pattern, the value will be lower than companies that lacked reliability for the period. To develop the value, we considered a scatter plot of operating margin and inventory turns for a specific company. Let d_{ij} denote the Euclidean distance between a pair of points i and j and let m denote the total number of pairs. The resiliency measure (R) is defined as the mean distance of all possible pairs of points at the intersection. That is,

$$ R = \frac{1}{m} \sum_{i} \sum_{j>i} d_{ij} $$

Figure A.2 shows an example of the operating margin and inventory turns intersection for an example company. Table A.1 shows the distances between every possible pair of points at the intersection. The resiliency is calculated from the mean of the distance values and is equal to 0.7335.

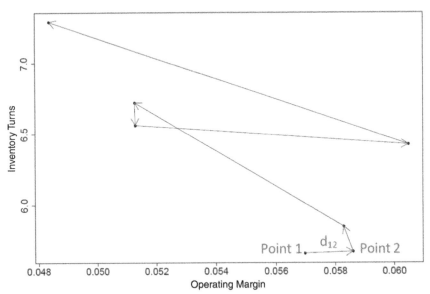

FIGURE A.2   Calculation of Resiliency at the Intersection of Inventory Turns and Operating Margin for a Given Company

TABLE A.1 Calculation of Euclidean Distances for an Example Company

Distance between Points	1	2	3	4	5	6
2	0.0133					
3	0.1887	0.1755				
4	1.0615	1.0484	0.8729			
5	0.9014	0.8883	0.7128	0.1601		
6	0.7666	0.7534	0.5779	0.2951	0.1351	
7	1.6306	1.6175	1.442	0.5691	0.7292	0.8641

Alternative Measures Considered for the Measurement of Resiliency

To develop the resiliency factor, we considered a number of alternative approaches. One method considered was Principal Components Analysis (PCA). It is a traditional method used to summarize multidimensional data. We considered measures commonly applied with PCA based on eigenvalues and eigenvectors (e.g., the condition index, percentage of variance explained by the first principal component). Although these measures were reasonable, they did not distinguish between orbit plots that were visually different as well as simpler approaches.

We also considered other measures based on the distances (e.g., sum, maximum, minimum, and the coefficient of variation of the distances). The mean distance was finally selected to measure the compactness of a set of points. In fact, a similar measure called *cohesion* is frequently used in cluster analysis to measure the compactness of a set of points. Rather than taking the sum of distances (as in cohesion), we consider the mean to account for the potentially different number of points for each company.

About the Author

LORA CECERE is the founder of the research firm Supply Chain Insights. The company is helping supply chain leaders pave new directions.

As a prolific writer, Lora is the author of the enterprise software blog *Supply Chain Shaman*. Lora's weekly posts are read by 6,000 readers. She also writes a blog for *Forbes*, is a LinkedIn Influencer, and is a featured columnist for *Supply Chain Management Review* and *Consumer Goods Technology*. Her book, *Bricks Matter*, coauthored with Charlie Chase, was published in December 2012, and her self-published book, *Shaman's Journal*, was published in September 2014.

As an enterprise strategist, Lora focuses on the changing face of enterprise technologies. Her research is designed for the early adopter seeking first-mover advantage. Current research topics include the digital consumer, supply chain sensing, demand shaping and revenue management, market-driven value networks, accelerating innovation through open design networks, the evolution of predictive analytics, emerging business intelligence solutions, and technologies to improve safe and secure product delivery.

With more than 30 years of diverse supply chain experience, Lora spent nine years as an industry analyst with Gartner Group, AMR Research, and Altimeter Group. Prior to becoming a supply chain analyst, she spent 15 years as a leader in the building of supply chain software at Manugistics and Descartes Systems Group, and several years as a supply chain practitioner at Procter & Gamble, Kraft/General Foods, Clorox, and Dreyer's Grand Ice Cream (now a division of Nestlé).

Lora writes from her home office in Philadelphia, Pennsylvania, and is frequently on the road working with clients. Currently, she is working on a doctorate of business administration (DBA) from Temple University. An avid gardener and quilter, Lora loves working with her hands; however, her favorite times are spent with her daughter and grandson.

Index

NOTE: Page references in *italics* refer to figures or tables.

Printed and bound by CPI Group (UK) Ltd, Croydon, CR0 4YY

12/03/2023

03200884-0005